I0887695

Thomas Ewing Jr.

Shades of Blue and Gray Series

The Shades of Blue and Gray Series offers Civil War studies for the modern reader–Civil War buff and scholar alike. Military history today addresses the relationship between society and warfare. Thus biographies and thematic studies that deal with civilians, soldiers, and political leaders are increasingly important to a larger public. This series includes books that will appeal to Civil War Roundtable groups, individuals, libraries, and academics with a special interest in this era of American history.

Thomas Ewing Jr.

FRONTIER LAWYER AND CIVIL WAR GENERAL

RONALD D. SMITH

University of Missouri Press
Columbia

University of Missouri Press, Columbia, Missouri 65211
Printed and bound in the United States of America

First paperback printing, 2018

ISBN 978-0-8262-2179-7 (paperback : alk. paper)

Library of Congress Cataloging-in-Publication Data

Smith, Ronald D., 1947–
Thomas Ewing Jr. : frontier lawyer and Civil War general / Ronald D. Smith.
p. cm.
Includes bibliographical references and index.
Summary: "Examines Thomas Ewing Jr.'s career as a real estate lawyer, judge, soldier, and speculator in Kansas and how he came to national prominence in the fight over the proslavery Lecompton Constitution, was instrumental in starting the Union Pacific Railroad, and became the first chief justice of the Kansas Supreme Court"—Provided by publisher.
ISBN 978-0-8262-1806-3 (hardcover : alk. paper)
1. Ewing, Thomas, 1829–1896.2 . Legislators—United States—Biography. 3. United States. Congress. House—Biography. 4. Generals—United States—Biography. 5. Kansas—History—Civil War, 1861–1865.6. Missouri—History—Civil War, 1861–1865.7 . Lawyers—Ohio—Biography. 8. Judges—Kansas—Biography. 9. Businessmen—United States—Biography. 10. Ewing family. I Title.
E415.9.E95S65 2008
328.73092—dc22
[B]

2008021866

⊗™ This paper meets the requirements of the American National Standard for Permanence of Paper for Printed Library Materials, Z39.48, 1984.

Designer: Kristie Lee
Typefaces: Adobe Garamond, Trajan Pro, and Johann Sparkling

To my wife, Marcia

CONTENTS

PREFACE

The Kansas legislature sometimes pays lip service to teaching Kansas history in the schools of the Sunflower State. It is a feel-good issue for lawmakers who are frustrated on the other important but unresolved issues of the day. Some students might have heard of William C. Quantrill but probably not of Charles Robinson. John Brown's name is familiar, of course; the famous John Stuart Curry painting of Brown adorns the wall just outside the governor's office on the second floor of the statehouse in Topeka. Perhaps even the names of Samuel Pomeroy, Cyrus Holliday, Daniel Anthony, or Jim Lane might be familiar. A few might associate the name of Samuel Lecompte with the old river capital of Lecompton, but they probably could not find the towns of Kickapoo, Big Springs, or Grasshopper Falls on a territorial map. They could not tell you which towns Abraham Lincoln visited in territorial Kansas in 1859 when he came to see where Bleeding Kansas had begun.

Alexis de Tocqueville, a student of democratic theory and ideas, wrote in 1840 that the American aristocracy was not the rich, who had no common ties. Rather, de Tocqueville nominated the country's judiciary and its Bar as his definition of nobility. American lawyers exercised an influence over government that became "the most powerful existing security against the excesses of democracy."[1]

One family that fit de Tocqueville's description came out to Kansas early, hung on during difficult guerrilla war and predatory land speculation practices, and made their mark across the nation. The Thomas Ewing family of Ohio were very prominent in Lancaster, and in Columbus, Cincinnati, St. Louis, and the other larger Midwestern cities. Their pivotal roles in the nation's growth and history in the last half of the 1800s are astonishing for a family that previously was relatively unknown.

1. Alexis de Tocqueville, *Democracy in America,* 2 vols. (1840), bk. 1, ch. 16, on the Internet at <http://xroads.virginia.edu/~HYPER/DETOC/1_ch16.htm> last accessed on April 5, 2008.

Taking different routes, four members of this Ohio family ended up in Leavenworth, Kansas, a dusty brawling river town. Not all of them practiced law, and for a time those who did practice law did so in near obscurity. Thomas Ewing, the patriarch, by the time of Bleeding Kansas was a real estate lawyer with a national reputation whose enormous fees had allowed him to purchase huge tracts of land in the St. Louis and Leavenworth areas. Hugh Ewing, Tom Ewing, and the boyish Charley Ewing all drifted in and out of the law firm's office at 2nd and Delaware in Leavenworth. There were two other Ohio natives. Dan McCook of the illustrious McCook family of Steubenville practiced for a time with Sherman, Ewing & McCook; and for less than a year William T. Sherman, a foster son of Thomas Ewing, managed the firm's business affairs and lending, biding his time while he waited for an entrée back into the army. It was a law practice that could scarcely be called distinguished. The local economy was sagging and filled with charlatans, claim jumpers, abolitionists, and border ruffians. Yet we can see in their lives reflections of the scrappy nation that first had to deal with the slavery issue at home before, as a nation, it could emerge as the international power it was at the end of the century. Sherman, of course, went on to a great career in the army, thanks to the fortunes of war. Tom, Hugh, and Charley became generals. So did McCook, though posthumously. Tom Ewing, especially, had extensive political and cultural connections with Bleeding Kansas and became part of the power struggle that was postwar Washington, D.C. All but McCook were present at some of the nation's most perilous postwar times.

Tom Ewing, though not the oldest of the four, was the firm's founder and unchallenged leader. During his boyhood, he was considered bright, but somewhat gullible to stories spun by his older brothers. His father, Thomas Ewing Sr, was a Whig senator from Ohio. As a teenager, Tom worked as private secretary to President Zachary Taylor and served an apprenticeship in the Department of the Interior, where he learned real estate law from perhaps the best lawyer on that subject in America—his father. Tom's life of privilege also included a wide array of projects in the business and political worlds—some successful, some not, but all of them interesting. He began life as a Whig and founded the Republican Party in Kansas.

After the war his constant ambition pushed him to ever greater efforts for the ideals he championed and a public life in the U.S. Senate, a goal he never achieved. He defended an unpopular conspirator, Samuel Mudd, in the Lincoln conspiracy trial. He championed the losing cause that was the presidency of Democrat Andrew Johnson, a political position becoming so shrill that a savvy cousin of his, Republican James G. Blaine, stated Ewing's "sacrifice" in personal prestige for Andrew Johnson was large enough to "free his action from the slightest suspicion" that his motives were anything "other than the conviction of duty." Later, in the fore of the Democrat-Greenback Party, Ewing achieved national acclaim on a broad array of economic issues and came within a whisker of winning the Ohio governor's chair, which, during the Gilded Age, had launched several later presidential campaigns.[2]

Ewing's family is remarkable, yet it is hardly known outside the circle of diehard students of Sherman who know the name and forebears of Sherman's wife, Ellen Ewing. Yet Tom Ewing was a remarkable person in his own right. Intensely ambitious as were all the Ewings, he rarely shied from a political fight. He loved the rough and tumble of courtrooms and smoke-filled political backrooms. Although he never achieved his goal of the U.S. Senate, he became chief justice of a new state and later in life a congressman from Ohio. When the rest of the country went to war, this neophyte without military training obtained a colonel's commission, raised a regiment, fought it well in northwest Arkansas and Missouri, and in a brisk battle in southeast Missouri in 1864 may well have saved Abraham Lincoln's presidency.

Through Tom Ewing's eyes we see a remarkable family. Through him we see how Kansas prairie politics soaked up a nation's anger and frustration and led to the Southern efforts that eventually spawned the catastrophic Civil War. Yet from his personality and these prairies also came the nation's economic and political future.

Above all, this story is an odyssey, of a family whose Ohio roots were dug up and moved into California, Washington, Kansas, back to Ohio, and then to New York. While comparing nineteenth- and twentieth-century living patterns is foolish, this story tells of a family on the move to those parts of the country where a nation's future was being written. Their presence in courtrooms and business suites at important times in the nation's development is one part of the story. The handprint of this extraordinary family is found in all these places, as well as in the lives of many men and women of influence who were touched by the Ewings. The Ewings' story is one of strong political men with sometimes strident views who also influenced presidents and kings. This particular story tells of one of the leading personalities and leaders of early Kansas. It is a story of faith and family, courage and despair, ambition, fame and disillusion, and ultimately reconciliation.

2. James G. Blaine, *Twenty Years of Congress: From Lincoln to Garfield,* 222.

ACKNOWLEDGMENTS

A work of this sort requires considerable support from people other than the author. I am indebted to many, and especially the staff at the University of Missouri Press whose encouragement to this neophyte writer was most helpful. I am most assuredly thankful to Candida Staempfli Steel, Thomas Ewing Jr.'s great-great-granddaughter, who is an administrative hearing officer for the Department of the Interior, of which her great-great-great-grandfather was the first secretary. Her early insight with the manuscript and her familiarity with the obligations of being a twentieth-century Ewing were helpful. Another of Thomas Ewing Sr.'s myriad descendants, the late Joseph H. Ewing of Wheaton, Maryland, provided great assistance and knowledge of Sherman's character by sharing family letters, some of which are unpublished elsewhere.

The Kansas State Historical Society's superior research and manuscript resources are exceedingly helpful to anyone interested in Kansas history. Anyone who has gone nearly blind attempting to read, at length, nineteenth-century handwritten correspondence in press books will identify with my thanks to an unknown writer during the Great Depression who, for meal money, typed and catalogued Thomas Ewing Jr.'s and Sherman's law office letters for the KSHS. Walt Busch, the curator of the Fort Davidson state battlefield park at Pilot Knob, Missouri, has written a PhD thesis on Tom Ewing's Order Number 11. His scholarship and understanding, and his guided tour of the remarkably preserved Pilot Knob battlefield, all were invaluable. My friends of too short acquaintance, Charles and Barbara Whalen of Bethesda, Maryland, are excellent resources on the McCook family. Charles was a congressman during the heady days of the civil rights movement. Their newest book, *The Fighting McCooks,* was published in early 2006.

Although we read the same material and came to different conclusions concerning a few items of Ewing material, the late professor David G. Taylor's insightful study of Thomas Ewing Jr. far exceeds my own meager efforts. Andy Papen, who runs the Missouri Department of Economic Development's community development division, continues to complain perennially about Missouri's tiger victimization by Kansas jayhawking. However, Andy has forgotten more about the Civil War in Missouri than I will ever know. His help reviewing this work is much appreciated.

Former national archivist and governor John Carlin and house minority leader Dennis McKinney are two Kansas pols with interests in history who graciously gave of their time to review this book. Dennis's efforts are particularly stellar since his hometown, Greensburg, Kansas, underwent a massive destruction by tornado in May 2007. My thanks to both.

Finally, my gratitude goes to friends and family who gave me space to think and work. Such space often is the greatest gift.

ABBREVIATIONS USED IN TEXT AND NOTES

AEC	American Emigrant Company
AT&SF	Atchison, Topeka & Santa Fe Railroad
ECE	Ellen Cox Ewing
EES	Ellen Ewing Sherman
EFP	Ewing Family Papers
EFP/LC	Papers of the Thomas Ewing Family, Manuscript Division, Library of Congress
EFP/ND	Thomas Ewing Family Papers, University of Notre Dame Archives, Notre Dame, Indiana
HBE	Hugh Boyle Ewing
HBE/OHS	Hugh Boyle Ewing Papers, Ohio Historical Society, Columbus
KSHS	Kansas State Historical Society, Topeka
LC	Library of Congress, Washington, D.C.
LP&W	Leavenworth, Pawnee & Western Railroad
NUP	National Union Party
O.R.	*The War of the Rebellion: A Compilation of the Official Records of the Union and the Confederate Armies.*
OHS	Ohio Historical Society, Columbus
POW	prisoner of war
SFP/LC	William T. Sherman Family Papers, Library of Congress
SFP/OHS	William T. Sherman Family Papers, Ohio Historical Society, Columbus, Ohio

SFP/ND	William T. Sherman Family Papers, University of Notre Dame Archives, Notre Dame, Indiana
TEJr.	Thomas Ewing Jr.
TEJr./KSHS	Thomas Ewing Jr. Papers, Manuscript Division, Kansas State Historical Society, Topeka
TESr.	Thomas Ewing Sr.
WTS	William Tecumseh Sherman

Thomas Ewing Jr.

Part One

HARDSCRABBLE

1

THE JUDGMENT OF HEAVEN ON A COUNTRY

Scottish-born Thomas Ewing, the first of several Thomas Ewings of America, settled in Greenwich, New Jersey, just before the Revolutionary War. Although Ewing's ancestry was traceable to Cadet Finley Colquhoun, an Orangeman allied with William of Orange in 1690 at the Battle of the Boyne, a century later during the American Revolutionary War Thomas's son, George Ewing, distinguished himself at Brandywine as a common soldier leading a section of artillery. George mustered out of the Continental army a dirt-poor captain who sold his inheritance to make ends meet. Destitute, like many new Americans the soldiers found fortune and a life in the West—the West at that time being western Virginia. George Ewing moved his family to a dirt farm in West Liberty, although some of his relatives complained that he "read too much" to become a good farmer. In 1787 the Founding Fathers were crafting the Constitution, with its slavery compromises prompting delegate George Mason to predict that the institution in America was a "slow poison," which would in time bring the "judgment of heaven on a country" where great sins would be punished with "national calamities." Two years later, a second Thomas Ewing in Finley Colquhoun's line was born. In 1792 George Ewing moved on, taking his young family further west, to Lancaster in central Ohio. This is where the family's meandering ended.[1]

1. Hugh B. Ewing, "Autobiography of a Tramp," 3. Mason's "judgment of heaven" speech to the

Lancaster at the time was not much more than a fortified stockade to deter marauding Indian bands. In politics George Ewing embraced federalism. Like the politics of the time, factionalism was taken seriously and could be virulent. When Aaron Burr happened to visit Lancaster in 1805, the young Thomas Ewing saw George Ewing being uncharacteristically rude to the former vice president. Only after the stranger left did the boy learn Burr's role in the dueling death of Alexander Hamilton.

By day Thomas Ewing labored on his father's farm and taught himself to read. Indeed he read books so rapidly that the family suspected some sort of genius within him. He was among the first American college graduates west of the Alleghenies. In 1816 Thomas was admitted to the Bar after studying with Philemon Beecher. When "Pa" Beecher went to Congress in 1818, Thomas Ewing began a renowned legal career. He was first a local prosecutor before building his civil practice in real estate law. While lawyers helped the less fortunate through pro bono cases, his important efforts were reserved for cases involving men of business. In January 1828 Thomas Ewing was admitted to practice before the U.S. Supreme Court.[2]

A patient man, he approached all things methodically. In 1819 he had to find a way to bridge the chasm between his own Presbyterianism and the Roman Catholicism of Maria Boyle, the daughter of the local court clerk and the woman he wanted to marry. He tolerated Catholicism because she demanded it of him. In return she bore him seven children, over seventeen years, all in the big house at High and Main streets in Lancaster. Three of his children became strong Catholics like Maria. Eleanor was known as Ellen to the family. Hugh, the second youngest boy, was a scrapper throughout his young life. Their daughter Maria eventually led a Catholic nunnery. Tom Jr. took on more of his father's deist ways. The oldest and the youngest were boys: Philemon and Charles, respectively. Furthermore, Thomas and Maria also raised three children of Ewing's sister Rachel, and a second cousin, Lewis Wolfley. For Thomas Ewing Sr. the phrase "devoted family man" was an understatement.

In addition Thomas Ewing took into his home nine-year-old Tecumseh Sherman, the sixth child of their neighbors Charles and Mary Sherman. The Shermans were also Revolutionary War refugees and had immigrated to Ohio after British

---

Constitutional Convention, August 22, 1787. See, generally, Robert Rutland, *The Papers of George Mason,* 966; *Notes of Debates in the Federal Convention of 1787, Reported by James Madison* (New York: W. W. Norton, 1966).

2. The information for this and the next few paragraphs is taken from *Guide to the Microfilm Edition of Thomas Ewing Sr. Papers,* 11.

Tories burned them out of colonial Connecticut. Charles Sherman had a small law practice that he was using to pay off debts from ill-timed efforts as a state tax collector in 1816. In Ohio in that era, Supreme Court justices were elected by the legislature, and Ewing had used his power there to get Sherman a position on the Ohio Supreme Court. The salary helped with the family debts, but then Charles Sherman died suddenly from a heart attack in 1829. Times had been hand-to-mouth even on Sherman's court salary. Now life became unbearable, and Mary Sherman had to divide her eleven children among relatives and friends. Extraordinarily loyal to his friends, Thomas Ewing took over Sherman's debts and volunteered to take Cump Sherman into his home. This was fine with Maria Ewing, except she insisted that no boy would live in the Ewing house without a proper first name, so the Christian name William was given to the redheaded boy.

Hugh Boyle Ewing was born on the last day of October 1826, and the attachment to the Catholic holiday All Saints Day colored much of his life. While All Hallows Eve had a pagan origin, Hugh Ewing always felt something very Catholic about his birthday. Much of his life he gave to the Catholic Church or at least its outward trappings. His religion formed patterns in his life, one of which was his dedicated journalizing of his every day. From him we learn much about the Ewing family, and that his earliest memories were religious in nature, a characteristic he shared with his older sister, Ellen, to whom he grew the closest. There was no Catholic church in Lancaster (the nearest was in Somerset, a half-day's ride away), thus Sunday mass was not always celebrated. When they stayed home the children and servants assembled in the big house, and Maria Ewing read aloud the mass prayers and led them in reciting the rosary. Catechism was rooted in reading Butler's *Lives of the Saints.*[3]

Although he was devout during his youth, Catholicism did not take root with Hugh until later in life. He was not the model son; this role was filled by Phil, the eldest. Hugh and Tom Ewing were three years apart and exceptionally normal, indeed ornery, in all respects. Hugh terrorized Tom and little Charley with whoppers about "hooper" snakes that could anatomically coil into a wheel and roll down hills, then skewer gullible younger brothers with their tail.

Smaller than his peers, Hugh was the "runt" of his crowd. The nickname infuriated him so much that he made up for it with an innate aggressiveness. If their gang needed a ringleader, Hugh was usually the one chosen. His first school was

3. The information for this and the next few paragraphs is taken from Ewing, "Autobiography," 6–7.

in a red frame building on Main Street run by Williamson Wright, a parson's son, a thoroughly unpopular and gloomy man. Wright's unusual ideas for punishment included forcing the boys to eat salty "bread pills." Hugh convinced the others that Wright's dreaded pills were dead flies wrapped in bread dough. Skipping school was another of his leadership decisions, and the episodes increased with the warmth of the season. Time was filled with swimming in the Hocking River, blackberry picking, building salt furnaces, collecting fossils from the coal mines in the region, hunting and fishing in nearby forests, and school if the boys could not think of reasons to skip.[4]

The same year he was adopted into the family, Cump Sherman joined Phil and Ellen Ewing and Sherman's little brother John at the Lancaster Academy. When the Sherman children had been divided, John had gone to live with a nearby relative, but he still came to the school. The academy was a private school for prominent families. The Ewings, Shermans, and fellow barrister Henry Stanbery had founded the place in order to educate their children. Headmasters Mark and Matthew Howe taught Latin, French, and Greek along with reading, English, algebra, geometry, and surveying. Grandpa Boyle's orchard was next to the academy grounds and provided the headmaster with an "immense supply of apple switches" for disciplinary purposes, most of which were focused on John Sherman. While John's childhood reputation was primarily as a talker, he once angrily heaved an inkstand at the headmaster. Howe whipped the back of John Sherman's legs until he was exhausted. John Sherman later decided that being a politician was his future since his aptitude as a rebel had its limitations.[5]

Hugh Ewing was another child prone to disciplinary problems. In 1836 a law student named E. B. Cone supplemented his income from Thomas Ewing by replacing the Howes as the headmaster at the family academy. At one point another student, Tom Hunter, knocked over a chair in such a manner it made Charley Ewing look responsible. Charley was an impish version of his larger-than-life father; although their facial features and heads were nearly identical, Charley was a small boy who would not cut a large figure when he grew to manhood. When Cone attempted to beat Charley, Hugh stepped in, Cone turned on Hugh, and they wrestled to the floor, out the door, and in each other's grip tumbled down the steps of the school into the dirt. Both were too stunned to continue and silently agreed their tussle had ended in a draw. Father Ewing had taught his sons to respect authority, and he demanded that Hugh apologize to Cone. Hugh refused.

4. Ewing, "Autobiography," 5–8, 11.

5. Ibid., 36, also 11–12, 15.

Charley was wrongfully accused, and no one should get a beating unless it was deserved. Thomas Ewing's anger increased, but Hugh held his position. Father Ewing also instilled in his sons a sense of justice, and he could hardly impose discipline in an already murky situation. Cone resigned over Ewing's inaction, and a new headmaster had to be hired. The younger brother of Lord Richard Lyons, the British minister to the United States, was hired. The Ewing boys liked Lyons and sensed their horizons were about to change. A second generation of young Ohioans was preparing for college.[6]

As he was with issues of authority, Thomas Ewing Sr. was stern but indulgent and preferred that his boys learn from life's experiences. A favorite teaching method he employed for his children was travel. At age fourteen, while his father was away campaigning for William Henry Harrison, Hugh was given permission for an all-week thirty-mile trip to Columbus, where he and Tom could learn the fascinations of a library and marvel at the sights of a city, which included an insane asylum and the statehouse. On the return trip, Hugh bought some sweet wine, which eleven-year-old Tom Jr. ("Tinker") threatened to report to their father.

On another unaccompanied trip, this time to Greencastle, Hugh and Tinker picked up an ornery cousin, James G. Blaine, a future Republican Speaker of the House and presidential candidate. Even as a boy Blaine had an irrepressible instinct to bait Democrats. When he taunted some Democrats at a Van Buren rally in Greencastle, as the carriage rumbled through town, Hugh was afraid the local men would recognize their father's carriage. Hugh warned Blaine if he acted up on the return trip, there would be hell to pay. While returning through Greencastle, Blaine leaped off the buggy and tore down the Van Buren flag. When he struggled to get back into the carriage, Hugh kicked him out and yelled that *gentlemen* did not destroy other gentlemen's property, even political property. If the Loco Focos did not cut his heart out, Blaine could just *walk* to his Aunt Morgan's house in Campaign County. Blaine, with imaginary wild-eyed and knife-wielding Democrats on his heels, ran cross-country to Aunt Morgan's, where he surrendered his ragged flag, taken in political combat, and was tossed unceremoniously into the carriage for the remaining trip to Lancaster.[7]

Thomas Ewing Sr.'s children grew up during Jacksonian Democracy, when the dominant parties were the Whigs and the Democrats. Andrew Jackson, the com-

6. Ibid., 37–38.
7. Gail Hamilton, *Biography of James G. Blaine,* 67–70; Ewing, "Autobiography," 27.

mon man's president, was tall, narrow-shouldered, and he moved on storklike legs. He was anathema to the Ewings' Whig household, and the children were taught the difference between Whigs and Loco Focos from an early age. Henry Clay led the Whig party of that era and gave color to its nationalism and its role as successor to the Federalists, whose rockets had long since dimmed.[8]

Thomas Ewing Sr. embraced Clay's ideology and the Whig Party as his political theology for the country's best future. In January 1831, the Ohio legislature sent Ewing to the U.S. Senate. At the time it was the legislatures that elected U.S. senators, and they did not hesitate to give senators "instruction" on how they felt about certain issues. When the Ohio legislature instructed Ewing to use his influence to scuttle the rechartering of the National Bank, however, Ewing not only disagreed with the theory that cheap money would benefit rural states such as Ohio, he disputed the legislators' authority to direct his vote. This sort of stubbornness became a family trait and was inherited by several of Ewing's sons. Jacksonian Democrats were quick to paint Ewing as an aristocrat who had speculated in Virginia land scrip before coming to the Senate and who had profited from that speculation by serving on the Committee on Revolutionary War Claims. Ewing did own Ohio scrip; he had taken scrip as legal fees in a cash-starved rural Ohio, where there was no national currency. Although no irregularities were proved, Jacksonians marked Ewing as a weakened foe, a flash in the pan, and a target in future elections.[9]

At the end of his first term, amid all the turmoil, a spot in the next West Point class became available for Ewing to appoint. While his first impulse was to check with Phil Ewing, the eldest son, generally Thomas Ewing believed the sons of a wealthy family should not be educated at taxpayer expense. Phil Ewing wanted to be a priest, not a soldier, and the other Ewing sons were too young. Cump Sherman, however, had always loved the outdoor life. Not only did an army career seem a better choice for him, but Cump was extremely interested in the possibility. When the appointment was offered, he wrote his foster father, "I received your letter with my appointment yesterday with great satisfaction. I have informed my mother and [sister] Elizabeth of my appointment." The sixteen-year-old Sherman entered West Point in the summer of 1836, one of Thomas Ewing's last appointments.[10]

8. *Guide, Microfilm Edition,* 5–6.

9. For an overview of monetary activities in antebellum Ohio, see David M. Gold, "Public Aid to Private Enterprise under the Ohio Constitution: Sections 4, 6, and 13 of Article VIII in Historical Perspective," *University of Toledo Law Review* 16 (1985): 405, 407–23.

10. Ewing, "Autobiography," 32–33; "my appointment" from William Tecumseh Sherman (hereafter WTS) to Thomas Ewing Sr. (hereafter TESr.), in Joseph H. Ewing, *Sherman at War,* 23.

Thomas Ewing Sr. concentrated on the politics necessary to be reappointed to the Senate, but even hiring a hall in Columbus with lavish spreads of food and drink did not persuade enough legislators to return him to the Senate. He was not hawkish enough against slavery. Ewing tried again in 1837 and 1838, but although he was a nationally known Whig, he failed again after some anti-Ewing gerrymandering in the state legislature eroded his support base. So Ewing returned home and reestablished his law practice, where he specialized in real estate matters and invested his fees in good property around Lancaster.[11]

His practice did not keep him from national politics, however. In 1840 he actively campaigned for William Henry Harrison and became cabinet material when Harrison won the election. Henry Clay and Daniel Webster were the polar personalities of the party, and each tried to mold Harrison's cabinet in his own image. Clay wanted John Clayton of Delaware appointed to the Treasury because of Clayton's strong advocacy for a national bank. Webster proposed Ewing instead. Harrison favored a national bank, but he wanted to avoid taking on a divisive issue and to concentrate on building the party instead. Ewing's moderate personality and ability to work with all sections carried the day. Harrison chose Ewing as secretary of the Treasury. On March 4, 1841, a raw, cold, and cloudy day, Harrison rode bareheaded and without a coat in his inaugural parade, then spoke to a crowd of over fifty thousand for more than an hour. His voice hoarse, he caught a cold, lingered three weeks, and died of pneumonia. Vice president John Tyler assumed the presidency.

Tyler was a Virginia Democrat who termed the slave trade abominable and who authorized Ewing to create a plan to reestablish a national bank. The target of angry Southern senators, who disliked the idea of a national bank, Tyler then reversed himself and told them privately that he was considering vetoing the bank bill. When the second national banking act was enacted, Ewing and Webster urged Tyler to sign the bill. The bank was vital to the growth of the Whig Party in the North. Tyler shattered what was left of his cabinet on September 10, 1841, when he vetoed the banking bill. Ewing and Northern Whigs felt Tyler had pandered to slave interests. Secretary of War John Bell, secretary of the Navy George Badger, Attorney General John Crittenden, and Thomas Ewing resigned en masse. Ewing wrote Tyler that he was "deeply hurt," since the president had not consulted him—as secretary of the Treasury—on the veto message itself.[12]

11. For the use of money in retaining these seats, as well as for an excellent tour de force as to why the direct election of U.S. senators may not be the best idea from progressive reformers, see Todd J. Zywicki, "Senators and Special Interests: A Public Choice Analysis of the Seventeenth Amendment," 1022; *Guide, Microfilm Edition,* 6–7.

12. *Guide, Microfilm Edition,* 8–9.

This resignation marked the passing of the first phase of Thomas Ewing Sr.'s national political era. He stayed on in Washington instead of returning to Lancaster, Ohio. His Washington law partnership included his son Phil. By 1842 Thomas Ewing's reputation as a man of influence had increased. The entire family came to Washington to live and work in a second home near the Capitol, which was an awe-inspiring location for young Tom Ewing and his brothers and sisters.[13]

In the fall of 1836 Cump Sherman left for West Point, in the Hudson River valley in New York state. He was tall, slim, and loose-jointed. His red hair, sunburn, and black eyes—which had earned him the nickname of "red-headed woodpecker" at the Ewing home—gave him the look of an untamed animal. His academy years were uneventful, and he finished high in his class, making many lifelong friends. He had maintained a long courtship of the oldest Ewing daughter, Eleanor, called Ellen. In 1844, the year Sherman first proposed to Ellen, the stubborn Hugh Ewing had bested his father in a test of wills and reported in July to West Point. Hugh had found an Ohio congressman who was only too glad to appoint Hugh, assuming that Thomas Ewing would approve. When Thomas Ewing reminded Hugh he had been a poor student with all his tutors and that West Point demanded academic excellence, Hugh promised this time things would be different. Father Ewing relented, but only because, if Hugh failed either the entrance exam or his classes, the boy would not hesitate to come home to an appropriate private career in Ohio.[14]

Two years later, America went to war in Mexico over the concept of Manifest Destiny, which stated that our national duty was to expand the God-given concept of democracy throughout the world. President James Polk had sent John Slidell to Mexico City to see if Santa Anna would allow the United States to purchase New Mexico and California, an overture that Mexican officials stiffly ignored. In the hot summer of 1845, Sherman and parts of the Third Artillery regiment to which he was assigned were sent to Corpus Christi, Texas, as part of a small military show of force. In December Polk ordered General Zachary Taylor's expeditionary force to cross the Nueces River and march to the Rio Grande. Santa Anna sent a force across the river at Palo Alto to block the Americans. In May 1846 Mexican troops skirmished with Americans, and Polk had his pretext to declare war.

13. Ewing, "Autobiography," 18–20.
14. Ibid., 40–42, 44.

Not everyone viewed the war through the religious purity of Manifest Destiny. The slavery-oriented land-grab nature of the war angered some Northern Democrats and Whig congressmen such as Abraham Lincoln, who was serving the only successful election campaign he ever engineered for himself above the state legislative level. Lincoln's public speeches were embarrassingly isolationist on the topic of Mexico, and he was part of the open Whig challenge to Polk in August 1846 with the Wilmot Proviso. Congress would fund the war if the territories acquired by the war would not support slave-oriented state constitutions. An objection to the proviso would telegraph the South's true intentions. Whigs delighted in watching Polk's men squirm. Polk wrote dejectedly in his diary, "Slavery will destroy the Democratic Party and may take with it the Union, too."[15]

The nation's professional army was now in motion, however. Cump's Third Artillery regiment was divided in half. The sections under Braxton Bragg went with Zachary Taylor into Mexico. Sherman's section was sent to California and saw no action, which left Sherman thoroughly disgusted. Still a cadet, Hugh spent a wonderful summer of 1847 on leave in Lancaster, but the war ended long before his graduation from West Point. Politics did appeal to him. His father was being touted by Whigs as a possible ticket-balancing vice-presidential candidate to Zachary Taylor in the upcoming presidential campaign. If this happened Hugh did not want to be stuck in a frontier posting when the family might again be in Washington. Hugh resigned his appointment to West Point and came back to Lancaster to study law.[16]

As the Mexican War was ending, Johann Sutter found gold in one of his mill sluices along the river above Sacramento. A gold rush of unprecedented proportions began. Sherman was in California, passed over for promotion, but still in the army. He complained to Ewingville, "I must remain here to my utter ruin and degradation." He did not disclose to his foster family his own speculative successes in buying and selling real estate near Sacramento.[17]

While Sherman was able to avoid the siren call of the Sierra Nevada streams and rivers, in Ohio Hugh Ewing and cousin Hamp Denman stunned Thomas

15. "Slavery will destroy" from James M. McPherson, *Battle Cry of Freedom: The Civil War Era,* 53–54.

16. Ewing, "Autobiography," 44, 48.

17. "Ruin" from Michael Fellman, *Citizen Sherman: A Life of William Tecumseh Sherman,* 27. Throughout this work I refer to "Ewingville" interchangeably both as a place and as a patriarch-centered state of mind for the family of Thomas Ewing Sr. The first characterization of Lancaster, Ohio, as Ewingville comes in WTS to his future wife, Ellen, January 31, 1846, in Thomas Ewing Family Papers, University of Notre Dame Archives, Notre Dame, Indiana (hereafter EFP/ND).

Ewing in late 1848 by declaring they also were headed to California to seek their fortunes. After thinking about it Thomas Ewing Sr. decided that at least his boy's youthful wanderlust had an economic goal. Ewing suggested they create a formal mining company, the stockholders consisting of the entire traveling party. The shareholders had never seen a gold mine, but in February 1849, the Lancaster Mining Company set out for California.[18]

In New Orleans there were more men headed for the gold fields than ships to take them. Ships that made it to California quite often did not return, if the crews decided to be gold miners. One vessel, the *Maria Burt,* broke down a day out of New Orleans and had to return. The Lancaster Mining Company caught the *Globe,* which was en route to Brazos Santiago. From there, sickened by heavy seas but eager to get going, Hugh and friends left Matamoras and struck out overland toward Mazatlan. It was a decision with tragic consequences. Cholera invaded the company almost immediately. The disease forced the party to travel in fits and spurts. James Corse was the first to die, on the mountain heights above Monterrey. With Corse's death, what had begun as a lark took a sobering turn. The travelers were disease-ridden and stranded in a land not entirely friendly to American gringos.[19]

The Ohioans pressed through the Sierra Madre Mountains at Rinconada, fighting howling winds on brown volcanic trails. On the western slopes, the cholera caught up with Hugh. Even though he feared he might follow Corse into the grave, there was no place to stop in that rugged country. Hugh took his supply of powders to fight the cramps, and laudanum to keep going.[20]

Hugh nearly died on the journey from Durango to Mazatlan. The "royal road" over the range turned into a mule trail. Hugh lost consciousness twice during this trip, the last time waking up in an Indian hut with a French doctor telling the party that Ewing needed a priest, not a doctor. After two weeks of rest, Denman brought Ewing out of the mountains and into Mazatlan to join the rest of the mining company. Sam Stambaugh told the British legation there that the son of the American secretary of the Interior was part of their party but was dangerously ill. The ship's doctor gave them some stout brown English ale and used it liberally until Ewing could handle food.[21]

From Matamoras the mining company in different groups, with Hugh in the last group, eventually made their way to San Francisco, a lifeless harbor in Sep-

18. Ewing, "Autobiography," 59.
19. Ibid., 51–53, 57, 59, 62, 70.
20. Ibid., 70, 74, 78, 79–81.
21. Ibid., 85–88.

tember 1849, where it appeared that half the ships in all the world were lashed gunwale-to-gunwale. The captain of the ship Hugh was traveling on, the *Olivia,* kept bearing up the river to Sacramento, knowing that if he stopped in the San Francisco harbor his ship would be anchored there forever. By the summer they had learned how to pan for gold, but panning earned them a total of nine dollars.[22]

Without prospects, Hugh Ewing and Hamp Denman looked up Sherman. Still in the army in a backwater assignment, Sherman suggested the gold fever would soon subside, and that when it did, agriculture and mining would take over as the mainstay of the California economy. If they could build a ranch on land Sherman had bought along the Cosumnes River, the joint venture might support all three of them. Sherman bought a team of oxen, and the three of them made plans for what was actually a large-scale "finishing" ranch where cattle would fatten up just before going to market, similar to a modern feedlot operation except there was more open grazing land. The longer they worked at it, however, the more they realized they had no abilities as farmers. Given the job of slaughtering a bull, Sherman assumed all that was needed was a gunshot to the head. He used a pistol—several times firing into the bull's forehead. The animal shook its bony head but never moved. Sherman "gave up," Hugh noted smugly in his journal, although Hugh had no better idea how to turn a bull into steaks than Sherman did.[23]

That winter in the high Sierra Nevadas brought the same sort of tragedy on gold seekers coming overland by wagon train as fell on the Donner Party in 1846. Several trains tried to negotiate the mountain passes before winter set in, and when the snows came early the wagons were marooned. The government organized a relief column from Sacramento to assure that as many as possible got out of the mountains before the snows fell. Major Daniel Rucker was the ranking army officer in Sacramento, and Sherman got the cash-starved Hugh Ewing and Hamp Denman a job on Rucker's rescue detail. Rescuing starving emigrants sick with both scurvy and malnutrition led Hugh to write home that he had spent his twenty-fourth birthday listening to a woman describe the taste of the frozen limbs of her first husband as innocently "as a Feegee Islander fresh from lunching on one of Sidney Smith's clergymen."[24]

22. Ibid., 100–101.
23. Ibid., 90–98, 101–2, 105; Sherman's attempt at slaughter at 119–20.
24. Ibid., 106.

Two compromises were engineered in 1850, one of a personal nature for the Ewing family and one with widespread national implications. The national compromise came about from the desire of the slave states to strengthen federal anti-runaway laws, which were sagging with age. The 1820 Missouri Compromise had introduced the concept of fugitive slave laws, which allowed a slave owner to use federal assistance to seek the return of his property if that "property" had fled to a free state. Such law was a necessary economic measure in the South that in the North was considered rank tyranny. Newspapers filled their columns with lurid stories of Southerners invading Northern states seeking their runaways. Often there was the bizarre spectacle of a man standing before the Bar seeking his freedom from an all-white jury, which was told there were no laws the jury was required to respect because the fugitive was black.

Before long, personal freedom laws in individual states made the pursuit and capture of blacks in the North a risky enterprise for Southern men, who were often charged with kidnapping. Jury nullifications wiped out the basis of their claim. Abolitionists routinely caught and charged with violating the Fugitive Slave Law were just as routinely acquitted. Antislavery societies became more vocal as they grew stronger. Abolitionists in Congress laying antislavery petitions before the House led to Southern demands for gag rules that threatened to disrupt the ability of the House and Senate to conduct its business if abolitionists persisted with the embarrassing petitions. By 1850 the thirty-year run of the Missouri Compromise had lost its focus. Northern states detested the necessity of compromise with slave interests, and the champions of slavery grew more radical every day.[25]

Thomas Ewing brought most of his family to Washington with him during these heady days of the Taylor administration. The secretary of the new Department of the Interior preferred these days above all others. Running a new department was a daily challenge. That his family could share those days with him gave him peace of mind. Sherman came home from California on army business and spent a lot of time in Washington with Ellen. He also spent spare time with Tom Ewing. The young man was working as Zachary Taylor's private secretary, totally fascinated by all things political, his keen intellect beginning to emerge. Tom had the look and build of his mother, not the bulky strength of his father. While he was considered a prize catch on the marriage circuit, young Tinker had no serious female interests. Taylor's private secretary made many Washington party lists where he was showered with interest from the eligible daughters of the high

25. Generally, Kenneth M. Stampp, *America in 1857: A Nation on the Brink,* 326; H. H. Crittenden, *Crittenden Memoirs,* 88–97.

and mighty. Between the secretary of the Interior's far-reaching patronage and Tom Ewing's being on the inside of the president's White House office, important political alliances and friendships were forged. With his son controlling the flow of information reaching the president, the secretary of the Interior found the nation's bankers, lawyers, and real estate merchants flocking to him as the go-to man in the Taylor administration.

It was a heady time for a twenty-year-old whose father preferred his pet nickname "the brat." Their alliance grew rapidly. Thomas Ewing Sr. came to rely on his namesake like none of his other sons, especially in political matters. This reliance from a man of such power in a presidential administration was heady stuff for the son. After a year at the White House, Tom moved over to the claims office at the Department of the Interior for two valuable years of learning real estate law in the Land Department, where he learned the politics and the law involved in refereeing state boundary disputes. The mundane work involved what some might deride as the alchemy of slog, but Tom Ewing saw his work as the statesmanship that set the boundary of what would later become West Virginia.

To the young Ewing, when he could get away to watch the Senate in action, the whimsical droning of Clay, Webster, and Calhoun concerning what they now called the Compromise of 1850 was an ongoing class in political science. Henry Clay waved a roll of papers at those who questioned his logic, stating that the only result if there were no compromise for a stronger fugitive slave act would be dissolution of the Union. And dissolution was unacceptable. The emaciated John C. Calhoun spoke slowly against the compromise and at times asked if Senator James Mason of Virginia could read his speeches for him. Accused of being untrue to his state because he did not recommend dissolution, Clay told his old friends, "I love Kentucky. But if Kentucky were to secede I would shoulder my old musket and be among the first to *put her down.*"[26]

Sherman described those days as "dangerous," and Clay as "pale and feeble in the extreme." The young bulls, testing themselves in the greatest congressional debate since the national banking bills and the Mexican War, championed ideology above all else. It took eight months for Clay's compromise—a free California, the end of slave trading in Washington, and a stronger fugitive slave law—to be accepted by a bare majority of lawmakers in each house. Millard Fillmore signed the

26. Sherman's memoirs mention days spent listening to the debates with Tom Ewing. Hon. Robert Miller, "Thomas Ewing Jr.: First Chief Justice of the Kansas Supreme Court," 3. Much antebellum Kansas history and information about this compromise can be found in William H. Taft, "Kansas-Nebraska Bill and Decoration Day, an Address by the Secretary of War at Topeka, May 30, 1904," 119n3; "put her down" from John F. Marszalek, *Sherman: A Soldier's Passion for Order,* 83–84.

bills later that year. Webster's epitaph and prayer was that the compromise would become a "finality that would give peace to a country."[27]

The personal compromise involved Sherman's long-anticipated wedding to Ellen Ewing. They had courted for over a decade. Each had stubbornly refused the other's more important demands—that he convert to what he later in life referred to as her "bigoted devotion" to Catholicism, and that she come to live with him at an army post before refusing its lifestyle. Up until their wedding day on May 1, 1850, they quarreled over these very topics. Ellen still wanted a life of luxury that would include complex religious travels to Italy, and Cump wanted a simple soldier's life free of a taint that might anger Protestant superiors in the army's hierarchy.[28]

Their wedding proved to be the Capitol's best social event of the season, befitting the marriage of a cabinet member's daughter. It was an opulent affair, hosted at the Blair House instead of a church. Much of the nation's leadership was in attendance, including the president, members of the Supreme Court, and senators Henry Clay and Daniel Webster, both frail and magnificent. Few American brides could brag to their diaries of receiving a wedding-day kiss from the president of the United States. An extended honeymoon in Philadelphia and New York began immediately after the ceremony. Ellen's younger brother, Tom Jr., went along. A honeymoon with a young male tagalong was not unusual for the times. The honeymoon was dampened a bit when, upon their return to Washington on the Fourth of July, after the president spoke to a large crowd at the dedication of the new monument to George Washington, the sixty-six-year-old Taylor complained of illness and five days later was dead. For the second time a president's death left Thomas Ewing Sr. a member in a cabinet serving a new president he personally disliked.[29]

The feeling was mutual. When Millard Fillmore moved into the White House, he put his own administration into place and fired some of Taylor's men, including Thomas Ewing. In Ewing's place at Interior he appointed Ohio senator Thomas Corwin, then Governor Seabury Ford tweaked Fillmore by appointing Ewing to fill Corwin's seat. Ohio's most ardent Whig would watch over Fillmore's irrational tendencies. The Old Salt Boiler (Thomas Ewing Sr.'s nickname since

27. "Pale and feeble" from William T. Sherman, *Memoirs of General William T. Sherman; By Himself,* 1:86; "finality" from Page Smith, *Trial by Fire: A People's History of the Civil War and Reconstruction,* xiii.

28. "Bigoted devotion" from Fellman, *Citizen Sherman,* 363.

29. Tom's role in the honeymoon from Marszalek, *Soldier's Passion,* 81–82.

his youth) savored each day, advocating internal improvements and a stronger banking system. In September Ewing proved that, had he instead of Fillmore been president, he would have vetoed Clay's compromise. He voted against the Compromise of 1850, a very unpopular vote back in Ohio. Four months later Ewing's term ended, Salmon Chase was named to the Senate that year, and Thomas Ewing returned to private life.[30]

Four months after finishing his term in the Senate, Thomas Ewing Sr. won the largest real estate lawsuit in American history up to that time, a quiet title action to considerable lands around St. Louis. Ewing's fee was one hundred thousand dollars, an unheard of sum. He invested most of his fee in huge tracts of land around St. Louis, titling the property in the name of his sons and daughters.

Now married to a woman with considerable property, Sherman was assigned to St. Louis at the sprawling facility at Jefferson Barracks. Even though she was a wealthy landowner in the region, Ellen stayed behind in Lancaster. Nine months from the date of their wedding, she gave birth to a daughter, Minnie. Ellen continued to resist living in St. Louis, at least at first. Sherman reminded her that St. Louis was hardly a frontier posting. They would live at the Planter's House hotel, the finest in St. Louis. Father Ewing sweetened the pot by offering Sherman the role of caretaker for the new family investments in St. Louis, hinting that Sherman first would have to build a home and live in St. Louis. Buoyed by the idea of living an extravagant lifestyle even if it was not in New York or Philadelphia, Ellen took up the challenge. Sherman purchased a small house ten minutes by omnibus from downtown St. Louis but stalled when it came to making any decision concerning whether he would quit the army and manage his father-in-law's properties. The Shermans lived a year in that home, sharing it with West Point classmate Stewart Van Vliet, who volunteered to contribute to the expenses, and Sherman accepted. In all, Cump and Ellen Sherman were married for thirty-eight years, but this time in St. Louis was the only time Ellen lived with him for any length of time.[31]

Like a lost stepchild Hugh Ewing missed Ellen's wedding, wanting just one last fling in the gold fields before he promised her to settle down to study law. His only significant find in the gold fields, a small packet of dust, he lost on a stream bank. Near Downeyville a tree fell on Ewing's ankle and broke it. A bit of malpractice by a local doctor left Ewing with a poorly set bone that promised a life-

30. Ford's appointment swap mentioned in Sherman, *Memoirs,* 1:85.
31. Marszalek, *Soldier's Passion,* 88.

time of rheumatism and a $250 bill he refused to pay. He wrote home that he had finished his last day as a miner.

After a short and fruitless career as a land speculator in San Francisco, Hugh contacted Calhoun Benham, and after assuring Benham he had no further itch to work the gold fields or speculate on any California lands, he began to read law. Sherman had written Hugh in 1848 that there were too many lawyers in California trying to earn a living where there were few courts. Now Hugh was seeing the problem firsthand. He was swindled out of speculation land he had bought in San Francisco when he could not come up with Benham's large retainer. There was also a dearth of women in California, which sent Hugh writing to Ellen with reminders that he had put on weight and was now a sour catch for a woman of any importance. "Having neglected the cultivation of my waist, it has grown out of all compass and my face has grown fat. I have sunk into an awkward, no shaped, fat-faced bachelor of 25 and must confess that my [romantic] prospects are gloomy, if not desperate."[32]

In June 1852 Hugh returned to Lancaster, renewing his law studies with the one lawyer in whom he had complete faith, his own father. Philemon Ewing was working with local bankers and had part of the Ewing properties under his wing, but Phil could not do it all. The obligations of sons to manage family affairs of the wealthy were strong pressures in the nineteenth century, and Thomas Ewing Sr.'s demands on Hugh in that regard were no different. One of his sons or sons-in-law was expected to handle the family affairs. If not Phil or Cump, then it would have to be Hugh, who had no attachment for army life and was unmarried. He became the logical choice once it was clear that Sherman was as yet not leaving the army. Hugh wrote a cousin that he was happy with his new life. The Ewing holdings in St. Louis were "rising in the market" making the ultimate value "enormous."[33]

While there was talk in Ewingville about new careers for Cump and Hugh, politics also formed part of the dinner table conversation. The Whigs tried to salvage something from Fillmore's disastrous presidency. The Compromise of 1850 had

32. The lack of courts to handle the territory's business may have been a conscious attempt to put more federal land agents into Kansas—who had a more direct impact on President Franklin Pierce's efforts there than did judges, whose political impact was less direct. See WTS to John Sherman, April 18, 1848, in Rachel Sherman Thorndike, ed., *The Sherman Letters: Correspondence between General and Senator Sherman from 1837 to 1891,* 39; "my waist" at Hugh Boyle Ewing (hereafter HBE) to Ellen Ewing Sherman (hereafter EES), March 24, 1852, from Ewing, "Autobiography," 160; Hugh Ewing's California days are generally at Ewing, "Autobiography," 122–68.

33. Ewing, "Autobiography," 176.

divided Northern voters and unified the South, leaving Fillmore with little to govern—even if he had been up to the task, which he was not. Sensing his weakness Democrats hammered at Fillmore's efforts to promote Whig legislation, blocking some of the agenda and chipping away at the rest. The country had wanted a war hero in 1848 and had voted for one, not a businessman. Fillmore's signature on the Compromise of 1850 doomed him to one fill-in term. At the Niagara Falls convention in 1852, Whigs sensed they needed a new leader, preferably a military leader to carry on Taylor's legacy. The Salt Boiler was scheduled to give an important nominating speech and again was being considered for high office, but he then took seriously ill with *cholera morbus.* Friends telegraphed Hugh to come to Niagara Falls immediately and to bring his mother. This last request frightened the sons. When Thomas Ewing had been fired from Fillmore's cabinet, Tom Jr. had left the Department of the Interior and had gone to Brown University in Providence, Rhode Island, to finish schooling. Providence was closer to Niagara Falls. Hugh wired Tom for assistance in getting their father home to Ohio. With Thomas Ewing gone from the scene, Fillmore's men worked to parry the challenge from Winfield Scott. On the forty-eighth ballot Scott was nominated.[34]

The best political weapon the Whigs could hope for that year was a divided Democratic Party, which was growing more attractive to Hugh Ewing. His father's vote against the Compromise of 1850 came with the viewpoint that the 1820 Missouri Compromise was a stronger way to keep the country together than the new law. Stephen A. Douglas was the darling of the Democratic moderates, but the Southern wing of the party would never support Douglas. What the Democrats did was nominate a nearly unknown New Hampshire lawyer who had been a brigadier in Scott's army, Franklin Pierce. When the Whigs self-destructed in the South and Scott's campaign never got going, Pierce swamped his former commanding officer in the general election. In his inaugural speech Pierce promised to use the power of the federal government to do nothing, especially where states rights were concerned. Democrats had finished the long road back into power, and the Whigs were bleeding profusely. "There is poetical rejoicing of the 'unwashed' victors," Hugh noted sarcastically.[35]

34. Ibid., 176–78.

35. "Poetical rejoicing" in HBE to Hamp Denman, November 5, 1852, from Ewing, "Autobiography," 180.

2

LE GRAND DÉTOUR

French explorers were the first to navigate the river that divides the state of Missouri and gives the state its name. In 1804 Lewis and Clark mapped the river area of northwest Missouri as they moved northwest on their "Voyage of Discovery." They passed through what the French called *le grand détour,* where the river divides Kansas and Missouri. The region came into sharper focus in 1853 when a new slavery "compromise" was rumored to be on the desk of a stumpy back-bench Illinois Democrat senator named Stephen A. Douglas. Two-thirds of the hundred thousand slaves in Missouri in the 1850s were congregated in the hemp- and tobacco-growing counties on the Missouri side of this river boundary. For Missouri planters these slaves were too close for comfort to the free state of Iowa, and the presence of untamed prairie land to the west represented for slave owners general enforcement problems under the fugitive slave laws. Slavery compromises had separated the Whigs into sharply divided camps, and Douglas was determined to keep his party from imploding along the political fault lines that consumed the Whigs.[1]

In later life Tom Ewing described his boyish self as "intensely antislavery" at that particular moment in the nation's history, "far more so than my Whig

1. Slaves in Missouri from Stephen Z. Starr, *Jennison's Jayhawkers: A Civil War Cavalry Regiment and Its Commander,* 4; H. Miles Moore, *Early History of Leavenworth City and County,* 6.

training would account for." He especially loathed the Fugitive Slave Law. His Brown College ties put him in touch with—and gave him more tolerance for—abolitionists. He did not openly embrace their theories, but he was not hostile to their views, at least not at that time. When word of the new compromise began to circulate in Washington, with rumors that it included a form of local decision-making about whether a territory would become a slave state or a free state (taking Congress out of the political mix), abolitionists were angry and Free Soil moderates were puzzled. For politicians such as Illinois state representative Abraham Lincoln, the issue was not the abolition of slavery but rather the fact that the federal government was reneging on a primary tenet of nationhood. Douglas's scheme was viewed by many as a public betrayal of Southern promises to forgo the spread of slavery into the territories. Lincoln later challenged Douglas with the dare: "These principles are an eternal antagonism. . . . When a white man governs himself it is self-government. When he governs other men, it is more than self-government; it is despotism. No man is good enough to govern another man without the other's consent." Repeal all compromises, Lincoln challenged Douglas, even repeal all history, but "you cannot repeal human nature." By implication, neither could territorial legislatures.[2]

On the floor of the U.S. Senate where waning Whig influence was the only true opposition to the act, young Tom Ewing watched the bombastic Massachusetts senator Edward Everett try to fight off the lure of Douglas's compromise. Ewing later wrote of Everett that he was "too cool, didactic, elegant, without a glow." Douglas spoke at length, saying that the political personalities of a territory, however jaundiced with prejudices, would—and indeed should—set the territory's political values. The South saw these debates from a very different point of view. Under this act they could expand slavery without going hat in hand to the Congress. With Southern support for the bill and a slow confused reaction from Northern Whigs, the act slipped through the political process. When the Kansas-Nebraska Act was signed on May 30, 1854, William Evarts, a Sherman relative, predicted that the Whigs' failure to oppose Kansas-Nebraska effectively was "an act of blindness." With President Franklin Pierce sympathetic to them, Southerners would launch a supreme effort—a test case—to preserve slavery's future

2. "Whig training" from Thomas Ewing Jr., "The Struggle For Freedom in Kansas," 1; Lincoln speeches from Larry Shapiro, ed., *Abraham Lincoln: Mystic Chords of Memory; A Selection of Lincoln's Writings*, 27–28.

on the prairie grasslands west of Missouri. Like bass in a pond, Southerners saw a glimmer of hope on the water's surface and rose to the bait.[3]

Even with politics as the best part of local theater, for the Ewings there was still time for family gatherings. On April 6, 1854, Henry Stanbery made the motion that Hugh Ewing be accepted as a member of the U.S. Supreme Court bar. The occasion prompted a Ewing family gathering, and most of the family came to Washington for the ceremony. Several weeks later Hugh confided in Ellen that he had come to Washington for more than just a Supreme Court sheepskin. He had come to meet Stanbery's daughter Clara. Hugh was not quite the eligible bachelor his younger brother Tom was, and Clara proved not to be the catch he was looking for. He might be a newly minted member of the Supreme Court bar, but Hugh's growing despair at finding a wife led him even to flirt with thoughts of a monastic life. Politically, the family followed the daily ebb and flow of debate on the Kansas-Nebraska Act, the subject of overwhelming interest that year in Washington. Hugh looked upon the act as Douglas preached it: a means of getting rid of slavery as an agent of national gridlock. He could tolerate Whigs because of his father's history there, but not the Republicans, who kept the issue alive with talk of abolition. "There may be such a thing as honor among thieves, but there is no such thing among Republican demagogues," he wrote Ellen.[4]

If Ellen Sherman's politics differed from her brother's, she kept her views private. Cump Sherman had been talked into leaving the army in order to enter the banking business in San Francisco for St. Louis banker Henry Turner. One condition her husband had set for his entry into private life was that she accompany him to San Francisco. While Ellen relished the thought of being a banker's wife, San Francisco had fewer amenities than St. Louis and she secretly prepared to welsh on the deal. San Francisco was an "outlandish place" she would go to for a short time only. "The Bible says 'let a man leave his Father's house and cleave unto his wife,'" she insisted in a letter to Hugh. She was man's "better half—and not his slave, and due regard to her taste, fears and feelings" must be paid. She would not give up family and friends "for all the gold in California."[5]

Mass emigration into the Kansas Territory began before the ink on the Kansas-Nebraska Act had a chance to dry. While settlers came from all over, the majori-

3. "Too cool" from Ewing, "Struggle For Freedom," 1; "blindness" from Chester Barrows, *William M. Evarts, Lawyer, Diplomat, Statesman,* 40.

4. HBE to EES, April 23, 1854; Ewing, "Autobiography," 197.

5. EES to HBE, May 3, 1854, EFP/ND.

ty came from the states of the old Northwest Territory. Abolitionist organizations such as the New England Emigrant Aid Society outfitted settlers and sent them to Kansas to form towns—buying their land for them, erecting hotels, mills, and stores, and organizing transportation. Settlers were to root out any proslavery men in the area and vote to organize the government along the Free State philosophy. Men such as Charles Robinson, a New England Company agent, and entrepreneur Cyrus K. Holliday were among the first into the territory. Holliday's letters to his wife boasted, "I would not exchange Kansas and its dirty shirts for Pennsylvania with all its elegance and refinement." Meanwhile Southern associations were playing the same game in reverse. With rumors circulating that Eastern bankers had raised $5 million to send twenty thousand armed abolitionists to Kansas, Southerners chose to believe that Northern prisons and immigrant shanty towns were being emptied and all the political flotsam of the East was en route to Kansas to burn out proslavery men. Organizations such as the Sons of the South, Social Bands, and Blue Lodges vowed to meet the challenge "with bayonets and blood" and formed for battle.[6]

Within two weeks of the president's signature on the Kansas-Nebraska bill, Leavenworth, Kansas, was founded primarily by proslavery men from Weston, Missouri, who set out the city's boundaries three miles south of the fort. It was a rough-as-cob place with crooked streets and an "almost impenetrable growth of underbrush which covered the entire tract," a smelly mixture of mud and horse dung. It was a hard place to grow dreams.[7]

With proslavery and antislavery elements in close proximity, claim jumping was common, and the regulation of land disputes became the most important government function on the prairie. The earliest government entities were squatter courts. The claims associations were formed at open-air mass meetings of settlers. They established crude rules of procedure to referee title disputes and administer claims. Squatter courts took it upon themselves to try all persons accused of claim jumping, even empanelling token juries, although there was no statutory basis for any of their operations. Josiah Miller, the probate judge of Douglas County, Kansas, held court in a meat market or, when a large crowd was expected, the new Congregational Church in Lawrence. The furnishings of the first Kansas courtroom of newly minted probate judge David Brewer was far from the

6. Carruth, "New England Emigrant Aid Company, 91; "dirty shirts" from Lela Barnes, "Letters of Cyrus K. Holliday, 1854–1859," 246; "bayonets" from Kenneth S. Davis, *Kansas: A Bicentennial History*, 40–41.

7. "Impenetrable growth" from the *Kansas Weekly Herald* (the first newspaper published in Kansas), September 15, 1854.

majestic mahogany chairs and bench of the U.S. Supreme Court he would later occupy. Brewer's probate court was a store on Nebraska Street in Kansas City, Kansas, where on more than one occasion the wooden stairway outside doubled as a scaffold.[8]

Rapid claim development in the territory not only caused claim jumping, it was a major blunder in the territory's development. A swarm of settlers like army ants came into the territory to squat on tribal lands. The cavalry assigned to watch the small numbers of relatively peaceful tribes were then both unable and unwilling to referee claim jumping. A large number of settlers held Southern loyalties, and Secretary of War Jefferson Davis certainly did not want them ejected. He refused to authorize more cavalry to go to Kansas merely to protect Indian lands that were going to be confiscated and sold off anyway. Entire Indian reservations became subject to de facto white settlement. Congress also was conflicted, promoting the mortgaging of public lands by railroads while at the same time promising settlers a nearly free homestead. Over 1.5 million acres of land, the eastern one-fifth of present-day Kansas, much of it Indian lands, went to railroads or settlers before, during, and after the Civil War. This change of policy in the Pierce administration and the rapid growth of partisan squatter courts and associations made Bleeding Kansas as much a story of speculation and claim jumping as a fight over politics and slavery.[9]

It was in Leavenworth that the Ewings would establish their first family presence in the Kansas Territory, but not immediately. Like the territory itself Leavenworth, the first boomtown in Kansas, expanded rapidly. In Leavenworth, just after the territory was opened in the spring of 1854, speculators offloaded from the steamboat *Martha Jewell* the first of many prefabricated houses for Leavenworth's growing population. The single hotel saw room rates begin at $2.75 per week, or $5.00 with board. Single meals cost twenty cents a day. Often the public rooms were unpainted, uncarpeted, and "as filthy as any incorrigible tobacco chewer

8. One of the better publications on the early Kansas bench and bar is Robert Richmond, ed., *Requisite Learning and Good Moral Character: A History of the Kansas Bench and Bar,* 30–31. See also Paul E. Wilson, "John Adams Halderman: Our Eldest Brother," 84.

9. Paul W. Gates, *Fifty Million Acres: Conflicts over Kansas Land Policy, 1854–1890,* 237–40. For Bleeding Kansas as land speculation, see Robert Gaston Elliott, "The Grasshopper Falls Convention and the Legislature of 1857," 183–84. "Bleeding Kansas" refers to the period 1854–1858 when settlers clashed violently over political efforts to make the territory a slave state in order to mirror the policy of the Buchanan administration.

would wish to have it." Men could not wait to have their own homes, even modest ones.[10]

With Free State interests now challenging proslavery men nearly everywhere, Missouri slave interests bragged to the *New York Tribune* that every Free Soil abolitionist was marked for "extermination." Taking their cue from editor Benjamin Stringfellow and U.S. Senator David Atchison, whose rhetoric gave Atchison's Platte City Regulators a quickening pulse for violence, the ruffians preyed on abolitionist sympathizers. In mid-April, Stringfellow destroyed the antislavery newspaper the *Parkville Luminary* and drove the editor and city namesake, George Park, out of town. The proslavery *Leavenworth Herald* warned its targeted readers, "Suffer not an avowed abolitionist to remain within your borders." The loss of a "free press" resulted in lurid stories about Kansas in Eastern abolitionist newspapers. This in turn encouraged more settlers to relocate, which led to more violence. The man who later in life would be known around the world as Buffalo Bill Cody watched his father suffer severe injuries inflicted by border ruffians wielding knives, and as a Kansas Red Leg during the war Cody would later take his revenge on Missouri ruffians. The violence was mindless. In 1855 Sam Fugate allegedly murdered a Free State settler just to win a drunken bet that he could "kill and scalp an abolitionist before dawn." Free State men retaliated. Malcolm Clark, a proslavery man, was shot dead at a squatters' meeting in Leavenworth in April 1855. Within a month the proslavery Vigilance Committee ordered abolitionist William Phillips to leave town. Phillips was stripped, tarred and feathered, and ridden a mile and a half on a rail. He was later shot to death in his home when a second mob set about to punish him once again, but not before Phillips had killed two of his attackers.[11]

A year after the territory opened, the sons of a spry Connecticut abolitionist settled a twelve-acre tract near Osawatomie. They wrote their father that Kansas was the place to make a life and raise the Sword of Gideon on behalf of the black sons of Ham. His spirit renewed, John Brown prepared to join his sons in Kansas and begin his own form of the Lord's work.[12]

St. Louis on the Mississippi River in the east of Missouri was too far east to have a direct hand in what was happening in Kansas. Since 1820 the city had

10. "Tobacco chewers" from Julia Lovejoy, "Letters from Kansas," 34.

11. "Extermination" from *New York Tribune,* March 26, 1855; "Suffer not" from *Leavenworth Herald,* May 11, 1855; "scalp" and Phillip's death from Richmond, *Requisite Learning,* 79.

12. S. J. Shively, "The Pottawatomie Massacre," 185.

grown into a cosmopolitan center. It was there, in the winter of 1854–1855, that Judge Alexander Hamilton accepted Hugh Ewing into the Missouri bar, largely on the strength of Father Ewing's legendary reputation. Thomas Ewing Sr.'s name was mentioned only in whispers among the local bar. There were things about the practice in St. Louis that were somewhat peculiar. The oath of allegiance required Hugh to support the Missouri constitution, which meant swearing allegiance to the state's slave code. It was a distinction that did not appear to bother Hugh's sensibilities.[13]

From Hugh's new law practice he wrote his father that "Cases are opened in our Courts as soon as the jury is sworn. The opening consists of explaining to the jury the nature of the case on the part of the plaintiff, as shown by the petition, and defense as shown by the answer and . . . outlining the testimony expected to be produced by plaintiff." The same jury often decided multiple cases. Trial income was scarce. The cost of a lawyer in a half-day trial in Wisconsin in 1861 was five dollars, about a dollar an hour. Such expertise could be hired in St. Louis for less.[14]

Hugh spent his days in advising friends and relatives about proposed Indian campaigns in Kansas being planned from St. Louis's Jefferson Barracks. Hugh's cousin Hamp Denman was in St. Louis and always coming up with new ideas, such as driving huge cattle herds overland to California behind the wagon trains. Denman's diversions aside, Hugh enjoyed his new surroundings. "I am making headway more rapidly than most beginners. There are a great many lawyers here, but the Bar is not distinguished for talent. I think most of them labor merely for a verdict money and not fame. I advise you to come here and nowhere else. But [not] Chicago. . . . It is flooded by Yankee attorneys, and a scanty living can't be picked up there."[15]

Hugh's enthusiasm for the charms of St. Louis did not extend to the caliber of its juries. His first trial uncovered "a hang-dog set of scoundrels as ever sat in a box," a jury that apparently held against his client. He assumed from their "ragged, half-starved" appearance that they were bribed by the other side. The thought that bribery was the only means of securing justice left him cynical. The lack of quality juries Hugh blamed on local judges. He quickly lost patience with Judge Hamilton when Hamilton refused to grant Hugh's client a new trial. Although he had been Hugh's sponsor earlier, Hamilton had become "the scoff of

13. Ewing, "Autobiography," 199.
14. HBE to TESr., January 12, 1855, ibid., 201.
15. HBE to Silas Wright, February 14, 1855, ibid., 201–2.

the city" and "an imbecile." He could understand Hamilton if his weakness was caused by bribery. To refuse Hugh's client a new trial because of "timidity" was sickening. "I, of course, say nothing here about Judge or jury but through motives of self-interest only. I would like to tell them what I think of them." During the day he handled low-paying unpopular causes, using his father's name and political connections to create a client base. "Men of first standing here at the Bar, have expressed to me their opinion that you stand at the head of the Bar of the United States," he wrote his father. At night he visited prominent families in St. Louis, "making acquaintances, which I hope to turn into clients." He handled a wide variety of matters at this time, mostly small collections, reveling in a daylong courtroom fight over the "bankrupt carcass of an old steamboat," where he netted his first fee (fifty dollars) as a creditor's attorney.[16]

While Hugh was beginning his career in St. Louis, Tom Ewing was also struggling, having decided not to finish his course of studies at Brown College where he had gone after his stint as Taylor's private secretary. By 1855 organized schooling was beginning to bore him. He attended law school in Cincinnati but again did not finish. Law schools were unusual in those days; the curriculum was more like graduate-level work in law and government procedure than the formal professional schooling of today. The Socratic method of teaching (students answering question after question from professors) was developed in the nineteenth century and remains part of modern law schools. Between classes on Kent's *Commentaries* on the common law, the program included debating societies and impromptu speaking, where young men learned to turn tables on each other and survive an opponent's gunfire of words. Tom enjoyed it enough that he took up public speaking for small fees. Politics provided the grist of his speeches, and the Kansas Territory and what would happen to slavery there was the main topic.

Hugh wrote Tom to encourage his younger brother away from the rigors of a practice in Ohio and to join him in St. Louis and bring his debating skills to the practice of law for the St. Louis upper crust. "I dine tomorrow with William L. Ewing," Hugh wrote once, "one of the first merchants and most wealthy men of the city. . . . We have agreed that we are related." That could mean much to a budding law practice. Tom thought seriously about Hugh's offer. He came out to look the place over and apparently liked what he saw, but it was uncertain whether a sparse St. Louis practice would support both brothers. Hugh reluctantly had to agree that finances, not desire, was the crucial stumbling block. "My dear fellow,

16. HBE to TESr., February 19, also February 26, 1855, ibid., 202–4.

[do you know] how hard a thing it is to get into practice [in St. Louis]? Since you left, I have had nothing upon the face of the earth to do." To Ellen Sherman, however, to whom Hugh bragged of his three new railroad cases and a probate matter, he wrote that his law practice was going in the right direction but not so his love life. Perhaps with a dig at Sherman, Hugh wrote Tom, "I am too poor to marry and too proud to live on the fortune of a wife."[17]

Beginning a practice in the West was going to require starvation wages for some length of time, and it was important to Tom that there be other means of earning a living. He began a law practice in Cincinnati in the spring of 1855 but kept his eyes on what was happening in the Kansas Territory. Henry Stanbery sponsored his membership into the Cincinnati bar. Ewing began as most new lawyers do, by soliciting clients through newspaper advertising. His father's name and reputation attracted work from other lawyers, especially appellate work in the U.S. Circuit Court. However, he had few paying clients. He supplemented his income with paid lectures. While the politics of the territory were interesting, so too were the land speculation schemes in Kansas. While Hugh worried about his matrimonial prospects, Tom tracked "every step of the struggle" in Kansas through the widely distributed writings of his first hero, Eli Thayer, whose lectures against the expansion of slavery were widely circulated.[18]

Reviewing the growing problems in the territory, Hugh lamented to Patterson Effinger the low ebb to which his father's Whig Party had sunk, "its members scattered like leaves before the wind." What truly concerned Hugh was the failure of his law practice to take off. He was better established in St. Louis than Tom was in Cincinnati, but his income was meager. His friends were taking advantage of him. "I tried a little case today, before the Justice, and gained it," he bragged to his father in June. "My client being a friend gave me no fee."[19]

One of Tom Ewing's lectures in Cincinnati was attended by the daughter of the Presbyterian minister in Lancaster. Tom Ewing was then introduced to Ellen Cox and they fell for each other quickly. In November, after a brief courtship, Tom proposed. On January 8, 1856, the young bachelor that nobody in Washington had been able to snare married Ellen Cox in the Presbyterian church of Lancas-

17. "I dine tomorrow" from HBE to Thomas Ewing Jr. (hereafter TEJr.), March 3, 1855, "get into practice" from HBE to EES, March 22, 1855, "too poor to marry" from HBE to TEJr., May 9, 1855, all in ibid., 205–8.

18. "Every step" from Miller, "Thomas Ewing Jr.," 2.

19. "Scattered like leaves" from HBE to Patterson Effinger, May 17, 1855, "no fee" from HBE to TESr., June 9, 1855, both in Ewing, "Autobiography," 208.

ter. Showing his early ability at internal compromise and external independence, and as Exhibit "A" as to why mothers always assume sons marry beneath them, Tom began attending a Presbyterian church with his new wife.[20]

Tom Ewing's law practice continued to languish. Cincinnati was filled with many established lawyers and firms. Anyone could practice law for nothing. In Kansas, on the other hand, the Ewings could be land agents and practice real estate law. It was fair to say that Tom Ewing also wanted to see where national history was being made. As Albert Castel wrote, Kansas was "an open field for his driving ambition." Cousin Hamp Denman was already in Leavenworth, eager to speculate in land and casting about for partners. Were Hugh and Tom interested in forming a land speculation company to go with the practice of law?[21]

The idea for a real estate speculation practice was hatched late in 1855. At least when dealing with land speculators, the Ewing sons were assured that the speculators had cash, a commodity with which their law clients in St. Louis and Cincinnati were not flush. Further, the Ewings had access to money through their father's influential Ohio friends. Surviving as speculators in an untamed frontier river town with consortium money seemed a better process than waiting for law clients to walk through the door. Within weeks of his marriage Tom Ewing traveled to Leavenworth and scouted the city and its prospects. Given that many recruiters for Kansas emigrants suggested its weather rivaled that of Charleston, South Carolina, Tom might also have been reviewing the scene as to what the weather might do to keep him healthy. In Cincinnati and before his marriage, he had suffered periodic bouts of malaria, a disease he first caught in Washington, D.C. The last time he had almost died, so his health concerns took on more importance. In Leavenworth Hamp introduced Tom around to some of the city fathers. Everyone he met, as so many others, had come there to make a fortune, not spend one.

In spite of ice running in the Missouri River, the decision was made, and both Ewing brothers made preparations to move to Kansas, where Tom felt "indomitable confidence in his capacity for self advancement." He spent time winding up his limited affairs and closing his Cincinnati practice. At about the same time Hugh finished his business in St. Louis by solidifying the family's friendship with Sherman's benefactor Henry Turner, who introduced Hugh to Turner's partner, James Lucas. Hugh wanted to cultivate Turner & Lucas so as to be the bankers' agents on the Kansas frontier. It was a financial liaison that would prove extremely

20. Marie Boyle Ewing was a devout Catholic. Tom married a Presbyterian, "beneath them."
21. Albert Castel, *A Frontier State at War: Kansas, 1861–1865*, 25.

beneficial for the next few years, and their ties with important financiers as far away as London would prove useful in the later railroad-building wars. Hugh wrote his father that Turner had invited him to spend Sundays at the banker's country estate, and that "Mr. Lucas says that Sherman is going to be a great man in California."[22]

Thousands of settlers who used Leavenworth as a jumping-off spot to the territory had no strong political affiliation over the slavery issue. They were in Kansas to acquire land and, with their families, build a life. What they faced was chaotic. Some officers in the territorial land office were the dregs of federal patronage, men from other states sent to Kansas as a favor for their Democratic leanings but perhaps unfamiliar with the job and using shoddy office procedures in the Lecompton land office. None of the patrons seemed to mind, however. Slow paperwork or even the loss of a record often worked to a squatter's advantage. Men who could work a patch of land appropriated from Indians in a cost-free manner could, over a year or perhaps two, make enough money to pay for the land when the specifics of the government sale of tribal land were completed. The hotheaded young editor Daniel R. Anthony came to Kansas to open a newspaper but wrote whimsically of the real estate business to his father: "If I had invested $1000 here six months ago, it would have been worth $10,000 now."[23]

While speculation was the main draw toward Kansas, the Ewings arrived during a remarkable period of lawlessness. The 1855 spring territorial elections were filled with voting frauds. Mobs from Missouri invaded Kansas and ran off twenty-nine hundred registered voters, electing their own legislature with over six thousand votes. First the more numerous Free Staters labeled the resulting body the "bogus legislature" and then ignored its edicts—such as the idiotic law that only proslavery men were qualified to hold public office. Proslavery elements even fought with Pierce's governor, Andrew Reeder, who then encouraged the formation of a "shadow" Free State government. So territorial Kansas began life with two legislatures, one self-appointed and the other elected by fraud; naturally they did not communicate with each other.[24]

Newspapers continued to arouse partisan hatred. The day after Christmas 1855, the proslavery *Kickapoo Pioneer* wrote, "It is this class of * * * [abolitionists] that Kansas must get rid of. We know of no better method than for every man who

22. "Indomitable confidence" from Miller, "Thomas Ewing Jr.," 5; "great man in California" from Ewing, "Autobiography," 200.

23. "Worth $10,000" from Starr, *Jennison's Jayhawkers*, 6.

24. Lovejoy, "Letters from Kansas," 43; Brian Moline, "Early Kansas Judiciary," 25; "shadow government" from Stampp, *America in 1857*, 272.

loves his country and the laws by which he is governed to meet in Kansas and kill off this god-forsaken class of humanity as soon as they place their feet on our soil." The *Pioneer* found itself in league with its more caustic neighbor to the north, the *Atchison Squatter Sovereign.* "In our opinion the only effectual way to correct the [situation] is to hang up to the nearest tree the very last traitor who was instrumental in [the] Topeka convention." Atchison wrote the *Charleston, S.C., Mercury,* to expect civil war within the year. "We are arming and preparing for it."[25]

In the midst of the efforts by the Pierce administration to restore order in Kansas, the scattered elements of the Ewing clan were assembling for a reckoning of their own. Throughout the spring and summer of 1856, while the nation's focus was on the aftermath of Massachusetts senator Charles Sumner's caning by a South Carolina congressman over Sumner's ill-tempered remarks about the "harlot Slavery," an economic and political slide began in San Francisco. Cump Sherman had been talked out of his army career by Henry Turner and was now running Turner's bank in San Francisco. Sherman wrote his father-in-law that, since the banks had failed, there was no money for operating loans, and without the sale of goods the city's tax revenues were falling precipitously. While Sherman's deft leadership had kept the Turner & Lucas branch solvent, the bank had just barely survived the panic.[26]

For every sow's ear there is a silk purse. While California was falling apart, the Kansas Territory was on the upswing, at least in places. The trip Tom Ewing had made to Leavenworth in the summer of 1855 encouraged him to make a permanent move to join Denman. In Cincinnati Tom had worked diligently for John Fremont's campaign for over a year. He did not particularly like Fremont, but between the light load of his law practice in Ohio and his efforts for Fremont, he was able to go out to Kansas in January 1856 to pick an office site in Leavenworth with Denman. Business operations were formally moved to Leavenworth in the spring of 1856, after the Missouri River shrugged off its winter sheen of ice. Tom then came out a few months later with Ellen. Leavenworth was not only their new base of real estate speculation, it allowed Tom to keep his fingers in politics, which greatly appealed to him. Politics in Kansas was never dull, as it had been in stodgy old Cincinnati. While Tom was uncertain whether his law practice would bloom

25. "Kansas must" from Shively, "Pottawatomie Massacre," 185; William E. Connelley, *Life of Preston B. Plumb,* 32; *Atchison Squatter Sovereign,* February 20, 1856; "We are arming" from George W. Martin, "The First Two Years of Kansas," 131n31.

26. "Harlot slavery" from McPherson, *Battle Cry,* 151; WTS to TESr., August 3, 1856, from Fellman, *Citizen Sherman,* 56.

in Kansas, he and Hugh were excited about the new venture and suggested to their sister Ellen that Sherman should join them.

The invitation to settle in Kansas was ignored by both Ellen Sherman and her husband, at least for the moment. Ellen was in San Francisco with Cump, and she was not anxious to go anywhere unless back to Lancaster. A muddy river town in Kansas was the last place he could ask her to go. Besides, Sherman was leery of pinning any hopes for a fortune on the quicksand of land speculation, in spite of the modest earlier successes he had made in Sacramento.

Tom took with him to Kansas a view of land as being the best of investment opportunities. He was twenty-seven years old and had never been elected to political office, nor had he operated any business. The politics of the young are always flexible. Ewing did not think slave owners were ogres; he simply disagreed with them on the policy surrounding the expansion of the institution. He supported Free State policies, but not abolitionists. At this point in his life the sun did not rise or set with the national Republican Party, which was trying to elect Fremont that year; the party was simply closer to his views on the important issues of the day than were Denman's Democrats.[27]

While Tom Ewing and Hamp Denman kept an eye on politics and potential violence, the brothers were trying to time Hugh's move of his St. Louis practice to Leavenworth. Obviously, if Kansas became a slave state, it would have more in common with Missouri—and Missouri money men such as Turner and Lucas—than if Free State sentiment prevailed. A frustrated Hugh wrote his father for advice, admitting that "I am [still] upon the list of waiters," and that most of his St. Louis clients were nonpaying. All the "beginners are in the same category, saving those who stoop to conquer, which I never will do." What he meant by "stoop to conquer" is unclear, but it appears his competitors apparently bent the rules on soliciting clients, perhaps by paying laypersons to refer clients to them. Hugh's wanderlust, like the recurring rheumatism from his broken foot, was acting up. He spent time in New York and Chicago raising investment funds for the Kansas speculation business from an increasing circle of acquaintances and then returned to Lancaster during the heat of the summer. Kansas had no special allure for him; Hugh often spoke of somewhere other than where he was headed. He asked one friend (known only as Kearney), "I have a great notion to go down to an interior town in Mexico, lie down under a palm tree, and let the world slide. Will you join me?"[28]

27. William E. Treadway, "The Gilded Age in Kansas," 14–15; David G. Taylor, "Business and Political Career of Thomas Ewing Jr.: A Study of Frustrated Ambition," 12–13, 17, 21, 26–27; Ewing, "Autobiography," 211.

28. "Stoop to conquer" from HBE to TESr., May 21, 1856, "palm tree" from HBE to Kearney, May 29, 1856, both in Ewing, "Autobiography," 209–10.

In the summer of 1856 Tom returned to Cincinnati to report to his father what he had seen and to finish putting together the Kansas investment and speculation consortium. Many Easterners invested in land speculation in groups similar to modern mutual funds. Most were Ohio friends and associates of Thomas Ewing Sr., men who had speculated from afar in other territories at other times. The consortium included J. D. Martin, a Lancaster banker, Phil Ewing who was in Martin's bank at the time, Henry Stanbery, and several others. They focused on the autumn sale of the Indian reserves. Business intelligence was important then, as now. There was no sense bidding blind on the properties if government information could be provided by men in the department who admired the former secretary of the Interior.

In addition to old friends in the Department of the Interior whom he contacted for tidbits of information, Thomas Ewing Sr. also asked Sherman to reflect on what he remembered of the perils of land speculation in San Francisco. Sherman candidly warned against any speculation in farmland since the "inexhaustible quantity of good land" in Kansas would keep prices down. "It will be a long time before land for the simple purpose of farming will be a valuable article of speculation." There was no indication of Ewing's response to Sherman's advice, but when Ewing, Denman & Company opened for business in November 1856, the company concentrated its purchases in town lots.[29]

Hugh's frustrations with his lack of matrimonial prospects decreased his desire to remain in St. Louis. "There are pretty girls in town, but by singular distinction the rich ones are all ugly or ill-tempered and the pretty ones are poor, [a] mysterious arrangement." His move to Kansas was made easier by this realization. By January 1857 the land speculating company had taken offices on the main floor at 60 Main Street, a stone's throw from the steamboat levees.[30]

The Ewing brothers put part of an advance on their inheritance into the consortium and established a banking relationship with Sweeny, Rittenhouse & Fant of Washington. Hamilton G. Fant would be one of the Ewings' more difficult investor-clients. A broker in military land warrants, Fant operated heavily in Iowa and Kansas. He would buy up the warrants from former soldiers, either those already in the East and Midwest or those immigrating into Kansas itself. Each soldier mustered out of government service had received a numbered warrant in Washington files, and while soldiers could sell the warrants for cash, proper endorsements by the purchasers of such warrants had to be documented. The bro-

29. WTS to TESr., October 5, 1856, in Papers of the Thomas Ewing Family, Manuscript Division, Library of Congress (hereafter EFP/LC), quoted in Taylor, "Business and Political Career," 40.

30. HBE to Philemon Ewing, April 4, 1856, SFP/ND, in Ewing, "Autobiography," 209.

kers simply hired firms such as the Ewings to spot soldiers who would sell their certificates at a discount. However they acquired the warrants, brokers such as Fant purchased land in Kansas for little or nothing and then sat on the property, waiting on appreciation, or sold it on mortgage with interest.

Using Denman and Ewing as agents to collect and remit funds, Fant's 10 percent annual interest rate for loans on Kansas land was thoroughly acceptable, considering that the common rate in Ohio was 5 percent per month. Interest rates on the frontier would continue uncontrolled until well after statehood, when the state legislature, to lure more homesteaders, enacted usury limits. During territorial days, however, lenders could take title on any land that a settler wanted and give the settler a contract to hand over the deed when the payment price was entirely paid. Since the seller retained title to the land until the full amount was paid, the price or the interest rate could be set very high and there was little a landowner could do if he wanted the land. In a growing economy, investors thought little about either interest rates or biblical injunctions against usury. Inflation in land values would grow the investors out of any financial difficulties as the value of the land increased faster than the lenders' interest rate. If Leavenworth grew at the pace envisioned by the family, tenfold profits on an eleven-thousand-dollar Ewing investment would be easy.[31] On the other hand, the land speculation business was also susceptible to the vagaries of Murphy's Law.

The late William Treadway—a Ewing scholar, law professor, and for a quarter-century the general counsel of the Atchison, Topeka & Santa Fe Railroad (AT&SF) at the railroad's home office in Topeka—described Ewing's Kansas practice as "town lot speculation and making loans to settlers." The Ewings were participating in the last and longest active period of public land speculation in American history. But the business was conducted in a town where riotous living was the norm. Mounds of freight were stacked on the levees and bluffs above the river, awaiting transportation inland. Freight lines such as Tutt & Dougherty and Livingston & Kinkead provided provisions to the army in Utah and towns along the Santa Fe Trail. The freighters were Irishmen and Welshmen, tough men who liked their whiskey and prostitutes and disliked anyone who tried to "clean up" the place. Pious Leavenworth neighbors disliked this sign of civic progress. "We are governed by whiskey . . . and the Sabbath is devoted to creating drunkards," one resident complained.[32]

31. Taylor, "Business and Political Career," 26–27.

32. Treadway, "Gilded Age," 14–15; "creating drunkards" from Walker Wyman, "Atchison: A Great Frontier Depot," 308.

The Ewings as speculators were buyers of land and the assumption was that speculators and buyers were on uneven playing fields. This was not always the case, however. As lawyers the firm's partners could often "host" a penniless settler who wanted land but needed a man to "front" pay for forty acres of land for the settler. The settler would "give bond" for the deed, essentially agreeing to pay the land off with interest within a year. The Ewings would hold a signed deed from the farmer, and if the note was not paid off, the deed was filed of record with the land office and the Ewing & Denman office would own another forty acres. Not being farmers, they would do what many modern farm owners do—rent out the land to a tenant farmer for a third of the crop—perhaps the same farmer who had given bond the previous year. Everyone in this sort of relationship won—the seller if he got his inflated price, and the buyer if the land continued to appreciate in value and crop prices remained good. If land bought at $1.25 per acre then inflated to $2.00 or $3.00 per acre in a short time, a speculator could still turn a profit.[33]

Speculators brought to a territory both cash money and credit, two items in rare but needed supply. Leavenworth lavished such men (men such as the Ewings and their banker friends) with powers not given to others. Their law office became a private banking house, similar to the type of practice of lawyers' offices in England after the Reformation. However, speculation fueled other problems. As one Wisconsin editor put it, speculation sucked up everything, like a gold rush. "Merchants have shut up their shops, lawyers have left the bar, farmers have laid down the shovel and the hoe, manufacturers have abandoned their business to turn [into] land agents and real estate dealers." While the Ewings were helped by not having to finance all their purchases (the purpose of the consortium), the speculators were easy targets for newspaper attacks. Smart editors taught their readers there was a distinction between speculators: the idle rich stayed in the East, invested their funds, and could care less about homes, schools, and churches in Leavenworth, Kansas, while local speculators such as the Ewings brought families to the territory and were helping build its infrastructure.[34]

Two years after its creation, and six months after Tom Ewing and Hamp Denman arrived to begin their business, the territory's population had mushroomed to eighty thousand. Leavenworth was the largest town with five thousand inhabitants, the site for the territorial courts and attracting the best members of the bar. Tom Ewing was one of the few lawyers in the territory with a formal legal educa-

33. Robert P. Swierenga, *Pioneers and Profits: Land Speculation on the Iowa Frontier,* 99–100, 215–16.
34. "Merchants" from Stampp, *America in 1857,* 218.

tion; and the Ewing name, with its ties to presidential politics and especially Thomas Ewing Sr.'s knowledge of real estate law and the Department of the Interior, placed his sons with an entrée into Leavenworth's business and political community. Both Tom and Hugh registered with the local federal and state district courts, as was required of lawyers of that day. The oath administered to new lawyers by Judge Samuel Lecompte swore allegiance to the Kansas-Nebraska Act and the Fugitive Slave Law rather than the Constitution of the United States and the "divinity of the Christian religion." This was a pragmatic view. The Fugitive Slave Act was more important to national stability than Christianity, at least at this moment—and from a Missouri slave owner's perspective.[35]

The biggest land sale of 1857 was in mid-November, when the Delaware treaty lands went on the sale block. Eastern capitalists who had no local agents of their own lurked in Leavenworth streets for a week. So much river traffic reached Leavenworth that steamboat operators had to negotiate parking at the levee. The government was selling 209,000 acres of Indian lands at an average appraised price of $2.09 per acre. The land was platted, and each "lot" was given a unique identity. While the proceeds of the actual sale would go to the tribe (at least this ostensibly was the government's intention), speculators had few eleemosynary impulses. There had been an unofficial auction before the real auction began in a furious market in buying and selling unofficial "preemptions." A preemption claim was land with an unsecured title because title had not yet been perfected from the government. Because a man might hold a preemption claim that was worthless if someone else bid higher for the land at the public auction, preemption claims sold for far less than land sold with a "patent"—the warranty of good title from the government. When one bought a preemption claim, however, it was with the assurance that no one else would bid on that property at the regular auction. Since nobody wanted to buy a preemption claim and then have to pay nearly full value for the land at the actual sale (paying more for the land than it was worth), the intimidation of possible bidders was necessary to keep the preemption market clear. If a speculator knew that buying a preemption would buy exclusive bidding rights at the regular sale, then the market in preemption certificates remained active.[36]

The Ewings participated in this huge land auction in the month of November. They were interested mostly in the eastern portion of the Delaware reserve, which

35. "Divinity" from Richmond, *Requisite Learning,* 77.
36. *Leavenworth Weekly Herald,* November 17, 1856; Taylor, "Business and Political Career," 23, 28.

included much of the city of Leavenworth. They were aware that squatter associations had already assured their members as to who "owned" the parcels. The *Leavenworth Weekly Herald* reported that outdoor rallies made it fairly clear that if anyone bid against a preemption claimant they might well get a bullet in the back before they could file their deed. Since a preemption claimant had to buy the land twice, the actual bid had to be kept artificially low to have both sales remain attractive when added together. The two prices together were probably closer to the actual value of the land, but the government (and their tribal beneficiaries) received only auction price. Because there were so many in the town associations, Hamp Denman suggested that the Ewings either become members of the squatter association or contract with someone in the association, a straw man, to buy the land and forfeit his claim to Ewing & Denman. Either way this environment led to wildly fluctuating prices and speculation well above the appraised value, but, with some of the more desirable properties, the Ewings had to "pay to play." Like other speculators they expected their squatter associations to protect their investment from interloping bidders at the government's title auction.[37]

The November sale was only marginally successful. Only fifty-five thousand acres of the treaty lands had been sold, forty-six thousand acres to squatters and the hundreds of speculators such as the Ewings. The remaining nine thousand acres went unclaimed at $3.50 per acre, the fairer but higher price. Leavenworth town lots went for $30 per acre.[38]

Tom Ewing bought ninety-three acres in the original Leavenworth town site sales, and because those lots were highly desirable (if the town grew rapidly the lots would double and triple in value), Tom ran into immediate problems. Hugh had gone back to St. Louis on business, and in early December 1856 Tom wrote him that two dozen other bidders each claimed title to their Leavenworth properties. This necessitated a time-consuming legal action known as a "quiet title" suit, which had to run its way through the local courts where litigation, then as now, was not a rapid undertaking. If the disputed lots were desired for purchase while still tied up in litigation, a sale opportunity and profits might be lost. Tom decided to shortcut the matter. "I shall bring up the [disputed] matter before the Squatter Court if survey is made this week. If not, I shall leave a brief for you and let you fight it out. I have made no arrangements as to who shall bid on our quar-

37. Richmond, *Requisite Learning,* 30; *Leavenworth Weekly Herald,* November 22, 1856; threats from Mary Jayne Newman Nice, "Frontier Life in Northeast Kansas during the Territorial Days," 31.

38. Denman letter to TESr., November 2, 1856, in Taylor, "Business and Political Career," 23–24.

ters. The first actual squatter must do it." The lawsuit was not complicated. Many of the speculators had purchased their position without getting anything in writing from the sellers. The Ewings had better documentation of their purchases and knew the ropes on real estate litigation better than perhaps any group in town. Tom wanted Hugh to come to Leavenworth to manage the business while Tom helped Ellen with the remainder of their move to Leavenworth. Hugh was single; Tom no longer was, and he was lovesick for his new bride.[39]

After the flurry of speculation that marked the beginning of their practice in Leavenworth, the Ewings were still trying to work out exactly the form of the business they had begun in Leavenworth. Denman had purchased the office at 60 Main Street where the main floor served as the local city magistrate's office and an unofficial hangout for all Democrats looking for political work. The traffic in and out of the first floor was nonstop. The Ewings' law office was above Denman's, and quite spare, but access was outside and along a rickety stairway and landing (nineteenth-century lawyers located law offices on upper floors to provide clients some measure of confidentiality). Within the office itself the lawyers had little privacy, working from simple writing desks in a large open room. The desk closest to the potbellied stove was coveted. There were no employees in the office to assist with paperwork unless the clerk was studying law. Regular employees were deemed unprofessional. Each partner kept his own accounts and files and wrote his own letters and pleadings by hand unless he was wealthy enough to employ several secretaries. Irreplaceable documents and cash for lending operations were kept in an office safe.

There was no substitute for the tedium involved in documentation in a law office, and the Ewing office was no exception. Mortgages had to be handwritten in time-consuming longhand. Copies of any document required infinite labor unless the copies were made using press books, an onionskin paper where the originals could be inserted and pressed while the ink was still wet, forming a crude copy of the document. As to the types of documents that were copied, Tom wrote Hugh that he preferred them doing business as "land jobbers" rather than half the business as landsmen and half as lawyers. "We will be regarded as half attorney and half land shark." Instead, Denman would front the land-buying organization from the first floor, and the Ewings would be silent partners and financiers. Father Ewing disliked this idea, suggesting that a lawyer carried more prestige in the

39. TEJr. to HBE, November 26, 1856, in Hugh Boyle Ewing Papers, Ohio Historical Society, Columbus, Ohio (hereafter HBE/OHS), cited in Taylor, "Business and Political Career," 26.

business world and that the Ewings might need that prestige at some point. The boys elected to go with their own plan, at least for the time being.[40]

When they had settled into their offices, they quickly began to take part in the clubs and civic luncheons that most businessmen attended to become known in the community. Leavenworth was different in that as a city it was large enough to have large and important transportation companies. Freighting and steamboat businesses were numerous and attracted investment interest throughout the territory. Most towns of any size west of the Missouri River would do practically anything to attract a terminus on the transcontinental railroad. The government, envisioning perhaps a half-dozen branches fanning out toward the Pacific, was in the process of choosing which roads would be part of the railroad bill. Among the railroads seeking capital that year was the Leavenworth, Pawnee & Western (LP&W), one of the railroads originally chartered by the 1855 "bogus" territorial legislature. While many engineers involved in the transcontinental road assumed the logical route through the Rockies would be in the western Nebraska Territory area (present-day Wyoming), the LP&W's modest route was Leavenworth to Lawrence, then up the Kansas River valley to Fort Riley and west to Denver, where it could link with other roads going north or south and then west across the mountains.

The original incorporators of the railroad were mostly proslavery gentlemen from the East and South led by James C. Stone and John Kerr of Leavenworth. Both these men saw the territory changing to a dominant Free State hue, and as businessmen first and ideologues second, they would need settlers to buy railroad land in order to finance the road's construction. Since they knew that later legislatures dominated by Free State men could easily decertify a railroad charter, like good businessmen they wanted their company's proslavery profile softened. Tom and Hugh Ewing seemed to fit the mold, and they were asked to join the LP&W management team, for a modest buy-in cost.

When Father Ewing got wind of the offer, he was skeptical. "Have nothing to do with them. And do not encourage your friends to help [with the investment]." Thomas Ewing Sr. had considerable experience investing in land but virtually none with railroads. Instinctively he felt a railroad investment was not feasible unless located between commercial cities. Building a railroad through an empty prairie would generate enormous costs long before it would produce profits. "It

40. "Land shark" from TEJr. to HBE, December 23, 1856, HBE/OHS, quoted in Taylor, "Business and Political Career," 29. In 1976, as part of the national centennial celebrations and in honor of this well-known firm, the Kansas Bar Association dedicated a plaque at the corner of 2nd and Delaware (the newer address) in Leavenworth. The plaque cites the law firm's original address, 60 Main Street, and the accomplishments of the members.

is all a humbug," he warned his sons. "A more unfortunate one for the place that attempts it."[41]

Father Ewing's advice went against the tide of local feelings. Stock subscriptions for the LP&W began on December 26, 1856. Although Ewing's railroad remained a paper corporation, the stockholder meeting of January 3 commissioned a survey of the proposed main line from Leavenworth to Fort Riley. One of the proslavery men who bought stock was a Louisiana-born and Pennsylvania-educated advocate of Southern rights, Andrew Isaacs, whose genteel alliance with Tom and Hugh Ewing would last two decades. The meeting was also the beginning of a Ewing association with an important group of capitalists, men such as William H. Russell, Alexander Majors, and Amos Rees. Tom Ewing was elected to the board of directors, and Hugh was named president. The January session of the 1857 territorial legislature officially ratified the formation of the LP&W.

Hugh Ewing and Andy Isaacs proceeded confidently to Washington to lobby for a grant of public lands for their railroad. Not only on behalf of the railroad but for business purposes generally, they needed to know how the incoming Buchanan administration would react to the rapidly changing Kansas political scene. Such information would be invaluable in raising the enormous sums necessary to get a railroad under way. As Douglas Democrats, Hugh and Isaacs were the logical choices to lobby the first overture. The promoters of the railroad knew the Ewing family ties to the Interior Department and that, even though Salt Boiler Thomas Ewing was not a stockholder or an officer, his name would gain them access to almost any congressional office in Washington.[42]

Tom Ewing had closely tracked the territory's politics before coming to the territory itself. There was excitement in the move, more than just the usual ebullient feelings for new work in a new town. The territory was brimming with opportunity, but with a touch of danger, too. Eastern newspapers were filled with stories about "Bleeding Kansas," and such stories did for the territory's entrepreneurial spirit what dangerous times do for any investment opportunity—they shut it down. The Ewings had money from their private investment consortium for real estate investment, but there was virtually none available for other business opportunities.

The new territorial governor for Kansas was John Geary, the appointee of the

41. "Humbug" from TESr. to HBE, January 2, 1857, also January 6, 1857, HBE to TESr., December 26, 1856, January 3, 1857, HBE/OHS, quoted in Taylor, "Business and Political Career," 8.

42. Treadway, "Gilded Age," 15; O. C. Hull, "Railroads in Kansas," 38; Gates, *Fifty Million Acres,* 234.

Pierce administration but who headed west with the blessing of the incoming president, James Buchanan. Geary had developed a plan to calm the territory and allow its orderly march toward statehood, which meant obtaining outside investments in the growth of the territory into statehood. Geary first suggested that Buchanan ask the bogus laws of 1855 be declared invalid by federal law and that Kansans reorganize under a new government. With Free Staters growing in numbers and affluence every day, this meant a Free State government, which Buchanan despised. Proslavery elements felt betrayed and viewed Geary as the worst politician imaginable, an idealist. Jefferson Davis's War Department denied Geary any authority to use federal troops to preserve order. Not content to get Pierce to undercut Geary's authority almost from the beginning, proslavery elements plotted to goad the governor into a gunfight, a frontier-style assassination. Geary was trying to govern a banana republic. His administration was largely a failure.[43]

While Geary's gubernatorial comet was fizzling in Kansas, Tom Ewing joined Hugh in Washington doing as much as possible for land grants for their Kansas railroad investment. He and Isaacs were able to get the bill out of a House committee, but it failed 55–85 on the House floor, where Northern abolitionists to garner opposition pointed to the proslavery makeup of the LP&W's incorporators. A Southerner, Andrew Isaacs had been brought along to help lobby the Southern congressmen who, it turned out, were down on all Yankee railroads. Failing to find support on either side, both Ewings came back to Leavenworth where everyone's railroad project was as "dead as Julius Caesar."[44]

Upon his return Tom campaigned for a delegate position to the upcoming Leavenworth Constitutional Convention and entered his first campaign to elective office as the Free State mayoral candidate of Leavenworth. He was soundly defeated by Marcus Parrott, a cultured South Carolinian who was the better orator. Parrott's win also showed the proslavery leaning of the current Leavenworth citizenry, but Tom suspected fraud. Seven hundred of the town's twenty-four hundred male voters were known to have gone west to the mountains, yet vote totals remained at the same level as in the previous mayoral election. Tom guessed there were six hundred fraudulent votes to go with the opposition efforts to paint him as a "black Republican" who intended for freed slaves to take Irish teamster jobs:

43. A full discussion of the plot against Geary is found at David E. Meerse, "No Propriety in the Late Course of the Governor: The Geary-Sherrard Affair Reexamined," 239–50.

44. "Julius Caesar" from TEJr. to HBE, Washington, D.C., February 7, 24, 1857, HBE/OHS.

> Through the influence of my special friends, not an Irishman voted for me. . . . There were not ten Irish in town who did not vote at least once, many of them twice, three and four times, all swearing to six months residence when challenged. There will be fifty to 100 criminal prosecutions on the strength of it. My special friends . . . [Lucius] Easton and the other old hellhounds of the Proslavery party [convinced voters and] the Irish took all they said on the stump for corn, and thought I was a traitor to my religion and a regular-built nigger stealer.

Tom Ewing's defeat in a minor election in Leavenworth was "rather a mortifying result, but such mortification is the fate of politicians." It was, in fact, a stinging disappointment for the man whose dream was the U.S. Senate.[45]

The weather on March 4, 1857, was overcast and gloomy all along the Eastern Seaboard. In Washington, on the east portico of the Capitol, James Buchanan stepped forward to place his hand on the Bible offered by Chief Justice Roger Taney and repeated the oath as president of the United States. During his otherwise boring inaugural address, Buchanan teased his audience with an indication that a case was about to come down from the Supreme Court that would speak great volumes on the issue of slavery. Four days later *Dred Scott v. Sandford* was handed down. Taney's court adopted a Darwinist view that a slave's station and character was created by birth and race and man's law could not change nature. Judge Robert Bork wrote that not only did *Dred Scott* "read into the law the legality of slavery forever," Taney had instructed the South that it no longer needed to compromise on the issue, which immediately put the constitutionality of the Kansas-Nebraska Act into question. If a slave had no rights and Congress could not give him any, having local governments determine whether a new state is a slave state or a free state was a useless exercise. Bork named *Dred Scott* as the worst nineteenth-century example of judicial lawmaking and wryly noted, "There was something wrong with a judicial decision that took a civil war to overturn."[46]

Like the rest of the country, which largely ignored Taney's decision, the Ewing brothers were too busy with their new business to concern themselves with thoughts of looming civil war. Until the spring of 1857 the Ewings concentrated on the sale of their land purchases and how this might relate to a future transcontinental railroad. Isaacs was hired by the LP&W to devise a way to purchase the

45. TEJr. to HBE in Lancaster, Ohio, early March (1857), HBE/OHS.

46. *Dred Scott v. Sandford,* 60 U.S. (19 How.) 393 (1857); Robert Bork, *The Tempting of America: The Political Seduction of the Law,* 29–30, 34.

Christian Indian lands, or at least secure an easement. Isaacs worked to have title to four sections vest with the Indians so that patents could be given and the railroad could buy the patent title. Although there were allegations that the railroad bought the land from chiefs after all-night rounds of drinking, this sale set precedent in that it was the first time Indian land had been sold by the government directly to an individual or group without its first becoming part of the public domain.[47]

The base for the building of the railroad was to convince a constant stream of settlers to buy land near the railroad. The first part of 1857 was a time of great optimism in the belief that Kansas businesses would expand, settlers would come, and land values would continue to grow. The brothers kept their Cincinnati investment trust appraised of how the developments were coming along. "The improvement [in Leavenworth] is great & prices are firm or steadily advancing." In speculation-prone Leavenworth there was only an upside. Hugh encouraged a cousin to "jump aboard a steamboat and come out first & look about." He reported to his Washington bankers that "Leavenworth is improving rapidly." A good sign was that land the Cincinnati speculation trust had purchased in May for $3,300 was sold for over $10,000. Not everyone was optimistic. Thomas Ewing Sr. warned against his sons' taking on further debt. He saw that economic winds were shifting. "The money market is becoming empty," he warned. "It may take a sudden adverse turn."[48]

The basic trust between businessmen that was needed for market speculation to succeed also turned against them. In the summer of 1857 the Ewing brothers met Dr. Madison Mills, a New Yorker with family money. Mills was one of the army's first professional surgeons, serving on early postings on the frontier and in Mexico, who now was stationed at Fort Leavenworth. Some men with vices choose gambling, liquor, or women; Mills liked to speculate in land. In May Ewing, Denman & Co. sank all the family and Cincinnati consortium funds into Mills's choice 337 acres in the Leavenworth area. The $78,000 investment, about $230 per acre, was an enormous purchase of land where so many others were buying no more than a town lot or a 160-acre basic farm. Mills's terms were $26,000 in cash and the remainder in four equal annual installments. Tom felt the total

47. The role of whiskey in the land sale alleged in Gottlieb Oehler to James W. Denver, June 20, 1857, quoted in Gates, *Fifty Million Acres,* 235.

48. "Steadily advancing" from TEJr. to Judge M. F. Moore, Sioux City, June 5, 1857, Thomas Ewing Jr. Papers (microfile edition), manuscript division, Kansas State Historical Society, Topeka (hereafter TEJr./KSHS); "look about" from HBE to Rachel Geraghty, Ft. Dodge, Iowa, June 5, 1857, and "improving rapidly" from HBE to Fant, June 5, 1857, both TEJr./KSHS; "money market" from TESr. to HBE and TEJr., jointly, June 2, 1857, HBE/OHS.

purchase was worth $150,000, the small fortune he had hoped to amass in his lifetime. He wrote Father Ewing that he would buy no more lands and retrench.[49]

A month after the purchase, tracts of this purchase already were selling for $260 per acre. But Tom discovered that Mills had sold fifty-four acres of the same land through a relative, Lafayette Mills, to another speculator, John Day. The Ewings demanded that Mills honor his promise to pass good title to them by returning Day's purchase money and forcing him to acknowledge the Ewings' title. When Mills declined, the Ewings could not resell the land without a lawsuit to quiet title. The master real estate lawyer, Thomas Ewing Sr., advised his boys to have patience. The Ewings had a written contract for their sale, and Mills's sale to Day was an oral contract. Then, as now, oral contracts concerning real estate were judicially unenforceable.[50]

The consortium decided to sue John Day and put Mills on notice that, if the Day suit failed, a cross claim would be filed against Mills for fraud. Mills was slated for frontier duty in Utah as surgeon to a detachment of dragoons. Tom Ewing drafted the pleadings against Day, and Hugh served the process papers on Mills at Fort Leavenworth "just as his foot was in the stirrup for Utah." The suit apparently caught Mills by surprise, and he was "pained" by the fraud allegations. He discussed settling the lawsuit for $2,500 if Hugh would retract the written allegations. The settlement negotiations fell through, however, when land prices that had soared now began to tumble. The Mills purchase would plague the Ewing brothers throughout their prewar careers, a constant reminder that their most lucrative property was tied up interminably and could not be sold during the best years of land speculation in Leavenworth.[51]

The California Shermans arrived in Lancaster, Ohio, in mid-June 1857. Cump Sherman was in a banking "retreat," having seen the San Francisco bank of Turner & Lucas closed because of economic conditions in northern California. He met briefly with his father-in-law, saw to the comfort of his wife and children, and then traveled to St. Louis to meet with Turner and Lucas about a new banking assignment the two businessmen were planning on Wall Street in New York.

In Leavenworth, Ewing, Denman & Co. went about their business of unloading their landholdings in a deteriorating market. While the brothers had anticipated that Father Ewing and Cump would both come to Kansas to review the

49. TEJr. to TESr., June 5, 1857, TEJr./KSHS.

50. TESr. to HBE, June 7, 1857, HBE/OHS. The requirement of a written contract or deed for a real estate conveyance is generally called the Statute of Frauds.

51. "Stirrup" from TEJr. to HBE, July 25, 1857, TEJr./KSHS.

progress of the speculation consortium, Sherman declined, citing Turner's need for him to report immediately to New York. "It is probably in NY I may be of service to your business [in Leavenworth]. To Tom and his wife, say that I regret that I cannot come up at this time." He promised to come out as New York affairs permitted. Then, perhaps viewing the New York job as a welcome reprieve, Sherman threw himself into the job of growing the Turner banking house into a thriving business.[52]

In June 1857, without Sherman Thomas Ewing Sr. traveled to Leavenworth by himself to review the vast landholdings that Ewing, Denman, & Co. had put together for the consortium. The purchase was an attempt to branch out from Leavenworth and possess the land where new settlements were most likely to start, another form of speculation that could bring huge dividends. Tom reported to his father that the brothers would purchase two sites across the Kansas River from Tecumseh, Kansas, nearly a thousand acres east of Topeka purchased "for our firm." The land was within a mile of the surveyed route of the LP&W and the military road connecting Forts Leavenworth and Riley. If the railroad came through, it would most likely mirror the military road, which would increase the value of the land enormously. Meanwhile, clearing this large farm would provide work for many Ewing relatives.[53]

The finances of the investment firm were tightening, however. After discussions with their father, Tom wrote Hamp Denman to avoid buying land unless it was precisely what the firm wanted. After his father had returned to Lancaster, Tom Jr. reported the farm purchase had swept their accounts clean of available funds.[54]

The Ewings' investment group brought with them a lending practice carried over from England before the advent of modern banking. Wealthy Englishmen deposited funds with lawyers, and the lawyers invested idle funds and paid third parties the sight drafts written by the patron, prepared mortgages and leases, collected the rents, and managed the properties. Such was the early law practice of the Ewings as well. Frontier banking practices have been described as loan-sharking without the broken leg, but the rates charged by the Ewings, although usurious under modern commercial practices, were not unreasonable for the frontier, since they reflected the high degree of risk. More money was needed for investments, and Eastern bankers provided it. Hamilton G. Fant, the Ohio consortium's Washington banker, sent a thousand dollars of the bank's idle funds to Denman for the

52. WTS to HBE, June 25, 1857, SFP/OHS.
53. TEJr. to TESr., July 25, 1857, TEJr./KSHS.
54. TEJr. to Hamp Denman, July 25, 1857, TEJr./KSHS.

company to loan. The firm began borrowing money from Fant at 10 percent and loaned it out at higher rates (up to 50 percent) to farmers, businesses, or other small-time speculators with good credit, taking mortgages and deeds of trust as security. The Ewings made 5 percent of the interest for administering the loans. At this time American banks were not regulated by any government, and anyone with money to lend could get into the business, even lawyers practicing law on the side. The ardor for land speculation had cooled somewhat, and the Ewings were finding it more profitable to loan money than to buy land, although they maintained the public facade that they were not in the lending business.[55]

The failure of a New York life insurance company coupled with the sinking of the steamer *Central America* in bad weather off Georgia, where hundreds died and $1.6 million in gold bullion went to the bottom of the Atlantic, is not the ordinary stuff that should spark a financial panic on Wall Street, but in 1857 just such a thing happened. Railroads foundered, along with the banks. Sherman was at first amused that others were suffering the same financial straits he had seen in San Francisco. However, when Wall Street stocks deteriorated, Sherman sensed a rising tide of new concern. "It seems that I am the Jonah of banking," he wrote his brother John. He passed on to Henry Turner a sense of impending doom. "We know now, too late, that we ought not be bankers." To his wife he confided, "Of all the lives on earth a banker's is the worst and no wonder they are specially debarred from all chances of heaven."[56]

The Panic of 1857 was more than a corrective economic blip. Like a blood supply when the heart stops, credit vanished, factories closed, railroads went bankrupt, and new construction halted. Men were thrown out of work, and millions more took pay cuts. There were food riots in New York. To make matters worse for Sherman, Turner and Lucas shut down their New York branch in early October 1857, only a few months after opening it. Sherman was stunned, out of work, and with his future as murky as it had ever been. By August 1858 Tom Ewing had brought up the idea that Sherman might want to consider a change. Kansas was, after all, the focus of the nation's attention. Many of Sherman's old army friends were at Fort Leavenworth. Sherman retreated into melancholy, writing that he had foolishly left the army and now was "as poor as a church-mouse," without a profession or confidence. It looked more and more as if he would be relegated to

55. TEJr. to TESr., July 14, 1857, and TEJr. to Denman, July 21, 1857, TEJr./KSHS; James C. Horton, "Business Then and Now," 144.

56. Sherman, *Memoirs,* 1:135; WTS to John Sherman, September 4, WTS to Turner, September 7, 1857, SFP/LC, quoted in Fellman, *Citizen Sherman,* 62, 64.

being an agent for his father-in-law, and he reacted like a fish being reeled in, trying every which way to flip its way off the hook. His dim views about working for Ellen's father naturally angered her. While he did not particularly like the prospect of becoming a lawyer, Kansas could provide other opportunities. Using John Sherman as a sounding board, Cump wrote, "We will have plenty to do in the war line. Mormon war, civil broils and strife, contests for political power growing out of slavery and other exciting topics, and perhaps a war with Spain, resulting in the conquest of Cuba."[57]

Part of the success of real estate speculation as well as financial investing is the ability of speculators and investors to convince outsiders, especially other buyers and investors, that matters are rosy even when they are not. The Panic of 1857 had caused chaos in the market. Land was not selling. Tom and Hugh Ewing worked desperately to sell their Leavenworth holdings in order to generate the cash to pay interest to creditors on their other properties. At the same time they represented to Ohio friends that all was well. "The city has increased beyond all hope and is growing hourly," Hugh wrote to assure his skeptical brother Phil.[58]

If the Panic of 1857 was not bad enough, President Buchanan then made it worse. In 1856 and 1857 no public lands had been scheduled for sale by the government. This was fine with homesteaders, or preemptors, who were given five or six years to save up to pay the government for their illegal act of squatting on the land and paying a token for it before original government patents were issued. In October 1857, however, Buchanan ordered forty-six million acres of Indian trust lands in Kansas sold for cash, not on credit, to raise funds for the failing Treasury hard-pressed by the financial panic. Speculators with their preemption rights had relied on the previous method of sale—a cash plus term repayment schedule. Now they had to come up with the purchase price in cash all at once. Those who could not do so lost their land.

Whatever buoyancy land prices had previously, Buchanan's new policy caused an immediate crash and achieved, indirectly, what the cavalry had been unable to do, which was to pour cold water on the mini–civil war that was festering in Kansas. Southerners who had bought preemption paper saw their land become worthless overnight. While Free State farmers were affected too, the policy drove out slave-owning interests to a greater degree, unless they had the cash. The policy directly affected political power in the territory because many with Southern

57. "Mouse" from WTS to TEJr., August 7, 1857, SFP/LC; Sherman, *Memoirs,* 1:138–39; "war line" from WTS to John Sherman, January 30, 1858, in Thorndike, *Sherman Letters,* 64.

58. "Beyond all hope" from HBE to Philemon Ewing, October 22, 1857, TEJr./KSHS.

leanings left the state, all the while cursing the president of the United States, their supposed ally.

During this lag in the economy, the Ewings were improving their Leavenworth alliances politically. Hamp Denman, a Douglas Democrat, was elected to a seat in the 1858 territorial legislature and later borrowed $2,500 for campaign and living expenses for all the Leavenworth Ewings. The 40 percent interest rate shows the times. Hugh sniffed around for a Democratic nomination for the territorial "Council," the equivalent of the state senate, but his frequent absences on business kept him from making a commitment. "I am spoken for the United States Senate but will not take a step; they may thrust it on me if they please," he wrote home conceitedly. The facts were that nobody was going to be a U.S. senator from Kansas very soon. The rest of his correspondence painted a gloomy picture of the economic rise and fall of Leavenworth. "Phil Stanbery is without money even to pay his board, and [is] getting quite seedy, [there is] nothing for him to do. He would have got on, I think, if he had been provided with a foothold." Hugh urged Thomas Ewing Sr. to contact his neighbor Henry Stanbery to help his son.[59]

Ironically, the Buchanan full payment requirements on public land sales in Kansas dampened speculation within the territory, but for reasons nobody quite understood it revived Leavenworth's local economy. Hugh was able to sell a few properties for gold, and those sales revived his enthusiasm. "Currency has never ceased to pass here," he wrote his father. Because a few properties had sold for gold, he crowed to Ewingville, "Everything looks bright," downplaying that the payment in gold usually came from the wealthiest of investors who recognized that landowners were in desperate straits and could be pushed into selling land for gold at a significantly discounted price.[60]

Hugh shifted his focus from the mercurial woes of speculation to writing Ellen for her recommendations for the "most captivating young lady" she knew in St. Louis. Ellen offered some suggestions but used her responses to grumble about Cump's constant harping on his beloved lost military career. Sherman wrote Hugh a few weeks later about the sorry shape of New York City. Cump was "used up" in the banking arena and wanted out with as little debt as possible. He soberly advised Hugh and Tom to make the wish he secretly desired for himself: "practice your profession and pay for the land as fast as possible and never make a note again in your life." If he were only footloose and single, Cump vowed, he would head

59. Denman's campaign expenses at HBE to TEJr., HBE to TESr., both October 23, 1857, TEJr./KSHS.

60. HBE to TESr., November 13, 1857, in Ewing, "Autobiography," 211.

for "one of those Pacific countries." It was an odd statement for a man to make to his wife's brother.[61]

In the midst of the panic, the Kansas Free State Party's convention of late August 1857 was held in the unlikely town of Grasshopper Falls. The purpose of the convention was to decide the Free State Party's voting policy after that fall's Lecompton convention produced its anticipated slave-oriented constitution. When Eastern newspapers urged Free Staters to boycott the Lecompton vote, the ire of the elder Ewing rose precipitously. He warned Tom against squandering his time and political future with any political party whose only answer to the crisis of the day was to boycott elections. For the Old Salt Boiler, Free Staters were "a strange compound of fraud and folly—fraud on the part of the leaders out of the territory—urging those in it to treason, and folly in those who suffer themselves to be led." However misguided the Union might become, the national will must be expressed in the political branches of government. Such was the essence of democracy. Free Staters who did not want to take possession of the territorial government legitimately would become tools of the unscrupulous. "Enter not into their counsel," Father Ewing warned. Tom was way ahead of his father on this one. He continually wrote of his wariness of colliding with the other forces in the party. "I have uniformly expressed my opinion that this move is a piece of unmanly and dangerous folly and I intend to stand clear of the political arena in KS while the leaders of the democracy are made up of political murderers and while the Free State party is but the football for the free-soilers of northern states."[62]

Tom Ewing's political career as a Free State advocate with statewide appeal got its beginning at the Grasshopper Falls party meeting. There he first opposed the war wing of the party led by James H. Lane and John Brown. One observer noted Ewing's princely appearance, possessed of the "most sturdy, massive and comprehensive mind of any man in Kansas," whose "measured oratory" spoke volumes from his "mental vigor." Those who heard him at the convention described him as "reserved and dignified." Lane and Brown wanted the territorial government to give them an excuse to use force. After conservatives such as Ewing argued against overreacting, Lane slowly came around to the "one more time"

61. "Young lady," HBE to EES, November 4, 1857, in Taylor, "Business and Political Career," 101; "practice your profession" and "Pacific countries," WTS to HBE, November 26, 1857, WTS/OHS, in Fellman, *Citizen Sherman*, 64.

62. "Fraud and folly" from TESr. to TEJr. at Leavenworth, July 23, 1857, Lecompton Constitution Manuscript Collection, KSHS (hereafter Lecompton/KSHS); TEJr. to TESr. at Lancaster, August 5, 1857, TEJr./KSHS.

crowd. In addition to the party's standing ready to oppose any slavery document that came from the Lecompton convention, Free State men would participate in the October legislative elections to choose a territorial legislature that would take office only if Congress ratified the Lecompton Constitution. It was a crucial election since this would be the legislature to implement any slavery provisions in the Lecompton Constitution. If the legislative election was stolen from them, Free Staters would support the Topeka constitution and government. If this meant war with officials of the Buchanan administration, so be it.[63]

October 5, 1857, saw the beginning of two days of voting for the post-Lecompton territorial legislature. While Lane's Free State militia were out in force, with many proslavery sympathizers having left the state because of Buchanan's change in land policy, Kansas saw its first relatively honest election. All that was left was to count the votes.[64]

With a Free State victory on the horizon, the Ewings were working tirelessly to arrange financing to resurrect their properties in the wake of the panic and the anticipated failure of one of the firm's Kentucky clients. George Sanders owned a Kentucky building company and was a major Ewing partner in a business venture to provide Leavenworth with dozens of low-cost prefabricated houses. Sanders also had been trying to convince army officers to buy prefab homes instead of living in barracks. Sherman had seen similar dwellings in San Francisco and considered an Indian teepee a better investment. Unable to pay his suppliers from the sale of these prefab homes, Sanders was headed for bankruptcy. The Ewings were concerned he would take them down too.[65]

The partnership was running on empty. Creditors could seek payment from any of the partners. While the Ewings felt their relationship with Sanders was that of an agent, here the agent was more solvent than the principal. "If Sanders pays but little more we shall be in the straits and it will require the hardest kind of rowing to get out," Tom warned, concerned that agency law might not protect the Ewings from being sued along with their principal. He was right, of course. Creditors would file suit first and determine liability later. The Ewings could not afford the spectacle of being named defendants in numerous civil suits. Hugh talked to their Washington bankers about taking property in lieu of payments so they

63. "Comprehensive mind" from John A. Martin, *Proceedings and Debates of the Kansas Constitutional Convention,* 658; "measured oratory" and "dignified" from Elliott, "Grasshopper Falls Convention," 186; "mental vigor" from Castel, *Frontier State,* 25–26.

64. Shalor Eldridge, *Recollections of Early Days in Kansas,* 145.

65. Teepee from Taylor, "Business and Political Career," 29–30.

could hoard their cash for an expected battle to come. "We shall have trouble in finding purchasers. I think we can get none in [Kansas]."[66]

The only booming market in the summer and fall of 1857 was in sheriff sales, and Hugh's banker friends wanted no part of bailing out Sanders. The always impatient Hamilton Fant worried about the indirect Sanders's loan he had made when the Ewings had loaned Sanders some money early on. Hugh reported that land sales were slow but the prospects were high, since three of Sanders's lots had recently sold for $1,600 in gold. This was fine with Fant. He suggested Ewing, Denman & Company loan money to Fant and take Fant's interest in the Sanders loan as collateral. Fant also had speculations and interest rates he had to cover, and his suggestion to the Ewings was an indication of the depth bankers had to go in order to preserve their liquidity. Hugh rejected the idea. "The loaning of money is not a branch of our firm business." The response conveniently ignored the fact that the firm had engaged in banking practices just months before. "I have no money to invest in notes and made no promise to endorse them. . . . Your money is secure." This rejection strained Hugh's relationship with Fant.[67]

In addition to his need to raise thousands of dollars for debt service, Tom Ewing was busy with a family crisis too. His brother Philemon was despondent over the fading value of his Leavenworth property. Tom's wife was weak from chills and fever caught on a riverboat trip to St. Louis. His son, Willie, took seriously ill, and his recovery was slow. The boy's brush with death frightened Tom. He needed help in the Leavenworth office and the real estate business. His correspondence again broached the idea that Sherman might come out to Kansas. Tom could use the help, especially with the Sanders mess looming. He did not appeal directly to Sherman but rather to Ellen, saying Sherman was gloomy about what had happened in New York, Turner would not have any self-respecting job for him, he was out of banking now, and "If a prospect were open in Kansas, he would go there." Considering how things stood for Sherman at present, the best course was for him to rely on *family.* Tom renewed his points that many of Sherman's old friends were in Leavenworth, and perhaps they were just the tonic he needed.[68]

Ellen agreed and suggested to her father that Sherman go to Kansas to examine their properties and put a mortgage value on them in light of the summer pan-

66. "Hardest kind of rowing" and "finding purchasers" from TEJr. to HBE, September 18, 1857, HBE/OSH.

67. HBE to Fant, November 3, 1857, TEJr./KSHS.

68. Illnesses from TEJr. to HBE, August 30, 1857, TEJr./KSHS, TEJr. to HBE, September 16, 1857, HBE/OHS; "prospect" from TEJr. to HBE, October 11, 1857, HBE/OHS.

ic, just in case they needed to sell out. While Ellen herself had no intention of living in Leavenworth, Sherman looked at the idea differently. He was so low on funds he had borrowed money from John Sherman in order to stay a few more days in New York. Cump had not been to Kansas since 1852 when he had inspected cattle at Fort Leavenworth. However, if the Kansas offer was real, he had to consider it.[69]

The Lecompton Constitutional Convention convened after the initial October 1857 election for the territorial legislature, but under a cloud of suspicion. Governor Robert J. Walker, a Pennsylvania Democrat who lived in Mississippi, had been appointed to replace Geary. He had reviewed ballots cast in several eastern county townships and found fraud. Walker believed that democracy would receive a "deadly blow" if such votes were allowed to stand. Walker declared the entire Oxford township vote for Lecompton legislators invalid, which changed enough votes to swing the majority of seats to the Free State Party. Free Staters were to control the legislature that implemented the Lecompton Constitution's slavery provisions.[70]

The proslavery convention opted for a "turkey or buzzard" choice. The only choice on the ratification vote was whether to adopt the constitution "with" Article VII allowing slave ownership in Kansas or adopt the constitution without Article VII. Voters were not allowed to reject the entire constitution. Buchanan's men had created a "political Ark of the Covenant," a proslavery document no human hands could touch or change.[71]

Everyone in the territory held their breath. Hugh Ewing and Hamp Denman tried to increase their positions within the fledgling Democratic Party in Leavenworth in order to keep track of what was happening. Walker had become an "intimate and strong friend" of the Ewing-Denman operation in Leavenworth. Walker spent some time there, sending telegrams to Washington from the only city west of the Missouri River that had a telegraph. In his telegrams Walker reminded Buchanan of the bargain they had made when Walker was appointed—that if Walker was to govern in the Kansas Territory, the ratification vote on a constitution had to be fair even if it offended proslavery obstruction-

69. Ellen's idea to father, from Fellman, *Citizen Sherman,* 65; borrowing from John, WTS to John Sherman, October 9, 1857, SFP/LC.

70. "Deadly blow" from Stampp, *America in 1857,* 262. See also "Fiftieth Anniversary of the First Free State Territorial Legislature, 1857," *Kansas Historical Collections* 10 (1908): 170n2.

71. "Turkey or buzzard" from E. Duane Elbert, "The English Bill: An Attempt to Compromise the Lecompton Dilemma," 221; "Ark of the Covenant" from Eldridge, *Early Days,* 145.

ists. When Buchanan did not respond, Walker went back to Washington for instructions.[72]

At this point Stephen Douglas decided to oppose the Lecompton Constitution. If Buchanan was not going to allow a fair up-and-down vote, it was clear that pro-Lecompton men wanted to destroy popular sovereignty before it was even given a fair test. Douglas would fight for a requirement that Kansans could either ratify or reject the whole constitution, not just parts of it. But if Douglas actively opposed Buchanan, he would doom his own presidential ambitions in the South. He did not care any more. As historian Kenneth Stampp put it, "Douglas had made Buchanan. Now he would unmake him."[73]

After the Lecompton debate began in the Senate between Douglas and pro-Buchanan supporters, a majority of Kansas Free Staters were agitating that the party boycott the local Lecompton vote. Because of the Ewing name, Tom was asked repeatedly for advice on what Free Staters should do. He consulted the best political mind in the family, his father, who advised the wise vote was to have the Free State men band together and reject the proslavery clause. "The framers of [Lecompton] did not intend you should vote, . . . but I would disappoint them, and I think [Free State men] have power enough to compel fair play." On the other hand, if Free Staters did not participate and Kansas did then become a state, proslavery men would sit in the U.S. Senate. Judges and other appointed officials would be against the Free State movement, and the entire machinery of government would become harder to control even if Free Staters continued to dominate the territory's population numerically. Father Ewing advised that it was folly to remain on the sidelines while Democrats controlled the state through Lecompton. "All who should resist such force in organized bodies with arms in their hands would be guilty of treason." Only those interested in "bloodshed and violence" would refuse to vote. There were other considerations. Thomas Ewing warned his sons to be careful that politics not overshadow why the Ewings went to Leavenworth in the first place. "If you cannot give a proper direction to [business] affairs [in a climate of anarchy], withdraw from them and let those that have a taste for such things indulge it."[74]

Tom Ewing saw in his father's reasoning the springboard he needed for his own political career. This tactic would propel him to the forefront of the moderate

72. "Strong friend" from HBE to TESr., November 20, 1857, in Ewing, "Autobiography," 211–12.
73. Stampp, *America in 1857*, 292.
74. Quotations from TESr. to TEJr. and HBE, December 10, 1857, HBE/OHS.

wing of the Free State Party. At a party meeting to decide how to respond, speeches were made by many of the leading members of the party. Tom Ewing offered his summation—a repetition of his father's influence and thinking. However, most Free Staters in attendance were in no mood to compromise with Buchanan or anyone else. Ewing's words were not persuasive. The Free State Party voted to boycott the ratification election for the Lecompton Constitution, an act that Ewing felt was a grave mistake. With Free State men boycotting the December 21 election, the official tally was 6,147 to 569 for the Lecompton Constitution's slavery clause. Over 3,000 of the difference came from just three small towns, Oxford, Shawnee, and Kickapoo, where fewer than 300 total males were lawfully registered to vote.[75]

On December 23, 1857, Charles Robinson presided over an emergency meeting of the Free State Party. The agenda items concerned what to do about the January territorial election to choose state officers under the Lecompton plan. Armed with his father's advice Ewing again addressed the convention, at the Congregational Church in Lawrence. His views echoed letters and newspaper editorials from the East, from men such as Senator Salmon P. Chase, an autograph hound who was a founder of the national Republican Party. Chase wrote Robinson that Free State forces should actively oppose the proslavery slate of officers on January 4, 1858. Tom Ewing read a letter from Congressman Samuel Vinton of Ohio who bluntly told the Kansans if they did not oppose the proslavery slate by all means available, influential Free State men in the East would "abandon the struggle in Congress" on their behalf. Ewing renewed his own previous efforts to get the party officially to oppose efforts to build a government under the Lecompton Constitution. He told the convention members he preferred a new convention that would draft a new document, but they had no time or authority for that course. He repeatedly advocated they do all in their power to elect Free State officeholders at the January election, otherwise they risked becoming the rebels in a revolution. Ewing wanted a Free State Party that could govern the state. Lane wanted only an excuse for guerrilla warfare.[76]

Ewing told the convention they had to fight back and their first battle should be the ballot box. It was a battle they could win. The constitution was slavery oriented. The government, however, could be Free State in outlook. Governments could change constitutions. Members attending the meeting such as Ben Simpson thought Ewing's remarks were "a wonderful exhibition of power in the dis-

75. Ewing, "Struggle For Freedom," 3.
76. "Abandon the struggle" from ibid., 3–4.

cussion of the question" of whether the party should vote. The Free State convention of that December, Ewing later wrote, "was the final struggle for freedom in Kansas." Winning in January was an alternative means of killing Lecompton itself without relying on a congressional vote. To the radicals who advocated fighting the federal force sent at them, Ewing declared, "Such a course is rebellion and Buchanan will deal with it as a rebellion."[77]

The views expressed by Ewing and also by another, Solon Thatcher, had almost carried the day when Edward Whitman, one of Lane's men, rushed into the church yelling that Jim Lane and James Montgomery's men were in a running battle with federal cavalry near Sugar Mound in Linn County. Every able-bodied Free Stater was expected to ride the sixty miles to Lane's rescue. Ewing and Robinson looked at each other. A military campaign at that moment, in the dead of winter, did not make sense. What did make sense to Ewing was that the hardliners were trying to sabotage the persuasiveness of the moderate wing of the party. Ewing leaped onto an altar table and yelled that Whitman's call was a trick and a fraud. "I was boiling over with suppressed rage and after a scuffle got the floor." Booed and cheered by respective factions, Ewing tried to keep the convention from breaking apart before it made a decision on the party's political position in the January election. In the bedlam Lane's people screamed for recognition, moved that the policy of voting in January be defeated, and called the question immediately. This was John Brown's doing, Ewing thundered in the bedlam. "He wants to be the instrument of expiation!" Explaining himself later in writing, Ewing declared that Brown's dream was "the abolition of slavery by Northern bayonets aided by the torch of the slave." In fact Brown was indeed scheming to kidnap John Calhoun and other proslavery officials along with the official Lecompton document and spirit them all to a secret location, in hopes that the Lecompton movement would collapse and that war in Kansas between militia and army would promote the fortunes of the Republican Party. This was unknown to Ewing and on the floor of the assembly. In a wild scene the motion to participate in the January 4 election failed 64–74.[78]

While Jim Lane and John Brown were busy orchestrating a pseudo war with Buchanan's federal appointees, Ewing and his friends decided to continue backroom efforts to give the Kansas Free State Party a modicum of respectability. Ewing persuaded Robinson to announce that those wanting to "bolt the action of

77. Simpson's remarks in Martin, *Proceedings and Debates,* 659; Ewing, "Struggle For Freedom," 3–4; "rebellion" from the *Lawrence Herald of Freedom,* December 27, 1857.

78. Ewing, "Struggle For Freedom," 3–5; Brown's scheming from Eldridge, *Early Days,* 147; "suppressed rage," "expiation," and "torch" from TEJr. to HBE, January 2, 1858, Lecompton/KSHS.

the convention" would meet at the Lawrence Masonic Hall that evening at seven o'clock. However, the bolters were pushed, shoved, and threatened by departing Lane men. "The result was that all our friends who had been swearing they would get up a [Free State] ticket, convention or no convention, grew mute and acquiescent—men like Dr. Davis, Pomeroy, W. Y. Roberts, and others." When the bolters met that night Lane supporters broke into the meeting and fistfights broke out. The bolters were forcibly ejected from the hall. Robinson kept them together and they decided to meet again, this time in secret.[79]

At midnight on Christmas Eve, Ewing met with Robinson and thirteen others who had voted to participate in the January election. From the basement of the printing offices of George Brown's *Herald of Freedom* this faction, known as Brown's Cellar Kitchen Convention, put together a Free State ticket for all Kansas state offices and the lone congressional seat, which, if elected, would take office if Lecompton was adopted by Congress. Ewing's bolters also made a post-meeting deal with the Douglas Democrats, who met in Leavenworth later that week. Ewing got Hamp Denman to convince his friends that Free Staters and Douglas Democrats had the same stake in defeating Lecompton. Douglas Democrats had no pull in Kansas politics since, rightly or wrongly, they were considered tools of Buchanan. Democrats in Kansas should be prepared to endorse any slate of candidates put into the field by the Free State bolters. Simply put, it was the Cellar Kitchen slate or none. George Brown was nominated for governor, with William Y. Roberts for lieutenant governor, P. C. Schuyler of Burlingame for secretary of state, and Andrew Mead of Manhattan for treasurer. Marcus Parrott, the anti-slavery South Carolinian, was nominated for the state's congressional delegate. Each man pledged that, if he was elected and if he later took office under the Lecompton Constitution, he would call another convention to frame a new constitution.[80]

Tom Ewing was appointed chairman of the party's executive committee to manage the Cellar Kitchen campaign. The first thing done was to tout the credentials of the Free State ticket, using falsehoods. George Brown's newspaper reported that the "voting policy" was adopted by a 47–44 margin when the convention had adopted nothing of the kind. Ewing paid livery men and volunteers

79. "Bolt the action" from Miller, Thomas Ewing Jr.," 6; "mute and acquiescent" from TEJr. to HBE, January 2, 1858, Lecompton/KSHS.

80. The Cellar Kitchen from Charles Robinson, "Topeka and Her Constitution," 304; Ewing, "Struggle For Freedom," 11.

nearly a thousand dollars out of his own pocket to deliver the *Herald of Freedom's* banner headlines all over the territory.[81]

Several things had to come together if Ewing's bolters were to get their men to vote for the candidates in a post-Lecompton state government and not succumb to the extremism of Lane and Brown. First, between Christmas and New Year's Day, they had to organize a get-out-the-vote effort on a shoestring budget. While newspapers were the fastest means of encouraging a vote, many Free State editors were Lane men and would not support the Cellar Kitchen ticket. Second, poll watchers had to have the means both to spot potential voter fraud and to deal with any violence.

Ewing had some advantages as he managed the difficult campaign. Previous raucous election results had pinpointed where to expect frauds—the four large townships of Oxford, McGee, Delaware, and Kickapoo. Again using his office's connections with Douglas Democrats, Ewing convinced the new territorial governor, James Denver, that a small number of troops in key townships could control the polling places and ensure fairness. While Denver had allegiances to Buchanan and the Democratic Party, he could hardly refuse Ewing's request since Ewing had championed Denver's request that the Free State men get involved in the election. Denver approved Ewing's request, which fit right in with Ewing's plan to trap Buchanan's men in a fraud. Ewing contacted Colonel William Harney, the grizzled Indian fighter in command at Fort Leavenworth. "I take a company of select men to Kickapoo and am bound to have fair play there."[82]

Not all Free State newspapers were happy with Ewing's get-out-the-vote campaign. The *Washington Union,* the Democratic Party's national organ, downplayed Free State efforts in Kansas, writing: "The whole population of Kansas doesn't equal a suburb of one of our Atlantic Coast cities. Why do we let them usurp a prominence in our affairs beyond that of our foreign policy, our financial condition and our widespread commerce?" Dwight Thatcher was the editor of the *Lawrence Republican,* a Lane paper. He was critical that Tom Ewing was allowed even to participate in the party's meeting in Lawrence. "No one can guarantee an honest election," Thatcher concluded, and the ploy "by misguided men" would have the tragic results of giving legitimacy to the proslavery men who were most likely to be elected to run the state. What Tom Ewing knew better than Thatch-

81. "Voting policy" from Taylor, "Business and Political Career," 65.
82. "Kickapoo fair play" from TEJr. to HBE, January 2, 1858, Lecompton/KSHS.

er, however, was how the city of Washington operated. One or two influential men given the right political ammunition could keep Congress from taking precipitous action, regardless of how the election went in January.[83]

One of the least likely problem areas was Leavenworth itself. Ewing called a mass meeting for December 28, 1857. Over a thousand people—one-fifth of the city's population—attended a cold outdoor meeting. Ewing addressed the crowd, hoping as many in the throng could hear him as possible. Leavenworth was nearly unanimous that the Free State men should vote in a town that was outwardly proslavery. Ewing was chosen to oversee the voting results north of the Kansas River. The question he pondered on New Year's Day was how to spring the trap.[84]

At midday on January 4, 1858, wrapped in a greatcoat, Tom Ewing rode slowly into Kickapoo, Kansas, along with thirty other Free State men intent on cataloging irregularities in a manner that would show those Missouri excesses to the world, or at least to the U.S. Congress. Ewing's men watched the small ferry operate back and forth on the river. In another month the river would freeze over. A cold and treeless place, Kickapoo was built without any planning on the bluffs west of a muddy ferry landing on the Missouri River, eight miles above Leavenworth. The firebrands who liquored up in clapboard saloons in Weston, Missouri, often used Kickapoo as their port of entry into Kansas. Yet that day, as fast as the boats could bring them across, Missourians were coming over to vote. Ewing watched the activities until their presence on the street was recognized. Intense excitement broke out. Bolstered by liquor the Missourians threatened to run Ewing and his Free Staters out of town—or worse. Two of the inebriated introduced themselves to Ewing as Horace Greeley and William H. Seward, and they had just voted for the makeup of the Lecompton legislature, and by God if Ewing did not like it, then they would just have to kill him. C. F. Currier, the chief clerk of the territorial house of representatives, nervously pulled Ewing aside and suggested he get his men off the street to avoid gunplay.[85]

Although the butt of jeers and oaths, Ewing kept his wits about him. He gave his own weapon to a friend and ordered all but himself and two others to head back up the road and wait, keeping alert to return if they heard gunfire. It was a

83. Ewing, "Struggle For Freedom," 6; "equal a suburb" from the *Washington Union,* quoted in Stampp, *America in 1857,* 322; Thatcher in the *Lawrence Republican,* December 31, 1857.

84. Taylor, "Business and Political Career," 68.

85. The narrative of events in Kickapoo comes from Ewing, "Struggle For Freedom," 7; Taylor, "Business and Political Career," 70.

gutsy thing to do. More than one man with antislavery views had been beaten or killed by these ruffians. Ewing did not just stand there; he, too, used the power of rumor. A talkative clerk in the Kickapoo land office whom Ewing recognized was told that Lane's militia was nearby at a telegraph office, armed and mounted, and that if the Missourians harmed any of Ewing's Free Staters, Lane would build the first bridge over the Missouri River with the ashes and stones of Weston, Missouri. Nobody knew if Ewing was bluffing, but they knew even less about Lane—except for his unpredictability, which was infamous.

Ewing remained in Kickapoo all day, watching the long line of Missourians walk into the voting office, swear to their Kansas residency, and vote. Under territorial law, citizens lawfully on the census could vote anywhere in the county where they lived so long as they voted only once. Several men got into line and voted two or three times, rerouting themselves to nearby saloons to refresh themselves. Even teenagers voted. When the polls were about to close, Ewing and Currier walked across the street, got in line, and voted, numbers 550 and 551 on the voting sheet. Two more Missourians voted behind them, and the polls were officially closed. Ewing later wrote that he and Currier were "loudly booed when finished, and under a shower of rotten garbage, [we] rode off."[86]

Although the Free State men smelled a fraud brewing in places such as Kickapoo, there had to be clear evidence. Before the territorial legislature could react to the frauds it had to investigate them. When the votes for the legislature were counted, at first it looked as if Free State men would control the house by fourteen seats and seven on the council. When word leaked out that proslavery majorities had been elected in both houses, Free State men knew the fix was in.

Ewing had seen the fraud with his own eyes, and within hours of the end of the election he swore out warrants to arrest the illegal Missouri voters he saw at Kickapoo. Free State marshals swung into Kickapoo and Delaware townships on the pretext of looking for perjurers and confiscated weapons stolen from the Liberty, Missouri, arsenal in 1855. Missourians in three counties across the river vowed revenge. However, the prompt arrests kept one of Calhoun's henchmen, a Missourian named Jack Henderson, from effectively falsifying the vote in another town, Delaware Crossing.[87]

When Calhoun reviewed the ballots from Kickapoo, he announced that over nine hundred men had voted there. This was four hundred more after Ewing vot-

86. Kickapoo efforts, threats, and "rotten garbage" from Ewing, "Struggle For Freedom," 7.

87. TEJr. to TESr., January 7, 1858, previously unpublished, in the private collection of the late Joseph H. Ewing, Wheaton, Maryland (used with permission of the family). A career army historian, Joseph H. Ewing was Philemon Ewing's grandson.

ed. When the Free State men went public with those numbers, telegraphing Ewing's remarks to Free State strongholds across the territory, anger erupted. Calhoun left for Washington, just ahead of a Free State mob that threatened to lynch him. Partly to calm the resentment growing in Free State ranks, Ewing convinced the existing territorial legislature immediately to enact a board for examining election frauds and to name him to chair it. Ewing's request was given a boost when word got back that Buchanan had adopted Calhoun's representations and intended to force Congress to approve the election results.[88]

Governor Denver could have vetoed the creation of Ewing's commission, but he did not. He made a last effort to convince Buchanan to give the Kansas territorial government authority to hold another election for convention delegates who would be fairly elected and send this constitution to Congress. Before Denver had transmitted his suggestion to Washington, Buchanan announced he would press on for the passage of the Lecompton Constitution. Tom Ewing recognized the treachery Buchanan was courting and the dilemma that his disdain for Denver's suggestion posed for Free State moderates. "If we are admitted and these Proslavery men have the power, there will be civil war," Ewing morosely predicted to his father. "The Calhoun faction does not number more than 1000 of 16,000 voters." However, it was the recklessness of the Free State Party's own "war" faction led by James Lane and John Brown that the younger Ewing feared most. "Kansas cannot be forced like a bastinadoed elephant to kneel to receive the paltry riders. I believe that the ringleaders of this [Free State] faction will be put to death the moment that Calhoun decides the election against us, and I would not be surprised to see the people unite in determined rebellion, although it is more probable that they will seize the state government by killing enough Proslavery men to give them a majority." It was clear that Ewing felt a lot more was riding on this constitutional fight than just politics.[89]

Tom also wrote Hugh, "If we can get our Free State ticket elected, as it really is elected, everything will be well and our success here will become certain. Otherwise, I fear we shall have a season of violence and probability of civil war, which would ruin us all." Further, Tom needed help in keeping the Leavenworth busi-

88. That TEJr. was to address the legislature, see TEJr. to Ellen Cox Ewing (hereafter ECE), January 12, 1858, TEJr./KSHS; Ewing's "voting frauds board" was created by Kansas statutes, *1857 Territorial Session Laws,* chapter 27, section 1.

89. Denver letter to Buchanan, January 16, 1858, Buchanan Manuscript Collection, Historical Society of Pennsylvania, Philadelphia; for Buchanan and the Lecompton effort, see Marcus Parrott to John Hutchinson, January 15, 1858, William Hutchinson Manuscript Collection, KSHS; TEJr. to TESr., January 18, 1858, TEJr./KSHS.

ness operation going. Hugh was riding out the winter in a St. Louis hotel. It was there that Tom found him. "I want you to come [to Leavenworth], now. There is a great deal to do and I cannot do it all! . . . We have to fight Redpath, Lane, Etc. and I want to be in that fight." Tom was spending so much time on politics that could pave the way to his Senate ambition that political uncertainties left the brothers' land speculation business in shambles. "If the decision on the Lecompton Constitution is delayed long, we shall have great difficulty in arranging the necessary spring sales. If the decision be adverse before then, we cannot meet our obligations at all, for in my judgment there will be violence almost at once."[90]

With the single-mindedness that formed an important part of his ability as an advocate, Tom threw off the thought of his own personal failures, and on January 26, 1858, his voting frauds commission began taking testimony from Calhoun's employees. Under Ewing's skillful examination, Jack Henderson confessed to forging 336 names onto the returns, on Calhoun's orders. The most uncooperative employee was Calhoun's clerk, Lauchlan MacLean, a sour blunt-faced man with few scruples. When the commission demanded to see the voting results, MacLean swore under oath that Calhoun had taken the returns with him to Washington. Ewing thought the story improbable since Calhoun had left so quickly and by himself. If he had taken the returns to Washington, Buchanan's congressional allies would demand to see the returns. The returns were in Kansas, somewhere. The pressure to find them was growing. Buchanan was going to certify the Lecompton vote to Congress within a few days.[91]

On the second night of the commission's work, Ewing's luck turned. He was summoned to a back-alley meeting with a lone stranger. Both men were bundled up against the cold, and both were nervous. The stranger produced a pistol, which gave Ewing a start—but the pistol was given to Ewing to show his good faith. The stranger swore Ewing to secrecy, or else the stranger would be dead by morning if word got out. He identified himself only by saying that he worked for the territorial government in Lecompton, but not for Calhoun. He said another man had seen MacLean and another employee hide a large box of voting returns under a woodpile outside Calhoun's office. When Ewing asked if the informant had seen MacLean's action in person, the informant said no. But Charley Torrey had seen it all. Torrey was a quiet, unassuming draftsman and messenger, who Calhoun's

90. "Season of violence" from TEJr. to HBE, January 10, 1858, TEJr./KSHS; "in that fight" from TEJr. to HBE, January 18, 1858, Lecompton/KSHS; "violence almost at once" from TEJr. to HBE, January 23, 1858, HBE/OHS.

91. Description of MacLean from Stampp, *America in 1857,* 153. For commission examination of witnesses to the voting frauds, see Eldridge, *Early Days,* 154–55.

people assumed was an alcoholic but who was actually a Pennsylvania Free State mole. Torrey had passed the word to the informant, who brought Ewing the best evidence Ewing could possibly want. To make sure there was no shooting war Torrey had also uncapped all the loaded muskets in the Lecompton arsenal and poured water down the barrels.[92]

Armed with crucial information Ewing wasted no time. He wrote out a longhand subpoena and a request for a search warrant. Since Calhoun was absent and certain witnesses had lied, in Calhoun's absence the commission had the lawful right to review the records. A probate judge in Lawrence agreed, giving the warrant to Sheriff Sam Walker to execute. Walker's *posse commitatus* found MacLean in his office and served the warrant. Walker informed MacLean he was under arrest for perjury and that they proposed to look for the returns under a woodpile. The terror-stricken look on MacLean's face was all the confirmation Ewing needed. Governor Denver was summoned in the dead of night and watched as the candle box was opened and the contents examined. Just as Torrey had stated, the woodpile hid the disputed election returns, showing among other things that at Kickapoo Township the vote had magically swollen by 442 names after Currier and Ewing voted. Henderson's attempt at skewering the Delaware Crossing vote was not even a decent forgery. Entire pages of a city directory had been crudely spliced into the list of names. Henderson's fraud and MacLean's role in it were complete. Ewing now had his own eyewitness testimony and proof positive for Congress of the fraud perpetrated by Buchanan's appointees. Sheriff Walker issued a warrant for MacLean's arrest, but MacLean had disappeared into the endless expanse of the Kansas prairie.[93]

Alerting Stephen Douglas was not the last thing Ewing did in the Lecompton fiasco. He spent a small fortune telegraphing news of the discovery of the returns to every influential Free State newspaper in the country. Then he completed the report of his investigating committee and his own abstract of the returns and set out for Washington. In his wake, the legislature promptly repealed the entire 1855

92. Compare the Eldridge text to the account in 1898 correspondence between Thomas Ewing III and William Brindle, formerly employed in Calhoun's land office, who claimed to be the informant who disclosed Torrey's name to Tom Ewing. In a letter to Charles Robinson dated four years earlier, however, Thomas Ewing Jr. named Henry Petrikin, an appointee of President Buchanan, as his source for locating the candle-box hiding place. TEJr. to Robinson, February 8, 1894, Robinson Papers, KSHS. See Thomas Ewing III, "Some Happenings Fifty Years Ago, Address at the Banquet of the Kansas Society," New York, January 29, 1908, 1–5, in Lecompton/KSHS.

93. Ewing, "Struggle For Freedom," 8–9.

code of bogus Missouri laws and called for a new constitutional convention. Denver signed the first bill but vetoed the second on orders from Buchanan.

Stephen Douglas had had enough. On February 5, 1858, while Ewing was still en route, Douglas declared that his party leaders (meaning James Buchanan) had betrayed popular sovereignty by seeking ratification of a document approved only through massive fraud. He urged the House of Representatives to take its time on the matter, and that key men from the territory would be among them soon to assist in the investigation of the "Lecompton doings." Buchanan charged Douglas with grandstanding. Congress should adopt the results and get on with deliberations for Kansas statehood as a proslavery state. Lawmakers could curry some presidential favors if they played ball and avoided any lengthy investigation. Douglas could not promise patronage, but he could promise House members whether their bills would have buoyancy in the Senate if they slowed the statehood process in Kansas and let the House Territorial Committee complete its investigation. The result was a narrow one-vote victory for the creation of a House Territorial Committee investigation. The ultimate watchers, with smiles on their faces, were the Republicans.[94]

Tom Ewing reached Washington at the height of this initial sparring. The information he placed on every congressman's desk "exploded in the capitol," defeating the alleged presidential "conspiracy" and driving the pro-Southern Democratic Party undercover. Abolitionists waxed eloquent, comparing Ewing with the Hebrew shepherd with the slingshot and the forged Kansas ballots as the stones "destined to pierce the helmet of the giant rebellion." For a month lawmakers discussed the Kansas question and the controversy surrounding the crooked voting scheme. Ewing's name was prominent in the discussions—a form of national advertising that was priceless. Lecompton finally came to a vote. The Territorial Committee, chaired by Georgian Alexander Stephens, offered the majority report, which, not surprisingly, favored Buchanan's views on Lecompton.[95]

On March 3, 1858, New York senator William Seward spoke at length on the "irrepressible conflict between the two 'antagonistic systems' of slave and free labor." In response Senator James H. Hammond of South Carolina snapped that the North "dared not make war on cotton. No power on earth dares make war on it. Cotton is King!" The bitterness and the feuding continued. Some Southern senators were having second thoughts about Hammond's "King Cotton" predictions. Among them was the former attorney general from Kentucky, John J. Crit-

94. Stampp, *America in 1857*, 309, 312, 319.
95. "Exploded" and "pierce the helmet" from Elliott, "Grasshopper Falls Convention," 189.

tenden, who in mid-March offered a new bill, which called for referring the whole process of Kansas statehood to Congress. While this move was contrary to Kansas-Nebraska, Douglas took Crittenden's actions as a sign that Southerners were deserting Buchanan. The administration, however, was still able to squeeze Lecompton past the Senate on a 33–25 vote.[96]

In the House the Territorial Committee recommended adoption of the Lecompton Constitution, but Buchanan's men lost traction among House Democrats. During the House debates, fisticuffs broke out as Republican Galusha Grow of Pennsylvania threw punches at Lawrence Keitt of South Carolina. For a moment, dozens of representatives to the U.S. Congress were swinging, pushing, and shoving in the well of the House while Speaker Orr gaveled them into order. Then the people's chamber voted down Lecompton.[97]

Newspapers reported no serious casualties except to pride; Congress was unable to organize even a brawl efficiently. Tom and Hugh Ewing had in a very short time in Kansas raised their visibility considerably, which brought on a measure of business success as both were now leaders in their political parties. Tom Jr. had not only begun a successful speculation practice, he was now a strong voice of moderation within the Free State Party. No one else in Kansas could claim they had successfully engineered a coup against highly organized and well-funded partisans of the U.S. president. Not only had Tom Ewing galvanized Stephen Douglas into taking action that backed James Buchanan into a political corner from which he could not recover, but Ewing had also prodded proslavery elements in Missouri and in Congress into seeing the folly of their activities in Kansas. While advocates of an ancient rhetoric rarely give up easily, and proslavery elements certainly did not give up, their banter in the press was less strident, and their threats of secession, especially, were somewhat less acerbic. They had to acknowledge defeat at the hands of a Kansas politician who was only twenty-nine years old.

One of the great milestones in Tom Ewing's life was his defeat of the Lecompton Constitution. In later years he would reflect back on what he did for freedom in Kansas much more than on his war record. It was not only the result of political luck, of which there was some; his achievements fighting the Lecompton Constitution showed a high degree of political acumen, an understanding of the human nature within his Free State Party, and an accurate comprehension of what

96. Stampp, *America in 1857,* 326.
97. Ibid., 327.

Congress would or would not tolerate. While, in any territorial situation, good and necessary men essential to a strong creative enterprise rise quickly to prominence, Tom Ewing's rise was indeed phenomenal. As Hugh might have described it with his own poetic flair, his brother had "brained the dragon" of Lecompton. But Lecompton was but a portent of what was to come.[98]

98. Hugh once referred to Douglas's role in fighting Lecompton as "fighting the dragon he had sired." HBE to TESr., October 15, 1860, in Ewing, "Autobiography," 231.

3

MORTGAGES, PRESS BOOKS, AND OFFICE BOYS

After providing the ammunition that Douglas and Congress could use to reject the Lecompton Constitution, Tom went back to Kansas, where he returned to pursuit of his fortune mixed in with the fallout from his participation in the failure of the Lecompton document. He still had not heard from Hugh on covering their business prospects. Two boats had brought out a hundred new settlers to Leavenworth, but none of them were buying land. Ewing reported to Hugh that the real estate market was "dull, and money very scarce." Even Governor Denver was in hock to lenders. Politics was taking a lot of time, and at the same time the land sales portion of their practice needed attention. They had to sell properties to pay debt. Tom complained to Hugh that the next six weeks were vital to their practice. "If you and Hamp are not out soon, we cannot expect to get along with our payments."[1]

The Ewing enterprises in Leavenworth were indeed suffering from neglect. Tom could not quit politics while Lecompton still twitched. Yet, Tom had reason to worry. Mortgage payments were due. The prefabricated housing was not selling. William Russell had agreed to make up for Sanders's activities, but the hous-

1. Both quotes from TEJr. to HBE, March 3, 1858, HBE/OHS.

ing was primarily aimed at Fort Leavenworth's soldiers, and they had not been paid in a while.[2]

The brothers were in fact having a minor falling out over which direction to pursue politically. While not entirely consumed with politics, Tom was intent on his work with the Free Staters, seeing it as a road to a political career in the territory. Like Cump he had soured on the idea of making money quickly. "I have no great faith in a 'great sale,' and hope you will not rely on one," he wrote Hugh at the very moment Hugh was trying to find a financier who could take some consortium lands off their hands at a discount. There was some movement in land sales, but not much. Added pressure came from the Ewings' old antagonist Madison Mills, who agreed to extend his mortgage payment terms on the land he had sold the Ewing consortium but only if the interest was paid. To raise part of that sum, Tom asked Eleazer Sherman to extend his notes for sixty days without interest, using the interest payments of one creditor to pay another. Property was being dumped on the Leavenworth market to compete with the organized sales of the Cincinnati consortium. Dumping was a bad sign. Rumors began circulating that Majors and Russell were moving their huge freighting company to Nebraska City, which if true would be an economic blow of monumental proportions to Leavenworth. Ewing found it necessary to squelch such rumors in some of his letters to out-of-town prospects.[3]

While his public face was positive, Tom Ewing had concluded that land speculation was a sorry investment fraught with danger where hard work was not always rewarded, fortunes disappeared overnight, and money was made only by the lucky or those fortunate enough to find rubes to buy land without regard to the price. He was ready to get out, and quickly if possible. If he could not get shed of the business, he wanted to scale down operations to more manageable levels. The practice of law, not speculation, could provide a good living and allowed him more time for his political work.

Hugh was aware of Tom's desires, but Tom was asking an avowed Douglas Democrat to support the Free Staters, indirectly, by handling Tom's affairs so Tom could continue his own political career. Hugh felt they would both prosper if Tom spent less time in his political adventures. The family knew of Tom's ambitions. If the Free State legislature became the first state legislature, it would name the

2. TEJr. to HBE, February 8, 1858, ibid.

3. TEJr. to HBE, February 19, 1858, ibid. For squelching out-of-town rumors, see TEJr. to TESr., March 29, 1858, TEJr./KSHS.

state's two senators. While it was no secret that the radical Jim Lane wanted one of the positions, Tom Ewing's strong work within the party might assure the other spot would go to a moderate. This diverging track caused some friction between the brothers. Hugh obviously did not come back to Leavenworth to oversee their investments as quickly as Tom desired, and the void brought an exasperated response: "I *cannot* abandon politics now. I can be of service in the Free State party for there is no man in it pretending to be a leader who can confront an aspiring popular move. You and Hamp should return now." Hugh, the family's Douglas Democrat, remained unimpressed.[4]

Stephen Douglas knew that while Congress was fighting off Buchanan's efforts to get the Lecompton Constitution ratified, others should be at work to create an alternative Free State constitution that Washington could live with. This meant compromising the key issues. Ewing's name, through letters to leading political figures and his work on the candle-box affair, moved him into the forefront of the Free State movement, which he used to obtain a delegate's position to the new Leavenworth Constitutional Convention. This convention met in early April 1858, concomitant with the period when Congress was debating whether to adopt the Lecompton Constitution.

The Leavenworth delegates eventually turned to the "Negro" question. This was not so much whether a black man should be free; freedom would be determined by some other entity or the gratuity of slave owners themselves. Which privileges and civil rights should the race have in Kansas, if any? The convention moderates did not want slavery in Kansas; they decided they did not want Negroes even to reside in Kansas, either. One way to discourage emigration was to leave them constitutionally without civil rights in local governments. Further, by not sheltering runaways who crossed the Missouri River to freedom, there would be no reason for runaways to come to Kansas and thus no temptations for slave-catchers to steal them back. Abolitionists were furious with this logic since it avoided the humanity question of the condition of slavery itself.

Abolitionist sentiment no longer held sway with Ewing, however. Since coming to Kansas he had considerably modified his abolitionist views, most probably because of the violence carried out in the name of abolition by the "war radicals" such as James Montgomery and John Brown. While Ewing did oppose slavery, his postwar references to "half-civilized Negroes" and his belief that integration must be gradual and supervised betrayed his true feelings, which resem-

4. TEJr. to HBE, March 3, 1858, Lecompton/KSHS.

bled those of his father. The Ewings were antislavery, but they were not for integration. As for the right to vote, Tom Ewing felt it was hypocrisy to give black men a franchise not yet available to white women (and he was not yet ready for that change, either).[5]

The radicals at the convention solved Ewing's polemical comparison of women and free blacks by enshrining in the Leavenworth Constitution a voting franchise for both blacks and women. The women's suffrage initiative was unique. As yet no state, North or South, had adopted such enfranchisement, however, and it was too radical for Ewing to remain silent. Women's suffrage was still a notion whose time had not yet come. He argued for patience. Let the Leavenworth Constitution be ratified by Congress, and then amend the constitution after statehood to allow women to vote—if this was the recommendation of the state legislature. Delegates to a constitutional convention were not as representative of the general population as were members of a duly elected legislature based on apportionment. He kept hammering to save their newest ideas for when the territory was a state and they could act without Congress looking over their shoulder, when Congress would be powerless to prevent concepts such as the enfranchisement of women. Tom Ewing's remarks carried great weight at the convention, but the radicals finessed him by leaving the question of voting rights to a territorial referendum.

Ewing had problems with other provisions, including one that required parents to send children to school through age sixteen—long past the time when a farm boy was strong enough to help with chores. Ewing labeled the idea, "tyrannical, unjust and anti-American." Although the argument sounds ludicrous now, laws prohibiting children from working in dangerous jobs was fifty years away from entering the conscience of Congress. Sixteen-year-olds formed an important part of the workforce. Ewing was concerned that mandatory schooling for young children was a bigger political issue. Governments should not coerce parents on how to raise their children. Ewing also was concerned that arguments for mandatory schooling, any mandatory schooling, would lead to the inevitability of the franchise for blacks and women.[6]

5. Mary Scott Rowland, "Thomas Ewing: The Reluctant Chief Justice," 17.

6. Ewing's discussions at the Leavenworth convention are best covered by "If Lecompton Had Prevailed," *Kansas Historical Collections* 10 (1908): 217–18. "Tyrannical" from Taylor, "Business and Political Career," 80. For Ewing's prominence in the Free State cause, see Martin, *Proceedings and Debates,* 664. The Leavenworth convention to some degree, and the later Wyandotte Constitutional Convention to a heavy extent, saw women such as Clarina Nichols work hard on the periphery of politics for full woman's suffrage. Radical suffragette Susan B. Anthony already had a contact with

Ewing and the conservatives had to fight several other radical amendments. James Winchell moved that if Kansas was admitted before a statewide ratification of the Leavenworth Constitution, then a clause would provide that the Free State Leavenworth Constitution would revoke the Lecompton Constitution and take immediate effect without a ratification vote. Ewing reminded the convention of its limits. Their charge was to create an alternative constitution to Lecompton. They had no authority to repeal anything. Ewing's supporters argued that Winchell's motion would make the Leavenworth Constitution no better than the Lecompton document. Ewing led the discussion on this sticky problem well into the morning of April 4, the final day of the convention. The report of the convention described Ewing's persistence in explaining that it was important to organize a Free State government under the Lecompton document and immediately offer the Leavenworth Constitution as a replacement. Patience, Ewing reiterated, was the key. All Free Staters had to do was maintain control of the legislature and, after statehood was granted, change the original constitution to whatever provisions they desired.[7]

Although there was a lot of stem-winding on these fundamental issues, Ewing's most bitter rivals agreed on the general document. The Leavenworth Constitution was not much different from the Topeka Constitution of 1855, with which even the radicals such as Jim Lane, James Montgomery, and John Brown had been content. Robinson and Ewing got Lane's allies to agree that the convention members should adjourn with solidarity behind them, something they had not achieved the previous December at the infamous bolters' meeting. Free Staters would present a united political front for Congress against the Democrats. Robinson especially, since he coveted the governor's position once statehood came, pushed Ewing's ideas of consolidation hard. They should work within the state system, keeping an eye on Washington but working the system regardless of what Douglas did.

Any agreement with Lane rarely lasted, however. Try as he might to convince Lane to be patient, Ewing could not affect the bloodshed that was spawned by Free State militia. As if to provide an exclamation point to the limits of the Leav-

---

Kansas through her brother, the publisher Daniel Anthony. The Wyandotte convention in 1859 would give women the right to vote in school district elections and also the right to own property. It would acknowledge the more radical idea that women should have an equal say in the custody of their children. See Martin, *Proceedings and Debates,* 303, 665.

7. Robinson to TEJr., March 24, 1858, Lecompton/KSHS.

enworth agreement, two weeks after the convention adjourned, Montgomery's jayhawkers surprised Hamilton's "Bloody Reds" at the Trading Post Saloon in Linn County. They destroyed the proslavery men's whiskey and herded the Reds toward Missouri with stern warnings that, if the ruffians crossed back into Kansas, shootings would be the kindest treatment they could expect. Newspapers reported hundreds of proslavery "refugees" trudging back into Missouri. The radicals kept their arms and secretly hoped for retaliation. For a month the militia companies remained on alert, sometimes sleeping in the fields so as not to be caught unprepared in their cabins. By the summer of 1858 in the Kansas Territory, the spirit that brought a diverse country together to fight two wars of independence from Britain had given in to sectional fighting. Each faction was intolerant and each of the competing labor systems practiced exclusivity. There was nothing left to compromise. The South once again threatened to secede if a version of Lecompton did not pass Congress. Ominously, Thomas Ewing Sr. reported to Hugh that Buchanan was sending more troops to Fort Leavenworth. The country was back to the same rhetoric it had faced in 1850.[8]

While Hugh had returned reluctantly to Leavenworth at Tom's request, he was now inundated with a pile of complaints. There was grumbling among their friends and acquaintances in Ohio who had been given a brighter scenario when they invested than the one now lying listless in the muddy river town they had never seen. George Sanders was the target of most of the concerns. Sanders's creditors swarmed the Ewings' Leavenworth office. Threats of foreclosure suits were coming from all directions. So angry were Sanders's creditors that the Ewings feared a lynching if the eccentric New Yorker came back to Kansas. Tom preferred that Sanders leave Leavenworth for good: "If Sanders can sell in NY let him do it by all means. He will be in our way out here. He will start fifty schemes and spend thousands and then all will fail." Madison Mills was pressing the brothers, as agents for Sanders, for payments on the property Sanders had bought from Mills, so Hugh authorized some interest payments to stave off suits. When Fant learned of the use of investment monies for this purpose, he sent Hugh a nasty note. Hugh fired back that he had given the banker *cestui que* deeds for Mills's property, that Fant should hold onto the deeds, and if the notes were not paid he could sell the deeds as collateral. Furthermore he no longer wanted to be Fant's agent in Kansas.

8. "Bloody Reds" from Stampp, *America in 1857,* 273; "refugees" from the *Lawrence Herald of Freedom,* May 29, 1858.

In words many lawyers would love to use with certain clients, Hugh wrote, "You are decidedly more trouble than you are worth."[9]

Similar letters went out to other creditors. Hugh wrote Warren Grigsby, Sanders's Kentucky partner, to come out at once and settle his business matters if he could, suggesting that Grigsby let Sanders go from the partnership. "How under the blessed sun he raised up such a cloud of creditors during his stay [in Leavenworth] is beyond my comprehension." In a later letter to Grigsby, he wrote, "I would give 20,000 dollars if he had never bought from us." Sanders had caused Hugh "endless trouble," and the firm now had serious credit problems. To Sanders directly, Hugh reported that the creditors intended to hold the Ewings responsible for damages: "We have been struggling like dying men with your indebtedness to Mills and must continue to do so with a fear of being sold out at every turn [by Mills]." Hugh was especially frustrated that the failings came when he was wanting to marry. He was closing up his property and heading for Europe and would "leave the affair" to others. This was not quite true, since between March and July the Ewings sold over fifteen hundred small lots. Sales dwindled after that, however. Unless Sanders had $12,000 in cash on him, there was no use in coming out to Leavenworth. "I am compelled under instructions to close the game" for Sanders. Hugh created a *cestui que* trust for the creditors and then headed for the arms of Henrietta Young and a European honeymoon.[10]

It was at this time that Tom finally recognized what he had been unwilling to admit before. The land speculation business tied him down too much and surely people such as Sanders did not mix with his political and legal ambitions. "I shall not remain in the real estate business in any event [we are getting out] this summer, if I can help it," he wrote Hugh. "Our interests must be rid of their entangling alliances."[11]

Hugh was concerned about his business affairs but excited about his new relationship with "Ri." His sloth in returning to Kansas was due to a slow-moving courtship. Henrietta was from a Maryland planter family, born on a two-hundred-year-old tobacco plantation called Geisborough, located south of Washington across the Anacostia River. George Washington Young, Henrietta's father, had resided at the plantation since 1833, and his family before then.

The Ewings knew of Hugh's concern that no one would have him, or at least

9. "Sell in NY" from TEJr. to HBE, February 19, 1858, HBE/OHS; "more trouble" from HBE to Fant, May 8, 1858, TEJr./KSHS.

10. "Cloud of creditors" from HBE to J. Warren Grigsby, May 3, 1858, in Ewing, "Autobiography," 212; "20,000 dollars" from HBE to Grigsby, May 28, 1858, TEJr./KSHS; HBE to Sanders, May 28, 1858, TEJr./KSHS.

11. TEJr. to HBE, March 30, 1858, HBE/OHS.

no one of sufficient station would have him, so when he announced his intentions to marry Ri, encouraging words came from his father and his mother, Maria Ewing. Henrietta had captivated Ewingville. "She is a fine little girl, and every one speaks well of her," Father Ewing wrote. Hugh's mother offered to accompany them on their planned honeymoon to Europe, just as Tom had accompanied Cump and Ellen in 1850. "Your anticipated marriage has caused quite a fervor in the city of Lancaster. Some of the young ladies I fear feel most fallen to think their chasings were not sufficient to captivate you." The one thing Hugh's wedding apparently would not do, she complained, would be to get the family together again. "What about Mr. Congress?" Maria wrote Hugh scornfully. "Tom has not written me a line since he returned to Kansas." She was thankful, she confided to Hugh, that Ellen Sherman was still with her. "A son is a son until he gets a wife, but a daughter is a daughter always," and she thanked God "the adage is verified in the only daughter I have married off."[12]

William English was an unassuming Indiana back-bench congressman and Douglas supporter who took great delight in his somewhat unrealistic views that if Congress were to contain slavery within the Old South, the seedy institution would die of old age, which is all the more reason to wonder at his solution to the political impasse in Congress over Lecompton. With Lecompton dead in Congress, English's idea was to send the Lecompton Constitution back to Kansas for a new vote on it with all its imperfections, including the slavery article, but to get all Kansans to vote up or down on the bill by attaching to it a public bribe. If Kansans ratified Lecompton, Congress would outright deed the new state government a huge chunk of public lands, which could be sold to anyone and the state could pocket the profits. Free Staters were furious. Buchanan was not only bribing Kansans, he was insulting them as well. With "paltry acres of land[,] unprincipled men have sought to purchase [our] manhood."[13]

Because federal officials in the Kansas Territory owed their allegiance to Buchanan rather than the Kansas settlers, a territory-wide vote on the English bill was scheduled in Kansas for August 2, 1858. Thomas Ewing Sr. scornfully warned Kansans to oppose the efforts "before new cliques have time to form." Rejecting Lecompton would require Kansans to wait for a new president before the territory would be eligible for statehood, but the wait, with heads held high, would be

12. "Fine little girl" from TESr. to HBE, May 13, 1858; "Mr. Congress" from Maria Ewing to HBE, May 4, 1858, both HBE/OHS.

13. Elbert, "English Bill," 223–31; "unprincipled men" from *Emporia Kansas News,* May 15, 1858.

worth it. "Your [Kansas] election in January defeated the Administration," a friend, John McLean, wrote Tom. "The eyes of the whole Country are on the people of Kansas, and I doubt not they will, in their future as in their past action, show that they know their rights and will maintain them."[14]

Not everyone was as convinced as McLean that Kansans would hang tough. James G. Blaine, a Ewing cousin who was seeking a state representative district in Maine, was concerned that Kansans would submit to the bribe in the English bill. Tom replied that his cousin maintained an "ungenerous lack of confidence" in the integrity of Kansans. Ewing railed at the "Arnolds and Iscariots" (Lane and Brown) for flooding Eastern newspapers with the charge that Republican conservatives were "covert Lecomptonites" who wanted a slavery-tolerant Free State government. Tom predicted:

> Your letter is the fifth or sixth I have received asking whether the English bribe may not meet with favor in the Free State ranks. The English bill . . . will not add a hundred votes to the strength of a naked Lecompton [constitution]. If the National Democracy makes no effort in its behalf it will be voted down by 8000 or 10000 majority. . . . The people of Kansas are poor, in debt, struggling to open their farms and build their homes, and have neither the numbers nor the wealth to bear the burden of a state government, [yet] they will not hasten to beleaguer the doors of Congress for admission.[15]

It was a polite way for Tom to tell Free Soil supporters to keep their shirts on. Matters were under control. He was right again. Lecompton's last hurrah—the August referendum on the English bill in Kansas—failed miserably.

The summer of 1858 produced a sensational criminal proceeding involving two of Lawrence's most prominent citizens, and Tom Ewing played an important part in it. James H. Lane was accused of murdering a neighbor, Gaius Jenkins, over water rights on a disputed claim. Jenkins was a popular abolitionist leader, and the entire town turned out for his funeral. Jenkins supporters, led by an avenging "Governor" Charles Robinson, called for Lane to be lynched. It was a measure of Tom Ewing's reputation as a lawyer that a frantic Mary Lane came to Leavenworth

14. TESr. to HBE, May 2, 1858, HBE/OSH; John McLean to TEJr., May 6, 1858, Lecompton/KSHS.

15. TEJr. to James G. Blaine, May 11, 1858, Lecompton/KSHS.

and asked him to defend her husband. Ewing knew of Lane's strong ambition to the U.S. Senate when statehood came, ambitions that matched his own. If by defending Lane an alliance could be created, and then if Lane were freed, he would owe Tom Ewing more than just a fee.

Mary Baldridge Lane got two for the price of one when she came to pour out her story to Tom Ewing, for Thomas Ewing Sr. was visiting his children in Leavenworth at the time. Both attorneys agreed that, without more, a murder charge could not be sustained without a showing of malice, and malice was hard to prove when a homeowner was attacked on his front porch. Mrs. Lane said that her husband, as usual, was without money and wanted her to ask the Ewings for bail, which Tom refused "as a matter of professional morality." Ewing did fight for Lane's bail, arguing that if the case did not involve malice, bail in some amount was automatic, and he knew that, when bail was set, Lane supporters would quickly raise it. Motions were heard and the bail was set. Ewing was right; Lane supporters immediately raised the bail amount. Lane faced a preliminary hearing in late June with a four-lawyer defense team against five prosecuting attorneys in front of a three-judge panel. The crowded and partisan courtroom left just enough room among the spectators for some newspapermen from St. Louis.[16]

At the time of the preliminary hearing for Lane, although Lane and Tom Ewing were unaware of the psychology involved (indeed neither man would have ever heard of the word "codependent"), beginning with their earlier political association in the Free State Party and the Jenkins murder investigation, each would become dependent on the other, if not intentionally then at least by circumstance. Lane was one of the Kansas Territory's more colorful characters. As historian Albert Castel described him: "Vulgar, tempestuous, of fluctuating courage and utterly unscrupulous, he was a cynic who posed as a zealot, a demagogue who posed as a statesman. His private life was that of a satyr and he was utterly irreligious except at election time." A Douglas Democrat intent on getting a bill of divorce from Mary, Lane had originally come to Kansas because the Democrat-dominated Indiana legislature would not give him one (she was the daughter of a highly popular former governor). He was "not one to carry party loyalty to unreasonable lengths." When the proslavery Kansas legislature would

16. Jay Monaghan, *Civil War on the Western Border, 1854–1865,* 108; "professional morality" from William E. Connelley, *James Henry Lane, The Grim Chieftain of Kansas,* 122; William E. Connelley, "The Lane-Jenkins Claim Contest," 21–22; Julia Lovejoy, "Letters of Julia Louisa Lovejoy, 1856–1864," 386–87.

not grant Lane such legislation either, he joined the Free State Party and began his association with Tom Ewing.[17]

Judge E. D. Ladd presided over Lane's preliminary hearing. A pretrial hearing is presented to a justice of the peace who decides whether a crime was committed in the jurisdiction, and whether it was likely that the accused did it. While most prelims were largely uncontested, Ewing decided to go for broke and seek a release and avoid a later jury trial, since it was easier to control the evidence going to a dispassionate judge than to control a jury that might contain Jenkins supporters. The first days were spent with the main prosecution witnesses, who established what had happened, the personal feud between Lane and Jenkins, and Lane's threats toward Jenkins before he was killed. The shanty over which the men feuded was a single rectangular room with twisted cottonwood planking and mud-chinked walls. Lane sold the property to Jenkins in 1855, but Jenkins made only part of the payments. Lane rescinded the contract, tendering back the sums, but Jenkins refused and claimed he owned the house and lands in spite of not having paid the full sums. Lane claimed he owned the property and submitted the dispute to the territorial land office for a decision, where it was languishing when the political feud broke into deadly violence.

Lane was in possession of the house, but Jenkins wanted access to the water on the property. Lane got wind of Jenkins's intent to take some water and threatened Jenkins to stay away. Jenkins came with allies, Ray Green and Henry Dufur. Testimony was contradictory as to whether Jenkins came armed, but Green and Dufur were armed. When the Jenkins group approached in the afternoon Lane, holding a shotgun, warned them away. When Jenkins moved toward the well with his hatchet, something prompted Green to fire his pistol. The percussion cap misfired, but the sound triggered a nervous reaction in Lane who fired on Jenkins, mortally wounding him. Green fired again, this time hitting Lane above the knee.

Chief prosecutor Frederick Stanton wanted to introduce evidence of who actually owned the disputed land. Ewing argued that for the law of trespass and defense of homesteads to apply, only "possession" of the cabin at the time of the incident was relevant. Ewing reminded Judge Ladd that, if ownership was to be the basis of the prosecution, Ewing would need to bring dozens of rebuttal witnesses of his own to establish Lane's right to the house and the water, adding nothing to

17. Albert Castel, *Civil War Kansas: Reaping the Whirlwind,* 19; Connelley, *Grim Chieftain,* 37; "unreasonable lengths" from Starr, *Jennison's Jayhawkers,* 12. The account in the following several paragraphs is taken from Connelley, "Lane-Jenkins Claim."

the law that the court must deal with but lengthening the hearing indefinitely. Faced with the prospects of spending a hot summer on an elevated bench in a muggy courtroom, Ladd sided with Ewing and rejected the prosecution's contention. Lane, still recovering from his knee wound, watched the proceedings ill at ease and in pain.[18]

George Smith, a rabid Robinson and pro-Jenkins partisan, was the primary witness concerning Lane's public threats toward Jenkins the day before the killing. On cross examination Ewing asked him: "Have you stated publicly that your evidence would convict General Lane of murder and you would walk fifty miles to give it?" The prosecution objected, but Ewing explained he was not impeaching Smith but rather showing Smith's animus toward Lane. Smith replied sardonically that he "opposed capital punishment," and Lane was so popular with juries that he would never get true justice—a rope. Smith volunteered, "The only way to deal with such men is shoot them down at the time." Smith opined that the two men who shot toward Lane should have taken better aim. Smith's irrelevant outburst having proved his point, Ewing excused Smith and called another witness.[19]

Ewing got Douglas County sheriff Sam Walker, a proslavery official, to admit he was first to arrive at the shooting where he interviewed witnesses. Green told Walker that, if he had used his pistol better, Jenkins would be alive because Lane would have been dead. This testimony favored Lane's version that he fired his shotgun after someone's pistol fired on him, which negated premeditation. When Green was recalled he admitted Walker was right. During Ewing's cross examination, Green glared pugnaciously at Lane, declaring that he himself would take on Lane or any Lane man with pistols at three feet. Lane snapped from the table, "I'd rather fight you at three feet than be assassinated." Green replied indignantly he would not assassinate anyone.[20]

The hearing lasted several weeks, and when the witnesses were through, Stanton began his summation. His main point went unchallenged—that Lane confronted Jenkins, retreated into the house for a deadly weapon, came back out, and used it. Stanton argued that under the law a man could not kill another in defense of his home until the intruder crossed the threshold. Jenkins was shot twenty-five feet from the house while moving toward the well, a long way from the threshold. The evidence, Stanton said, could not support self-defense. Lane knew the law enough to go get his gun, kill his "ancient enemy," and then claim self-

18. Connelley, "Lane-Jenkins Claim," 133.

19. Ibid., 143–44.

20. Ibid., 164; also "The Homicide at Lawrence: Fourteenth Day," *Daily Missouri Democrat,* July 8, 1858.

defense. He was not in danger from Jenkins's axe but rather from Green's pistol. A defendant with no malice in his heart would have shot Green, not Jenkins.[21]

Tom Ewing took his time with his rebuttal summation of the evidence for the defense. His arguments were classical—set up the elements of what had to be proved by the prosecution, then demolish the proof one piece at a time. He first reminded Judge Ladd of the panel's narrow duty. "In the eye of the law, all men are equal in right and [the law] makes no distinction in station." It was not the judge's duty to try Lane's guilt. The prosecution had charged that the felony was intentional. Evidence had been presented. The court had to determine from that evidence whether the killing of the "great public man," Jenkins, was deliberate. The evidence, Ewing said, showed Jenkins and his cohorts were trespassers, and the court had to apply the common law of trespass to the facts. English common law since Magna Carta prevents even the king's men from trespassing into a house, and the possessor of the land could use deadly force to resist such an invasion. Stanton's argument was appropriate for a killing on a highway, but not for a case of defense of a home.When Green fired his weapon first, Lane did not have to choose among his tormenters when using deadly force. Jenkins was killed and that was unfortunate, but it was self-defense, not murder.[22]

Ladd announced the court's decision—that Lane was freed on the prosecution's failure to show probable cause the crime was willful. The courtroom erupted with competing cheers for Lane and outrage from Jenkins's supporters. Ewing's unusual argument—that Green's errant first shot turned a felony into justifiable homicide of another man—carried the day.[23]

While the English bill was completing the fight over Lecompton, John Easter came to Leavenworth with a report by two Delaware chiefs that placer gold had been discovered along Cherry Creek, in the mountains near Pikes Peak in Kansas Territory. What was left of Bleeding Kansas died in the gold fields of the mountains in the western part of the Kansas Territory. Footloose Free Staters and border ruffians forgot their political differences and headed west. Leavenworth merchants quickly saw their lean times evaporate. The outfitting of prospectors became a booming business. When the word reached Eastern cities, riverboats floated into Leavenworth to unload more eager young men. Sherman was skeptical as to whether now was the right time to come to Kansas. Outfitting prospec-

21. Connelley, "Lane-Jenkins Claim," 168.

22. Ibid., 171.

23. Ibid., 176. As to secret deliberations of the panel, see John King to TEJr., July 1, 1858, TEJr./KSHS.

tors did nothing to improve the practice of law, and if farmers and skilled craftsmen abandoned their farms and shops eastern Kansas would dry up. Sherman, Hugh, and Hamp Denman had seen it often enough in California to dampen any enthusiasm they might have over a gold strike. "Thus far Kansas has been settled by lawyers and politicians instead of farmers and mechanics."[24]

Henry Turner had run out of reasons to keep Sherman on the banker's payroll, however. The loss of his status as a banker was a bitter end to a civilian life Cump had not wanted in the first place. He sardonically reminded Turner of the security he had given up in the army. "When I leave here, I shall accept some post . . . with Mr. Ewing where at least I can do no harm if I can't do good." Instead of Turner, Ellen became a substitute object of his frustration. "I will stay here as far into the year as I can keep Mrs. S. quiet, but she is disposed to be insubordinate." To his father-in-law he complained, "She professes great willingness to live in a log house, feed chickens, or milk cows, but I know better. She cannot come down to that." His only demand was that he not be forced to live in Lancaster, which may have represented home to Ellen but for Sherman only reminded him of the death of his father and the splintering of his family. In Leavenworth he could bring order to a law office that needed a steady in-house manager, and he would be close to army friends while running the errands his father-in-law might have there for him. A Kansas law partnership with Ellen's brothers became an agreeable compromise, of sorts.[25]

By the end of July, however, Sherman was back in Lancaster where Ellen was making all preparations for Hugh's wedding and final decisions on what Cump would do next in his life. Sherman's indecisiveness at this point caused Thomas Ewing Sr. to twist the knot a bit differently, again asking Cump to manage the family's saltworks outside Lancaster. Sherman initially resigned himself to the offer, then he resisted, quietly enlisting his sister Elizabeth in avoiding the doldrums such a mind-numbing career would put him in. Elizabeth and Ellen quarreled over whether Ellen had, by her petulance, forced Cump away from the California he loved. The heat of August passed without resolving the problem. Sherman's memoirs suggest that Hugh did not like managing his father's property around Leavenworth, and Cump disliked Lancaster.

At the Leavenworth firm Sherman could take over the mundane investments and manage Thomas Ewing's Kansas properties while assisting young Tom with

24. For gold strike ends Bleeding Kansas, see Monaghan, *Civil War,* 109; for Sherman's skepticism, WTS to EES, September 25, 1858, quoted in Taylor, "Business and Political Career," 44.

25. WTS to Henry Turner, April 7, 1858, EFP/ND; "log house" from WTS to TESr., April 7, 1858, quoted in Fellman, *Citizen Sherman,* 41; Sherman, *Memoirs,* 1:139.

the business affairs of the law firm. Sherman wrote Tom that all he wanted in Kansas "is a start, and I think I would settle down and not budge unless some unexpected good luck should turn up." Tom could not believe his good fortune. Sherman had more of a stick-to-business mind than Hugh did, which would relieve Tom of the pressure and constant need to be in the office. Sherman would bring management to the firm. Although the old man approved of the Leavenworth venture, Thomas Ewing felt it might be short-lived. He detailed to Tom and Hugh that, if "Captain Sherman" remained in Leavenworth, a building site was to be chosen for Ellen from among the old man's properties.[26]

Tom and Hugh were in severe debt, over $25,000 not counting the notes to Madison Mills. Their father had told them repeatedly to sell everything they could, until the market picked up, but above all else buy nothing more and keep hold of their finances. Tom did what he could, becoming conservative in his debt service to the point where he acknowledged his debts to Father Ewing, who had been keeping the boys afloat, and resolved to ask for nothing more. "On fully considering the state of my affairs I have determined to ask you to make no effort to aid me further at present. I believe that I can get through unaided—perhaps with little or no property left but still I feel sure that by good management, whether matters grow much better than they now are or not—I can get through." If he failed, he felt it would be because Leavenworth "came to a dead halt" and if that happened, everyone would break. Things were tight enough that he let one servant girl go, Maria Maher, with a letter of recommendation for further employment. Tom was just thankful that Sherman would soon be out to assist their efforts to stay afloat.[27]

Hugh Boyle Ewing's problems with Kansas real estate were the farthest thing on his mind on a sultry early August evening in 1858 when he married Henrietta Elizabeth Young. The wedding party spread out on a grassy flower-covered knoll near the main house at Geisborough, her father's estate. The wedding was one of the highlights of the summer season for that portion of lower Maryland and attracted guests even from Washington City. Hugh's father-in-law, George Washington Young, was a descendant of Benjamin Young, a commissioner of Crown lands in Maryland, and of Cuthbert Fenwick, who settled in Maryland in 1734.

26. "Not budge" from WTS to TEJr., August 9, 1958, EFP/LC, quoted in Fellman, Citizen Sherman, 66; "Captain Sherman" from TESr. to HBE, October 15, 1858, HBE/OHS.

27. Ewing's debts from TEJr. to Charles Goddard, "affairs" and "dead halt" from TEJr. to TESr., both dated September 5, 1859, TEJr./KSHS.

The plantation boasted one of the largest numbers of slaves in Maryland. Hugh's groomsmen included his younger brother Charley and Ri's brother, Washington Young. Tom did not attend—his politics could tolerate slavery in reality where he might fight it in theory, but his high profile in the congressional battle against the Lecompton Constitution would have made the Southern guests of George Washington Young uncomfortable.

A month after Hugh's wedding, in early September 1858, Cump Sherman traveled to Leavenworth to reinforce Tom and Hugh in their law office outpost. Sherman stood along the rail of a nondescript steamboat packed with officers, soldiers, and the families moving to Kansas for a new life. As he wrote later in life, remembering the trip out: "Although in the course of my military reading I had studied a few of the ordinary law-books, such as Blackstone, Kent, Starkie, Etc., I did not presume to be a lawyer; but our agreement was that Tom Ewing Jr., a good and thorough lawyer, should manage all business in the courts, while I gave attention to collections, agencies for houses and lands, and such business as my experience in banking had qualified me for." Sherman paid the ten-dollar passage from St. Louis and hoped Leavenworth would provide him a measure of independence and perhaps some fortune. He had no illusions about living out his life there. His wife would see to that. If he could make a bit of money there, as he had done in California, he would move on. Further, John Sherman was still watching for openings in the officer corps, and if by chance a telegram awaited him in Leavenworth announcing a new posting, Sherman would be on the first boat back to St. Louis. He would swallow his pride and return to the army even at a reduced rank. Even a colorless paymaster's position would be fine.[28]

Tom Ewing noticed that when Sherman arrived in Leavenworth he was thin in comparison to his army days, but he was still the same old Cump Sherman, nervous, introverted, with a sandy red beard worn short. He stayed with Tom and Ellen at their home at Third and Pottawatomie, newer streets in town with larger homes but without trees. Ellen Ewing was pregnant, and even though the house was big enough for all, it was going to fill up rapidly when Ellen Sherman came out with the Sherman children. Sherman was disappointed when he saw the law office. Sherman later remembered the Leavenworth office in his memoirs: "The law office was not grand. It was located on a main street on the second floor of a ramshackle building with an outside staircase that frightened anyone who ventured to climb it. Some even said the shingle was dingy." The wobbly outside stair-

28. Sherman, *Memoirs,* 1:140.

case that accessed the office on the second floor was frightening to just about everyone, including the firm's newest partner.[29]

If he were going to be part of a profession, then Sherman felt he should have a license. Tradition from the old English Inns of Court held that each judge provided a means of testing lawyers on their suitability to practice law. Samuel Lecompte knew of Sherman's connection to Thomas Ewing Sr. and that Sherman would be practicing law with the old man's sons. "He admitt[ed] me on the ground of general intelligence," Sherman wrote in his memoirs. Sherman joined 160 other Leavenworth men who had signed the judge's rolls. Most of these lived in Leavenworth, but there were differences of opinion on the quality of the bar. Future senator John Ingalls described the nearby Atchison bar as an "ignorant, detestable set of saddle-headed numskulls and blackguards." It was hardly possible that Atchison drew all the numskulls while Lecompte signed up only scholars. The members of the bar having colorful reputations did not mean that trials were lively, however. Judge Josiah Miller of Leavenworth reported listening to a dreary drawn-out three-day lawsuit between inexperienced attorneys seeking replevin of a calf worth four dollars. Miller offered to pay for the calf if it would end the lawsuit. Agriculture being a serious occupation of the state, Judge David Brewer once had a jury of farmers leave the court without permission, when it looked so much like rain the farmers decided they must go home to look after things.[30]

This was the world Sherman stepped into when he arrived in Leavenworth with little more than his father-in-law's blessing. He had taken on a profession that could provide high drama one minute, but mostly it was mundane and routine. Managing Thomas Ewing's holdings around Leavenworth was not much different from what he had been doing for Henry Turner in St. Louis, San Francisco, and New York. Lawyering was apparently an afterthought. Sherman had run into his share of oddballs in the California bar, and he came to Kansas with higher expectations for land jobbers and speculators than for lawyers and jurists. Sherman's correspondence gave Ellen the impression that a frontier law firm was not as idyllic as banking or even the army, but he intended to give it time.

An old friend, Stu Van Vliet, was stationed at Fort Leavenworth, and Sherman used him as a means to reconnect with his old army friends. Van Vliet gave Sher-

29. Ibid.

30. Ibid.; "saddle-headed numskulls" from Richmond, *Requisite Learning,* 35–37, 39; Judge Miller and the calf from James C. Horton, "Business Then and Now," 148; Michael J. Brodhead, *David J. Brewer: The Life of a Supreme Court Justice, 1837–1910,* 14.

man the job of overseeing a crew repairing worn spots on the military road connecting Forts Leavenworth and Riley, 140 miles to the west. Sherman had not had a field assignment in nearly ten years, and he relished getting back outdoors. When he arrived at Fort Riley he could meet the parties coming out of the mines. "If there be real gold placers, it will provide Leavenworth what it needs, a market on which she can rely to support her present population." More than once the thought crossed his mind to drop everything, point his horse west, and keep going.[31]

Sherman wrote few letters to Ellen from Kansas, but those he did write communicated this wandering sentiment, which unnerved her. She was concerned about his mental health and realized that perhaps he should have stayed in the army, even though it was a dangerous profession. She did not see her constant absence from him as triggering his despair. She did not want to lose him: "even religion could not sustain me were you to die without my seeing you again." She loved him and promised to live a plain life. He did not respond. She had suggested the same before, when he was in San Francisco and in New York. It did not surprise him that she would try to mold his Kansas experience in the same way. He was tiring of the game. Either she would make peace with Leavenworth or she would not. He had seen Leavenworth for what it was, a large town with only three main businesses—military spending, freighting, and land speculation. It was a city of adventurers and "back-trailers," whining constantly about how wonderful things were anywhere else but Kansas, views that he shared.[32]

Still, he knuckled down to business, encouraging new settlement when he felt he could. "I cannot advise you to move here if you are doing even tolerably well as there are many here seeking places," he wrote a friend. For clients needing the traditional collection of overdue accounts, Sherman vowed that Sherman & Ewing would provide excellent legal results. One matter involved a prejudgment attachment of a store's inventory owned by Paul Hamey. Such attachment required the filing of a bond in case the court ruled for the property owner. Lecompte disliked such attachments. The firm was going to test Lecompte on this action and had several other cases with attachments ready to file, depending on how Lecompte decided the case. Even if the motion was denied, Sherman vowed, "we will follow these Hameys as long as the law allows."

31. Van Vliet's offer in Sherman, *Memoirs,* 1:141; "gold placers" from WTS to EES, September 25, 1858, quoted in Taylor, "Business and Political Career," 44.

32. "Were you to die" from EES to WTS, October 11, 1858, EFP/ND, quoted in Fellman, *Citizen Sherman,* 46; "back-trailers" from Wyman, "Frontier Depot," 298.

Several days later Lecompte granted the attachments, and the other cases were quickly filed, along with other bonds. Then, as now, "hell hath no fury like a lawyer on a contingent fee."[33]

Two months after arriving in Leavenworth, Cump asked Ellen to come out and at least see the town before making any lasting decisions on where the family would live. She would have a special role to play in Leavenworth, as part of the civilizing force that women gave a frontier town. Sherman felt Leavenworth was going to be home enough to drum up new business, sending cards to some New York acquaintances he had made through his banking connections. Of the firm Sherman & Ewing, he wrote, "I am associated with two sons of the Hon. Thomas Ewing of Ohio who have been here two years, and we propose to make this our *future* home." It was interesting that while Sherman wanted Ellen to make Leavenworth her future home, in his own mind Leavenworth was not yet his own home.[34]

Dan McCook was another of the young lawyers casting for a foothold in Leavenworth. Dan was the sixth son of Judge Daniel McCook, from a Steubenville, Ohio, family prominent in Democratic politics. He possessed sad features, and his constitution was "delicate and nervous." Frail from boyhood, when he repeatedly fought chronic chest colds, he played mostly indoors as a child and read nearly everything in the large family library. His friends described him as affectionate, warm-hearted, and unselfish. In Leavenworth he was six feet tall, wiry and thin. His steel-gray eyes covered an aggressive spirit. Sherman later characterized McCook as the only real lawyer in the firm, but it is not quite clear whether Sherman was impressed with McCook or just frustrated with the way Tom Ewing's politics overshadowed his legal work. The Northern winters affected the boy's health, and in 1854 Dan was sent to Florence, Alabama, ostensibly for his education but also for his health, entering the LaGrange University at Leighton. One biographer indicates that McCook possessed "an over studious mind, so much so that at one period his health was undermined." The school gave military training, but young McCook took up forensics and debate. He graduated in 1857 and went back to Steubenville to read law in his brother's law office. George McCook was a power in Ohio Democratic politics and a law partner with Edwin Stanton. Stanton at the time was attorney general in the Buchanan administration. Two months

33. WTS to H. E. Ring, November 1, 1858, WTS to the law firm of Spalding & Parsons, November 2, 1858, both TEJr./KSHS; "hell hath no fury" is probably apocryphal but also was used in a U.S. Senate speech on tort reform by the late Pennsylvania senator John Heinz.

34. "Our future home" from WTS to William T. Coleman, quoted in Marszalek, *Soldier's Passion,* 117.

before his twenty-fourth birthday, Dan began practicing with the firm of Stanton & McCook.[35]

Four months later Dan informed his brother George that he was off for Leavenworth, where he arrived the same month as Sherman. There was an open position with Pendrey & Bailey, which he took. Tom Ewing saw something in McCook that he liked besides his connection to the McCooks of Ohio. His credentials would fit well with those of Hugh Ewing and Hamp Denman, both of whom were Democrats but not popular sovereignty Democrats. Neither was Dan McCook. After coming to Kansas Dan wrote his family in Ohio on several occasions that Judge Stephen Douglas was misguided on issues surrounding admission of Kansas to the Union under a popular sovereignty mantle. Tom saw that McCook, unlike Hugh, would actually be around the office long enough to practice law, which, along with Sherman's presence, would free Tom Ewing from his trial work as well as from office matters. Four months after Sherman's arrival in Leavenworth, Dan McCook was asked to join Sherman & Ewing, which changed to Sherman, Ewing & McCook. When Hugh learned of the change he was still in Maryland, and he noted to Ri's brother that at the moment at least he was not involved in the new firm. "McCook is a very active, good lawyer. He was not in Leavenworth in your time. I have just closed my trust business, and am resting this summer on my oars. I have not yet determined on my future course, but will probably settle in Leavenworth for life."[36]

Sherman, Ewing & McCook sailed on without assistance from anyone other than the three partners who, like most business partners, looked after one another's schedules and clients, since financial loss attendant to a case affected all of them. Without salary and modern technology as an overhead expense, with clients paying the court costs up front, and with no income tax on the fees, any fee was profit. The only problem was the lack of law-related work. In Leavenworth just before statehood there were too many lawyers. McCook's skills were such that he was not treated as a newcomer. He more than held his own with experienced lawyers on important cases, including one high-profile murder case.[37]

35. "Delicate and nervous" from Whitelaw Reid, *Ohio In The War For The Suppression Of The Great Rebellion,* 2:904. Colonel Leslie Perry, who helped edit the *Official Reports of the War of the Rebellion,* indicated that McCook attended Alabama University at Florence, Alabama, not Leighton. Nixon B. Stewart, *Dan McCook's Regiment, 52nd OVI: A History of the Regiment, Its Campaigns and Battles,* 206. The "Fighting McCooks" as a family are best described in Charles Whalen and Barbara Whalen, *The Fighting McCooks: America's Famous Fighting Family,* 291–93.

36. "Resting on oars" from Ewing, "Autobiography," 216.

37. That four lawyers formed a law firm in 1858–1859 was unusual for the times. As late as 1960 two-thirds of American lawyers were in solo practice. McCook's murder case is in the *Tazewell Register,* May 12, 1859, quoted in Whalen and Whalen, *Fighting McCooks,* 259.

Sherman's attitude concerning his own legal abilities apparently grated on McCook and Tom Ewing to the point that they set him up to see how he could cope with a real situation. One of McCook's Irish teamster clients was being evicted for nonpayment of rent. Sherman was alone in the office when the client came in, all spiffed up and ready for trial. Trials in the territorial courts were not set for any certain date. Rather, when a "term of court" convened, lawsuits were bunched on the docket and called into session one after the other. Most firms kept office boys in the back of the courtroom with a list of cases, and when the case in front of their case was called the boy raced back to the office to warn the attorneys in time to get to court. The teamster's trial was ready. Where was McCook? Sherman panicked. No case was scheduled, as far as Sherman knew, so their office boy was not down at the courthouse. Sherman ran down to the courthouse and asked for a continuance, but it was denied. Sherman had to handle the teamster's matter without preparation. Sherman stammered through a few unprepared questions of the landlord and his witnesses but did not shake their claim to the property.[38]

Sherman and the dejected client were still in the office when McCook returned. The client did not mind the ejection (the land was not his), but he had paid good money for the prefabricated house and stood to lose this too. McCook had conceived of a private solution all along. The teamster should simply get a dozen friends together, undo the mooring nails, lift the small house off its foundation, and move it to another location. The teamster brightened, found some of his friends, and followed McCook's advice that night. Sherman may have appreciated McCook's clever post-trial solution. More than likely, however, he disapproved. He was used to associating with bankers, not lawyers whose problem-solving solutions seemed concocted in the back of a saloon.[39]

Sherman was given the opportunity to practice in the courts but there was no particular appeal in it for him. Trial rules were loose and based more on custom than statutes. Some judges admitted certain types of hearsay evidence, others did not, and attorneys had to learn and use each judge's proclivities. Sherman attempted to settle most of his matters that were headed for trial. One client would not settle a scheduled lawsuit, so at trial Sherman faced Lewis Burns, who came to court with six witnesses and a box of law books. The witnesses, Sherman noted, knew little about the sale of the calf, which was the subject of the lawsuit. Sher-

38. The setup is in the *Leavenworth Times,* January 22, 1911; duties of office boys from Barrows, *William M. Evarts,* 50.

39. Some of the house-moving story was reprinted in the *Topeka Capitol-Journal,* October 5, 1958, 12B.

man felt he had won the lawsuit, but in his closing statements to the justice of the peace, "Colonel Burns" began pulling books one at a time from the box and quoting from them with thundering phrases. Sherman felt he might as well have been reading from the Koran for all the sense it made, but the confused judge listened to Burns's irrelevancies and awarded judgment to Burns's client. Dejected again, Sherman advised his client to forget the appeal since the cost would be more than the calf. "If this is Kansas justice, I want no more of it," he later told friends.[40]

Sherman's reluctance to reenter the courtroom is evident in later writings. He wrote collection letters but informed clients that, if Tom Ewing was gone, Dan McCook would attend the depositions and if necessary handle the trial. Cump had learned that working with paper was not as slippery as working with human beings. The whole concept of a law practice bothered Sherman. In California, a collection lawyer Sherman had hired to collect accounts for Turner's bank had first pilfered the recovered funds and then claimed he did not have to repay the funds because of his insanity. Between California's insane lawyers and frontier lawyers who babbled irrelevant quotes, Sherman's initial irritability with his new profession worsened. Much of the Leavenworth practice was transactional office work focusing on real estate law. Given his father-in-law's reputation, the firm's name was highly prized when such problems arose. Government land giveaways and people moving frequently into, and out of, the territory meant that lawyers needed to draft deeds, mortgages, and deeds of trust, advising their clients in other states about land purchases, and then acting as agents to buy or sell the property. By December 1858, Sherman had retreated solely into an office practice where in the drafty upstairs room he could battle his asthma, and Dan McCook could weather his chronic bronchitis.[41]

One developing arena of litigation for the trial lawyers of Sherman, Ewing & McCook was commercial litigation, and the crown jewel of a river-town practice was steamboat litigation. Steamboats had remarkably short commercial life spans. High winds could tip them over or boilers could explode without warning. Right after the Civil War, the *Sultana* had been ferrying survivors of the Andersonville POW camp home when the steamer exploded near Memphis and sank with the loss of over fifteen hundred lives, a greater loss of life than even the *Titanic*. Steamboats operated on rivers with thousands of snags, and their wooden hulls were

40. "Kansas justice" and Colonel Burns from Moore, *Leavenworth City and County,* 333–34.

41. Reluctance for courtroom from WTS to T. T. Garrett, December 28, 1858, TEJr./KSHS; Sherman mentions his own role as office collector and manager in Sherman, *Memoirs,* 1:140; for WTS's asthma, EES to Minnie, November 22, 1858, SFP/OHS.

highly flammable. Repeated groundings on sandbars acted like sandpaper on their thin hulls. Like the depreciation of a new automobile as it is driven off the lot, a steamboat's value depreciated quickly, often by 25 percent in the first year. It took a good deal of luck and volume of business to make a steamboat investment pay off. Before the widespread use of casualty insurance, lawsuits were the only means of protection against the negligence or fraud of others wrecking a steamboat business.[42]

The firm took on several steamboat cases. One lucrative one involved the *Isabella,* owned by Captain John Keiser of St. Louis. A storeowner, James Dixon, went into business with a silent partner, Judge M. F. Moore of Lancaster, Ohio, who was a Ewing family friend. During the winter of 1857–1858, Dixon had ordered some flour shipped to Leavenworth by boat. The *Kate Howard* dropped the flour off at the levee at Providence, Missouri, for the boat's draft kept it from coming further up the Missouri River. The lighter *Isabella* was hired and its crew loaded the flour for delivery to Leavenworth. Before unloading it, Captain Keiser sought payment on the freight charge of $1.50 per sack. Dixon refused to pay. The *Isabella* then carried the flour back down the river. By the time Dixon arranged other shipment of the flour, the river had iced over and steamboats could not run. Keiser, meanwhile, was incurring storage costs on the flour in another city. By the time Dixon's flour was delivered overland, Keiser filed a claim for an overdue bill. Dixon's counterclaim argued that Keiser's freight charge was too high and the storeowner had lost profits on the flour, which could be sold for a much higher price in Leavenworth than elsewhere. In December 1858 Keiser hired the Ewings to obtain a judgment from Dixon and his partners. In April 1859 the firm received written information from George Parker in Providence that Dixon had given Parker instructions to hold the flour until further transport was arranged, and, given the lateness of the year, Dixon was aware of the risk of bringing a riverboat up the ice-bound Missouri. Dixon's instructions were followed and Parker believed the freight charge was reasonable. Tom Ewing asked Parker to write Ewing a letter describing his view of the transaction. "We desire very much to beat [Dixon] in the cases for they have acted badly with the steamboat. It very much depends on your evidence." Parker apparently provided the narrative Ewing needed. By the middle of the summer, he had obtained a judgment in Keiser's favor against Dixon, but recovery would be difficult.[43]

42. Phil E. Chappell, "The History of the Missouri River," 291.

43. TEJr. to Captain John Keiser, St. Louis, December 10, 1858, WTS to Alexander Smith, February 12, 1859, TEJr. to John Keiser, June 30, 1859, TEJr. to George Parker, March 2, April 4, 1859, all in TEJr./KSHS.

Older lawyers who disliked the travel requirements of circuit riding would hire younger men to do it for them. McCook spent his spring in the northern counties until the court resumed work in Leavenworth. At age twenty-seven he was now an intense man to whom everything was a challenge. He loved the combat of the courtroom. He had more in common with Hugh Ewing's puggishness than Tom Ewing's erudite manner. But law firms needed different personalities and political persuasions in order to make the practice work. When the economy soured, lawyers turned to clients who needed bills collected. However, the territorial legislature had conspired against the firm's efforts. The numbers of new settlers coming out to Kansas were lagging. In order to encourage more emigration, legislation was enacted that barred suit on any claims from outside the territory unless brought within two years of making the contract. Settlers with debts more than two years old could move to Kansas and be safe from collection suits. This left settlers free to spend their money on new land and personal property in the territory, or borrow more money without repaying old debts.

While perhaps bending the Full Faith and Credit clause of the Constitution to the breaking point, the real impact of this law was the box in which it placed creditors—and their attorneys—if they waited too long to collect their notes. Many Eastern businesses that had lent money or credit to persons now residing in Kansas had no way of knowing of the new law. Even with these legislative setbacks McCook was confident. "I am doing well in my profession," he bragged to a friend. "I am in partnership with the son of Old Tom Ewing of Ohio and with Captain Sherman, Ewing's son-in-law." Still, McCook's youthful naiveté was evidenced when a witness in a deposition came into the Ewing office. After Cump administered the oath and questioning began, the witness asked to go to his house to find papers to help him better explain his position. McCook let the witness take the client's letter with him, but the witness disappeared along with the original letter. "It is hard to catch and keep witnesses here," Cump lamely wrote the client, asking for a new letter outlining deposition issues.[44]

Sherman's reluctance to litigate made him an unlikely lawyer in a slave-catching episode, but such a trial was just the sort of political theater Tom Ewing sought. In January 1859 men came into Charley Fisher's barbershop in the Planter's House Hotel. Fisher was a mulatto. He found himself accused of theft, and when he was lured outside his abductors tied him up and hustled him across the Missouri River. To those who asked, the slave-catchers insisted Fisher was a Kentucky

44. McCook to James Roberts, April 17, 1859, WTS to A. Garesche, April 29, 1859, TEJr./KSHS.

runaway and they had federal authority to take him back into slavery. Fisher escaped his capture and swam the icy Missouri River back to Kansas, alerted friends, and went into hiding. When the slavers returned they were arrested by antislavery deputies, taken before the city judge, and charged with kidnapping. They argued that they were carrying out their duties under the Fugitive Slave Law. The prosecutor countered that Charley Fisher was not an escaped slave but, rather, a free man.

Sherman, Ewing & McCook got involved because of McCook's efforts for a slave-catcher named Campbell. McCook applied to Judge Lecompte for a habeas corpus petition, and Lecompte promptly released all the slave-catchers. Rain Hutchinson, a Kentuckian, then filed a claim in Leavenworth County that Fisher was a fugitive slave who belonged to the estate of two infant children and that Hutchinson was their guardian. Returning the fugitive to Kentucky for resale would provide funds to allow the children to survive their orphan status. Lecompte served a subpoena on Fisher to appear in federal district court to defend against Hutchinson's allegation and ordered Fisher to stay in the Leavenworth jail while awaiting a court hearing. Judge George Gardiner of the local probate court provided a new writ for Fisher's supporters, Leavenworth's local abolitionists. While en route to Gardiner's hearing, abolitionists struck, stealing Fisher away by overpowering the sheriff. The mulatto was never again seen in Kansas.

Enraged, Judge Lecompte had Gardiner and eight others indicted for violating the "obstructing capture" clause of the Fugitive Slave Act: the eight for forcible abduction and Gardiner for issuing a writ that let Fisher into the open where the abolitionists could get to him. Trial was set for September 1859. Between indictment and trial a new federal territorial judge—John Pettit, an Indiana Democrat with no particular leanings for slavery—was appointed to preside over the actual trial.

Tom Ewing had just turned thirty and was in the middle of his career both socially and politically. Ignoring McCook's previous representation of one of the slave-catchers, Ewing jumped at the chance to represent Gardiner and the other antislavery defendants in federal court. It was a show trial on the Fugitive Slave Law. Ewing was still a power in the Free State Party and still harbored ambitions for the Senate. He was not pandering to the abolitionists; rather, he felt strongly that the Fugitive Slave Law was being wrongfully misused. With his success in representing Lane, a successful defense in what came to be called the Fisher matter would place his star even higher in the heavens.

Arguments for and against the validity of the Fugitive Slave Act were passionate affairs, complete with vocal cheering for the litigants. Pleadings in such cases were handwritten and copies of important documents were made by hand or kept in press books. The Fisher case would be lawyering by the seat of the pants. A sharp mind and the ability to keep juries focused on slight variations in facts was all that was fundamentally necessary. Appeals to prejudices or political viewpoints were usually irrelevant but commonly done, since until the early twentieth century, common law juries were allowed to decide both the facts and the law governing a case. This common law tradition of jury nullification allowed jurors to become legislators and decide whether a law enacted by the elected Congress should be enforced. In this way a Free State jury not only controlled proslavery-oriented judges but also the authority of the Congress to enact laws with which the jury disagreed.[45]

Legislatures of the day were bombastic arenas, full of pomp and foolishness, posturing and picayune jealousies that might or might not result in good laws. Nineteenth-century lawyers and judges smugly thought their own branch of government was above contemptible lawmakers or pompous governors and their patronage-laden supporters. One certainly could not look to legislators for justice against the railroads, banks, and big corporations when legislators were wined and dined by those very interests and thus obligated to the ubiquitous "them." Courts were forums where individuals could obtain justice—or at least the best opportunity for justice.

The Fisher case had all the earmarks of a brawl. Most residents knew of the legal issues and many made side bets on the outcome. The Fisher case divided the bar in Leavenworth along individual allegiances to slavery. Pettit was determined to run an orderly trial without the theatrics that had taken over in South Carolina. He generally felt the Fugitive Slave Law was constitutional, which led Free Staters to label him another Buchanan stooge. However, he was new and no one could predict his rulings.

Ewing's antislavery "Gardiner defense" was a legalistic argument of multiple points, layering the facts so that Ewing could attack the validity of the Fugitive Slave Act solely on its application to the facts in Fisher's case. Rather than fight the case after impaneling a jury and take the luck of the draw that the jury might have proslavery sympathies, the defense filed a pretrial motion to quash the indictments, which required an evidentiary hearing the lawyers hoped would never allow the prosecutor to put his case in front of a jury. After arguments on the

45. James Durham, "*U.S. v. Lewis L. Weld:* Judicial Creativity or Judicial Subversion?" 8–11.

motion lasting several days, Pettit adopted Ewing's view that since the 1850 amendments to the Fugitive Slave Act imposed heavy fines and penalties, it was a penal law and thus must be construed strictly against the government. In short, the slave-catchers had to prove every element of the law or Fisher could not be labeled a fugitive slave.

Having persuaded Pettit to agree to view the Fugitive Slave Act as penal law, Ewing attacked the minuses of the 1850 act itself. It allowed runaways to be recaptured only by the owner, or agents or attorneys of the owner. The slave-catchers argued they were agents of the owner, but Ewing's arguments painted Fisher's abductors as agents of the guardian. Infants were not legally capable of contracting with an agent, nor could they offload that responsibility on a guardian. The category of guardians thus being excluded from the list of those lawfully empowered to reclaim their slaves, the Fugitive Slave Act did not allow agents of a guardian to recapture anyone.

To Pettit, there were good reasons Congress had limited slave-catching authority to owners or agents of owners and not those tinged with "the rashness and indecision of youth who may have no interest in or kind feelings for the Negro." In language seen in modern Supreme Court cases, Pettit reasoned it was not his job as judge to supply words not put there by the Congress. The criminal indictments against Ewing's clients were dismissed, to great bursts of applause outside the courtroom.[46]

In the spring of 1859, most of Ewingville came out to review the large new farm and other Ewing investments in Kansas. The farm was a thirteen-hundred-acre portion of "half-breed" tracts (two of the twenty-three platted tracts), heavily wooded patches of land along the Kansas River between Topeka and Lecompton. The tracts were purchased for ordinary sums—perhaps $2.50 per acre. However, if any railroad ran through the area, which was likely since the road would need timber for ties and fuel, the value would skyrocket. It was a pleasant visit, but to no one's surprise, when Thomas Ewing returned to Lancaster, Ellen and the children went with him. Cump's parting shot at her was for her to be sure to keep track of what her father provided for her so someday he could repay it![47]

Further discouraged, and with Tom back in town, Sherman got out of the office by agreeing to supervise the building of improvements on Thomas Ewing's farm. This labor included breaking sod, building a house, digging a well, and

46. "Rashness" from ibid., 11; Fisher in family correspondence from TEJr. to TESr., April 21, 1860, TEJr./KSHS.

47. "Repay" from Marszalek, *Soldier's Passion,* 118.

building rock fences. Sherman hired the Kistler brothers of Topeka to do most of the heavy work. Lonely and dispirited, he would walk the acreage for hours without talking with anyone. He rarely went to town, and when he did he hung around with the lawyers. Part of his time was spent corresponding with John Sherman, who was embroiled in several nasty political fights, and giving unwanted political advice. "There is no outlet for the Negroes of *our* country; and we have no right to displace the population of Mexico to put slaves there. Slavery must stay pretty much in its present boundaries."[48]

Few others solicited his advice. Sherman hit an emotional rock bottom during that spring while he was at the farm. He had invested $2,000 in seven thousand bushels of corn to sell to miners headed for Pikes Peak. So many others had the same idea that the territory was bursting with corn and prices for it were low. Most of the corn went unsold, killing the market. Sherman faced another personal failure also. His depression bottomed when John wrote he was traveling to Europe. Cump enviously desired to wander the European battlefields with John, but no invitation was extended for a joint venture. He wrote John to think of him from time to time "out here on the pampas of Kansas."[49]

The Kansas political landscape was changing rapidly. Republicans had been weak and ineffective in 1856, but three years later most Free Staters were switching their allegiance to the Republican Party. The party's strength for the 1860 campaign was growing exponentially, partially because its main national plank was blocking the spread of slavery into the territories, the national issue attracting former Whigs such as Abraham Lincoln to its ranks. Tom Ewing threw himself into the formation of this new political base as a logical extension of his family's Whig politics and his own admiration for Lincoln and William Seward. Ewing convinced doubters such as editor George Brown that although Free State men had won the battle in Kansas the party had no national base. It would be a "great disgrace" if the Democrats carried Kansas. "If we fail there, we shall have good reason to stand aloof from both parties, or to organize [a party] whose principles and policy will be consistent with our views."[50]

The first Republican convention in Kansas began on May 18, 1859, at the Osage

48. Farmwork from *Topeka Capitol Journal,* March 27, 1955, 13A; "no outlet" from WTS to John Sherman, April 30, 1859, in Thorndike, *Sherman Letters,* 69.

49. Taylor, "Business and Political Career," 44; "pampas" in WTS to John Sherman, April 30, 1859, in Thorndike, *Sherman Letters,* 69.

50. "Great disgrace" from TEJr. to George Brown, April 13, 1859, "stand aloof" from TEJr. to A. C. Stafford, April 14, 1859, both in TEJr./KSHS.

Valley House in Osawatomie. Tom Ewing attended the convention, as did Horace Greeley, who timed his California trip perfectly so as to attend the Kansas meeting at the request of the radicals. Greeley's agenda was pushing for states such as Kansas to adopt a plank promoting a transcontinental railroad. To avoid rancor the leaders of the two wings of the Free State Party, Charles Robinson and Jim Lane, stayed away. Because of his preconvention letters to other conservatives such as Preston Plumb and W. Y. Roberts, Ewing's supporters had the upper hand, even blocking efforts by abolitionists to let non-delegate Greeley address the convention. O. E. Learnard described Ewing and his performance at this charter Republican convention: he was "an imposing figure and had a commanding presence, tall and straight as an Indian." He spoke deliberately, with a tremulous voice, which was his style, and argued the resolutions designed to assure the nation that Republicans did not want to replace slavery where it existed, only that Kansas desired to be a free state. They must reject abolitionist planks and concentrate the party's efforts on putting good men into public office.[51]

The speech greatly affected the convention's final resolutions. By the fourth day the platform committee that Ewing had virtually appointed returned a document on which both wings of the party agreed. Much of the text found its way into the 1860 Republican national platform. Ewing wrote five of the eleven main planks, which opposed the slave powers by legal means, declared the new party submissive to the Constitution and laws of the United States, acknowledged the existence of slavery in the old South, condemned the "perversion of the power of the Supreme Court of the United States," but upheld the right of territories to create their own governments.[52]

There was more to the formation of the Republican Party in Kansas than just putting together a statement of principles. There was also considerable angling for nominations to coveted offices. Ewing's eyes were on one of the U.S. Senate positions that would be available to a new state. His rapprochement with moderate Free Staters included pushing Robinson for commissioner of Indian Affairs in the next Republican administration. Through that appointment Robinson could have influence over patronage in Kansas. A man with a federal job because of the appointment of one man indirectly could help Ewing's long-term senatorial aspirations by influencing legislators through their important constituents. In the time between the end of the formation of the party and the Wyandotte Constitutional Convention, Ewing also began writing Free Staters and Republicans who

51. Greeley at the convention from Mark A. Plummer, *Frontier Governor: Samuel J. Crawford of Kansas,* 3–4; "imposing figure" from O. E. Learnard, "Organization of the Republican Party," 312–16.

52. *Lawrence Republican,* May 26, 1859.

were assured of legislative office about his own desire for the U.S. Senate appointment. But radicals at the convention felt Ewing was too conciliatory toward slavery interests, and Democrats would not support him because of his role in killing Lecompton. His opponent for the Senate nomination was Marcus Parrott, who was the better orator. When it became clear that many were already committed to Parrott and were not going to switch to Ewing, Tom suggested to his father that he might seek another position within the Republican Party. Chief justice of the supreme court paid $1,800 per year, the second-highest salary in state government. Such sums could come in handy even for the son of a wealthy attorney. His father found no fault with the logic. Learnard eventually stepped in to mediate the situation between Ewing and Parrott and agreed with Ewing. Parrott's forces and the Republican Party would nominate Ewing for chief justice if Ewing agreed not to oppose Parrott for the Senate position. Ewing's choice was a good one. Legislatures appointed senators, whereas the voters elected members of the Kansas Supreme Court. Even had the party endorsed Ewing for the U.S. Senate, it was not a direct election, and the candidates were at the whim of the band of lawmakers chosen by the electorate.[53]

By the spring of the Republican convention, the Pikes Peak gold rush had flopped. Disheartened men returned through northeast Kansas with wagons ruefully lettered "Pike's Peak or Bust-ed" with the "or" painted out. That spring Tom's son William was battling a bad case of boils, and Ewing asked his chief creditor, Dr. Madison Mills, to treat the boy. Ewing was asking more than just credit for his son's illness. The brothers did not sell a single lot that spring. "There is no market for property at any price whatsoever." Mills would have to go unpaid—at least for his mortgage with the Ewings. While the military doctor was wealthy in his own right, there was a limit to his patience, and he continued to pressure the Ewings for payments.[54]

Sherman sensed the despair of his foster brothers. He had asked to come to Kansas to help out, but there was nothing he could do about horrible economic conditions. Cump wrote John, now in Europe, "I wish I were there to watch the operations and changes, but alas, I am in Kansas." His letters to Ellen dug into

53. Ewing's initial desires for the chief justice position from Rowland, "Reluctant Chief Justice," 31. For the chief justice election, TEJr. to HBE, July 27, 1859, HBE/OHS, TEJr. to HBE, August 6, 1859, and to TESr., April 13, 1859, both in TEJr./KSHS.

54. Calvin Gower, "The Pikes Peak Gold Rush and the Smoky Hill Route, 1859–1860," 158–66; "busted" from Davis, *Bicentennial History*, 75; "no market for property" from TEJr. to TESr., April 21, 1859, TEJr./KSHS.

her a bit when he complained it was a wife's duty to live with her husband. This brought crisp complaints from Ellen that she was not a squaw and her needs for comfort were "more numerous and expensive" than those of the field hands he was supervising! She was pregnant again and her hormone-laced mood was lousy. "Does it ever occur to you that the pangs of labor are terrible and that from the oppressive weight of child bearing I shall find relief only in agony?" she wrote. Sherman had no response to that. He was marooned on a dry prairie, afraid of more failures to come, and unless he visited bordellos like a common soldier he faced an unaccustomed celibacy. Sherman had a good reputation with the legal community in Leavenworth but he knew he was out of his element. The highlight of his day was sorting the mail and wandering the large tract of Thomas Ewing's land to run off squatters. Even his banking years were not worthy of pride. Tom Ewing's reputation in Kansas was growing. Leavenworth knew little about Sherman in those days. It had been six years since he left the army, six years of aimlessness. He wrote Ellen, "I am doomed to be a vagabond. I look upon myself as a dead cock in the pit, not worthy of further notice."[55]

While Sherman did not think much of his situation in Kansas, there were always other opportunities coming along for which his name popped up. The Cincinnati consortium was interested in obtaining overseas investments in a transcontinental railroad. Perhaps knowing that Sherman's wanderlust was unsatisfied in Kansas, Hugh suggested Cump move to London and head up the consortium's operations there. The salary was $7,500 the first year, and $10,000 thereafter. Sherman did not jump at the chance. The salary barely equaled what Lucas and Turner had paid him to go to San Francisco five years earlier. Sherman would not be in charge of anything, being hired simply to follow orders. For a time he did not respond to Hugh's overture, suggesting that if Hugh had any influence Sherman preferred a position as an army paymaster. "The more I see of the precariousness of civil life, the more I think of getting back [into the army]." However, Sherman was allied with Tom Ewing, and since the Lecompton vote anyone associated with Tom Ewing was now persona non grata with the Buchanan administration, which recommended appointments, including the War Department. Hugh advised Sherman that Buchanan was "bitter against democrats who opposed Lecompton" and he had better wait until a new administration was in office.[56]

55. "I wish I were there" from WTS to John Sherman, May 25, 1859, in Thorndike, *Sherman Letters,* 72; "numerous and expensive" and "pangs of labor" from EES to WTS, June 1, 1859, EFP/ND; "vagabond" from WTS to EES, April 15, 1858, in Fellman, *Citizen Sherman,* 67.

56. London offer and "bitter against Democrats" from HBE to WTS, July 31, 1859, from Ewing, "Autobiography," 218; "precariousness" from WTS to HBE, July 5, 1859, SFP/OSH.

Ellen kept up her barrage of guilt-laced letters, however, suggesting that Sherman simply needed to settle down in Ohio and take his rightful place in her father's operations, not go gallivanting off to another dusty God-forsaken military post or hanging around frontier courthouses. She predicted, "you would be happier than you now imagine," which meant of course that she would be happier. "It is a poor house [here] with the father gone," she wrote. "The children are constantly expecting you."[57]

Sherman was uncertain. He was hanging on in Leavenworth in part to give Tom and Hugh time to live up to their bargain. Tom had promised Sherman in 1858 to "look to his profession." Thus far, Sherman wrote cryptically to Hugh, Tom "has done nothing" to build a real law practice, and Sherman claimed McCook was also unhappy. Sherman was "ready to go to any quarter of the world where I can do anything" and work for "a common salary." He put the blame squarely on Tom, whose ambitions for higher office were affecting the firm. "Still I hope that it would awaken him to his own true interests. He would eschew politics entirely and do as I understand him to promise last fall—look to his profession. . . . But if Tom will now put in hours and be in the office during all business hours, I do not yet despair that we could catch enough business in time, which in connection with the prosperity here would maintain us." Yet, Sherman predicted that Tom Ewing "utterly loses all chance of professional positions and will be swept away by current extractions."[58]

The summer of 1859 saw Kansas Democrats running a reverse Lecompton strategy on the fledgling Republicans. While Buchanan Democrats were unable to get control of the state when facing the Free State cause, they were finding the going somewhat easier when facing the new Republican Party, which was promptly labeled the party of the "black Republicans" and the "Negro Question." Hugh Ewing and Hamp Denman were involved in pushing this winning Democrat strategy, and there was a surprisingly strong showing in the elections in June 1859 to vote for representatives in the Wyandotte convention delegation. Democrats swamped the Republicans, at least in Leavenworth. While Democrats were still outnumbered in Kansas, and Hugh was involved with the party long distance, from Geisborough, there were enough Democrats in the delegation to make their presence felt and allow Buchanan to have input into the crafting of the Kansas

57. "Happier" from EES to WTS, June 6, 1859, EFP/ND; "poor house" from EES to WTS, October 28, 1859, quoted in Fellman, *Citizen Sherman,* 47.

58. WTS to HBE, June 8, 1859, SFP/OSH.

constitution. "Secretary [of War John B.] Floyd was in ecstasies at our success," Hugh wrote Hamp, trying to discourage Hamp's considering possibly running for governor when the new state constitution was implemented. "Do all you can to help the party without spending money, and bide your time," Hugh advised. Then, as if tweaking Tom's ambitions, he wrote, "Any man who goes into politics for barren offices, unless he has plenty of money, ruins himself, and becomes the shuttlecock of low politicians."[59]

However, Hugh could not help crowing at Tom when the Democrats carried Leavenworth's convention delegate elections. "You expect *your* party to walk over the course this fall [in the elections]. . . . You have heard of the tortoise and the hare." Besides, Hugh had a new concern then, and he sent proud words to Leavenworth that on July 13, 1859, his first daughter, Edith Ewing, was born at Geisborough.[60]

In spite of the political successes in Leavenworth, the brothers' political efforts gave way to being on the receiving end of lawsuits. In early 1859 a St. Louis lumber dealer, Adams & Mattox, who had supplied lumber to Sanders, filed suit against Hamp Denman. As Sanders's agent Denman was accused of fraudulently inducing the lumber men to sell to Sanders. Tom Ewing felt the lawsuit was vexatious and suing Denman was chasing the only deep-pocket investor behind Sanders. The Denman & Ewing speculation business had not assumed agent status for Sanders, and Hugh demanded if Ewing & Denman's "flag goes down," it would be by the "shot of the enemy." There would be no settlement with the St. Louis business. The Ewings were spoiling for a fight, but Sherman worried the lawsuit was a portent of things to come.[61]

Meanwhile Sherman's backstairs contact with former friends in the army had provided positive feelers about his potential as superintendent of an academy. Don Buell wrote of an opening for a superintendent at a new military academy, the Louisiana State Seminary of Learning. Sherman was uncertain. Such jobs were more political than military in nature, but after rejecting the idea initially, he sensed that Louisiana was a job that could keep him in touch with key army personnel, while not garnering the enmity from Ellen that could come from a return to active duty. Sherman asked George Mason Graham, the half brother of Sherman's commanding officer in California, about the opportunity.[62]

59. "Floyd was in ecstasies" and "shuttlecock" from HBE to Hamp Denman, June 24, 1859, in Ewing, "Autobiography," 216.

60. "Tortoise" from HBE to TEJr., August 12, 1859, ibid., 219.

61. "Flag goes down" from HBE to TESr., July 31, 1859, ibid., 218.

62. Marszalek, *Soldier's Passion,* 120; Fellman, *Citizen Sherman,* 69.

4

MR. CHIEF JUSTICE AND A MAN NAMED LINCOLN

On October 10, 1859, John Brown and eighteen other men fought their way into a musty federal arsenal at Harpers Ferry, Virginia. Hoping to provoke a slave uprising, they took hostages and fought for a day to hold off a local militia company. Lieutenant Colonel Robert E. Lee led a company of marines to retake the arsenal, killing ten men inside, including two of Brown's sons. Within weeks Brown was on trial for inciting an insurrection.

Four days after Brown's Harpers Ferry raid was suppressed, Kansans went to the polls in record numbers under their proposed new Wyandotte Constitution. While the convention had hosted controversies over women's suffrage, black suffrage, apportionment of the first legislature, and homestead laws, the general product was one that most Kansans could support. Democrats balked at efforts to cut off the western border of the state and let the portion that now runs from eastern Colorado to the Continental Divide remain a territory. Wyandotte was different from all previous constitutions, which had preferred the larger state. While Republicans and Free Staters such as Ewing in general approved of the Wyandotte Constitution, Douglas Democrats such as Hugh, Hamp Denman, and Dan McCook did not. The constitution purposefully contained a poison pill for the territory's Democrats. Its provisions on apportionment of the first legislature virtually guaranteed Republican successes in battles for legislative seats, which meant a considerable uphill battle for Democrats to dominate future state legislatures. Legislatures controlled the makeup of U.S. senators from Kansas. The apportionment wrangle was a Republican gift to Buchanan's Democratic Party for all the heartache it had caused Kansas.

The Wyandotte Constitution also allowed black children to be educated in Kansas's public schools, but this was as far as liberality between the races would go in 1859. The constitution did not guarantee an integrated education. Dan McCook relayed to his father that Kansas Democrats nominated Saunders Johnston, a former federal judge from Ohio, as their standard-bearer and intended to oppose the Wyandotte Constitution. Not to do so would allow the rigged apportionment section of the constitution to entrench Republicans in Kansas in such a way that it would take a "10,000 vote popular majority to beat this apportionment." McCook was right. The long dominance of the Republican Party in Kansas is the result of the efforts of this initial constitutional convention to rig the political scene from the beginning. Because of this skewed apportionment issue, none of the Democrat delegates signed the document.[1]

When territorial voters went about approving the convention's handiwork, they did not know that the Wyandotte Constitution would remain the Kansas state's core document for over a hundred years. Its adoption—combined with the trial of John Brown for Harpers Ferry—marked the political end of "Bleeding Kansas" and radical Free-Soil politics. As Kansas lamented the passing of John Brown after his execution for treason, Tom Ewing complained several times—once after a eulogy for Brown given by Senator Edward Everett—that Brown's "victims" were forgotten in all the speeches about him. Had Brown succeeded in forcing a war between Free Staters and the American government, "all the nations of the world would have stood with the prestige of the South and the General Government while the North would have been divided, overwhelmed and conquered." Writing on the subject in his later years, Ewing noted that the Civil War had intervened, "no doubt divinely directed to unify and purify our people for their glorious mission," in order to foil John Brown's mad scheme. For the first time in Kansas, all settlers cast a full and free vote for the constitution, this time not intimidated by warring factions.[2]

The Wyandotte Constitution required another election of potential state offi-

1. Democrats' problems with the Wyandotte Constitution from Plummer, *Frontier Governor,* 4; "10,000 vote popular majority" from McCook to his father, Daniel McCook Sr., August 20, 1859, Stephen A. Douglas Papers, Special Collections, Manuscripts, University of Chicago Library.

2. TEJr. to Senator Edward Everett, December 21, 1859, TEJr./KSHS; Rowland, "Thomas Ewing Jr.," 12; "prestige of the South" from Ewing, "Struggle For Freedom," 11.

cers, who would automatically take office if Congress granted statehood. Eleven days after the constitutional ratification vote, the Republicans nominated Tom Ewing for chief justice. Within a week the Democrats nominated Judge Joseph Williams, Buchanan's latest appointee, to oppose Ewing. Tom was elated. Williams was an Iowan long on political contacts and short on Kansas roots. Ewing sensed that given the importance of the courts in interpreting statutory policy in a new state, the last thing Kansans wanted was a carpetbagging chief justice with open ties to Buchanan. "There is no earthly doubt of my election," Ewing predicted to his father. "I will get the vote of half the Democrat lawyers in Leavenworth."[3]

Ewing spent the rest of 1859 trying to secure Jim Lane's support for his chief justice nomination while avoiding giving Lane a reciprocal endorsement for senator. Although Ewing represented Lane in the Jenkins murder trial, he did not trust Lane. Tom was getting considerable pressure from other Republicans to support Lane, even though Ewing had given his word to Parrott. The Seward Club of Lawrence tried to get Ewing to support Seward for president. Ewing deflected the inquiry by pointing out that, as chief justice, he was not part of the legislative process and wanted no influence in the decision. As a leader of the party, however, his opinion on leadership was important. He found ways to sidestep such questions. "I am unaware that the fact that I am nominated on the state ticket makes it incumbent on me to say whether or not I intend to support anyone."[4]

His politics-on-the-one-hand-but-not-on-the-other attitude was a bit disingenuous considering he sent any number of agents, such as Preston Plumb, through Republican circles to ensure that Kansans voted for Ewing as chief justice. Further, a reluctance to get in the senatorial battle did not stop him from working behind the scenes to ensure that James Montgomery, the Kansas territorial delegate to Congress and a Lane man, was not put on the Public Lands Committee. John Sherman and Marcus Parrott were both asked to see that Montgomery was dumped. Montgomery was a major landowner in Atchison and would not be someone Ewing could work with on a Leavenworth railroad operation. Besides, Ewing just plain did not like Montgomery.[5]

When Kansans went to the polls a second time later that year, thirty-year-old Tom Ewing was elected chief justice of Kansas and was the state's top Republican

3. "No earthly doubt" from TEJr. to TESr., October 26, 1859, TEJr./KSHS.

4. "That I am nominated" from TEJr. to various men, October 24, 1859, TEJr./KSHS.

5. TEJr. to John Sherman, December 16, 1859, TEJr./KSHS. For background on the ethics of such political involvement by sitting judges, see *Republican Party of Minnesota v. White*, 536 U.S. 765 (2002).

vote-getter. He would take office whenever Kansas was admitted as a state. Ewing had proved that it was possible to create a Free State government out of proslavery beginnings, using the law and political procedure rather than violence. He had led his moderate Free Staters to triumph as a leader in the new Republican Party, where their numbers dominated the so-called war wing. This had led to the enactment and the triumph of the Wyandotte Constitution, the constitution that would lead the territory into statehood. All this was juxtaposed to John Brown's recklessness at Harpers Ferry, which Ewing knew had caused innocent people to die for no good reason.

The triumph of Kansas settlers in presenting to Congress the terms of statehood embodied in the Wyandotte Convention did not ease the growing tensions that had reverted from the prairies of Kansas, where such actions were focused in 1854, to a national division and unease. Harpers Ferry had reminded Southerners that radicals in the North might start the most feared of antislavery actions: a slave uprising. The Nat Turner episode in the 1830s was still legendary in the South. Kansas might be ready for its own statehood, but Southerners spitefully opposed the effort.

Tom Ewing was the Kansas Territory's chief justice–elect, but he had much to do before taking office, and during this hiatus he continued his law practice. But he was always on the lookout for others to replace him within the Leavenworth firm when he went on the bench. One prospect was his younger brother Charles Ewing, who had just finished law school in Cincinnati. Tom wrote Charley a letter introducing the idea. "The politics of the firm will be well-assorted, I being Republican and McCook a Democrat and you, 'not a democrat but a Buchanan man.'" Also approached was James Coombs, a Washington-based lawyer who was handling a case with Thomas Ewing Sr. The lawyer who joined the firm could continue an active partnership with a supreme court justice whose very name alone might bring in important clients. "If we are admitted [to statehood], I can propose you a good offer," Tom wrote Coombs. At the same time Ewing's correspondence was discouraging other lawyers from locating in Leavenworth unless they could support themselves for a year without fees.[6]

Nothing further came of these overtures, even after statehood when Ewing took the bench as chief justice. Ewing's proposals aside, there were opportunities to make significant legal fees during this period. Tom's work with the Fisher mat-

6. "Not a democrat" from TEJr. to Charles Ewing, June 27, 1860; "propose you a good offer" from TEJr. to James Coombs, October 20, 1859; downplaying Leavenworth from TEJr. to T. T. Abrams, September 22, 1860, all TEJr./KSHS.

ter attracted a man named Cline to Ewing's office. Cline had gotten into a fight over a slavery issue and was beaten. Ewing sued the batterer and won a $5,000 verdict for pain and suffering, a large verdict for that era.[7]

Another fee came from a major real estate case that carried such notoriety in Leavenworth it promised all sorts of future clientele if the firm were successful. John Fackler was a partner of Madison Mills and a significant landowner in Leavenworth. When Tom and Hugh had initially created their law office, Fackler contacted Hugh about representation in a test case on disputed territorial land titles. Fackler's personality had some of Mills's sharper edges, and given Hugh's preference to avoid problem clients such as Fant, he referred the case to another Washington attorney. John Ford, the other party, had hired Thomas Ewing Sr. The matter had worked its way through the federal territorial courts and was scheduled for argument in the U.S. Supreme Court.

The facts were simple. In 1856 Ford contracted with Fackler and Mills to buy Fackler's sixty acres in the old Delaware Indian reservation along with the "Fackler Addition" to Leavenworth. As part of the $10,000 deal, Fackler promised Ford the rights to extend a ferry across the Missouri River onto the south part of the Fackler Addition and a half-interest in the addition itself. After obtaining title Fackler realized that a viable ferry operation made the acreage worth more than the amount for which he had agreed to sell to Ford. Fackler tried to renege, offering to return Ford's down payment with interest. Ford declined. He sued Fackler for specific performance of the contract.

Fackler's defense to the suit threatened to undo the entire fabric of territorial land acquisition practices and deals made since the 1830s. A thirty-year-old congressional law punished all those who by whatever means entered into "combinations or conspiracies" to prevent others from bidding on land sales. Fackler argued the government had defrauded the Indians by selling the land below its value, and since Fackler obtained the Fackler Addition from the government, he and Ford were a combination or conspiracy and should not be allowed to perpetuate the fraud by completing the contract. The U.S. Supreme Court did not buy this argument, in fact labeling it "impertinent." The Supreme Court held unanimously for John Ford and ordered specific performance by Fackler.[8]

Sherman spent New Year's Day 1860 preparing for what he hoped would be a long stay as superintendent of the Louisiana Military Academy. Ellen Sherman

7. Cline suit at TEJr. to HBE, September 8, 1860, TEJr./KSHS.

8. *Fackler v. Ford,* 65 U.S. (24 How.) 322 (1860), at 327–29, 331–33.

had not gone south with him and was far from happy about his move to Louisiana. In the spring she enlisted Hugh and Ri into hosting the Shermans at Geisborough. Many wealthier Northern businessmen and politicians such as Stephen Douglas owned Southern plantations, complete with slave labor, and ran them as absentee landlords through managers. She thought, incorrectly, that Sherman had enjoyed working on her father's large Kansas farm, that Thomas Ewing's money and power could buy a Southern plantation, and that Sherman would aspire to a genteel Southern society with wealth and privilege, although it was still unclear whether she intended actually to live on such a place. Ellen was being petulant. Her husband loved the outdoors, but this did not mean he loved farming or being a farm overseer. He did not understand agriculture and had never shown any special aptitude for it. Sherman had spent only a few months at the Kansas farm, and when Henry Clark arrived to farm it, only a tenth of the acreage was ready for use.[9]

In February 1860 Hugh was still urging his sister Ellen to convince Cump to accept Roelfson's offer to manage the European banking house, another idea that would take him even further from Lancaster. Hugh wrote Sherman that he could get him a two-year contract. "If you accept, the sooner you leave Red River the better," he wrote Sherman. To a Roelfson aide, Hugh predicted, "We all feel satisfied that Sherman will resign his place in the south."[10]

Once again Hugh was wrong. The country was not enjoying a strong economy. Sherman instinctively knew that 1860 was not the time to give up a good job either to invest in a Southern plantation or to go gallivanting away to England. The Brits were a territorial race, and operating a successful English banking house required English roots, not American. Roelfson was not one of Sherman's friends; he was a member of the Ohio consortium of his father-in-law's. Sherman might have gone to London to work as an agent for Turner, but not for Roelfson. "I have concluded to stay [in Louisiana]," Sherman wrote Ellen in mid-February 1860. "I am going to take the bit in my mouth, and resume my military character and control my own affairs." He tried to pass up the London option in a lighthearted manner. He was a "Jonah" at banking, having "blown up" banking houses in San Francisco and New York. If he ran a bank in England, it "would signal the downfall of a mighty empire."[11]

9. Sherman, *Memoirs,* 1:141; *Topeka Capitol Journal,* March 27, 1955, 13A.

10. "Red River" from HBE to WTS, January 26, 1860, TEJr./KSHS; Roelfson's offer mentioned in HBE to WTS, July 25, 1859, and "Sherman will resign" from HBE to Tucker, January 15, 1860, in Ewing, "Autobiography," 218, 221.

11. All quotes from WTS to EES, February 13, 1860, SFP/ND.

Ellen disliked Cump's cavalier attitude and demanded that he reconsider Roelfson's offer immediately. Instead of just saying no, in March 1860 Sherman engaged in more deception of the sort that regularly characterized their feckless disagreements. He sent a letter of resignation to the academy, with private instructions to Graham to keep the letter in his safe. Sherman agreed to visit Ohio to investigate the London offer. He finessed the situation by demanding a salary that the consortium would not pay. The bank was to wire him $3,500 in cash and a written and guaranteed employment contract for $15,000 for each of the next two years. When Hugh, Sherman, and Ellen dined with David Gibson, one of the senior partners in the bank, Sherman was straightforward. He did not want to be stranded in London. He wanted to be paid for two years whether the venture went through or not. Gibson replied that the bank could not possibly front two years' salary. This was fine. Sherman proposed that Gibson guarantee the salary personally. Roelfson could take over payments upon his return. Again Gibson declined. He was not going to guarantee more than his partnership interest. Understanding the game that Sherman was playing, Hugh offered to back Sherman's salary on his own account, but Sherman wanted Gibson as his guarantor. Gibson said no. Then Sherman went back to Louisiana where, for the time being, his tent was pitched.[12]

Ellen took out her anger on Tom. During McCook's absence in Colorado on a collecting tour for the firm's creditors, Tom received a choleric note from Ellen. She had grown crotchety at the lost opportunity in London and at Cump's decision to remain in Louisiana. In her view both Tom and Dan McCook were blameworthy for their collective inability to sustain Cump in the law profession and keep him away from army people. Specifically, Sherman had given McCook instructions to use the small amounts he had collected from debtors on the use of her Leavenworth property and apply it to taxes on her remaining Leavenworth properties. She insisted McCook was misapplying the funds, and she wanted all the interest on those properties returned to her. Tom responded patiently that, "I don't know your instructions to McCook, but Cump was positive to pay taxes with the proceeds of these notes." Tom had some "negotiations" and understandings with Sherman concerning Ellen's property in Leavenworth, which he was trying to trade in order to spur some sales of his own property. Ellen's independence regarding her property was going to mess up the deal. Tom offered her twice as much land from what he owned northeast of Topeka if he could take her Leavenworth properties and create a package of lots for eager buyers. Tom did not re-

12. Marszalek, *Soldier's Passion,* 131; the Gibson dinner from Ewing, "Autobiography," 225.

solve the issue with Ellen and assured himself of future doses of animosity by teasing her with "We are all delighted that Cump gave up the London project and hope you will find a pleasant and healthful home in Louisiana."[13]

Sherman knew of Ellen's letters to Tom and felt some sympathy for his foster brother. Ellen was playing the role of spoiled sister. She was pouting, even refusing to come out to Kansas for the marriage of McCook to Julia Tebbs of Platte County, Missouri. Tom kept after them. "McCook is committed in that [marriage] direction and is beyond hope of redemption," Tom reported. Whatever else Sherman might have thought about the tax flap, he seemed genuinely happy that Ellen was unhappy, since she had not bothered about his feelings of living alone in Louisiana. If Ellen came south, he predicted flippantly that her white abolitionist servants would probably quit. "Then she will have to wait on herself or buy a nigger."[14]

Ellen's pique with Tom boiled over and caused her to hire a Lancaster law firm to sue Ewing & McCook in order to recover $36.15. When Tom got the demand letter from Hunter & Sons, he was livid. "If McCook did not communicate the full situation to you, he deserves censure, but not such an overflowing and overwhelming measure of it." He was "under instructions from Cump," her implied agent, which made the lawsuit ludicrous. If she had problems with Cump's instructions, talk to him about it. As chief justice he had been sued by his own sister, an embarrassment that might have political repercussions. His mood was not alleviated by the fact he was suffering from hemorrhoids. "[Your letter] has given me *offense*!" Tom would have McCook send all the money to Ellen without revealing that she was angry with him, but he took the opportunity to make her another offer, to take some of her eighty lots in the Ewing-Roelfson addition for some of his property near the downtown.[15]

None of this interested Ellen, whose heart remained firmly fixed in Lancaster. Since she had decided against going to Louisiana to live Sherman exercised his prerogatives as husband to demand that Ellen send their children to Lancaster public schools instead of to a Catholic school. She tried to dissuade him, spicing her letters with tales of teacher immorality and a story that some public school boys had peed on Minnie. She demanded that he reconsider. He would not, and their relationship twisted on itself again.

The family's inner pettiness boiled over into other relationships. For the first

13. TEJr. to EES, June 6, 1860, TEJr./KSHS.

14. "Julia Tebbs" and McCook's commitment from TEJr. to EES, June 6, 1860, TEJr./KSHS; "wait on herself" from WTS to TEJr., June 21, 1860, EFP/LC, quoted in Fellman, *Citizen Sherman*, 75.

15. TEJr. to EES, July 3, 1860, TEJr./KSHS.

time in their association, Tom and Hugh began to experience problems communicating with each other. Hugh was perturbed that, by giving Tom some of his Cincinnati trust property, he could not have choices in the "central" subdivision of Leavenworth, and he accused the chief justice of Kansas of having exceeded his authority as Hugh's agent. Tom reminded Hugh that the property was mortgaged to Madison Mills, so neither of them could trade it to anyone. Exasperated and slowly going broke on his stagnant properties in Leavenworth and St. Louis, Hugh decided to take his father's offer to head up the Lancaster saltworks. Thomas Ewing Sr. intended to spend two years in Europe on an extended vacation. Afterward Hugh would be given an option to buy a half interest worth $200,000 from his father for $14,000, a 7 percent investment.[16]

Like an addiction he could not shake, Senate politics continued to occupy Tom's time. Most of the state's elected officials had been elected the previous autumn, but when Kansas became a state that legislature would then elect two U.S. senators. Already men were angling for the plum positions, usually through the difficult process of determining who would be elected to the first Kansas legislature and convincing them to vote for one candidate or another. Lane was disliked by Kansas politicians, but he was strong with the voters, and Tom predicted this would force the politicians to support Ewing's old client. "Lane is a decidedly bad man but I know of no decidedly good and sound Republicans to take his place. I cannot entirely forget Lane's service to the cause before the [Free State] convention of December 1857. For since then he has done nothing I know of but mischief."[17]

Lane's primary opponent was James Winchell. Ewing found himself aiding Lane indirectly when he received authority from a New York City client to sue Winchell for some old debts. Hard times had dogged Winchell. He knew the suit was coming, but he had written Coe & Wallis, the New York firm, that he was destitute and needed more time. He had offered to "negotiate" a judgment but demanded in return "Messrs E and M not commence suit." Coe & Wallis instructed Winchell that he had to do his negotiating with Ewing & McCook, much to the delight of that firm.[18]

Samuel Pomeroy was dueling Marcus Parrott for the second Senate spot, but Parrott's alcoholism had caught up with him. As bad as Lane or Winchell might

16. EES to WTS, October 24, 1860, EFP/ND; Ewing, "Autobiography," 228.
17. TEJr. to John Hanna, January 26, 1860, TEJr./KSHS.
18. Correspondence on Winchell, Coe & Wallis to TEJr., January 30, 1860, TEJr./KSHS.

have been for Ewing's own political aspirations, Pomeroy would be worse. A short, stout, balding man with a Mona Lisa smile, he was called by his enemies "Pom the Pious." Pomeroy was tied closely into Cyrus Holliday's AT&SF railroad. Ewing played some politics of the situation, suggesting to publisher Mark Delahay that the newspaper should point out Pomeroy was a radical, not a Lincoln man, and would be bad for Leavenworth. Although he had made a deal to stay out of the Senate race, Tom quietly kept his dark horse possibilities alive in case Parrott's battle with the bottle proved too much for reconciliation and Pomeroy otherwise failed to attract enough votes.

But Tom Ewing was overconfident—a weakness his father recognized right away. Getting into a Senate campaign after pledges had been made would prove fruitless after Parrott had alienated many of his friends. For political and business reasons Pomeroy would be their senator in spite of his radicalism. When he realized his father was right, Tom urged that the Ewing clan work to get Hamp Denman appointed federal land agent in Lecompton. The job was a good appointment, a presidential position that paid more than the chief justice's salary. Hamp had the assistance of the anti-Lecompton Democrats in Kansas. Further, even if a Republican won the presidential campaign and all the Democrat officeholders were sent packing, the Ewing strength in the Republican Party might keep Hamp's job intact. Tom Ewing orchestrated town support for Denman. When the recommendation came to Washington from Kansas Democrats, however, someone in Buchanan's camp spotted Denman's connection with the Ewings, and someone else was appointed. "Buchanan has paid you the only compliment in his power to bestow!" Tom wrote the dejected Denman, who was fighting bankruptcy. "Like a toad he grows more ugly and venomous with increasing age. If the devil don't get him, then there is no sense keeping a devil. There is no place in hell hot enough for that scoundrel."[19]

To make things worse, in the summer of 1859 the heavens stopped giving moisture to most of Kansas. Except for isolated patches of rain, no moisture fell in Kansas for the next seventeen months. For Kansans who had seen border warfare, and who were slowly recovering from the Panic of 1857, the drought was the last straw. Livestock had to be slaughtered or they would starve, and without livestock that winter, starvation loomed. Tens of thousands left the territory, and those who stayed faced dreadful circumstances. Florella Adair, who left that summer to return to Ohio, wrote to her husband and daughter remaining in Osawatomie, "It

19. TEJr. to Hamp Denman, February 23, 1860, TEJr./KSHS.

seems to me that the territory is cursed of the Lord, and that it is fighting against him to try to live there and do any thing but barely to exist."[20]

Even law practices began to melt in the heat and drought. In February 1860 only three civil cases were tried from a thousand pending matters in Leavenworth. There were more lawsuits than courts to try them, and debtors knew that if they stonewalled a demand on a note or mortgage, lenders had little recourse. Garnishments were unheard of at that time, and even if there had been such a remedy, there were no incomes or accounts to garnish. If a man had only modest funds he usually carried most—if not all—of those funds on his person, and the garnishment of the era consisted of bill collectors' simply tracking down the debtor and demanding payment on the account, sometimes at gunpoint. Judicial inactivity "mired" the business community just as the lack of water in the fast-disappearing Kansas and Missouri river basins. The bright side was that taxes were not levied, and the courts were so slow that tax foreclosures disappeared. Everyone was living on borrowed money.

Between the ongoing drought and the slowing economy, all that was holding Leavenworth together was the hope that Congress would admit Kansas as a state before the land dried up and blew away. John Ford, the Ewings' successful client in the Supreme Court, bought some of Tom Ewing's distressed Leavenworth properties at fire sale prices, as a means of paying part of Thomas Ewing Sr.'s fee. Tom spent the time juggling interest payments on overdue notes to keep other properties from the court system and sheriff's sale. The Leavenworth branch of Smoot, Russell & Company also sued Denman and Ewing in an attempt by William Russell to obtain cash to rescue his foundering Pony Express operation. By October 1860 Russell no longer could borrow money at local banks, and Hugh had seen Russell on an Ohio River steamboat looking so "broken up" he had to slowly count his pennies to pay for a telegram.[21]

The Ewing & McCook law practice called in their own notes owed them by clients and pushed hard on notes placed with the firm for collection. Hugh tried to unload all his holdings in Leavenworth to a local investor consortium for $64,000, a fire sale of the first magnitude. "If this is not good speculation, no such thing as speculation exists." But there were no buyers, which left Tom and Hugh incredulous and concerned for their own future. "If you will keep a sharp lookout, you may be able to run down a speculator on Third Street some bright morning, and sell him enough to get out of debt. But why get out of Debt? It is the

20. F. Adair to Samuel Adair, November 21, 1860, Adair Family Papers, KSHS.
21. Russell from Ewing, "Autobiography," 231–32.

normal condition for western speculators." Never again would Tom be caught overextended "with all my sails set, if ever I am able to reef them."[22]

Statehood had become an imperative. It was the only remaining means to attract attention in Congress and to name the state's railroads as part of the transcontinental railroad legislation. If this were done, investment would pick up almost overnight. "Unless something is done for Leavenworth," Ewing wrote the railroad board, "this generation of property holders will break down and pass away, and the . . . money lenders will take the town. For the present property holders, it is half a loaf or no bread." The Ewings, as first-generation speculators, were going to be easy pickings for the second generation, and Tom Ewing knew it but did not seem to care. In July 1860 Ewing sought Otis Berthoud Gunn's later involvement in the LP&W on the theory that Gunn was one of the "capitalists who will take control of the company and build the road themselves. . . . It will give me pleasure to endorse your application favorably as I regard you as being fully competent [to engineer and build a railroad]."[23]

In April 1860 Kansas Republicans began the process to choose convention delegates to their first national presidential convention. Americans were cautiously eyeing the new party to see if it would nominate another lackluster dilettante such as John Fremont or a wild-eyed fanatic in the John Brown mold. Tom Ewing had opportunities to set his friends straight on the difference, although usually with tongue-in-cheek humor. "I hope you will not educate yourself up to the standard of ultra republicanism," he wrote college chum Thomas Vernon. "That wing is composed chiefly of nullifiers. . . . Their theory of state's rights, . . . would result in . . . the general government could only have the power to execute a given law in localities where the law [was popular]."[24]

But slavery was not the only issue at the Kansas Republican convention. A transcontinental railroad plank was in the platform. How the country handled this issue spoke volumes about the importance of expansion. Ewing was in Washington hiring some lobbying for the LP&W spur in this railroad plan, and walking a tightrope between support for legitimate businesses and public bribery. On March 30, 1860, he asked Charles Robinson to meet him in Washington along

22. "Not good speculation" from HBE to James Stone, January 16, 1860, in Ewing, "Autobiography," 221; "sharp lookout" from TEJr. to Charles Ewing, January 26, 1860, in Taylor, "Business and Political Career," 48; "reefing sails" from TEJr. to J. D. DuBois, January 25, 1860, TEJr./KSHS.

23. "This generation" from TEJr. to James H. McDowell, February 14, 1860, also TEJr. to HBE, September 8, 1860, HBE/OHS; TEJr. to Otis Gunn, July 24, 1860, TEJr./KSHS.

24. TEJr. to Vernon, March 25, 1860, TEJr./KSHS.

with C. W. Babcock or George Deitzler, and the Lawrence men should get up a fund of "$10,000 to $15,000" and some Lawrence town properties with which to "secure aid from the rapacious lobby." This lobby group comprised men who had influence over key government officials. "Among them are gentlemen of character and influence who, for a reasonable fee in property made contingent on the passage of the bill, will go to work for the bill and do it substantial service." Ewing suggested to Andrew Isaacs that Leavenworth businessmen would need $25,000 to $50,000 "to aid the passage of the land grants," a similar tactic. Ewing sarcastically noted the character of the influence peddlers. While Ewing's call for organized contributions was blatant, it was hardly unusual and is not evidence of any wrongdoing. Whether the *politicians* received assistance indirectly from these unelected friends is unknown—and this unknown quality was precisely the reason the method was employed.[25]

Ewing's railroad was in a position to make the best run at being the Kansas portion of the transcontinental railroad. It was ideally situated to link the major river port in Kansas with the territory's major cities. Other competitors were quick to realize this. In December 1858 the competing Kansas railroads, with Robinson, William H. Russell, Luther Smoot, and W. F. M. Arny, met in Washington and agreed to get the Delawares to sell their diminished reserve for the LP&W's benefit. For much of the last half of the nineteenth century, Washington's reason for being was to act as a political protectorate of large business concerns, the so-called Gilded Age. Ewing did not make these rules; he only used the rules to his own best advantage. There is little practical difference between the rapacious "lobbying" of men who, for a fee, claimed special entrée to nineteenth-century congressmen and senators and the K-street Washington lobbyists of today. Former congressmen who lobby their former colleagues fit this nineteenth-century mold, too. Politicians survived on the good graces of moneyed friends, then and now. The only difference was that, in the nineteenth century, campaign contributions were not reported to a federal election commission and hence there was no limit on the amounts given.

25. "Rapacious lobby" and "gentlemen of character" from TEJr. to Charles Robinson, March 30, 1860, "aid the passage" from TEJr. to Isaacs, April 2, 1860, both in TEJr./KSHS. The late Professor David Taylor argues that this letter by Ewing is the foundation for a bribe. While this is one conclusion that could be drawn, it may overstate the situation. Ewing's feeding of the rapacious lobby was not directly bribing public officials. He was gaining access to the friends of politicians, and acting through close friends or relatives was how one best influenced nineteenth-century lawmakers. Then, as now, it was not illegal to pay a friend of the congressman to influence the congressman so long as the friend obeyed the law. The only difference between then and now is that today, if anyone takes money to influence public officials, he or she must register as a lobbyist. Current federal and most state laws require much more public exposure concerning the use of such funds.

Kenneth Stampp argues that major businesses often had more power in courts than with state and federal governments of the day, which were small, and their investigative commissions had nothing like the financial backing of the trusts. "Politicians of the time," Stampp notes, "often invested in western lands, town properties, railroad projects or banks." If the Congress of that day was debased, other institutions were debased, too. Even the haughty rarified air of journalism could be "rented" by the well-placed fee. Ewing knew all these things. This does not make his actions of organizing town businessmen to pay for lobbying a crime. After all, Ewing became one of the more expensive of postwar Washington lobbyists. While he was a friend to many important persons and while corporations paid him to influence those persons, there is no indication that money went improperly from the payor to the politician via Ewing.[26]

Ewing's railroad concerns were not his only issues that month. Kansas Republicans sent six delegates to the national convention with ideas for the platform and instructions to vote for Seward. Having given up on Bates in favor of Lincoln, Tom was asked if he wanted to be a delegate. He declined, citing pressing business matters. He did toy with going to Chicago just to meet privately with Lincoln's friends. He was concerned that Lincoln might hold it against the Kansas Republicans that Seward was the delegation's choice when, in December 1859 the state had turned out so mightily for Lincoln on his visit to Bleeding Kansas. Delahay was—and is—a Lincoln man, Ewing wrote the future president, but the delegation chose Daniel Wilder, who was for Seward. It turns out that some of the problem lay in Delahay himself—a newspaperman who thought he was a lawyer. A kinsman of Lincoln, when Delahay later sought the U.S. attorney position in Kansas, Sol Miller wrote, "The only bench Delahay is suited for is the one with a hole in it." Ewing assured Lincoln that the "Seward instruction" was only for the first ballot and thereafter the delegation could go for Lincoln. Kansas Republicans would be united, he promised, and would "complet[e] the destruction of the Democratic Party which ought to have quietly and gracefully died when the old Whig Party gave up the ghost."[27]

While Hugh had little interest in his brother Tom's Republican politics, a bit of political luck fell on him that spring. While en route home to Kansas from

26. Stampp's analysis is from *America in 1857,* 28, 136. Bribery in the late 1850s is defined at chapter 52, section 7, 1855 Laws of the Kansas Territory.

27. TEJr. to Abraham Lincoln, May 6, 1860, TEJr./KSHS; more pro-Lincoln letters in TEJr. to J. J. Osborne, June 4, 1860, TEJr./KSHS; "Delahay's bench" from Castel, *Frontier State,* 166; "gave up the ghost" from TEJr. to Lewis Wolfley, May 1, 1860, TEJr./KSHS.

Cincinnati in mid-April, he happened to meet H. Miles Moore and John Halderman. The Democratic Party had decided for general unity to hold its national convention in the South, but Moore and Halderman expected a long convention and Moore could not stay that long. Would Hugh Ewing go in his place? Hugh jumped at the chance. He wired Ri and his father of the travel change, set off for Memphis by boat, and then traveled across the South by rail. As his train passed through the plantation country in middle Tennessee, Hugh had little warning that he had been given a ticket to one of the pivotal meltdowns in American political life.

The convention began on April 20, 1860. Charleston did not roll out its famed Southern hospitality. Northern Democrats received a very cold shoulder. Visitors had a difficult time finding housing and transportation to and from the convention. The balmy weather outside the convention disguised a bitterly divided Democratic Party inside. Stephen Douglas was the party's lightning rod, and in the end its scapegoat. Douglas demanded that the party embrace popular sovereignty as the only unifying issue with which to fight Republicanism. Southerners who watched Kansas slip away from slavery's camp were not about to agree with this view. There was no slave state admission on the horizon. They had compromised with Douglas in 1856. It was time he compromise with them. This required adherence to *Dred Scott*—a slave was property and would always be property. Douglas had a majority of the delegate votes, but he needed two-thirds for the nomination. The price for Southern support for Douglas was that the *Dred Scott* resolution be part of the Democratic Party platform.

Stephen Douglas was the front-runner, but the convention's icon was William L. Yancey of Alabama, who had engineered promises from six Southern states that their delegates would bolt if the slave-as-property resolution failed to become a platform issue with Douglas. The platform had to be agreed upon before the nomination process began. Hugh watched Yancey take the floor and defend the ultra-Southern position, supporting Buchanan's views of Lecompton and attacking Douglas's treachery. To loud boos from the Douglas delegates, Yancey thundered that defeat on principle was preferable to victory achieved on ambiguous issues. Ohio's George Pugh retaliated heatedly, "Gentlemen of the south," he roared. "*we will not do it*!" Hugh hastily scribbled in his journal that "nothing will be done. No harmony." He was right.[28]

The last day that antebellum America saw an undivided Democratic Party was

28. Ewing, "Autobiography," 225; Robert W. Johannsen, *The Frontier, the Union, and Stephen A. Douglas*, 160.

April 30, 1860. The section pledging that Douglas would stand by decisions of the Supreme Court on slavery was voted down. Southerners walked out amid wild applause from South Carolinians in the galleries. The centrist party of Andrew Jackson lay ragged and dying on the convention floor, without a nominee. Disgusted, Hugh left for Leavenworth the same day. Douglas's last efforts at nomination were complete. The Democrats had retreated into irreconcilable sectionalism. Although Democrats reconvened in Baltimore, where the Southern states were neither welcomed nor invited, and nominated Douglas, within weeks Southern states nominated John C. Breckinridge as their Southern candidate for president. Republicans privately and publicly rejoiced. Their enemy was divided and would do battle that fall as much against each other as against the Republican nominee. All the Republicans had to do was exploit the middle.[29]

By early summer the population of Kansas hit 106,000, enough to be admitted as a state under the pre-English rules, enough, that is, if the Senate members were of the same mind, which they were not. Tom Ewing made several efforts to persuade reluctant Southern friends such as Senator John Crittenden to get the Senate off the dime on Kansas statehood. Crittenden balked. In the aftermath of the Charleston convention the party was too raw. A portion of the Wyandotte Constitution spoke to suffrage by "aliens." Southern senators were suspicious the phrase meant voting rights for blacks. Southerners believed in their paranoia, in spite of Ewing's assurances to Crittenden that aliens did not mean blacks. However, Jefferson Davis and James Hammond did not want to deal with two new Kansas senators such as Jim Lane or Samuel Pomeroy in the Senate if there was any opportunity for Democrats to have a greater voice in the legislature and perhaps elect a moderate compromise.[30]

The drought in Kansas in 1860 might have had some Kansans eating acorns, but it stirred unusual movement among some of the state's railroad entrepreneurs. The Hannibal to St. Joseph railroad swung a spur from Cameron, Missouri, thirty-five miles east of St. Joseph, then southwest toward Weston. If this happened, Leavenworth would be bypassed. Leavenworth businesses organized a bond subscription of $100,000 to entice the Hannibal & St. Joseph Railroad to bridge the river at Weston and proceed south through the fort and into Leavenworth.

After much thought Tom Ewing was not as concerned as many of his business associates in town. A spur from St. Joseph to Kansas City made no sense. A ra-

29. Johannsen, *Stephen A. Douglas,* 146, 149, 159–58, 162.
30. TEJr. to John J. Crittenden, June 5, 1860, TEJr./KSHS.

tional railroad man would not throw expensive trunk lines within a mile of a territory's largest city and fail to run a bridge across to it. The LP&W's board advised Leavenworth city fathers to be patient. John Forbes and James F. Joy, the St. Joseph road's money men, were wanting others to finance their railroad for them. In fact Joy did offer the LP&W stockholders rate concessions if other railroads would spend their own capital to run a spur to the Hannibal & St. Joseph road. This would require Kansans to spend money for the expensive bridging of the Missouri River. Tom Ewing wanted none of it and urged the bond vote be defeated. The *Leavenworth Daily Times* adopted Ewing's views and predicted the $100,000 initial capitalization was just the down payment and more would be extracted if taxpayers gave in to Joy, even just one time. Without the LP&W behind the effort, the bond issue fell through. Ewing was later proved correct. Joy and Forbes were not interested in the Cameron to Weston spur if they had to fund it themselves.[31]

In June 1860 Isaac's railroad efforts in Washington proved fruitful. Ewing was notified that Congress would soon grant special authority to the LP&W to negotiate with the Delaware tribe for the sale of their trust lands. Eighty acres of timbered land in northeast Kansas had been assigned to each tribe member, and the railroad was given exclusive authority to purchase this acreage from tribal members "in trust" for them and pay the government price for the 223,000 acres available. In turn the sale of that land would finance the railroad's development through northeast Kansas.

There was a catch. Marketable title would not pass from the tribe to the government, and then to the railroad, until the railroad had raised private funds sufficient to lay twenty-five miles of good track west of Leavenworth. This reservation was fine with the railroad because its directors did not want title in the roads and adjacent lands until they had a viable railroad or they would be taxed on a nonproductive entity. At this point half the lands purchased would be deeded to the railroad and the other half were available only when the railroad had built its way to the western edge of the reserve. Another condition was that acquisitions had to be purchased in gold, not scrip. And the entire project had to be accomplished within a "reasonable time" or the deal was voided. This put a premium on solid private financing, the road's Achilles Heel.[32]

31. Joy's efforts from Taylor, "Business and Political Career," 92; TEJr. to E. Peabody, June 24, TEJr. to TESr., June 30, 1860, TEJr./KSHS. For Leavenworth county bond sales for railroad development, see the *Leavenworth Daily Times,* July 2, 1860.

32. David G. Taylor, "Thomas Ewing Jr. and the Origins of the Kansas Pacific Railway Company," 158–59.

Naturally, such favoritism showed to one railroad made other railroad investors hostile to the entire idea. To buy off possible opposition from competitors or organizations who complained the deal exploited the Delaware, the railroad earmarked substantial tracts of the land for mission schools and churches as well as "retainers" for the tribal chiefs. The treaty's details set off "wild enthusiasm" in Leavenworth, replacing the gloom of the drought. James Stone and Jim McDowell immediately sought the million dollars in gold needed to buy the treaty lands. Within eighteen months from beginning production, they predicted the line could be to Fort Riley with Leavenworth, Lawrence, Topeka, and Manhattan along its route. Denver was the natural western terminus. The transcontinental railroad would be one-third complete, and Leavenworth would be its eastern terminus. Treaty enthusiasm spurred a midsummer growth spurt in the town. Properties began to sell in anticipation of hosting railroad business development, especially repair and locomotive yard facilities. The Ewings sent a flurry of letters to other influential persons and investment trusts urging them to get on board for the investment of a lifetime.[33]

As with other efforts of the U.S. government telling tribe members how to dispose of their land, the appraisal system for the Delaware lands was not a model of ethics. Andrew Isaacs worked all that spring to get the Interior Department's assurance that the lands would be appraised at the legal minimum of $1.25 per acre, an amount the land was worth without a railroad on it, rather than at the increased value the land should bring with a functioning nearby railroad. The landowners were, after all, just Indians. While racism was involved here, there also was practicality. Nineteenth-century governments did not ordinarily use tax revenue to fund internal improvements.

Most states and the federal government got involved indirectly, however. One easy subsidy by government was to allow railroads to buy their right-of-way land at an artificially low appraised price. Land was something the government had plenty of. With land subsidies, railroads could mortgage the land and use the difference between the appraised value and the actual value of the land they sold to homesteaders to run the railroad. Appraisers eventually ruled that 224,000 acres could be purchased by the LP&W for $286,000, about $1.28 per acre, perhaps half of its true value. A year later the land sold for $6.50 per acre. Since this process was approved by the Department of the Interior, it could not exactly be called a swindle. However, had the acreage been owned by whites, it is doubtful the right-of-

33. Clara Gowing, "Life among the Delaware Indians," 189n9; Castel, *Frontier State,* 220; Taylor, "Origins of the Kansas Pacific," 158–59; Anna Heloise Abel, "Indian Reservations in Kansas and the Extinguishment of Their Title," 89; TEJr. to George Purkins, June 13, 1860, TEJr./KSHS.

way would have been purchased in the same manner. Having received the subsidy, Tom asked Hugh to intercede with Roelfson to see if they could raise a million dollars in England in order for the railroad to buy access across the Delaware reserve.

On August 27, 1860, Congress formally approved the LP&W treaty with the Delawares. While publicly enthusiastic, Hugh expressed private doubts that the railroad's current board could pull off the financing without English capital getting involved at a hefty premium. Ewing alerted his father to the treaty's problems. Now that the basic law was in place giving statutory rights to the LP&W, the former secretary of the Interior was just the man to work on some amendments.[34]

The movement in the nineteenth century for a transcontinental road first had to be financed. One means of enticing banking investors in railroads such as the LP&W would be to show that the railroad was developing a given service territory between Leavenworth and Denver with little or no competition. In September 1860, prominent Kansans scheduled a railroad convention to see if a territorial agreement might be obtained among the various paper railroads for where the transcontinental railroad and trunk lines should be laid through Kansas.

The Kansas railroad convention convened on October 17, in Cyrus Holliday's turf in Topeka. While the LP&W was on the inside track to being the major road in Kansas because of its Delaware rights, Ewing also realized there were too many railroads and there had to be a way to limit their competitive nature or they would compete each other to death. His realization also left him ripe for a double-cross. Whether he saw one coming or not is unknown. Tom Ewing asked Marcus Parrott to send a letter to the convention commenting on the probability that the transcontinental railroad legislation, the Vandover bill, would go through if Kansans united behind a single railroad interest. With this document Ewing had two goals at the convention. Long-term, the LP&W men would use their influence on the next president and the Republican Party to push an intercontinental railroad terminus in Kansas as public policy. The other goal was to delay the final payment date for the building of their railroad, which would give them some liquidity. In the short term they would use their "rights" in the treaty lands as leverage to be named the preferred line, thus attracting more investors.[35]

34. Appraising the acreage from Taylor, "Origins of the Kansas Pacific," 159–60; TEJr. to TESr., September 8, 1860, HBE/OHS.

35. Competition was bad for railroads, Taylor, "Business and Political Career," 102–3, 105; "Vandover bill" from TEJr. to Marcus Parrott, September 27, 1860, TEJr./KSHS; postponing payments from Rowland, "Thomas Ewing Jr.," 13.

However, the LP&W had to keep an eye on Holliday's Atchison-Topeka consortium, which was working just as hard to outfox Ewing. The ten-man Leavenworth delegation to the convention included Ewing, Carter Wilder, and Jim McDowell, a Douglas Democrat and another close Ewing associate. With staunch Democrats such as Hamp Denman and McDowell, Leavenworth had become a stronghold for Douglas Democrats, and the rest of the Republican-dominated territory knew it. It was well-known that Stephen Douglas wanted an intercontinental railroad, and Republicans were not automatically going to let that prize go to a Democrat city. They would try to exclude—or seriously diminish—Leavenworth input. Anticipating that his railroad could pull it off, Ewing went counter to his father's advice and scrimped and saved every dollar he could find for a down payment on twenty-three sections of "half-breed" land west of Leavenworth, nearly fifteen thousand acres. This investment, solely for speculation, would be worth a fortune if the line came through even a portion of these lands.[36]

Charles Robinson, a Ewing ally at the convention, was the first to test Holliday's support. Robinson gave a speech on the importance of fairness. He moved to apportion convention delegates based on a county's proportionate population to the territory as a whole. This would give Leavenworth its share of votes. Chairman Ben Stringfellow tabled that motion and presented the Holliday substitute—that each territorial county should have one base vote, plus all other votes based on proportionate population, which greatly increased the rural voting strength. Even sparsely settled western counties had at least two votes. By offering the amendment Holliday was making indirect promises to potential customers that, if they played along with him, the rural counties would be rewarded by his railroad. It was wrong, Leavenworth delegate Tom Means argued, for smaller counties whose delegates represented nothing but prairie to assume a fourth of the voting power at the convention. Holliday's men pandered to the farm vote, arguing that farming was the future of Kansas, so the state's agricultural base should have a strong position at the table.

When this motion passed, Leavenworth found itself as the largest county but only the fifth-largest vote count at the convention. The county was playing against a rigged deck. The Leavenworth delegation abandoned the convention after the first day, followed by other counties, which left Holliday's Atchison and Topeka delegations in charge. The convention decided on five main lines, the fourth being the current Atchison, Topeka & Santa Fe line (AT&SF), a road from Atchi-

36. Purchasing fifteen thousand acres from TEJr. to TESr., March 9, 1860, also TEJr. to M. Parrott, June 12, 1860, both in TEJr./KSHS.

son northwest into the Colorado territory along the top tier of counties in Kansas that later became the Chicago & Rock Island. The line from Kansas City through Lawrence, Topeka, Manhattan, Ft. Riley, and west to Salina, Russell, and Hays would figure prominently in the 1862 Pacific Railroad bill as the eastern spur of the Union Pacific. Leavenworth was given a token spur line up from Kansas City.[37]

Ewing had no intention of letting Holliday and Stringfellow create additional railroad interests at the expense of the LP&W. If the LP&W could link with a Missouri road before Holliday's AT&SF, pressure would build for a bridge at Leavenworth and further expansion west. The other "planned" roads could be bypassed as johnny-come-latelies. Ewing asked Alfred Gray, another Washington confidant, to steer lawmakers toward working with Charles Robinson's Quindaro railroad interests in the Vandover bill and ignore the other lines recommended by the railroad convention. His recommendation to Gray was an indication that, as rivals, he could work with Robinson but not Holliday. Derailing Holliday would give Ewing time to work on an alliance with a Missouri road and begin discussions with George Park in Boston about a spur from Parkville, Missouri, to Leavenworth.[38]

While the railroad developments were exciting, with the splintering of the Democrats in Charleston presidential politics overwhelmed everything during the summer of 1860. John Bell, a Whig senator from Tennessee and a Southerner who could work with Northern interests, was initially reluctant to campaign on the Constitutional Union ticket, but among his old Whig colleagues who persuaded him otherwise was Thomas Ewing Sr. Ewing argued that Bell was one of the few Southerners to vote against Lecompton in the Senate, which meant that Northerners could trust his integrity. The whole country had to fear the results if Lincoln and Douglas split the vote and Breckinridge's hardliners slipped into power. A Lincoln presidency would present some problems for the Republic, but a Breckinridge presidency was certain war.

As was the custom the presidential campaigners did not actively seek the office, instead letting surrogates in each state carry their message. Lincoln, especially, was silent. Douglas sensed an opportunity and traveled into the South, seeking direct support. By the autumn, with Bell not catching on in the South, Thomas Ewing

37. Page Smith, *The Rise of Industrial America: A People's History of the Post-Reconstruction Era,* 111; railroad convention from George Glick, "The Railroad Convention of 1860," 467–78.

38. Anti-Holliday efforts, see TEJr. to Alfred Gray, December 4, TEJr. to George Park, December 16, 1860, TEJr./KSHS; Taylor, "Origins of the Kansas Pacific," 157.

Sr. made it known in Ohio circles that he was supporting Lincoln over Douglas, partly because of Douglas's "recklessness" with Kansas-Nebraska but more likely because the Republican convention produced a platform grounded more closely to Whig monetary policies. His late-summer change of allegiance made his name anathema to Democrats and to a very puzzled old friend, John Bell.[39]

Hugh's in-laws were among the Southerners perplexed by Thomas Ewing's switch. Lincoln frightened slave owners. For Hugh, helping to run Geisborough that summer meant helping his brother-in-law Washington Young purchase slaves in Alexandria, Virginia. Young intended to ship the slaves to their Louisiana sugar plantation on the Bayou Tèche. Hugh Ewing's presence allowed him insight into Southern thinking, both from the Youngs and from their neighbors in Maryland and Virginia. Hugh's political reports back to Ohio were gloomy. He wrote Hamp Denman, "The Giant [Douglas] is dead" in the South. Southerners expected Lincoln's victory and were "like Huguenots, picking their flints." Hugh had no love for Douglas, however. To his father he wrote, "He fought the dragon Lecompton and for that, I mourn him. But then again, he sired the dragon and deserves no credit for braining the devil he raised."[40]

The drought had burned the life out of the Kansas economy during the summer of 1860. Without moisture for seventeen months, the creeks and rivers had dried up. Hundreds of thousands of buffalo and cattle died, leaving a stench even the prevailing southern winds could not entirely erase from the prairie. When crops failed, many settlers left, sporting a new territorial motto: "In God We Trusted; in Kansas We Busted."[41]

Congress seemed oblivious to what was occurring in Kansas, the talk being of the Democratic schism and a Republican nominating convention. Relief efforts were organized, including a symbolic check for $100 from President Buchanan. Charles Robinson lobbied Congress for help, too. New Yorker financier Thaddeus Hyatt helped organize the relief effort and, as a friend of Buchanan's, asked that the government not only assist in moving tons of food and clothing into the territory along largely uncharted roads but also to postpone land sales in Kansas in the Homestead Act.[42]

The drought and Buchanan's reaction to Hyatt's suggestion figured into presidential politics, however. The new Homestead Act specifically extended the time

39. Campaign of 1860 from Johannsen, *Stephen A. Douglas,* 165.

40. "Giant is dead" from HBE to Denman, "fought the dragon" from HBE to TESr., both October 15, 1860, in Ewing, "Autobiography," 231.

41. "Kansas We Busted" from Kenneth S. Davis, "Portrait of a Changing Kansas," 33.

42. Robinson's efforts for drought relief in Congress from TEJr. to Charles Robinson, November 22, 1860, TEJr./KSHS; drought relief from Glick, "Railroad Convention," 482.

that Kansas homesteaders had to pay the government price for their lands. Buchanan originally told Hyatt he could support the postponement. Many farmers had gone into debt at usurious rates and sold livestock in order to hang on to their claims, providing hungry families with meat through hunting. Just before the election, however, Buchanan vetoed the Homestead Act. Thousands were unable to make their payments, and their farms—into which their life savings had been poured—reverted to the bankers, speculators, and government land agents.

The veto was a political goof of major proportions. Anti-Democratic bitterness grew to fever pitch in Kansas. First Buchanan had tried to foist on Kansas a slavery constitution, and his appointees had fostered voting frauds to achieve the goal. Buchanan's change of heart led Kansans to desert the Democratic Party in droves. Never again would the Democrats in Kansas have the ability to contest numerically for control of all state and local offices, not even during the popularity of Franklin D. Roosevelt.[43]

A few nights later, in the chilly night air, Springfield, Illinois, hosted the cheers of hundreds gathered outside Abraham Lincoln's home. Election returns were already showing the magnitude of his victory. Eight of every ten men of voting age had voted, a turnout unequaled in American history. Lincoln amassed 1.8 million votes, but he was a plurality president, his three opponents collecting 2.8 million between them. Lincoln carried none of the Southern states, and in five of them he did not receive a single vote. However, he carried 180 of the 303 electoral votes. John Sherman was glad of Lincoln's outright electoral college victory because it saved the country from a "discreditable scramble in the House" where Lincoln's votes would have been subject to an unhappy Democratic House of Representatives. In a letter that he no doubt wanted circulated in the South, John Sherman noted the election was a contest for the possession of Kansas and New Mexico, not a general Republican assault on slavery. "If Buchanan had submitted the controversy in Kansas to its own people and had closed it by admitting Kansas as a free state, the Democratic party would have retained power." Still, he rejoiced in the Republican victory. "Lincoln will do much to dissipate the feeling in the South against the North by showing what are the real purposes of the Republican Party."[44]

John Sherman was wrong. The election of 1860 simply put the Southern states on a course of secession. In South Carolina conventions were called and delegates

43. Impact of Homestead veto, Castel, *Frontier State,* 14, 17, also Castel, *Whirlwind,* 17.

44. Election results from Shelby Foote, *The Civil War: A Narrative,* 1:34; all quotes from John Sherman to WTS, November 26, 1860, in Thorndike, *Sherman Letters,* 87–88.

selected. Two days before South Carolina voted to secede, Hugh wrote Cump, "You will find the South too warm before long." Cump's fallback position was to send new overtures to his brother John that he no doubt hoped would be passed to John's friends in the War Department. He wrote his wife that "If Louisiana remains in the Union I will serve her honestly and faithfully. If she quits, then I quit too." Sherman loathed the talk of war. "The true position for every gentleman North and South is to frown down even a mention of disunion." He felt he should not be held accountable for John's abolitionist views any more than all Southerners were accountable for slavery. But matters were sliding beyond anyone's control, Sherman wrote. Later he wrote a thoughtful note to Graham, "War seems to be coveted by those who understand not its cost. I fear my duty here is drawing to a close."[45]

In Kansas, where the country's troubles had led to a national schism, the last month of 1860 contained beginnings as well as endings. On December 5, Dan McCook married Julia Tebbs, the daughter of a transplanted Virginian, Algernon S. Tebbs. The Platte City wedding was a large gala attended by many members of the bar, including Tom and Ellen Ewing. It was Ellen's first public venture since early November when she had fought a serious and debilitating illness. Her recovery had been slow and worrisome for the family, but she did not want to miss Dan and Julia's nuptials. Their world in Kansas was being turned upside down with events nobody could control. Julia Tebbs, the daughter of Southern gentry, was marrying the partner of the city's most renowned Free State advocate, whose foster brother was coming home from the South to fight slave owners. The talk was polite and subdued, but filled with dread.[46]

Hugh had responded to Charles Ewing in Ohio that the South was made up of "besotted fools" and would face "a mighty avalanche" if they fired on federal installations, that "Egypt's" social and political organizations had no indigenous strength and would go down beneath the heel of the North's "war horse." Brother Philemon predicted to Hugh that Buchanan was so beholden to Southern interests that the president would surrender Sumter without a fight. Lincoln, however, was a fighter. Hugh's Lancaster friend Henry Myers got in his licks, too, suggesting that any war the South would start would be over in a year.[47] Myers was half right.

45. "Too warm" from HBE to WTS, December 8, 1860, in Ewing, "Autobiography," 234; "then I quit too" from WTS to EES, December 15, 1860, in Marszalek, *Soldier's Passion,* 135; "true position" from WTS to Y. Mason Graham, January 6, 1860, SFP/ND; a year later "War seems to be coveted" from WTS to Y. Mason Graham, January 6, 1861, SFP/ND.

46. *Leavenworth Daily Times,* December 7, 1860.

47. HBE to Charles Ewing, January 23, 1861, and Myers prediction in Ewing, "Autobiography," 235.

On a blustery cold day, January 7, 1861, the Kansas territorial legislature met in Lecompton for a brief session before adjourning several days later to the better creature comforts of Lawrence. There, the lawmakers met for nearly a month, speculating on what Washington was doing regarding the growing list of secessions of Southern states. The legislators quietly hoped that 1861 might be their last session as a territory. As the Southern states seceded, Southern lawmakers abandoned Washington, which left only Northern men in Washington and lowered the quorum to do business in the Senate. The talk now was of Dixie. What would the South do? How should Lincoln respond?

Phil Ewing had been right. Buchanan's inaction gave the South a clear signal that the federal government had no stomach to prevent secession forcibly. On the second day of 1861, when Secretary of War John B. Floyd resigned and was replaced by Joseph Holt, Texas secessionist Louis Wigfall urged South Carolina major general of volunteers M. L. Bonham to "cut off supplies from Anderson and take [Fort] Sumter as soon as possible." Three days later the steamer *Star of the West* loaded up in New York with two hundred reinforcements. When the ship entered Charleston harbor without South Carolina's permission, rebel batteries on Morris Island fired across its bow and drove the ship back out to sea. When there was no immediate response, South Carolinians rejoiced in new drumbeats. War seemed imminent, but the federal government was impotent. Although he spent his presidency using cavalry to force Kansans to accept an unwanted state government, in the days before Lincoln's inaugural Buchanan decided against retaliation against South Carolina's actions. Buchanan had little with which to retaliate, and the Southern states knew it.[48]

The war talk caused Tom Ewing to reassess his political positioning. Lane wanted to be the state's first senator, but he would not be able to resist leaping to the colors for the political results that might be brought by a field commission. Since general officers were approved by the Senate, senators could not serve in the army while in the Senate. If Lane left for the army, then Ewing, the best vote-getter in the previous November's election, was a logical consideration for an interim appointment to the Senate. The key to this appointment remained getting Charles Robinson to be appointed Indian Commissioner. "If 'R' is appointed, I will go to the Senate sure!" If statehood came with the war and Lane resigned the Senate to seek glory, Governor Robinson would appoint an interim senator just

48. *The War of the Rebellion: A Compilation of the Official Records of the Union and Confederate Armies,* 1:133–38, 140, 240, 252 (hereafter *O.R.* with either volume number and page or sometimes volume number, part number, and page); "*Star of the West*" at Mark Boatner, *The Civil War Dictionary,* 79.

before Ewing's influence persuaded Lincoln to appoint Robinson to the federal post.[49]

This unexpected backdoor way to the Senate rekindled Ewing's Senate ambitions and caused him to focus all his efforts on Robinson's appointment. He contacted his father for help as well as other influential Ohioans such as Governor William Dennison. Ewing persuaded Robinson to postpone the first meeting of the state legislature for as long as possible, knowing that supporters of both Lane and Parrott were agitating for a quick election of senators. Ewing needed time to discuss Robinson's appointment with Lincoln and keep Robinson focused on contacting the right people without the daily distraction of working with a legislature controlled by Lane. Outwardly Ewing was maintaining a position of neutrality because of his pending judgeship, but supreme court judges of that day were hardly nonpolitical. As Indian Commissioner Robinson would control considerable patronage, and the appointees in turn would be important persons in many legislators' districts. They could pressure state legislators into voting for whichever Senate candidate Robinson wanted. Ewing turned up the heat, asking John Sherman and Jacob Collamore to use their influence with Lincoln on Robinson's appointment. During these anxious days Tom let off steam by poking fun at his Democrat friends such as future U.S. attorney general Richard Olney, inquiring whether Olney had supported Lincoln and thus was "sound enough on the goose" to write Lincoln a supportive letter on Robinson's appointment.[50]

The war talk also helped the Ewings stall their creditors. Ewing knew that foreclosure would require his creditors to assume tax burdens on idle ground. By keeping the debtors going and by paying taxes at whatever interest he could, the lender was better off. Smart debtors knew these facts. Nobody was buying properties in Leavenworth at that time, not even distressed properties. Mills's Leavenworth property would sell for nothing. Ewing used these facts as a polite means of telling Mills that his threats of a lawsuit against the Ewings, even if successful, would merely net Mills title to land he could not sell and judgment for money against Ewing he could not collect. The limits of Tom's stubbornness were seen when Mills asked him to borrow from his father to pay the debt. Ewing refused. "I will not call on Father for help for reasons satisfactory to me." He offered Mills a deed

49. Ewing's Senate positioning from Castel, *Frontier State,* 25–26; "If 'R' is appointed" from TEJr. to HBE, January 17, 1861, TEJr./KSHS; Rowland, "Reluctant Chief Justice," 31–32.

50. TEJr. to HBE, January 17, to John Sherman, to Jacob Collamore, to Richard Olney, to J. J. Coombs, all January 22, 1861, to TESr., January 20, to William Dennison, January 24, to Robinson, January 24, 1861, all in TEJr./KSHS.

to the property in return for Mills's agreement not to sue for a deficiency, but Mills preferred to extend the note. It was the last time until after the war that these debts became an issue.[51]

Louisiana had planned its secession convention for January 26, 1861. Anarchy and sedition were being preached in the streets of Alexandria and going unpunished, which caused Sherman to want nothing further to do with the federal government he described as "pusillanimous." He wrote Graham of the coming ugly war. "The storm is upon us and we must each to our own ship." Hugh reminded Cump that Louisiana could secede on paper but in reality only if the North let her go, for "King Cotton is not so potent as His worshipers imagine." Sherman was not so sure. Braxton Bragg sent Cump a bittersweet letter, from one old comrade to another. However, the time had come. Sherman resigned from the Louisiana academy on January 28, 1861, collected the $500 owed him by the state, and made appointments to clear up his business affairs in Louisiana.[52]

One day later, with Southern senators called home from Congress, the remaining senators voted Kansas into the Union. All of Leavenworth took to the streets, celebrating in the chilly air. Tom Ewing and two friends, Tom Fenton and Jim McCahon, rolled the old Kickapoo cannon from its public moorings to where the abolitionist publisher Daniel Anthony's home overlooked the bluff above the river. They tore up two volumes of the laws of the bogus territorial legislature, stuffed the barrel with the paper, and fired it at Missouri, belching paper all along the bluffs while a crowd cheered. While the Wyandotte Constitution had thought of almost everything, the state was without a motto still. Ewing had suggested *ad astra per aspera,* "to the stars through difficulties," and was gratified when his suggestion was chosen. Tom Ewing was thirty-two years old and the chief justice of the newest state's supreme court. He was sworn into office on February 9, 1861. After the ceremony, flat broke, he left Leavenworth to attend the nation's final effort at intersectional reconciliation.[53]

Not all Southerners were eager to leave the Union, and not everyone north of Virginia wanted its preservation. A peace conference was called for early Febru-

51. TEJr. to Mills, January 19, 1861, TEJr./KSHS.

52. "Pusillanimous" from WTS to EES, January 8, 1861, in Mark DeWolfe Howe, *Home Letters of General Sherman,* 109, quoted in Fellman, *Citizen Sherman,* 79; "storm" from WTS to Gen. G. M. Graham, January 20, 1861, SFP/ND; "King cotton" from HBE to WTS, January 28, 1861, in Ewing, "Autobiography," 236; Bragg to WTS, January 28, 1861, in Marszalek, *Soldier's Passion,* 138.

53. Cannon vignette from Daniel R. Anthony, "Address To The Kansas Historical Society," 410; state motto from Ewing III, "Some Happenings Fifty Years Ago," 14.

ary at the Willard Hotel in Washington in hopes of holding the country together, for economic reasons if nothing else. Although couched in the words of political reconciliation, in large part this was a final effort by Northern capitalists to protect their investments in the South. Seven slave and fourteen free states sent representatives. Most of the representatives were moderates who had voted for Bell or Douglas not Lincoln or Breckinridge. Thomas Ewing Sr. was one of the Ohio representatives. Governor Charles Robinson was given the task of forming a Kansas delegation. Robinson suggested Tom Ewing as the delegation chair, but Ewing declined when he found out the delegation was mostly Democrats and would be under no compulsion to support Lincoln or the party's viewpoints. He planned to attend, but he also sensed the convention was a waste of time. Much of his time in Washington would be spent with his father and James Stone, discussing a transcontinental railroad bill with any congressmen who would listen.[54]

The convention began with high hopes. Since the delegates were not sent with instructions from their state legislatures, however, convention decisions were not binding. Republicans attending the conference could agree only to something Lincoln would approve. Thomas Ewing Sr. was frustrated by the "sickening sentimentalism" injected by abolitionists into the conference discussions. His rationale was curiously Southern. Slavery benefited the North, since that region was not ready for general emancipation and a slave kept in the South was one less family in the North seeking work with white workers. Lincoln himself held the view that slavery eventually would die in the South and right-minded Southerners would eventually liberate their slaves. The old Whig conceded that making concessions to slavery—especially financial concessions—might be impractical, but a measure of impracticality was preferred to war.[55]

At the same time as the peace convention, which ended in disarray, another more important convention was taking place in Montgomery. Alabama firebrand William Yancey introduced Mississippi senator Jefferson Davis, declaring, "The man and the hour have met!" and that "all who oppose the south will smell Southern gunpowder and feel Southern steel!" A new song, *Dixie,* was unleashed for the occasion, and the Confederacy was formed with Davis as its new president. In this

54. Ewing declines Kansas delegation chair from TEJr. to TESr., February 12, 1861, TEJr./KSHS.

55. Peace conference at Taylor, "Business and Political Career," 56, 159–61; "sentimentalism" from Lucius Eugene Chittenden, *Report of the Debates and Proceedings in the Secret Sessions of the Conference Convention, for Proposing Amendments to the Constitution of the United States, Held At Washington, D.C. In February, A.D. 1861,* 472–73.

new aristocracy there were no Republicans or Democrats, only factions that would either support or oppose Jefferson Davis's policies.[56]

Lincoln arrived for his March 1861 inaugural by a circular route, amid rumors of an assassination attempt. Pressed as to his intentions against hot blood states such as South Carolina, he was careful to convey he was not going to war with anyone unless someone made war on the federal government. He had a duty to protect federal property in the South. He let reporters observe him reading a book on how Andrew Jackson had handled the South Carolina nullification crisis.

The newly appointed senator from Ohio, John Sherman, made an appointment with the president immediately after the inaugural, one of those squeezed-in meetings that any incoming chief executive schedules during the hectic early days of a new government. Cump Sherman had returned to Ohio in late February. Henry Turner heard of his change of circumstances and offered Sherman a $200 per month job to run a St. Louis streetcar company. Sherman had stalled Turner and gone to Washington to visit with his brother and see if Lincoln had any offer worth considering. Lincoln chatted for a while, preoccupied with minor appointments, apparently unconcerned with Cump's information of war preparations in the South. War was not yet inevitable, the president insisted. Slavery was in a moral decline. Lincoln said he agreed with Charles Sumner, who was advising Lincoln that a few months of isolation and the "petulant children" would be humbled.[57]

Nothing came of this meeting with the president. There might or might not be a commission for Sherman. Even if there was, it was unclear as to what rank. Those were War Department issues, the domain of Simon Cameron. Cump Sherman was "mortified" at his visit. He quickly saw Lincoln had no administrative experience. He had been no captain of industry, no governor. Moreover, unlike Jefferson Davis, Lincoln had received no training in how best to move a brigade from point A to point B, or what to do with it once it arrived. Their meeting was the source of immense foreboding for Sherman. Afterward, Cump Sherman petulantly lectured John on the holocaust toward which the nation was marching, thanks to the politicians. How could Sherman serve in an army commanded by

56. "Man and the hour" from McPherson, *Battle Cry,* 259. Professors Herman Hattaway and Richard Beringer point out that Davis and his military advisors decided most Confederate policies and submitted decisions to the Confederate Congress only for approval. Herman Hattaway and Richard E. Beringer, *Jefferson Davis: Confederate President,* 39–40.

57. Shapiro, *Mystic Chords,* 38–39, 41–42; "petulant children" from Phillip S. Paludan, *The Presidency of Abraham Lincoln,* 28.

Lincoln? He told his family he intended to take Turner's streetcar presidency position in St. Louis. Ewingville was stunned by his decision. What kind of nonsense was going on in Washington that could run off West Pointers such as Sherman?[58]

John Sherman was just as frustrated by the meeting. There were cards he could play in all this, however. He was the new senator from Ohio, named to that position when Salmon Chase became Lincoln's secretary of the Treasury. John vowed to get Ohio governor William Dennison to appoint Cump the commander of the state's militia with a brigadier general's commission. Cump was intrigued with the idea but decided he would let John carry the water this time. He was tired of groveling to politicians. Besides, he had learned in California that turning militia into an army was a horrible task for any true military man, the equivalent of giving a starving man a bowl of ground glass. Sherman waited several weeks until the news came. It was not good. John Sherman's efforts had fizzled, and Dennison had appointed George McClellan to the militia command.[59]

After the presidential inaugural, the watering holes in Topeka began to fill with supporters, come to lobby their state representatives and senators on behalf of various candidates. Samuel Pomeroy rented a house and turned it into a free restaurant and bar for state legislators (ridiculed by his opponents as "Fort Sumptuous"). On March 26, 1861, the Kansas legislature convened its first session, handled a bit of work, and settled down to elect the first senators. Tom Ewing followed the meetings closely. He had worked behind the scenes for weeks, trying to circumvent Pomeroy's bid to be senator, primarily because he felt Pomeroy was weaker than Lane but also because of Pomeroy's ties with Cyrus Holliday's AT&SF railroad. There was also interest in seeing Lane defeated. Ewing's preference for a high federal position for Governor Charles Robinson, something he had worked on since before Lincoln's inaugural, "would go far to secure Lane's defeat." He had written his father two months before the senate elections that Robinson's position would be something that "can be used in his favor effectively with influential Republicans, but which I must use carefully if at all." As chief justice Ewing was trying to maintain "a position of armed neutrality between Lane and [Frederick P.] Stanton."[60]

58. Sherman, *Memoirs,* 1:162, 167–69; "mortified" from HBE to Charles Ewing, March 10, 1861, in Ewing, "Autobiography," 237.

59. Foote, *Civil War,* 1:59; Ewing, *Sherman at War,* 27, quoting Lloyd Lewis, *Sherman, Fighting Prophet,* 157–58.

60. Castel, *Frontier State,* 32–34; all quotes from TEJr. to TESr., January 20, 1861, TEJr./KSHS.

As a new state, the legislature had to elect both senators at the same time, but to staggered terms. Each state representative and senator cast two ballots simultaneously when the clerk called his name. At least, these were the anticipated rules. A Robinson supporter offered a resolution to vote on the senator who would come from south of the Kansas River and vote immediately, using independent votes of the house and senate. The Kansas senate, which had been elected in 1859, still included a majority of Robinson supporters. If the vote went in that manner and Lane was defeated in the senate, the Robinson men could argue that the only fair thing was that a senator must be someone popular enough with lawmakers to be individually elected in both chambers: Tom Ewing.

The gambit almost worked. Robinson's resolution was adopted and the senate voted 16–9 for Frederick P. Stanton over Lane. However, no vote was taken in the house. Pomeroy and Lane then joined forces and, after a day of politicking, persuaded the senate to back off its earlier rule and meet with the house in a joint session for a single vote for senator, where Lane only had to win a majority of the combined votes.

With this, the vote for senator fell into the disarray of a parliament with six parties. Each side jockeyed on the floor, making last-minute compromises on other issues in exchange for votes. Fifty-eight lawmakers changed their votes at least once. Several of them changed six times. Some 297 votes were cast in all, and the clerks were unable to keep an accurate tally. Pomeroy and Lane won both positions by narrow margins. Moderates moaned that Kansas had been delivered from slavemongers only to be given to radical abolitionists, one extremist group for another. George Brown, the editor of the *Kansas State Journal,* had the flag above his building lowered to half-mast. With Pomeroy's election Ewing's LP&W stock slid, and Cyrus Holliday's AT&SF railroad stock went to the head of the Kansas railroad class.[61]

While Kansas was basking in the organizational efforts of statehood, behind the scenes opposition was growing to the head start given to the LP&W railroad in the transcontinental sweepstakes. John Wright, an Indiana banker and railroad speculator who coveted the Indian lands for a competing railroad, hired John Usher, a real estate litigation specialist, to represent a group of the Delaware Indians wanting the treaty overturned. Usher informed congressmen that the Delawares had not been paid for their land as required under the May 30, 1860, treaty and if the government backed a bogus railroad effort by the LP&W, it would be per-

61. Castel, *Frontier State,* 32–34.

petrating a "nefarious fraud." If he could get the treaty rescinded, Wright's backers would begin their own line.[62]

Tom Ewing and James Stone got wind of Wright's efforts but did not panic. Usher was good, but Wright's weakness was his business arrangement with Usher, who took the assignment on a contingent fee from Wright equal to 25 percent of whatever value a reappraisal for Wright's interests might set above the earlier government estimate of value for the LP&W. Wright's efforts to increase the per-acre price of the land for a second railroad might make him popular with the Delaware tribal chiefs, but it would make it more difficult to sell the land to finance the railroad. Since making a railroad more difficult to finance was not in the government's interest, the Interior Department would be foolish to adopt Usher's recommendation. Ewing counseled patience, then let Stone convince Usher he was saddled with a contingent fee that would net him zero. Then Stone hired Usher to oversee the LP&W's efforts to rework the existing treaty, a classic example of buying one's way out of a problem. Although Wright could have sued Stone and the LP&W for interference with his contract with Usher, this was not the kind of contract that businessmen liked to see discussed in open court. When Usher defected, Wright's efforts collapsed.[63]

There was not an initial rush of new cases to the Kansas Supreme Court to review, so Tom was in Washington much of the spring of 1861 prepared to meet with anyone who could help with amendments to the Delaware treaty. Skeptics attacked the LP&W treaty adjustments, which made Lincoln nervous. The railroad was proposing acquisition of enormous tracts of Indian lands without paying anything for them. Unfavorable political publicity was the last thing the railroad—or Lincoln—needed. The president was an old railroad lawyer and knew how railroads were financed, including the reasons for the unusual new options. But what the railroad wanted was too rich for his blood. He needed cover. He suggested that if the Indians selling the right-of-way also preapproved the financing through government bonds, the sailing would be smoother. Further, the company could not patent the lands until they were paid for, another blow at unrestricted acquisition efforts.

Lincoln directed that the company give 6 percent of the bonds to Lincoln's friend, Kansas district judge Archibald Williams. A hundred thousand acres for which the LP&W paid nothing was put in a trust for the Indians, securing another 124,000 acres that the LP&W could sell at its leisure. Lincoln knew what

62. "Nefarious fraud" from Taylor, "Origins of the Kansas Pacific," 161.

63. Elmo Richardson and Alan Farley, *John Palmer Usher: Lincoln's Secretary of the Interior,* 15–16.

was happening, of course. It was a classic end-justifies-the-means political supposition. A transcontinental railroad, however procured, would spur emigration, expand the country westward, and improve the economy of the entire nation. Lincoln's party had campaigned on the issue.

On July 2, 1861, the amended treaty language was approved by the Republican-dominated Congress. Ewing was thrilled, since now the LP&W was more than a paper railroad. It had acquired a favored position among the roads being considered and now had enormous lands without paying anything, land it could mortgage for operating cash. If the tribe approved the changes, Ewing stood to make enough money to get out of debt. Having done the Ewings a favor with the railroad treaty, Lincoln opted to keep peace with Lane by appointing William P. Dole rather than Charles Robinson as Indian commissioner.[64]

On April 14, 1861, a rebel artillery barrage opened on the squat stone fort that dominated the harbor in Charleston, South Carolina. Within a few hours Fort Sumter was surrendered, falling also as a metaphor for the power of the federal government in the spring of 1861. The loss of life was minimal, but the nation's pride was seriously wounded. Congress was not in session, so Lincoln could not ask for a declaration of war. Using his stated constitutional powers to suppress a rebellion, he called for seventy-five thousand volunteers from all the states that had not seceded. "Companies were forming and there was great excitement," Hugh noted in his journal while in Ohio. The excitement carried over to the newest state too. The day after the fall of Sumter, Kansans from all walks of life, including state officials, volunteered for military duty. The American that de Tocqueville wrote "takes pride in the glory of his nation; he boasts of its success, to which he conceives himself to have contributed; and he rejoices in the general prosperity by which he profits" had watched his nation reach its ultimate schism.[65]

Leavenworth, the largest town in Kansas, at the war's beginning supported three newspapers, several hotels, a college, and a great number of saloons and brothels. As befit the town that was the terminus of overland trade with inner cities in Kansas, the town sponsored a great many early volunteers. Recruiting

64. The amended treaty from Taylor, "Origins of the Kansas Pacific," 162–63; Castel, *Frontier State,* 220; Taylor, "Business and Political Career," 119, 121; Abel, "Indian Reservations," 90; Lincoln's understandings from Howard G. Brownson, *History of the Illinois Central Railroad,* 4:301, 323.

65. Eldridge, *Early Days,* 167; Ewing, "Autobiography," 238; de Tocqueville, *Democracy in America,* bk. 1, ch. 5 (1840) on the Internet at <http://xroads.virginia.edu/~Hyper/detoc/1_ch05.htm> last accessed March 28, 2008.

grew into religious fervor. Out of an entire combined population of less than fifteen thousand, Lawrence and Leavenworth mustered sixteen infantry companies (a hundred men each) in the first ten days.[66]

Among the instant volunteers was Dan McCook who with a friend, Jim McGonigle, organized the Shields Guards, a militia company of Leavenworth men they had trained for over six months. The Guards were ready to go. In fact, the cocky McCook had tendered his sixty men to the War Department two months before Fort Sumter. He was indignant when he heard nothing in reply. War Department reticence before the firing on Fort Sumter left both Hugh Ewing and McCook unsure of their allegiances should war come. McCook had thought on it the most. "Everything seems dark to me. We are borne on a relentless overwhelming tide to anarchy." As usual he fell back on his classical education for inspiration. "My old army fever returns. But like Huns as they hovered upon the Danube menacing both Constantinople and Rome, I am hesitating against which empire to turn my 'weighty sword.' The tangled woof of wrong enwraps *both* causes. . . . Public sentiment is divided [in Leavenworth]. . . . I know not whether to support the Administration or oppose 'coercion.'" He had been educated in Alabama and had marital ties to the South. He preferred a Southern lifestyle, as did Julia. And the McCooks came from a long line of rebels—Dan's great grandfather had been one of the Whiskey Rebellion's ringleaders who fought the infant country's veteran army under George Washington. If he sided with the South he would be fighting his brothers, cousins, perhaps even his father. But rabid Douglas Democrats such as the McCooks also looked askance at fighting for a Republican president. That reticence was just fine with Julia, who preferred that Dan remain neutral. "[Julia] says if I go into it she will look upon it as a breach of one of the implied conditions of the contract. She says moreover that she discarded a captain in it for me and this she considers should settle the question conclusively against the army and in favor of the law."[67]

Fort Sumter changed everything. The whole country was arming, and Julia's concerns now were irrelevant. The commander of Fort Leavenworth's arsenal was concerned. Not only could Missourians be expected to obstruct military traffic on the river, he felt the fort's arsenal was in peril, since there were not enough reg-

66. Smith, *Trial by Fire,* 3; Castel, *Frontier State,* 8; "religious" nature of enlistments see Thomas C. Grey, "The Constitution as Scripture," 3.

67. The Shields Guards would become part of the First Kansas regiment, which would suffer enormous losses at the Battle of Wilson's Creek. See James A. McGonigle, "First Kansas Infantry in the Battle of Wilson's Creek," 292. Dan McCook's tendering of his militia company to government service at *O.R.* 3:1:63. McCook quotes are from Dan McCook to George McCook from Leavenworth, March 10, 1861, quoted in Whalen and Whalen, *Fighting McCooks,* 261.

ulars to protect its grounds from a determined attack. Until the regulars arrived from Fort Kearney in the Nebraska Territory, Kansas governor Charles Robinson sent three Leavenworth militia companies, including Dan McCook's Shields Guards, to assist the fort's commanding officer.[68]

Hugh Ewing faced a dilemma similar to that of McCook, for his wife also was from the plantation South and had many friends with Southern sympathies and pedigree. Apparently the South had a strange magnetic appeal for some men in Northern states—the concept of being part of a rebellion. However, like McCook, Hugh ultimately chose to serve the Union. The Ewing family had spent too much time getting a posting for Sherman to have Hugh go south to the Confederacy, even though some of Ri's brothers and cousins eventually would wear gray uniforms. Hugh convinced Henrietta that he had to stand with Ohio even if it meant disappointing his Maryland in-laws. Until something better was offered him, he wanted Governor Dennison to let him serve under McClellan as a captain in charge of drilling Home Guards at Camp Anderson, outside Cincinnati.[69]

Even after Fort Sumter fell, the lack of preparation in Washington left Tom Ewing apprehensive. He was in Washington when the war broke out. When Lincoln called for volunteers, Ewing felt the president had acted too precipitously. He wrote his father, "Your last advice to the President was, if he had to draw the sword, not to blow the trumpet first. He has [forgotten the advice] and as a consequence he can't get his sword out and is likely to lose his trumpet. And his only excuse to the country is that he has been so busy peddling high offices that he has not had time to save the nation." Modern Lincoln scholars indicate that a good many other than just Ewing felt the same way about their ambling indistinctive president in those first days, that he was a man unfit for the enormous new task. The regular army was in disarray, more than half its officers having gone over to the Confederacy, and Lincoln was depending on half-trained militia regiments to win the war. Tom had had long conversations with Cump Sherman, and he also was unconvinced the government was ready for this crisis if it had to rely on volunteer regiments. McCook might have great faith in the Shields Guards, but Tom disdainfully described another Leavenworth militia company to his brother Philemon as "Invincible in peace, invisible in war."[70]

68. For early requests for help at Leavenworth, see Harney to the War Department, *O.R.* 1:662, 667–68, 670, 677.

69. Ewing, "Autobiography," 238–39.

70. "Blow the trumpet" from TEJr. to TESr., April 24, 1861, unpublished letter, Joseph H. Ewing Collection (photocopy in possession of the author); "invisible in war" is TEJr. to Phil Ewing, January 25, 1861, TEJr./KSHS.

Indeed all the Union regiments seemed to be invisible. Only five regiments were in the Washington area, and only the Eighth Massachusetts—the first regiment to reach Washington—was decently trained. The rumor that a rebel army was marching on Washington to hang Lincoln from a tree began the strangest paramilitary organization of the war, the Frontier Guard. Claiming five or six organizers, including Jim Lane and "Judge" Daniel McCook, the Guardsmen numbered about sixty who had been recruited in the Willard Hotel to guard the White House, although the press reported the Guard's sentinels once arrested the building's chief occupant during a nocturnal presidential wandering of the White House corridors. Tom Ewing spent some time with the unit, but part of his days were spent working with congressmen on Robinson's abortive appointment and trying to find a military job for Cump Sherman.[71]

On the day Fort Sumter was bombarded, Cump Sherman was a fifty-dollar-a-month streetcar president in St. Louis. After Fort Sumter Sherman's star as an administrator had risen again. Every department was looking for quality administrators. Montgomery Blair asked if Cump would take a clerk position in the War Department until Blair had time to persuade Lincoln to appoint Sherman assistant secretary of war. Sherman did not want to be in Washington while his classmates were fighting this war; he had missed the Mexican War and he was not going to miss this one. However, he was not going to take a command opportunity that was less than what he felt he deserved. One persuasive angle Tom Ewing used with the War Department was that Louisiana was still trying to recruit Sherman to lead its forces; if Louisiana had that sort of faith in Sherman, why did not Abraham Lincoln's War Department? Sherman agreed with Ewing's approach. He wrote Tom that, while the family was "displeased with my apparent apathy" about the service, he did not care. Either he would be an officer at the level he deserved, or he would remain in St. Louis and run the streetcar company. There would be no compromise.[72]

The beginning of the war shattered what was left of the law firm of Ewing & McCook and what was left of their practice. Sherman had been gone a year—first to Louisiana and then back to Ohio, awaiting employment in the U.S. Army. Even though Tom Ewing was on the bench as chief justice, he still maintained a small

71. Frontier Guard at Ewing, "Autobiography," 237, and Castel, *Frontier State,* 34–35; sentinel from *Washington Evening Star,* April 19, 1861; job hunting from Marszalek, *Soldier's Passion,* 144.

72. Blair's recommendation from Sherman, *Memoirs,* 1:170–71; an example of letters enticing Sherman to serve the Confederacy was S. A. Smith to WTS, April 24, 1861, quoted in Ewing, *Sherman at War,* 26; "apparent apathy" from WTS to TEJr., April 26, 1861, EFP/LC, quoted in Fellman, *Citizen Sherman,* 88.

private practice, and Hugh continued with land sales while he prepared for a position among Ohio's regiments. Dan McCook was gone, readying himself for the coming conflict with his brothers, who had received West Point training and would soon be in the thick of it. Many of their debtors whom they looked to for payments on debt had gone into the ranks of the first Kansas regiments to muster in. The war would soon consume everything.

Ewing family patriarch, Whig senator and cabinet member to two presidents: Thomas Ewing Sr. Courtesy of the Library of Congress, LC-USZ62-43497.

Major General Hugh B. Ewing. Courtesy of the Library of Congress, LC-BH831-947.

Early Civil War photo of Thomas Ewing Jr., possibly late 1862.
Courtesy of the Kansas State Historical Society.

Ewing's most famous murder client and political nemesis: Kansas senator James H. Lane. Courtesy of the Kansas State Historical Society.

Early war photo of Colonel Daniel McCook Jr. William T. Sherman called McCook the "only true lawyer" in the Leavenworth firm. This photo is courtesy of the Library of Congress, LC-USZ62-104988.

Part Two

THEY'D AS SOON FIGHT THE DEVIL AS TO FIGHT KANSAS MEN

5

A WORLD WAS WATCHING

When Lincoln's first call went out to the states for seventy-five thousand troops to suppress the rebellion, the federal government had never before raised an army of that size for any military purpose, including its wars with Great Britain or Mexico. The costs, initially borne by the states, were staggering. The paperwork of mustering state regiments into federal service was monumental. In Ohio, Governor Dennison considered both Hugh Ewing and Cump Sherman as men who could provide organizational and inspirational value. Both were considered for posting with Ohio militia units.

Although Hugh was willing to start the war as an officer in an Ohio militia unit, Sherman was not. He had moved his family to St. Louis in preparation for Turner's streetcar job. John Hunter and Charles Ewing had formed a law partnership in St. Louis and were sharing rooms with Sherman at the time. At Secretary Simon Cameron's urging, Sherman was asked to provide the War Department with an assessment of Southern preparations as he had seen them when he came north before the war. Cump's assessment was pessimistic. The Confederacy was preparing for a long war. Ohio historian Henry Howe indicates that, during this hiatus between Sherman's initial conversation with Lincoln and this overture by Cameron, Sherman wrote Cameron, "You might as well undertake to extinguish the flames of a building with a squirt-gun as to put down this rebellion with three months troops." A "gigantic war" that would "call out the whole military power of the country" was the nation's future. Sherman put in another plug for himself, offering to serve as a colonel or higher rank, but only so long as the post was attached to a three-year commission in the regular army so that "an officer can prepare his command and do good service." Coming from a former captain with no combat experience such a demand was somewhat cheeky, but his predictions were accurate. Cameron ignored Sherman's initial request.[1]

Missouri had remained neutral when the states were choosing sides. It would soon be a battleground coveted by both armies. Jefferson Davis had sent muskets to assist pro-Confederate Missouri militia in St. Louis. On May 10, 1861, Union troops forced the Missouri militia to surrender at Camp Jackson. Hugh, Cump, Sherman's son Willie, Charles Ewing, and John Hunter were part of the large crowd that came out to watch the captured Missouri militia be marched off to a federal camp where they would be paroled. The decidedly pro-Southern crowd continued to grow and taunt the Union guards. A drunk fired a wild shot and hit a federal officer in the leg. The untrained federal volunteers brought their muskets to their shoulders and returned fire indiscriminately in several directions. Charles Ewing threw Willie Sherman into a ditch, and he and Cump covered him as Hunter and Hugh Ewing sprinted away from the line of fire. The ominous whack of lead on bone raged above them. A woman and her child fell near where Sherman crouched, two of the twenty-eight civilian dead among scores of wounded. The ugliness of what would become the border war in Missouri was brewing. At Wilson's Creek later that summer, more men died per number of men engaged than in any subsequent battle. The First Kansas lost 284 of 644 engaged. Shelby Foote described Wilson's Creek as "a reciprocal form of murder."[2]

Tom Ewing kept working on Montgomery Blair to make inroads in Cameron's War Department for Sherman. Four days after the St. Louis riot, Sherman received a telegram of his commission as a colonel in the new Thirteenth regiment of regulars. Sherman was thrilled with the offer, although obsequiously telling friends that if he had given away his pride and answered Lincoln's first call he would have been a major general. The colonelcy was "as much as I could ask for," he wrote Tom, thanking him for his assistance. Ellen was sent back to Lancaster, and the family was instructed to "trust to the fate of war." On the same day Sherman was commissioned, orders came for Hugh Ewing to report to the Third

1. "Squirt-gun" from Henry Howe, *Historical Collections of Ohio,* 596; "do good service" from WTS to Cameron, May 8, 1861, in Sherman, *Memoirs,* 1:171–72.

2. Sherman, *Memoirs,* 1:169, 173–74; Ewing, "Autobiography," 239; "reciprocal murder" from Foote, *Civil War,* 1:94.

brigade of the Ohio militia at Camp Dennison as a brigade inspector with the rank of major.[3]

Northern drill depots were less cordial to officers with slaves, but Camp Dennison, nestled in a small range of hills, was comfort enough for new majors such as Hugh Ewing. He soon disliked sleeping in a tent and found lodging near Cincinnati in a room provided by a wealthy farmer. Other officers at Camp Dennison at that time were William Rosecrans and George McClellan. Ewing knew Rosecrans from their West Point days, but McClellan was younger, and although Hugh had had prewar dealings with him it was during this time that Hugh got to know the reserved and tactful McClellan well. In the early regiments, the officers were elected by the men, and many stiffened their popularity by letting the privates shirk guard duty. West Pointers such as Hugh spent much their time instilling in the volunteers the importance of duty. Hugh noted in his journal that the German regiments, especially those whose ranks were filled with veterans of European armies, drilled the best, but few regiments in those early days had the snap and polish of regulars.[4]

Even before Sherman's arrival in Washington to receive his colonelcy, Tom Ewing was putting out fires with Cameron and General Winfield Scott. He was still promoting a brigadier's star for Cump but then found out why Sherman was a colonel while former soldiers with lesser achievements were being elevated. The cabinet had its doubts as to whether Sherman was "sufficiently sympathetic with the government" to be promoted to general. Sherman confirmed the administration's concerns in a letter to Tom when he wrote that "the constitution has given [slave] owners certain rights which I should be loath to disturb." When Cump arrived in Washington, he found the Thirteenth regiment of regulars was a paper regiment—someone else was still recruiting the unit. Sherman found a hotel room, hung around the War Department, and awaited an assignment. Even with nothing to do, he was back in the army, and it felt good.[5]

While Washington prepared its bureaucracy and counted its soldiers, and while Ohio organized, in Kansas a new state government saw its young taxpayers rush off to war and its tax coffers remain largely empty. Kansas was immediately sad-

3. "As much as" from WTS to TEJr., May 23, 1861, EFP/LC; "trust to the fate of war" from Sherman, *Memoirs,* 1:175.

4. Ewing, "Autobiography," 240, dated May 20, 1861.

5. TEJr. to TESr., May 22, 1861, unpublished letter, Joseph H. Ewing Collection (photocopy in possession of the author); "loath to disturb" from WTS to TEJr., May 23, 1861, EFP/LC; Sherman, *Memoirs,* 1:177.

dled with the costs of funding its own quota of regiments, and every available tax dollar was spent for military purposes. While Tom Ewing had convinced the federal government to get involved in financing railroads, in 1861 he was begging New York bankers to buy Kansas bonds so he could purchase law books for a supreme court library. There was no capitol building in Topeka, no government offices, no court or library. Many of the first books for the library were kept in the homes of the court clerks.

In the hiatus between Fort Sumter and the first winter of the war, in September 1861 the LP&W railroad hired John Usher and Saunders Johnston to take the new treaty amendments in the federal legislation and obtain treaty ratification with the Delaware and Pottawatomie tribes. If the optimists were right and it would be a short war, then Ewing wanted his railroad positioned to move quickly on the transcontinental project. The new treaty was Tom Ewing's roadway to a fortune and away from the embarrassment brought him by his idle landholdings in Kansas. He was upbeat about the prospects. Both Usher and Johnston were experienced men, and if they did their job well the railroad would stretch from Leavenworth to Fort Riley within two years. The freight hauling between Fort Leavenworth and Fort Riley and towns along the route would pay for itself in only a few years. One of Tom Ewing's shortcomings was that rampant optimism so common to entrepreneurs. While the line to Fort Riley would indeed be an important segment, at that rate of development, the road would take the better part of two decades to go from Leavenworth to California. However, entrepreneurs also believe that success breeds more success. If the first part of the railroad was successful quickly, then it would attract more money for building the remainder of the line. Ewing spent the fall of 1861 writing his creditors with the now familiar litany of needing more time to pay the interest on his notes.[6]

Governor Charles Robinson had good reason to wonder where the chief justice might be in any fight over railroad or government policy. The governor did not trust the Kansas senior senator in Washington. The LP&W treaty with the Delaware had to have Jim Lane's assistance, and with Ewing's having defended Lane in the Gaius Jenkins matter, Robinson was suspicious of Ewing. On the other hand Lane trusted nobody. Ewing's railroad had previously added Robinson and Robinson's friend Robert Stevens to the board of directors. When Usher and Johnston got to Washington and met with Lane, Lane's terms for approving changes in the treaty were that the railroad had to dump Robinson and Stevens from the board and replace them with Lane's friends Josiah Miller and Chester

6. Hiring Usher and Johnston from Taylor, "Business and Political Career," 122.

Thomas. In this way Lane would have a direct pipeline into the road's building decisions. Lane also wanted a section of railroad land for someone to be named later and to select twenty-two hundred acres of Delaware land for himself. The railroad could hardly refuse this solicitation. There were too many other railroads that would leap into the void if the LP&W did not play ball. By December 20, 1861, the board changes were made and Ewing's break with Robinson was public and complete. Later in life Ewing would attempt to reestablish their friendship, but in late 1861 Ewing and Robinson were enemies.

Robinson tested how far the falling-out had gone when he sent George Brown to Ewing to see if Robinson could continue to own an option on railroad land. Ewing told Brown that Robinson was not entitled to any option until the Pottawatomie treaty was ratified. As part of the bargain Robinson was to help the railroad whenever it sought help. Rumors had arisen that Robert Stevens would try to scuttle the Pottawatomie treaty because he had been dumped from the board. Ewing told Brown that, if Stevens fought the treaty, it would be hard to believe Robinson was not involved. If this happened, the land on which Stevens and Robinson had options to buy would be forfeited. Brown was enraged that anyone would question Robinson's good faith. Ewing reported to fellow investor James Stone "unjust suspicion was the penalty honest men paid when they slept with thieves," a dagger thrust at Robinson's partnership with Stevens. Robinson was furious at being cut out, but Lane held all the trump cards. The railroad either dealt with Lane or watched its road die.[7]

In early November fellow LP&W stockholder James Stone convinced the Pottawatomie chiefs to sign a deal similar to the Delaware treaty. The tribe selected 80-acre tracts, but the remainder of the 340,000 acres would be sold to the railroad for $1.25 per acre. The St. Mary's Catholic Mission and Baptist Board of Missions were granted 320 acres each for their schools and churches in return for their support among the Pottawatomie. Ewing was pleased with the terms, which allowed the railroad to postpone its first payments on the land until three years after ratification of the full treaty. But investment funds remained scarce.

The railroad tried to obtain additional funds from selling land on the right-of-way to settlers, but news of the drought had gone nationwide, and it kept outside interest in Kansas at a minimum. Some speculators offered to buy some land if the railroad guaranteed their investment. Others wanted a premium, buying the land for about $1.00 an acre for which the railroad would pay $1.20. There were

7. Castel, *Frontier State,* 220; Taylor, "Origins of the Kansas Pacific," 166–67; "penalty honest men paid" from TEJr. to James Stone, December 20, 1861, TEJr./KSHS.

signs that Ewing had similar concerns. He asked Hamp Denman to write Caleb Smith, the secretary of the Interior, to inquire about the "relative risk" of having to forfeit any land he purchased from the railroad if the road later went bankrupt. He also asked Usher to contact Caleb Smith requesting the same information, in order to check if the answers were similar.[8]

Ewing's frustration shows the nearly impossible task of trying to raise venture capital in the middle of a war. His financial woes were exacerbated when he took a fall in a gully behind his neighbor's house, which left his knee badly swollen. The injury forced him to postpone a trip to Washington to meet with Fant and other bankers. Further, Ellen Sherman was still carping about the minor amount McCook had applied on taxes at Cump's direction. It perturbed Tom greatly that his sister expected him to reimburse to her a $30 tax debt when he could not get financing for a major link in a transcontinental railroad.[9]

The first session of Ewing's Kansas Supreme Court began on November 28, 1861. The days just prior to the opening session were spent selecting clerks and reporters of cases, adopting rules, and admitting to practice the few attorneys who had cases ready for consideration by the high court. Many of the counties of modern Kansas were yet to be incorporated, and appeals had yet to move through the system. For the first time since coming to Kansas, Ewing was paid a salary, in scrip, worth only 60 percent of the arbitrary greenback rate. He spent much of his time working on the financing of the LP&W from his Leavenworth office while handling the claims of private clients in the lower courts, a conflict of interest that would not be allowed in a modern judiciary.[10]

There remained a lot to do before construction began on the railroad. Lane had gotten into the deal by Ewing's direct involvement. Now Samuel Pomeroy let it be known he wanted "neutralized" too, something Ewing could not ignore. He wrote, reluctantly, "If you desire *anything* done for any of *your* friends in connection with the Leavenworth, Pawnee and Western Company or road, please advise me and your wishes will be complied with as fully as practicable." To John Usher, Ewing let it be known that the Pottawatomie treaty had to be in front of the Senate immediately at their December session, and the provisions enacted before Christmas. He wrote Usher that Pomeroy should be "friendly" by then. Ewing as-

8. TEJr. to Usher, November 9, 12, to Denman, November 12, 1861, all TEJr./KSHS.

9. The flap with Ellen and McCook in TEJr. to TESr., November 12, 1861, TEJr./KSHS; Taylor, "Origins of the Kansas Pacific," 162.

10. TEJr. to Major Kinsey, to Robert Campbell, to John Usher, all October 24, 1861, TEJr./KSHS; clerks and rules from Miller, "Thomas Ewing Jr.," 20.

sumed that Pomeroy's neutralization regarding the LP&W meant the senator's ties with Cyrus Holliday and the Atchison railroad group would be neutralized too. "You cannot give too much weight to this suggestion," Ewing instructed Usher.[11]

Ewing used direct persuasion on one of Pomeroy's friends, Junction City newspaper editor Robert McBratney, inquiring what routes the LP&W should take through his area and asking him to get Pomeroy to support the Pottawatomie treaty. Obviously McBratney, if he owned any land nearby, would suggest the road go through his property, which would indirectly increase his own wealth. Any help McBratney could give would be "appreciated and reciprocated" by the company. There was also evidence that Willis Gaylord, Pomeroy's brother-in-law, was given shares in return for his influence. Whether any of the stock or any railroad land ever found its way to Pomeroy is unknown, but clearly the letters acknowledge the fact that a senator's own political organizations were as important to politicians as any political party.[12]

On February 5, 1862, Missouri congressman James Rollins introduced the LP&W's treaty bill in the House. Pomeroy introduced a similar bill in the Senate. With Usher and Johnston working the bill, the treaty went through in April 1862, but construction on the railroad would not begin until November, near present-day Kansas City. With two others, Ewing now owned twenty-six thousand acres of the Indian lands north and east of Topeka. In nine months the railroad had spent $50,000 and had one graded mile to its ledger. The railroad was bankrupt, and everyone knew it. His railroad investments were pinching him hard. While Ewing would remain a director for a while longer, as happened with many railroads of the time a new group of investors would have to inject cash in the railroad to keep the dream alive.[13]

The Lane-Robinson feud ran deeper than just the matter of a seat on the board of directors of a Leavenworth railroad, and this animus directly affected Tom Ewing's career as chief justice. Lane wanted a brigadier's commission and command in the district of Kansas, but a U.S. senator could not serve on active duty in the military. Lane wanted military glory but was loath to relinquish his Senate seat. If he commanded in Kansas, he would steer government contracts to his sup-

11. TEJr. to Pomeroy, November 8, and to Usher, November 19, 1861, TEJr./KSHS.

12. TEJr. to McBratney, November 27, December 27, 1861, TEJr./KSHS. Castel believes the McBratney letters are evidence a bribe was being engineered with Pomeroy. See Castel, *Frontier State,* 221. What Pomeroy was doing was extortion.

13. Ewing's land from G. Raymond Gaeddert, *The Birth of Kansas,* 114; Richardson and Farley, *John Palmer Usher,* 17.

porters, and he did not want Robinson nosing around. Lane pulled Ewing further from Robinson's political orbit by hinting that someone Lane could trust would have to go to the Senate if Lane were commissioned, a suggestion Lane knew Ewing could not ignore.[14]

Lane feared Robinson's political organization. The main gubernatorial power with the army was the naming of the officers of state regiments. Arguing that a special crisis called for special rules, Lane went to Washington and finagled a special appointment from the War Department for himself to raise the Kansas regiments while still a senator and that he, not the governor, would name the new regimental officers. Robinson fought back. If Lane was a commissioned officer capable of raising regiments, then he was no longer a senator. When Lane came to Kansas to recruit, Robinson declared Lane's seat vacant and appointed Frederick Stanton as the interim senator while the legislature considered a new position. Lane rushed back to Washington to persuade judiciary committee members that Robinson was playing politics and to postpone a decision on the vacancy since he had not really accepted a posting of brigadier general of the provisional Kansas brigade (even though in fact he had).[15]

Lane then retaliated by getting the new legislature to charge Robinson with participating in a bond scandal, and impeachment was ordered. The effort was so orchestrated by Lane that the trial in the senate began in early February 1862 with little defense preparation. Ewing as chief justice presided over the trial. Auditor George Hillyer was convicted and removed from office. The Robinson-dominated senate acquitted Robinson by a vote 18–2, but his reputation was permanently damaged, however.[16]

In addition to efforts to impeach Robinson, Lane got the Republican Party to call for a statewide election in November 1861 to elect a new governor and legislature. Lane's allies declared Robinson's two-year term was up in January 1862, only a year after statehood but two years after Robinson was elected under the Wyandotte Constitution's initial elections clause. George Crawford was Lane's gubernatorial nominee to replace Robinson. Robinson and the existing executive branch officers ignored the election and Crawford won unopposed. Robinson refused to vacate the governor's office, and Lane's allies filed a mandamus with the Kansas Supreme Court to get the board of state canvassers to declare the office to

14. Castel, *Frontier State,* 77–78.

15. Rowland, "Reluctant Chief Justice," 31; Davis, *Bicentennial History,* 81; Lane authority to recruit, *O.R.* 3:2:444; see also T. J. Anderson, *Report Of The Adjutant General Of The State Of Kansas, 1861–1865,* 198.

16. Castel, *Frontier State,* 70–77.

be Crawford's. The key to this action was Tom Ewing. Lane had so snookered the situation that Robinson's legal fate was Lane's litmus test of Ewing's loyalty to Lane.

The mandamus was heard directly at the supreme court, not having to go through the lower courts first. Ewing wrote the opinion in *Crawford v. Robinson* within three days of the oral arguments. This case, the first important interpretation of the Wyandotte Constitution, denied Crawford's claims and Lane's writ. Instead, Ewing validated the powers of a duly constituted state government, gave the new constitution judicial approval, and established Ewing's reputation as being fair and impartial—at least in the eyes of surprised Robinson supporters. Had Ewing adopted Crawford's reasoning, then the lower house of the 1861 legislature would have had its terms end in November 1861 also, and the dozens of laws it had enacted since the 1859 election would have had no legal existence—including its appointment of Lane as a U.S. senator. The opinion strongly promoted less judicial involvement in political matters. However, the *Crawford* decision poleaxed Lane. Afterward, he was observed outside Ewing's office in the snow, poking fingers at Ewing's buttonholes, trying to convince the chief justice to change his mind. Ewing held firm. Lane's support for any future Ewing senate candidacy evaporated. In his first case as chief justice, Ewing dealt a self-inflicted blow to his own ambition. But he felt he was right on the law.[17]

The other cases heard in Ewing's court and where he authored the opinion during that first winter and spring after statehood had little to do with the war and were mundane in their holdings. One tested as to whether two laws enacted by a legislature with conflicting statutes of limitation were to be construed together or separately. Another reined in a district judge who kept referring to the defendant as "this murderer" as a violation of due process. A third defined the contours of appellate practice. A fourth, *State ex rel Ross v. Robinson,* was a squabble over who had the right to a state printing contract. Edmund Ross, a future Ewing ally, was the winning litigant as Ewing finished his term as chief justice.[18]

Although he was chief justice for less than a year, Ewing's court worked well. As he tracked the war news, he was the only former partner of his law firm not in the war. Sherman was in Tennessee with Grant. Young Dan McCook—with no

17. *State ex rel George Crawford v. Charles Robinson,* 1 Kan. 17 (1862); Castel, *Frontier State,* 70; Robinson's worry about Ewing from Rowland, "Reluctant Chief Justice," 31; Connelley, *Preston B. Plumb,* 91; "buttonholes" from *White Cloud Chief,* January 22, 1862.

18. *Elliott v. Lochnane,* 1 Kan. 125 (1862). *Horne v. State of Kansas,* 1 Kan. 47 (1862); *State v. Hitchcock,* 1 Kan. 173 (1862); *Gallaher v. Southwood,* 1 Kan. 141 (1862); *McCracken v. Todd,* 1 Kan. 146 (1862); *State ex rel Ross v. Robinson,* 1 Kan. 182 (1862).

more military training than Tom Ewing—occupied a staff position with the division of his brother Alexander McDowell McCook in the Army of the Ohio, Dan having pompously announced he would win either a general's star in the war or a soldier's grave. Hugh was going to be in the western Virginia mountains with his own regiment under Rosecrans. Tom's brooding and introspective style meshed well with the other court members, but he frankly was bored. Later Chief Justice Robert Miller described Ewing as a "strict constructionist" and thought that, had Ewing wanted a long judicial career, he could have had it, perhaps even a federal appointment under Lincoln. As the first winter of war gave way to the spring of 1862, the political career Ewing wanted in Kansas was not as chief justice. Ewing wrote his wife that the war was "between two systems of civilization for the mastery of the continent" and must be "settled by the sword." He would have to risk something in order to solidify his future in politics. That "something" turned out to be risking his life.[19]

While new commands fell on Sherman, even after his unspectacular start as a brigade commander at Bull Run, Hugh Ewing had to push a bit harder. After several frustrating weeks under Charles Schleich's thumb, on August 7, 1861, Hugh asked relatives and friends Wager Swayne, John Hunter, and George McCook to call on the governor of Ohio and plead for a regiment of his own. Ohio was rapidly churning out new regiments, and on August 15, Hugh was commissioned colonel of the Thirtieth Ohio volunteers, reporting for duty at Camp Chase, just outside Columbus. He was met there by Lieutenant Colonel Theodore Jones, the regiment's second in command, who had actually raised the Thirtieth. The new colonel with political connections and the son of a famous Whig senator raised some eyebrows when he brought his former slave, Black Ike, to the regimental headquarters. Hugh Ewing had just enough time to sew silver eagles onto his shoulder boards when the Thirtieth Ohio received orders for western Virginia. Brigadier General William Rosecrans was forming an army of occupation for a region of small unit actions commanded by the "Bully Dutchman," as Rosecrans was known.[20]

The terrain of western Virginia did not lend itself to movement and maneuver. Without local guides, whole divisions could get lost in the forests and mountains. Confederate generals John Floyd and Henry Wise commanded small rebel forces

19. Ewing's tenure on the court from Miller, "Thomas Ewing Jr.," 10–11; Richmond, *Requisite Learning,* 81; McCook's boast from Prentice to Whitelaw Reid in Reid, *Great Rebellion,* 2:904–5; "settled by the sword" from Castel, *Whirlwind,* 38.

20. Davis, *Bicentennial History,* 80; Ewing, "Autobiography," 243.

in the area and had no real means to defend the sprawling Kanawha Valley. At Birch Mountain, Rosecrans attacked Confederate entrenchments, the first action for the Thirtieth Ohio. Some of Hugh's men were "too sick" to fight. Others, even officers, retired at the first sounds of battle. One colonel who had reportedly shunned fire in a recent skirmish was determined to be brave. He stood behind his line of battle, mounted on horseback, until a rebel sharpshooter put a bullet in his forehead. "We fought until dark," Ewing wrote, "[b]ut did not succeed in forcing the entrenchments. It was . . . a grand scene. The men moved back, worn and dull and the dead and wounded were carried back." The rebels fled their entrenchments that night. The few dozen dead men were the first war casualties Hugh had ever seen. But nothing strategic was happening in the western Virginia theater.[21]

The boredom they suffered in western Virginia fostered long discussions among the idle officers, who all came from differing political and intellectual backgrounds. Hugh had brought along his black servant, Ike, whom he outfitted grotesquely in a white turban and rifle, making the regimental headquarters resemble a French Foreign Legion post. Their discussions and topics were far-ranging, yet when Ewing and other officers began discussing the merits of slavery, Hugh changed the political views he had taken with him to Charleston in 1860. He no longer thought Kansas-Nebraska was good policy for Democrats or Republicans. Slavery was not something to be viewed in the abstract anymore. The South had grown complacent and greedy. Slavery could no longer be merely tolerated. It had to change. Emancipation should be gradual and tied to the "Christianization" of blacks. When he put the gist of these conversations in letters back home, he realized his views would not be popular with his father and his father-in-law. His political views outpaced even the president's. "We generally think [here] that the Union can be restored only by abolition." To his father he wrote, poetically, "I am sorry to hold an opinion adverse to one held by you, still I cannot help feeling it is our destiny and policy to carry the war into Africa."[22]

The Thirtieth Ohio spent the autumn on garrison duty near Little Sewell Mountain, where Ewing's legal background allowed Rosecrans to appoint his former pupil as the command's senior courts-martial officer. While most such assignments were routine, the trial of Confederate colonel James W. Spaulding of the Sixtieth Virginia was not. While visiting family in the Union-controlled area,

21. *O.R.* 5:128–32, 145–46; J. A. Palmer to Folks at Home, December 30, 1861, in Lester L. Kempfer, *The Salem Light Guard, Company G, 36th Regiment Ohio Volunteer Infantry, Marietta, Ohio, 1861–1865,* 36; Ewing, "Autobiography," 245.

22. HBE to TESr., November 12, 1861, EFP/LC, quoted in Taylor, "Business and Political Career," 172.

Spaulding was captured in civilian clothing and was charged with spying. Hugh's court-martial found him guilty and sentenced him to be executed, but everyone assumed Washington would overturn the sentence as there was no indication Spaulding was actually obtaining important information for the Confederacy. When no clemency came down, Rosecrans was ordered to proceed with the execution. The inability of the court-martial board to obtain clemency for Spaulding angered Major Rutherford Hayes of the Twenty-Third Ohio, who commanded a sister regiment with Ewing. Before he was shot Spaulding left pictures of his wife and children with Ewing to return to Spaulding's family. On October 31, 1861, his thirty-fifth birthday not long after Spaulding's execution, the waste of watching a man die for such a small indiscretion weighed heavy on Hugh Ewing. He spent his birthday brooding in a tent, writing notes in his journal. Most of his men were sick of the dark mountains of western Virginia, and so was Hugh. "I dreamed that Tom and Charley were killed by the enemy and lying in a room with others, covered with a cloak."[23]

While Sherman's candid thoughts had been sought out by the War Department prior to the war, now that he was back in uniform he learned the hard way that others did not want or appreciate his bluntness. In mid-August 1861 Sherman was appointed as General Robert Anderson's deputy and sent with Anderson to Kentucky to organize the Department of the Cumberland and keep Kentucky in the Union. In early October, Anderson abruptly resigned from the army, citing mental fatigue as the reason. Sherman was named department commander. His first message to Washington advised that he would need sixty thousand men to hold Kentucky and two hundred thousand if he was ordered to invade Tennessee and put down the rebellion in the West. He wrote similar pessimistic letters to his brother and his father-in-law. "My force is too small to do good, and too large to sacrifice." Incredulous at these numbers, Secretary Cameron came out to Louisville to discuss the issue with Sherman. He brought along Simon Wilkerson, a *New York Tribune* reporter who later blindsided Sherman with an article making Sherman out to be loony.[24]

On November 8, 1861, racked by fatigue from twenty-hour days and a poor diet, Sherman's body rebelled. A captain on Sherman's staff telegraphed Ellen to

23. Ewing, "Autobiography," 249.

24. Marszalek, *Soldier's Passion,* 160–61; Fellman, *Citizen Sherman,* 93–94; WTS to TESr., September 30, to John Sherman, October 5, 1861, quoted in Ewing, *Sherman at War,* 34; "too large to sacrifice" from Sherman, *Memoirs,* 1:209; Wilkerson's article was in the *New York Tribune,* October 30, 1861.

come relieve General Sherman of the "pressures of business" although there was "no occasion for alarm." Ellen and her father rushed immediately to Louisville's Galt House with good reason for alarm. Few in the army knew of Cump's bouts with depression (Charles Sherman also suffered from melancholia). Cump had endured depression when Turner's San Francisco bank failed, and he reached rock bottom when he exiled himself in Kansas. The mess in Kentucky had so troubled him that again he thought of suicide, but he told John the thought of Willie and the children stopped him.[25]

In the nineteenth century, depression was considered a character flaw not an illness. Depression was common in the army, especially in remote assignments. Many soldiers fought it with liquor. The Ohio Ewings were supportive of Cump, and this made all the difference in Cump's reaction to the challenge. However, the political pulls on John Sherman were strong. When Ellen asked John to speak out against those in Washington who were making rumors about his brother's illness, he declined. John prided himself on his contacts in the War Department, and they said Cump was wrong on the crisis in Kentucky and was laboring under delusions. It is odd that John preferred to believe his political friends rather than his brother, especially knowing that melancholia ran in the family. Before going to Louisville, John wrote a curiously uncaring letter: "Your mind casts a somber shadow on everything. Your manner is abrupt and almost repulsive, so unlike your usual manner." Somehow, Cump had to snap out of it.[26]

Sherman's salvation came in the form of his old California friend Henry W. Halleck, who was sent to Missouri to replace Fremont. A balding forty-seven-year-old soldier, Phi Beta Kappa scholar, and lawyer whose distracting walleye gave him a comical look, "Old Brains" Halleck had made a fortune in a law practice. He took Sherman to Missouri with him, hoping the change of scenery would do his old friend good. Upon Sherman's arrival, in a letter to Phil Ewing, Halleck noted his ill health but passed it off to long hours and "continuous excitement and responsibility." Sherman relapsed, and Halleck decided Sherman did indeed need more rest, but he explained to Phil Ewing that Sherman should not let "these squibs" trouble him. To McClellan, on the other hand, Halleck wrote that Sherman was "physically and mentally broken by duty."[27]

25. The gist of the captain's telegram is in EES to John Sherman, November 10, 1861, SFP/LC; the pressure Sherman was under in Marszalek, *Soldier's Passion,* 163; suicide contemplated in WTS to John Sherman, January 2, 1862, in Fellman, *Citizen Sherman,* 107.

26. John Sherman to WTS, November 17, 1861, SFP/ND.

27. Halleck to Phil Ewing, December 18, 1861, *O.R.* 8:441–42; Halleck to McClellan, at *O.R.* 8:389–90.

Relaxing in Lancaster was foreign to Sherman's nature. He spent hours poring over different newspapers for war news. The *Cincinnati Commercial*'s headline of December 11, 1861, ended his tranquility, its headlines shrieking, "General William T. Sherman Insane!" The *Commercial*'s attack was even more damning since publisher Murat Halstead was Sherman's cousin. Sherman's foster family again became an abatis against further attacks. Phil Ewing fired off letters to Cump's friends Halleck and Buell to help the family blunt the criticism. Hugh and Thomas Ewing suggested a libel suit, but John Sherman, perhaps trying to find solid ground in some embarrassing family quicksand, urged the Ewings not make more out of the stories than was there. Halstead later was apologetic for his newspaper's part in the whole affair, after some dutch-uncle work by Philemon Ewing. It was John Sherman who met with the only man who counted—the commander in chief—and asked whether Lincoln had lost confidence in Sherman. Lincoln was noncommittal.[28]

Two days after the damning headline, the *Commercial* published Phil Ewing's letter rebuttal denying all the charges. At the prodding of the family, Halleck also published a friendly letter through Phil Ewing. "Those who saw [Sherman in St. Louis] may have drawn wrong inferences from his broken-down appearance and rather imprudent remarks." Sherman merely needed a rest, not institutionalization. Ellen was not sure this was enough. She laid the conspiracy at General John Pope's feet when she saw an article praising Pope in the same edition of the *Commercial* that had blackened her husband's name.[29]

On January 7, 1862, Sherman returned to duty in St. Louis, still plagued by a sense of failure. Halleck assigned him to duty at the training barracks. His spirits plummeted. The only difference between him and a drill sergeant was that he wore a star. He broke down and asked Ellen to redouble her efforts to see the president and urge him to intercede with the War Department for a better assignment. She traveled to Washington with her father and kept an appointment with Lincoln on January 29. Lincoln put her at ease, and she promptly launched into her army-Pope-conspiracy theory. Lincoln said little. Ellen was beginning to sound like Jessie Benton Fremont in the impassioned meetings with Lincoln on behalf of her husband. Lincoln told Ellen he had high regard for Cump and he was not about to cashier good officers on the myopia of newspaper editors.[30]

28. The entire "Sherman Insane" matter in the Ohio press is covered in Marszalek, *Soldier's Passion*, 163–66;

29. Castel, *Whirlwind*, 41. For the exchange of letters for this period, see Sherman, *Memoirs*, 1:216–18; Fellman, *Citizen Sherman*, 133; Phil Ewing to Murat Halstead, December 12, 1861, *Cincinnati Commercial*, quoted in Ewing, *Sherman at War*, 44–45; Halleck to Phil Ewing, December 18, 1861, *O.R.* 8:441–42; "conspiracy" from EES to WTS, December 19, 1861, EFP/ND.

30. Fellman, *Citizen Sherman*, 105.

On February 8, 1862, Halleck telegraphed McClellan that, due to the restructuring of western commands, he wanted to give Sherman one of the open division commands in the force Grant was making ready at Paducah, Kentucky. "His health has greatly improved," Halleck noted. After the battles for Forts Henry and Donelson, Major General Ulysses "Sam" Grant landed his troops at Pittsburg Landing, further up the Tennessee River toward Nashville, and slowly closed in on Corinth, Mississippi. The city's rail network fed Vicksburg, the ultimate prize of the campaign. Sherman was ecstatic and quickly telegraphed the news home. When he learned Ellen was continuing to warn Washington officials to watch McClellan, who was a Confederate spy, her home-front effort was the last thing Cump needed. Cump did not have the time to deal directly with Ellen's conspiracy theories and he dared not order her to stop her letters, but he asked an aide to write Tom to ensure quietly that her letters were intercepted before someone important read them.[31]

At Shiloh, American history was changed dramatically. Two of the four Leavenworth Kansas law partners were present on the rainy field. On the night of April 5, 1862, patchy clouds raced across the face of the moon. Then clouds covered the night sky and the sound of the rain on tent canvas was all the Union men heard. In the woods to the southwest, however, beyond the Pittsburg and Corinth roads, rebel skirmishers had turned into regiments and brigades, then divisions, forming as quietly as Major General Albert Sidney Johnston could coax them to do. As Johnston prepared to unleash his divisions on the southern perimeter of Grant's camps, Grant wrote Halleck: "I have scarcely the faintest idea of an attack (general one) being made upon us, but will be prepared should such a thing take place."[32]

At three o'clock on the morning of April 6, Colonel Everett Peabody's Union pickets reported noise. Two skirmishing companies in the woods were fired on by Confederate pickets. Behind those pickets fifty-four hundred men of Major General William Hardee's Third corps were advancing in line of battle on Peabody's camp, and Sherman's Fifth division. Sherman galloped four hundred yards forward then halted abruptly as he saw a massed rebel corps "coming down on me as far as the eye could see," bayonets gleaming from the sun behind him. Deadly rebel fire toppled one of Sherman's aides from his saddle. Initially federal units such as Colonel Jesse Appler's Fifty-Third Ohio melted away at the sight, Appler

31. Halleck to McClellan, *O.R.* 7:595; Halleck orders Grant to move, *O.R.* 7:674; Lieutenant Drayton to TEJr., March 5, 1862, quoted in Marszalek, *Soldier's Passion,* 173.

32. Grant to Halleck, *O.R.* 10:1:89.

screaming, "For God's sake, fall back and save yourselves!" an order that was promptly obeyed. Other Union men were paralyzed with fear. "Shoot! Shoot!" one Illinois lieutenant yelled at a cowering private, who yelled back he could not see anything but smoke. "Shoot anyhow!" the officer shouted in his ear.[33]

The raw recruits of the Union army learned quickly that day how to shoot back. For two days the armies fought and men died fighting as formations sloshed across bloody fields littered with wounded and dismembered men. Sherman was slightly wounded twice but held his division together and helped save Grant's key positions around the embattled Pittsburg Landing. Buell's Army of the Ohio was ferried across the river, and on the second morning of the battle Alex McCook, along with his aide Dan McCook, sent McCook's division forward to help lead Grant's counterattack. By midday, the Confederates were retreating toward Corinth, Mississippi.[34]

There had never been an aftermath like that of Shiloh. The casualties exceeded any battle on the North American continent to that date. Wagons hauled piles of dead rebels to burial pits, where bloated bodies were placed in the trenches "like sardines in a box." Twelve Iowa regiments fought at Shiloh, most of them green recruits such as Iowan Cyrus Boyd, who wrote in his diary, "My God, can there be anything in the future that compensates for this slaughter?" After two weeks of cutting off mangled limbs, surgeon Daniel Yandell alerted his relatives back home that he had "mistaken his calling." He joined the cavalry as a private. After the battle Dan McCook recognized one dead rebel as an Alabama friend from college days. He buried him in a single grave in the Tennessee mud. Ambrose Bierce, a private in the Ninth Indiana, saw a Union sergeant with an exposed brain wound suffering horribly from convulsions. To a suggestion that they should bayonet the man as an act of mercy, Bierce declined. "Too many are looking."[35]

Sherman's personal esteem among his fellow and senior officers was rising because of his performance in the battle, however. His support of Grant when Grant was accused of not having been prepared cemented their relationship. Halleck wrote the War Department, "Everyone here had the opinion that . . . Sherman

33. "As far as the eye could see" from Sherman, *Memoirs,* 1:230; Appler's order at *O.R.* 10:1:264; "Shoot anyhow!" Victor Hicken, *Illinois in the Civil War,* 57.

34. Albert Castel, "Dead on Arrival: The Life and Death of General Albert Sidney Johnston," 36.

35. Daniel McCook Jr., "The Second Division at Shiloh," 3, 5, 6; "sardines" from Marszalek, *Soldier's Passion,* 181; Cyrus F. Boyd, *The Civil War Diary of Cyrus F. Boyd, 15th Iowa Infantry,* 37–38; Yandell's remark in Joseph A. Frank and George A. Reaves, *Seeing the Elephant: Raw Recruits at the Battle of Shiloh,* 159; surgeons overwhelmed from Wiley Sword, *Shiloh: Bloody April,* 429; Alexander Downing, *Downing's Civil War Diary,* 43; Ned Bradford, ed., *Battles and Leaders of the Civil War,* 89; "Too many looking" from Peter Cozzens, "The Tormenting Flame," 50.

saved the fortunes of the day on the 6th and contributed largely to the victory on the 7th." The Union had a new hero, the self-doubting, henpecked William T. Sherman.[36]

Although Sherman's star was in ascendancy with some friends, there was criticism too, primarily from regimental officers that Sherman and Grant had been unprepared. Sherman's whining about unreliable volunteer soldiers returned. "The common soldiers and subordinates ran away and now want to blame their commanders," he wrote John Sherman. John was careful that such statements did not become public. His father-in-law again put the Ewingville support system into action to help defend Cump and suggested Tom Jr. visit Lincoln while in Washington and give him a copy of Halleck's post-Shiloh report, which supported Sherman. Thomas Sr. then also suggested Tom relay the point that, if Sherman had commanded at Pittsburg Landing, his innate "caution and appreciation of danger" that caused problems for him in Kentucky and Missouri would have resulted in breastworks being employed, which would have easily repulsed Johnston. This argument was stretching things a bit. Whether Sherman would have had his men dig breastworks is sheer speculation. Further, Grant had not stifled initiative; he had not ordered his division commanders not to dig breastworks. Halleck was the force that stopped the bickering. When Union troops slowly marched south of Shiloh toward Corinth, Mississippi, he summarily ordered Sherman to stop the backbiting with his critics and get back in the war.[37]

Both Sherman and McCook had met their testing in battle with cool dispatch, and the Gods of War had smiled on both men. The carnage at Shiloh had shown the mettle of the volunteers now commanded by Sherman, Hugh Ewing, and Dan McCook. These Western boys would stand in withering fire and slug it out, dying in great numbers but with a spirit that did not allow retreat. The casualty list at Shiloh dwarfed that of Bull Run, which the Army of the Potomac, as the Eastern army was now called, bragged on. This Western toughness would add mettle to the armies, but it was a peculiarly American mettle found in the Southern armies, too.

The notion of a short war died with the thousands of casualties at Shiloh. Now the only question was which side would run out of men first. The war would drag on, and soon it would be Tom's, Charley's, and Hugh's turns to be thrown into the maelstrom.

36. *O.R.* 34:3:171, 10:1:110.

37. WTS to John Sherman, April 22, 1862, quoted in Fellman, *Citizen Sherman,* 125; TESr. to TEJr., April 22, 1862, TEJr./KSHS; Halleck's order to stop bickering from WTS to Phil Ewing, July 13, 1862, quoted in Ewing, *Sherman at War,* 63–64.

6

EWING'S LIGHT ARTILLERY

In the spring of 1862, with the casualty lists from Shiloh dominating the war news, action in Congress for the transcontinental railroad was almost forgotten. Congress ratified the Pottawatomie treaty for the LP&W. The railroad had not laid a single rail of track yet, but by congressional fiat it owned the paper rights to a small fortune in land on the Delaware and Pottawatomie reservations. The road still had problems attracting investors, however, which unnerved Tom Ewing. Pomeroy and Lane were now behind the treaty, but corporate railroad subscriptions were sometimes self-fulfilling prophesies. The longer it took to attract private capital, the longer investors waited on the sidelines. A great deal of investment monies in America during the war already were tied up in railroads, and now there were new investment opportunities as the antebellum nation of small shopkeepers turned to making the tools of war.

For the first time Tom wrote his father that he was unhappy with prospects, and if stock sales did not increase there was talk among the directors of selling out. The war had no end in sight; Shiloh had seen to that. Stalemate would deplete investment capital and kill railroads. He was even becoming weary of shuttling back and forth to Washington. The only good thing on the family's horizon was their universal pride in Cump's achievements. Tom reported home that he had overheard officers at the Willard Hotel bar say, "Bonaparte, had he commanded at Shiloh, would have made Sherman a field marshal on the field."[1]

1. Taylor, "Origins of the Kansas Pacific," 167; "Bonaparte" from Marszalek, *Soldier's Passion,* 182.

Even without investment capital in his road, Tom lobbied the May 1862 session of Congress for another railroad bill, which nailed down that the LP&W would be the main eastern terminus of the transcontinental railroad. The Campbell bill, as it was known, was the most important of transcontinental railroad legislation. Its initial proposed route was across the Kansas prairie to Denver, then north and west through Wyoming. Ewing argued to any congressman who would listen that the Kansas route was more practicable since Kansas was more populous than the desolate prairie Nebraska Territory. Just as the modern interstate highway system arose from the military's need to move large bodies of troops and transport easily throughout the nation, Lincoln's government had similar reasons to support a transcontinental railroad. Internal lines of transportation, like internal lines in battle, meant a need for fewer seaports and fortifications. It was an argument that sold well among interior state congressmen, but not with those from the New England coastal states.[2]

In the summer of 1862 the Pacific Railroad Act was debated in Congress. While work began on the act just after Fort Sumter, the 1862 act incorporated a national company later known as the Union Pacific (UP). Section IX of the act allowed the LP&W to construct its road as part of the UP system, and its tracks would make up the eastern terminus of the UP, which ran roughly from Forts Riley and Hays on the frontier back to Leavenworth.

The bill was not without its flaws. The federal subsidies were small. Only ten sections of land per mile were granted in the bill, and at prevailing land prices their sale by the railroads would not generate enough for construction costs on a per-mile basis. The prairie railroad was eligible for a government bond subsidy at $16,000 per mile, but each forty-mile segment required new presidential authority. One controversial point was that construction loans made by the government had to be repaid by an annual deduction of 5 percent of the railroad's earnings after the roads were in operation. This made the government a stockholder in railroads while investing only public lands in the project. Yet even with these enticements, financial interest in the LP&W was insufficient to help it grow.[3]

It was not hard to drum up opposition against the Campbell bill. Coastal shipping interests argued it was cheaper to send goods from New England to San Francisco by sea, and they continued to maintain this position even in the wake of the numbers showing they were wrong. Jim Lane defended the Kansas railroad and berated other senators with irrelevancies of how Kansans were more patriotic than their Eastern colleagues.

2. Taylor, "Origins of the Kansas Pacific," 170.

3. Government per-mile subsidy from "Business and Political Career," 139–40.

The Senate passed the Campbell bill on June 20, 1862, with LP&W interests whittled down but nevertheless still in the bill. There was a fortune at stake with this legislation and the locusts were already in the field. Lane was supportive, but Pomeroy was double-crossing the Leavenworth railroad and working behind the scenes for Holliday's Atchison-Topeka road. Efforts were redoubled to distribute "favors" to those Kansans who could be persuasive with key congressmen and senators. The bill was falling apart, and now the rush was to pass something before the entire effort was lost. The main route was changed from the Kansas River at Kansas City to near Fort Riley and then northwest to a connection at the 100th meridian between the Platte and the Republican rivers, where it connected with the main track of the proposed UP line out of Omaha. Even Tom Ewing's relationship with Lincoln could not halt the changes in the bill. Lincoln could not pressure congressmen in favor of any road without enraging other sections of the country. Many good ideas would fall by the wayside before the transcontinental link could be finished, and one of them was the viability of the LP&W. Lincoln signed the heavily amended Campbell bill on July 1, 1862.[4]

Tom Ewing's railroad hopes were now limited. It was uncertain whether the value of the investment he had made in hopes the road would blossom into a major part of the transcontinental railroad would ever materialize. Wealth from a railroad was still possible; the East was covered with wealthy short-line roads connecting prosperous towns. However, if it was difficult to attract investors to the main line of the transcontinental railroad out on the prairie, it would be more difficult to do so for a prairie trunk line. Tom Ewing returned to his mundane life on the Kansas Supreme Court, disappointed in the Campbell bill and his own efforts, and trying to find solace in his court work.

While the work with the court was intellectually satisfying, the war was still an overriding concern of every Kansan. With the fall harvest now over, Ewing sensed it was time to do something more. He had been eyeing the possibility of an entry into the army, if a commission would advance his overall political aspirations. Hugh offered Tom a staff position in the Thirtieth Ohio, but he warned Tom that, in western Virginia, his Ohioans had hit dull duty, and the least he could do was share it with his brother. Tom preferred a Kansas command, and Jim Lane had a better alternative.[5]

4. Taylor, "Business and Political Career," 137, 139–40; Taylor, "Origins of the Kansas Pacific," 170; "favors" and details of the Campbell bill from Castel, *Frontier State,* 221.

5. Hugh's "dull duty" from HBE to TEJr. July 25, 28, 1862, in Ewing, "Autobiography," 271.

When Lane was advised that Ewing was interested in leaving the court and raising a regiment, Lane jumped at the offer, though not from altruistic reasons. He could control Ewing better as a military subordinate of some of his own appointees, men such as James Blunt or Samuel Curtis, than as an independent jurist. Ewing had no military training, but Lane did not care if Ewing's regiment ever saw action. Even if it did, a failure by Ewing would work to Lane's advantage. Ewing's appointment by Lane was calculated to infuriate Robinson, Ewing's recent enemy.[6]

When, in the summer of 1862, Lincoln called for another three hundred thousand volunteers, Lane was authorized to recruit three new regiments from Kansas. Recruiting was not going to be easy. The drought had driven off a third of the state's population two years previously, and most of the available footloose men were already in the existing regiments. Only family men—farmers and mechanics—were left. All were poor and just getting started in their lives. Missouri border ruffians were still active, and the western Indian tribes were threatening to attack settlements. It was not a good time for three thousand men to be absent from their homes.[7]

None of this deterred Lane. Fort Leavenworth's Camp Lyon became Ewing's headquarters, and the new colonel was given power to appoint the officers of his regiment, which was another affront to Robinson, who it was doubtful would ever have appointed Ewing to a regimental command. Until curtailed by directives from Stanton, the energetic Senator Lane even tried to get men from Illinois and Missouri to come over to fight with his Kansas regiments. Caught as he was between Lane's authority and his previous tactical alliances with Robinson, if Ewing thought Lane had exceeded his authority he did not say. Lane had so much authority with Secretary Stanton that he was told if Robinson did not commission Lane's officers, the president would. The year of fighting with Lane was the last straw for Robinson. Why, he asked Stanton rhetorically, would the general government give the power of a loyal governor to a U.S. senator? Robinson reminded the secretary of war of the type of "problem" Lane had been to the government early in the war. "What shall I say to the people who elected General Lane U. S. Senator and myself Governor, that [General] Lane is both Senator and Governor by consent? . . . [Y]ou have the power to subvert for the time being the State Government of Kansas but you have not the power to get my approval of the act." Although equity lay with Robinson in this squabble, Lane's wing of

6. Richmond, *Requisite Learning,* 81; Kim Scott, "The Preacher, the Lawyer, and the Spoils of War," 209.

7. Anderson, *Adjutant General,* 198.

Kansas Republicans commanded more supporters with Lincoln's state organization, and when Lane ran roughshod over Robinson, Lincoln looked the other way.[8]

The strength of the Eleventh Kansas was in its young officers, a development that had Ewing's hand in it. Among the company captains were two publishers, Preston Plumb and Edmund Ross. Like their commander, Plumb and Ross had no military training but brought with them considerable energies and a political following. Ewing knew he needed a steady regular as an executive officer to glue his regiment together, and he found one in Thomas Moonlight, a twenty-nine-year-old former sergeant in the regulars. He was a Leavenworth lawyer whom Ewing had known before the war. A Scottish immigrant who had stayed on the prairie and tried farming, he went back to the army at Fort Leavenworth and after Fort Sumter raised a volunteer battery. As a former regular, Moonlight might have warranted a regiment of his own, but his former status as sergeant kept him from the top job. Moonlight had the right political associations (he was a Lane man) and resigned his commission in the regulars to help lead Ewing's volunteer regiment. If Ewing had any doubts about Moonlight's allegiance, the Scot turned out to be a marvelous soldier and leader, and Ewing was glad to have his assistance.[9]

The Eleventh Kansas regiment attracted a variety of men. Dan McCook had gone from his brother's command in northern Mississippi back home to raise a regiment of his own. However, unlike McCook's concurrent efforts raising the Fifty-Second Ohio regiment around Steubenville, Ewing did not have a particularly difficult time filling the ranks of his regiment. The Eleventh regiment of Kansas volunteers came together in just under six weeks, in part from the patriotism that still flowed in Kansas and partly from the Eleventh's convincing squads and companies of men from other recruiting areas to slide into its own recruiting zone. Plumb was especially good at this poaching. He advertised in the *Emporia News* that the state's chief justice would hold a "war meeting" at Neosho Rapids, Emporia, Americus, and Council Grove over a four-day period. All four towns were south of the Kaw River, but Plumb's inducement was an annual bounty to their families if they crossed north over the Kansas River and signed up with the Eleventh. If he had any second thoughts about where the bounty would come from, this was in no way apparent. Plumb encouraged Ewing to speak at these ral-

8. Lane's out-of-state recruiting halted by Stanton, but presidential commissions in lieu of Robinson's, see Stanton to Lane, August 23, 1862, *O.R.* 3:2:444; "power to subvert" from Robinson to Stanton, August 26, 1862, William Connelley Collection.

9. Moonlight's abilities by Samuel Sturgis, May 5, 1862, *O.R.* 13:370. Moonlight would retire as a brigadier general.

lies, but later he may have reconsidered. Ewing was "able but cold in temperament," and the chief justice's speeches came across as wooden.[10]

If Ewing's well-chosen but stiff words sounded unnatural, Preston Plumb's oratory made up for it. Using the same sincerity and persuasiveness that would one day make him a U.S. senator, Plumb tracked down footloose men and convinced them not only to join Ewing's regiment but to bring along others with them. Harrison Hannahs, an energetic private who would become Ewing's adjutant, enlisted on August 15 and brought a squad of boys to help complete Company H. He reported that another squad of recruits was available at Burlingame, but this was outside Ewing's territory. Ewing sent Hannahs to Lane for permission to have them muster with the Eleventh. Hannahs apparently augmented Ewing's request with timely persuasions of his own, since the Burlingame boys were slated for the Twelfth Kansas to be commanded by Lane's son-in-law, Charles Adams. Ira Hodgson had come to Wabaunsee County with his father before the war; at fifteen he had been a teamster on the Santa Fe Trail. He walked a hundred miles to Leavenworth to enlist in Ewing's Eleventh regiment. Other stories were similar. Samuel Worthington enlisted in spite of chronic breathing problems. Newspaperman S. H. Fairfield was one of seven original abolitionists who founded the Beecher Bible and Rifle Church west of Topeka. The thirty-two-year-old German immigrant Henry Grimm would survive the bullets of the Civil War only to suffer debilitating arrow wounds during the 1865 Indian wars. He farmed two thousand acres in Wabaunsee County and fathered fourteen children. To all these men Plumb stressed duty to the Union over health or family considerations. The message worked. Twenty wagons were needed to haul the new men to Fort Leavenworth.[11]

While Ewing was busy raising his regiment, he had one person whom he knew he had to convince that his decision to enter the army was the correct one. Although Thomas Ewing Sr. did what he could to get Cump Sherman a field commission early in the war, he did not necessarily want his sons in harm's way. At least Cump Sherman and Hugh Ewing had some military training. Neither Tom nor Charley Ewing had any. Tom knew all this, but what carried him forward and convinced him he was making the right decision was the feeling the men had of his abilities. He wrote his father on September 5, 1862, "Officers and men without a solitary exception urgently insist on my taking command of the regiment."

10. The Eleventh's "poaching" within the state from Harrison Hannahs, "General Thomas Ewing Jr.," 277; "cold in temperament" from Connelley, *Preston B. Plumb,* 101.

11. Ira Hodgson, "Reminiscences of an Old Civil War Veteran," 2; Worthington's enlistment at December 16, 1862, Samuel Worthington Manuscript Collection, KSHS; Connelley, *Preston B. Plumb,* 100–105.

Even so, he recognized he was no starry-eyed patriot. In the end, he was moved by the sacrifices other men were making:

> When I asked your advice I had not begun recruiting. If I had not undertaken to raise the regiment, I could have remained out. But as I have raised it, of men every one of whom have made personal sacrifices, as great to them as any sacrifice I make is to me, I cannot without selfishness refuse to lead them. Besides, ever since the war broke out I have felt uncomfortable accepting a position which, however honorable in place, I do not regard as conferring honor now on an able bodied young man. During the war the Chief Justice of Kansas should be an old man or a cripple.[12]

Ewing was not a military man like Sherman or Grant. However, this letter is consistent with what was happening on the war front in Kansas. Kansans were flocking to the colors, even men who had no business volunteering. Already eight regiments had been formed, which meant over seven thousand potential politicians at the end of the war, many of them wanting to be U.S. senators. If those men became legislators, a man such as Ewing, without a military career behind him, would have to look to the veterans for an appointment to the Senate, which was unlikely. Ewing hints of this concern in a letter to his father. "The people are greatly aroused, and the men of the highest character and intelligence are going in as privates. In Jackson County, every lawyer volunteered—three ministers, three merchants, and every county officer save one. There will be a great deal of competition for the company and field officers, there being so many qualified for the places."[13]

The risk was there, of course—a soldier's risk. He might not only die or be horribly wounded, his lack of military education might lead him to botch the job horribly, causing his regiment to be slaughtered. However, for Tom's dreams the risk of inaction was higher. That military service was to be almost a necessity for Kansas politicians is evident in the postwar political careers of Ross and Plumb, who parlayed military exploits in the Eleventh Kansas all the way to the U.S. Senate.

Furthermore, Tom Ewing was now a true believer. Slavery had assaulted the original design of the Union. Slave powers threatened not only good order but the origins of national liberty. To root it out—to ensure that slavery would never again imperil the Union—depended now on the sword, not logic or rhetoric.

12. TEJr. to TESr., September 5, 1862, EFP/LC, quoted in Scott, "Spoils of War," 209.

13. Scott, "Spoils of War," 209; "great deal of competition" from TEJr. to TESr., September 5, 1862, quoted in ibid., 208.

"I appreciate fully there are reasons enough to excuse me were I to stay out—but my heart is in the service, and I must go also."[14]

On September 15, Governor Robinson dutifully commissioned the Eleventh Kansas regiment into federal service. Tom Ewing was finally in the war. On September 24, 1862, Kansas became part of the new Department of Missouri under the command of a Lane man, Major General Samuel Curtis, the victor at Pea Ridge. Ewing wired Curtis that the state's newest regiment was ready for service.

In early June 1862, Colonel Dan McCook was also giving speeches encouraging enlistment in his Fifty-Second Ohio. The work was part tactician, part orator, and part evangelist, and this was right up McCook's alley; he was much better at this sort of martial persuasion than Tom Ewing. Like Preston Plumb, McCook did not particularly care for the pedigree of his recruits. Twenty new privates came from the Ohio State Penitentiary, pardoned on condition they would fight for the Union.[15]

There was precious little time now. As fast as Ohio could muster new regiments, they were sent to central Kentucky. The Fifty-Second Ohio crossed the Ohio River into Kentucky with 1,019 men. Private Nixon Stewart's first train ride was in the "palace cars," but he predicted they would come back in other ways, if they came back at all. McCook's regiment saw its first action covering the exhausting retreat after General William "Bull" Nelson's fiasco in central Kentucky at the Battle of Richmond, where Nelson lost only a few hundred casualties but also five thousand prisoners to Kirby Smith's army of Shiloh veterans.[16]

While McCook's regiment stumbled across Kentucky in their abortive shield of Nelson's retreat, the man that Ellen Sherman trusted only slightly less than the devil, the flamboyant John Pope, was given command of the new Army of Virginia. Jacob Cox, a protégé of Pope's, invited his Kanawha division into the fight. On August 30, Hugh Ewing's Thirtieth Ohio led the advance regiments of Cox's division out of the mountains to Warrenton Junction, Virginia, to join Pope's army, which was attempting a flanking operation while McClellan's Army of the Potomac remained on the Peninsula.[17]

14. TEJr. to TESr., August 6, 1862, in Scott, "Spoils of War," 209.

15. Reid, *Great Rebellion,* 1:314; convicts from "Reunion Program, McCook's Brigade, Davis's division, 14th Army Corps, Army of the Cumberland, 1901," from *Roster of the Survivors of Col. Dan McCook's 52nd Regiment, Ohio Volunteer Infantry, 1907. Third Brigade Second Division, Fourteenth Army Corps, Army of the Cumberland,* Thirty-First Annual Reunion at Steubenville, Ohio, Aug. 28 and 29, 1907, cited in Stewart, *McCook's Regiment.*

16. Stewart, *McCook's Regiment,* 11, 17.

17. *O.R.* 12:3:451.

Bragg had campaigned into Kentucky and sent Union armies reeling. Now it was Robert E. Lee's turn. Lee's army slipped away from the slowly retreating McClellan. Lincoln ordered McClellan back to Washington to support Pope. Before those armies could link up, Lee sent Stonewall Jackson's divisions to hammer Pope's forward units at Cedar Run, southwest of Culpepper. When Washington sent more troops toward Culpepper, Jackson's and A. P. Hill's divisions swung around Pope, looped into the Shenandoah Valley, then down the Thoroughfare Gap and through Gainesville onto the old battlefield at Manassas. Pope was unaware of this movement and was oblivious to the size of the alley fight coming his way. In northern Virginia on August 29 and 30, first at Groveton and then on the old Bull Run battlefield, Pope's army was hammered like a punching bag. Pope fought like a small boy, eyes closed, swinging wildly under the stiff-arm of an adult. Then, for a second time, the main federal army in the East fled from Centerville for safety among the forts around Washington.[18]

From the estate at Geisborough, Hugh Ewing could hear the rumble of artillery but had no way of knowing if his regiment had gone into action. Cox's rapid movement from western Virginia and the Kanawha River to Washington had left Hugh physically ill. Then he was sick with disappointment at having missed his first major action. The Kanawha division fell back with the rest of Pope's army to prepared positions at Munson's Hill near Alexandria, having played a very small part in the Second Battle of Bull Run. The rout complete, Lincoln had no use for the separate Army of Virginia, which Lee, Jackson, and Longstreet had just carved up like Thanksgiving turkey. McClellan was ordered to resume command.[19]

Lee did not give Washington time to reorganize. Stuart's cavalry moved north and west of Washington, toward Harpers Ferry, ahead of the rebel infantry, carrying the war into the North for the first time. The army would replenish itself off farms in Maryland and Pennsylvania. At least this was Lee's plan. To implement it, he divided his force and laid out his marching orders in Special Order 191, a copy of which fell into the hands of a Union corporal and, eventually, reached McClellan.[20]

18. Part of Second Bull Run at *O.R.* 12:2:78, 176–78, 325–46, 550–76, 600–605; Whitelaw Reid, *Ohio In the War; Her Statesmen, Generals and Soldiers,* 2:234.

19. Ewing, "Autobiography," 273; Second Bull Run at Reid, *Ohio . . . Statesmen,* 2:235; "fell back" from Lieutenant J. A. Palmer to parents, September 5, 1863, quoted in Kempfer, *Salem Light Guard,* 84.

20. *O.R.* 19:1:144–56.

On Sunday, September 7, the Kanawha division left Washington as part of the Ninth corps, which was in pursuit of Lee. They marched on hot dusty roads at the vanguard of McClellan's army, a parallel march through Leesborough, Brookville, and Damascus, toward the rolling hills of western Maryland. Colonel Rutherford Hayes of the Twenty-Third Ohio indicated, "Straggling and confusion and disorder [was] everywhere." The slow march enraged McClellan's senior officers, among them Major General Jesse Reno, the Ninth corps commander. Reno exploded with rage when he caught some of Hayes's and Ewing's men stealing straw from a haystack. Ewing explained that, if the men slept in the rain and mud, instead of fighters he would have a regiment on sick call. Western army commanders, he informed Reno, took care of their men first. Reno apologized for his angry language but then snapped, "I suppose you westerners think your troops are better than those back here," indicating the veterans of Second Bull Run behind them. Ewing replied that his men were good, and he intended to keep them in fighting trim. Reno vowed that in the coming battle he would put Ewing's men in the front ranks and find out![21]

Major General Joseph Hooker wrote that South Mountain was "precipitous, rugged, and wooded, and difficult of ascent to an infantry force, even in absence of a foe." Near the crest were some hardscrabble farms carved from the forest. From the forests it was hard to see thirty feet into those clearings, which made it easy for ambushing troops to hide in the tangle. Two roads—the turnpike over Turner's Gap and a backcountry route through Fox Gap—crossed the southern summit. The old Boonsborough Pike crossed the north side of the mountain. Lee's captured orders informed McClellan that the Confederate main body was forming behind this mountain. Lee gave the assignment to contest the passes through South Mountain to Daniel Harvey Hill. Major General Alfred Pleasonton's cavalry reconnoitered Turner's Gap the evening of September 13, skirmishing with Hill's arriving infantry. In the dark Pleasonton learned the rebels were entrenched on the summit, but there were two side roads around the positions at Turner's Gap. Pleasonton called on McClellan for infantry. Reno's corps was closest, and General Eliakim P. Scammon's brigade with Hugh Ewing's Thirtieth Ohio looped over the initial range of hills northwest of Frederick and was nearing South Mountain before dawn, along with a heavy concentration of artillery.[22]

21. Ewing, "Autobiography," 274; Rutherford B. Hayes, *Diary and Letters of Rutherford B. Hayes,* 2:346.

22. *O.R.* 19:1:214.

Reno's test of Ewing's Western men was now upon them. Scammon, a fussy, unpopular math professor at West Point and a stickler for discipline, had the brigade working its way forward in the dark. At daybreak on September 14, Ewing sent out a skirmishing company, and the Thirtieth Ohio led the Kanawha division up South Mountain. Scammon's brigade angled left at Koogle's Mill behind the cavalry screen to the Old Sharpsburg Road that ran through Fox Gap. Almost immediately federal batteries began shelling the high ground from long distance, with the spherical shot jangling federal nerves if those rounds fell short. Slowed by the winding road and in the oppressive September heat, by midmorning the men were sweating profusely and beginning to drop out. As Ewing's men neared Fox Gap and onto scattered open fields, a rebel battery opened from a stone wall below the summit of the gap. Scammon's and Crook's brigades went into line of battle, swinging back down the mountain as they formed a line of nearly three thousand men. The formation went forward. From the federal lines and behind the rebel-held stone wall long volleys erupted, filling the woods with a flat rippling sound and dense smoke.[23]

The Kanawha brigades had butted into Brigadier General Samuel Garland's brigade of five North Carolina regiments. Garland had nothing in the terrain on which to anchor regiments. If they could keep their cohesion, the federal units could swarm Garland's flanks in thick undergrowth and there was little Garland could do about it. Scammon placed batteries of the Ohio light artillery in the federal lines close enough to use canister, but sharpshooters of Captain James Atwell's Twentieth North Carolina worked onto the flanks of the artillerymen and knocked down enough gunners that the guns were abandoned. Then George Anderson's Confederate brigade charged, the first of three counterattacks that afternoon. But they were not up against Pope's men in an open field at Second Bull Run. Union volleys cut down the Carolinians. The charge blunted, all along the lines the soldiers crawled back into the trees, leveled their muskets, and opened up a shooting gallery. Men began to fall on both sides.[24]

Cox called for reinforcements, and Reno sent the divisions of Samuel Sturgis, Orlando Wilcox, and Isaac Rodman swarming up the national road. With the light fading in the late afternoon, Cox's whole line finally went forward seven hundred yards along a ridgeline. They struck the stone wall where the Twenty-Third and Twelfth North Carolina regiments waited. The recruits gave way, and in the melee of a counterattack by the Thirteenth North Carolina, Garland was mortal-

23. Ibid., 461, 469, 471.
24. Ibid., 1039–41, 1045–47.

ly wounded. The Tarheels of the Twenty-Third hugged the stone wall and held fast, giving as good as they got. The armies traded fire for another hour and a half. Late in the day the Tarheels came screaming out of the woods at a battery that had been shelling them. They regrouped and came again. Each time the fire from Hugh's brigade left gray bodies on the ground. Then the rebels delivered their own volley, and men around Ewing began to drop.

South Mountain became a soldier's fight; each man dropped his weapon butt first into the ground and stabbed into the open cartridge box for the next round, tearing at the paper with his teeth, tasting the saltpeter in the gunpowder, ramming home a round, shouldering the gun, and firing at anything moving beyond the smoke and haze. Smoke hid everyone. Where the lines warped together, soldiers used clubbed muskets on each other. Henry McElroy noted that the Thirty-Sixth Ohio's rapid fire stopped the rebel advance, and the slow but steady movement of the rest of Crook's brigade through the woods drove the attacking force back into their tree line.[25]

At five o'clock, under Reno's impatient supervision, Cox formed the Kanawha division in the woods and sent them forward with a loud yell that could be heard across the valley. Hugh Ewing's regiment went forward on the left in a column formation behind a heavy skirmishing line led by Lieutenant Colonel Ted Jones, his second in command. The first line roared around both flanks of the Twentieth North Carolina and passed into the rear of the Twenty-Third North Carolina. The regiment's column took artillery fire from rebels on Ewing's left. He skillfully ordered the regiment to wheel on his flanking company and charge the battery, then wheel again, reversing position on the same company. Men were falling around him as Hugh ranged back and forth behind the line, shouting orders. Mexican War veterans in the Thirtieth Ohio later told Hugh they had not seen a place as hot as the open fields and mountain tree lines of South Mountain. "Although outnumbered, we held on," he later wrote, misjudging his own resources versus his enemy's.[26]

The Twenty-Third Ohio, a sister regiment in Crook's brigade, drove forward into the fighting on Ewing's right. One of the two future presidents in the regiment, Colonel Rutherford B. Hayes, fell in front of his regiment, a bullet in his arm. A North Carolina volley into the face of the advancing federals staggered the Ohioans. Vicious hand-to-hand fighting erupted. When the rebels counterattacked, the green Seventeenth Michigan and Forty-Fifth Pennsylvania regiments

25. Ibid., 1026; George Crook, *Autobiography*, 95.
26. Ewing, "Autobiography," 276.

from Willcox's division were ordered to fill the gap between the Twenty-Third and Thirtieth Ohio regiments, which they filled with their bodies. Over 260 men in these two regiments fell within a few minutes, but they halted the North Carolinian counterattack.[27]

As evening fell Hill ordered further attacks, and Ewing's men saw two counterattacks coming. His men were shooting too high in the excitement, and several times he screamed orders to cease fire, cool off, and "steady their nerves." Reno and his staff galloped to where Scammon and Ewing were directing fire. The volleys rang out again, this time with greater effect, leaving rebel dead in the fields and behind the wood lines. Reno scanned the littered field, then roared at Ewing, "You have kept your brag!" More musketry from the North Carolinians at the well-mounted Yankees across from them left Reno dead on a tiny road near the crest of the mountain, among the last to die on South Mountain. Reno's death meant overnight command changes in the Ninth Corps. Cox moved up to command the corps, and Scammon took Cox's division command. With Rutherford Hayes wounded, Hugh Ewing was ordered to command Scammon's brigade.[28]

For a day McClellan dithered, concentrating his army, and thus missed the best opportunity to strike Lee a blow with overwhelming force. McClellan's morning attack on September 17 came in three Napoleonic waves, north to south. John Palmer in the Thirty-Sixth Ohio in Crook's brigade listened as "the ball opened early" to the north of their position.[29] Hooker's corps led the dawn attack against Stonewall Jackson's undersized divisions on Lee's left in the West Woods and the cornfield. While nearly ninety thousand men and three hundred artillery pieces engaged in the hardest fight of the war, Major General Ambrose Burnside was ordered to turn Lee's flank south of Sharpsburg, carry the town, and strike the deathblow against the Army of Northern Virginia. With only a day's rest since the exhausting bloody fight at South Mountain, Ewing's Kanawha brigade was ordered into line as part of Burnside's flanking attack.

The roads west of Sharpsburg that led to the Potomac River fords and Harpers Ferry were a jumble of horse paths and footpaths. If the Army of Northern Virginia retreated down these roads, the straggling that had dogged Lee when the army came to Maryland would destroy his army. It took a long time to form up, but Burnside ordered his entire corps—thirty-five thousand men—across Antie-

27. *O.R.* 19:1:49–50, 429, 463; Stephen W. Sears, *Landscape Turned Red: The Battle of Antietam,* 128–31.

28. *O.R.* 19:1:187, 214–15, 469; quotes from Ewing, "Autobiography," 276.

29. Kempfer, *Salem Light Guards,* 89.

tam Creek and forward. Had he accomplished this feat an hour earlier, Ambrose Burnside would have been one of the storied heroes of the American Civil War and Hugh Ewing would have shared a measure of that glory. It did not happen.

Above Snavely's Ford, Colonel Ewing's Ohioans drove in the rebel skirmishers on the east side of the stream, but rebel cannon showered the Ohioans with a hail of grapeshot from the west bank. From the ridge above the creek, they saw the spires of Sharpsburg. Rodman's division, with Ewing's brigade guarding its extreme left, moved in echelon with Willcox's division. When Willcox hammered the rebel line, Rodman's division would sweep down the Harpers Ferry Road, through Sharpsburg, and shatter Lee's right flank. Instead, Rodman inexplicably slowed his advance and gave the defending rebels a stunning reprieve.[30]

On the Ninth corps's exposed left flank, Ewing was worried. Harpers Ferry had been reduced the previous day. This meant a rebel force was out there, somewhere, south of Ewing's position. Before crossing Snavely's Ford Ewing sent a squadron of cavalry south to report to him any large Confederate movement. Almost immediately a rebel column was spotted marching north through hilly tangled woodland, and word was sent to McClellan. Nobody knew how long it would take for the rebs to reach the field south of Sharpsburg. Had McClellan effectively used his cavalry to block A. P. Hill's approach, the Union cause at Antietam could have made its own luck. It was not to be. Hill's scouts led the rebel light division masterfully onto Burnside's left flank at the height of Rodman's attack on Sharpsburg. The brigades of Gregg, Archer, Branch, and Toombs came at Ewing's flank. As the Ninth corps's reserve on Rodman's left, Hugh Ewing turned his brigade to stem a division-sized attack before it rolled up Rodman's flank.[31]

Unable to determine the size of the attacking force, Ewing pushed his three regiments into an inverted "L," placing the Twelfth and Twenty-Third Ohio regiments to the south with the Thirtieth Ohio facing west along the Otto Farm rock wall. In the twilight the Twelfth Ohio mistook the rebels for federal reinforcements and waited to fire until the rebels fired a volley. The right-angle development of Ewing's brigade was done under a shower of canister, a deadly slaughterhouse unlike anything the Kanawha men had seen even in the chaos at South Mountain. Ewing's aide Lieutenant Reese Furbay fell dead in a rebel volley with three wounds in the chest. Lieutenant Charles Duffield was wounded in the leg and died that night from loss of blood. Colonel Augustus Coleman, commanding the Eleventh Ohio, fell dead near Ewing. Lieutenant Colonel Ted Jones, Ew-

30. Crook, *Autobiography*, 97–100; *O.R.* 51:1:844, 19:1:437–38, 865, 898–99, 917.
31. A. P. Hill's report at *O.R.* 19:1:980–82.

ing's successor with the Thirtieth regiment, was wounded and briefly captured. While trying to rally support for Ewing's disintegrating brigade from Toombs's and Archer's brigades, General Isaac Rodman went down, mortally wounded.

The maelstrom of Hill's advance—which came on steadily, knocking down Ewing's men like matchsticks—terrorized everyone. Every officer on horseback had his animal shot down, including Ewing whose favorite horse, Hettie, crumpled in a fusillade. Enlisted men fared little better than the animals. When the Thirtieth's colors were erected at the wall, Color Sergeants Nathan White and Williams Carter defiantly waved the national and regimental colors. Both were shot dead for their efforts. Others were wounded carrying off the colors. After withdrawing to a supposedly safer rock fence in the Otto cornfield, the brigade took more enfilading fire and decided to go back to its original position. A section of the First Ohio light artillery sent forward to help the brigade took Confederate infantry fire, which killed or wounded the entire gun crew and killed Lieutenant George Crome, the section commander. Ewing's brigade fought back desperately. Then Archer's and Branch's brigades were on them, and Ewing's men fired several volleys to stagger the Confederate advance, giving Harlan's brigade time to clear out. Then the Kanawha brigade withdrew, firing as it retreated.[32]

Just how close Ewing's and Rodman's attacks came to crippling the Confederate cause is found in Henry Benning's accounts. "If General Burnside's corps had once got through. . . . it would soon have been in the rear of our whole army, and have been disastrous." However, this sort of élan was no longer in the Ninth corps. Now the battered Union lines were fighting not to be overrun, and Confederates were fighting cautiously, not wanting to be shot in the growing twilight. Cox ordered his division to retreat backward to the hills above the Rohrbach Bridge, out of harm's way, giving up several hard-won ridges in the process.[33]

General Scammon had never particularly liked Hugh Ewing. Scammon was a fussy professorial type while Ewing had never in his life met a teacher he could not irritate. In his after-action report, the tired and somewhat disgusted division commander did not try to tell his own story about the attack on the Union left but simply passed along the reports of his subordinates. However, he felt compelled grudgingly to report, "While I leave it to brigade and regimental commanders to make special mention of their officers and men, I must claim the privilege of testifying to the energy and skillful bravery of Colonels Ewing and Crook."

32. *O.R.* 51:1:871; Ewing, "Autobiography," 276.
33. *O.R.* 19:1:426; Benning's assessment at *O.R.* 51:1:164–66; Sears, *Landscape Turned Red,* 285–88.

Ewing's division commander did not share Scammon's views. Cox's official report does not mention Ewing's name.[34]

Later historians credited Ewing's attack at the stone wall in the Otto cornfield with "saving the Union left from being completely driven in" by Hill's attack. Hugh bragged to his journal that an aide to McClellan had watched the charge and claimed it was the "finest he had ever witnessed." It was some consolation for a hard two weeks of fighting. His favorable mention by Burnside led to his star. First recommended by Rosecrans in January 1862, his actual promotion would not come for nearly a year.[35]

That night, after the battle, an intermittent cannonade rumbled over all the five-mile-long battlefield where sixteen thousand wounded lay between the lines, screaming. The next day both armies lay exhausted, sniping at each other only sometimes. Neither army attacked. Hugh reported in his journal, "[We] lay on our arms, worn out. [An] advance this morning brought on a light fight. Gen. Sturgis came over to the rear of my brigade and lay all day with me. Relieved at dark, and went over the Antietam." His journal reported a lot more of that grisly field. He had seen two of his aides die quickly around him, and scores of his men fall. Ewing's men had captured some Confederate wounded that afternoon and placed them behind a straw stack. The stack was set afire by a shell and they burned to death before anyone could reach them. He also reported that seventeen other Confederate wounded lay under a tree on the bluff where Ewing's regimental surgeons were dressing wounds. A Confederate battery trained on them and killed all the wounded but one "whose leg was being amputated at that moment." The rebel artillery, from the advantage of height, "had delivered an awful fire of canister on us." The night of September 18, Lee melted away through the woods south of Sharpsburg along Boteler's Road and escaped. Like a dog scratched hard by an angry cat, McClellan was content to let Lee go.[36]

Hugh Ewing had been ill even before the battle, and he took a month's sick leave after Antietam. He did not rejoin the Kanawha division until late October. What he had seen affected him. Men of high rank such as Reno and men in the ranks who bore his flags all had died—and had died in ways that carried no glory. He was upset with Cox and Scammon. Crook came by and claimed he would never draw his sword again while commanded by either Scammon or Cox. Dur-

34. Scammon's report at *O.R.* 19:1:462.

35. "Saving the Union left" from Reid, *Great Rebellion,* 2:853; the assessment by McClellan's aide from the self-praising Ewing, "Autobiography," 276 (Burnside's recommendation at 277).

36. McClellan's report, *O.R.* 19:1:32–65; Ewing's official report at *O.R.* 19:1:470–71; "lay on our arms" and later quotes from Ewing, "Autobiography," 276.

ing these days Hugh wrote few letters and remained introspective. He seemed most affected by—and much appreciated—his brigade officers who stopped at Geisborough to check on his recovery.[37]

On September 29, 1862, while the Eastern armies were recovering from the carnage, caring for the tens of thousands of wounded from the Antietam battlefield, the Eleventh Kansas regiment formed a column, shouldered arms, and marched south behind its new colonel. The eagles on Tom Ewing's shoulders did not give him any military insight, however. He assumed, never having walked thirty miles in one day in his life, that his men could do it with packs and heavy muskets. For the Eleventh Kansas, a shortage of decent muskets forced them to draw heavy .79 caliber Prussian muskets at the Leavenworth arsenal. These 1818 vintage weapons were heavier than the Springfields. Moonlight informed Ewing that fifteen miles was about as much as infantry could average, given the "light artillery" the regiment was toting. But Ewing was impatient to join Blunt. On the march, the regiment struggled but repeatedly kept going well past a fifteen-mile limit. This resulted in officers scattered along the entire march, herding stragglers. Private Worthington found that he could not march as far as his peers. He was not alone. The Eleventh Kansas arrived at Fort Scott in straggling squads and broken companies rather than in one proud column.

Ewing used the days in Fort Scott to continue training. Arms were not the regiment's only problems. Plumb's bounty also came due at that time. When army payroll funds were not available in Fort Scott, Colonel Ewing had to arrange payment with his Leavenworth banking friends to keep Plumb's promises. The men were given manual of arms training by the post's ordnance officer and were told to prepare to march to meet Blunt's Union force in the field. After a few days' rest and securing ammunition for their ancient muskets, on October 12, 1862, Ewing's regiment set a slower pace, escorting Blunt's ammunition wagons southeast, toward Arkansas.[38]

The Kansans moved on soggy Arkansas roads through the rugged Boston Mountains, a land of patchwork farms and forest inhabited by strong East Tennessee Unionist farmers. While Arkansas was not as glamorous as northern Virginia or Kentucky, the Eleventh Kansas joined Blunt's army at the old Pea Ridge battlefield. After covering 275 miles in fifteen days, Edmund Ross was justifi-

37. Hugh's sick leave at Reid, *Great Rebellion,* 2:853.

38. Outdated weapons from Castel, *Frontier State,* 89; Anderson, *Adjutant General,* 200; Connelley, *Preston B. Plumb,* 108.

ably proud of his company's marching. "Not a man in my company has given out."[39]

By mid-October rumors of a large Confederate force recruited from among the Cherokee and Choctaw Indians became fact. Confederate regiments skirmished near Newtonia, Missouri, with a small Union force, intent on swinging through southeast Kansas on a destructive raid. After Newtonia they retreated into Arkansas and divided their forces racially. Ten thousand white troops remained with General Thomas C. Hindman in Arkansas while five thousand Indians with Colonel Douglas Cooper and Stand Waite, the Cherokee leader, moved into the Indian Nations. Blunt's force at Pea Ridge was the only effective Union force confronting these Confederates.

Tom Ewing had, above all else, remained practical. Given his earlier bouts and weakness from malaria, he did nothing about his elected public office in Kansas until he was sure he could stand the physical rigors of campaigning. In northwest Arkansas he concluded he was fit for this new work. On October 20, with rumors swirling about the Confederate forces coming toward Blunt, Tom Ewing hurriedly wrote out his resignation from the Kansas Supreme Court and mailed it to Governor Robinson. Then Blunt ordered the Army of the Frontier into motion to find Hindman.[40]

Within a week of Ewing's resignation from his judicial post, Blunt's force surprised Cooper's Indian regiments in their camps near Fort Wayne. Samuel Crawford, a future Kansas governor, led five companies of the Second Kansas cavalry in a wild charge against rebel cannons before the Confederate Indian force could organize. The six hundred men of the Second Kansas—infantry veterans of Wilson's Creek, now mounted—went after Cooper's force, which was ten times larger. They went in without bayonets, driving the Confederates from their artillery.

When Ewing's men heard the firing, they were slogging along a dirt road three miles behind the Second. The Eleventh Kansas began jogging forward, shedding blankets and knapsacks on the run. Cooper's Indians had rallied and were forming for a counterattack when the Tenth and Eleventh Kansas regiments came up. The Kansans decided that nobody fought Indians—even Indians intent on fighting the White Man's way—like Napoleonic regiments. They fixed bayonets on

39. Blunt's advance, see *O.R.* 13:20:691–92; Pea Ridge battlefield from Anderson, *Adjutant General*, 200; Edmund Ross to his wife, October 20, 1862, Edmund G. Ross Manuscript Collection, KSHS; "Unionist farmers" from Samuel Worthington letter to Father and Mother, November 7, 1862, Worthington Collection.

40. Connelley, *Preston B. Plumb*, 96, 108–10; Ewing's resignation from Edwin A. Austin, "The Supreme Court of the State of Kansas," 98.

the fly and ran bunched up, keeping a column as best they could. "The rebels could not stand the sight of our fixed bayonets in heavy column coming over the hill on a full run," and the Indians "ran like the devil," scattering into the mountains, disappointing Edmund Ross, who was hoping to get into the regiment's first fight.[41]

At Camp Babcock, Arkansas, Ewing received his official commission, and the Eleventh Kansas drilled and waited for another opportunity to get at the rebels. Although bushwhacking was commonplace (two officers were shot when they took a recreational ride), his men felt sympathy for the inhabitants of this rugged tree-covered hill country. William Haynes wrote his wife, "There isn't a good-looking woman in the whole country. The people see hard times here." Then, reminded that the same situation existed back in Kansas, Haynes instructed his wife, "Do the best you can till I get home. Home to me is all the world."[42]

Blunt's efforts in Arkansas that year were important to the success of Grant's Vicksburg campaign. Halleck was stripping the western commands in order to send troops to Grant's force now preparing to advance on Vicksburg. However, Blunt informed his superior, Brigadier General John Schofield, that he was determined to keep pressure on the rebels in Arkansas even with a reduced command. "I have no doubt of my ability to sustain myself during the winter at Fort Smith, . . . and be in a position to move down the Arkansas Valley to operate in conjunction with [Steele's Union] forces against Little Rock should the enemy concentrate their whole force at that point for defense." Schofield authorized Blunt cautiously to press Cooper's Indians toward Fort Smith and keep the scattered rebel units from forming a cohesive army.[43]

While he had now settled in to his army existence and cut his ties with his prewar life, Tom Ewing was learning to live with the less exciting aspects of a backwater assignment in the war. Part of his frustration with the army was having to take orders from his intellectual inferiors. An early nemesis was Colonel William F. Cloud, Ewing's brigade commander, an Ohioan of more humble origins. Cloud had served as a sergeant in Mexico and had come to Kansas in 1858 to pastor a small church in Emporia. A haughty Bible-thumping martinet, the former preacher felt Ewing's regiment had been too slow to support Cloud's cavalry at Fort Wayne. He demanded that Ewing train his men to Cloud's more exacting

41. Connelley, *Preston B. Plumb,* 108–10; Plummer, *Frontier Governor,* 14–15; Blunt's report at *O.R.* 13:325–28; quotes from Edmund Ross to wife, October 25, 1862, Ross Collection.

42. William C. Haynes to Letia, November 23, 1862, William C. Haynes Manuscript Collection, KSHS.

43. Schofield to Curtis, *O.R.* 13:760–61.

specifications. Ewing felt Cloud was acting like an impudent sergeant rather than an officer and a gentleman. "If he had any brains I could stand him better, but he has none," Ewing wrote his wife.[44]

If Blunt was aware of this friction, he did not intervene. When some of Ewing's men did some scavenging, Cloud held Ewing personally responsible, asking for duplicated written explanations that Ewing categorized as useless paperwork. Apparently, however, and even with men like Moonlight in his officer corps, Ewing was unable to control his men's adventurism totally. Even Blunt said something to Ewing when men from the Eleventh got out of hand during foraging operations. Considering Blunt's ruthlessness in earlier Missouri operations with Lane and his lingering suspicions of Ewing's loyalties from the territorial days, Ewing thought Blunt's statements hypocritical. "I shall have trouble here with Blunt as well as Cloud."[45]

There was not much time for Ewing to change the Eleventh's reputation. The Confederate army in northwest Arkansas had looked forward to wintering in the Fayetteville area in the midst of the region that produced famous peach and apple brandies. The Boston Mountains south of the town rise to more than two thousand feet and constitute the highest part of the Ozark Plateau. In late November Blunt sent his four thousand men and thirty cannon to strike at General John Marmaduke's eight-thousand-man command. They met at Cane Hill, Arkansas, a cotton-milling region twenty miles southwest of Fayetteville.

With the Second brigade in reserve, Ewing deployed the Eleventh Kansas. Their long-barreled muskets were double loaded with a .79 caliber ball and buckshot, turning the weapons into crude long-range shotguns that were effective only if they got close enough to an enemy formation. Also in the battle line was Colonel William Weer's Tenth Kansas, Colonel William Phillips's Third Cherokee regiment, the Ninth Wisconsin, and the Sixth Kansas cavalry. Ewing's men were on the move at dawn and four hours later were still tramping rugged bush country. Cloud kept up a constant stream of messages to Ewing to hurry his men forward.

The exhausted regiment formed its lines with the booming of cannon distinct on the horizon. Ewing watched four companies of the Second Kansas cavalry go forward into a rattle of musketry, with the infantry to follow at the double-quick. With Rabb's and Hopkins's batteries in support and Weer's regiment on the left, the two regiments swept forward and the rebel force fell back, retreating through the town to a wooded area four miles south of Fayetteville. Marmaduke formed

44. Scott, "Spoils of War," 212.
45. Tom quoted in ibid.

a line that could not be flanked and waited on Blunt's next move. Marmaduke's forces were primarily cavalry, and without infantry support they could not hold a determined assault. The Union bayonets advanced rapidly, and with Blunt and Cloud cheering them on, the Kansas brigade went forward into a thick volley of fire. When their attack stalled, a well-timed cavalry charge by half of the Sixth Kansas cavalry regiment attempted to break the rebel resistance, but the Confederates fired by volleys, into the horses, then retreated. The cavalry's commanding officer, Colonel L. R. Jewell, fell with a mortal wound.

Late in the day only the Eleventh Kansas was in a position to pursue the rebels down the Cove Valley toward Hindman's sanctuary beyond the Arkansas River. What had begun awkwardly in fact "ended gallantly." The infantry had traveled thirty-five miles with full packs, and yet Cloud berated Ewing for the inability of his infantry to keep up with the brigade's cavalry. "The puppy!" a sore-footed Ewing complained after the battle.[46]

A week after Cane Hill, Union scouts reported that Brigadier General Thomas Hindman was marching on Fayetteville with a force that outnumbered Blunt's four to one. Prudence dictated that the outnumbered Blunt should retreat. Unimpressed with the fighting abilities of the Confederate forces at Cane Hill, Blunt telegraphed Curtis for reinforcements and made new preparations to confront Hindman.[47]

The nearest Union reinforcements of any size for Blunt were camped among the graves at the old Wilson's Creek battlefield outside Springfield, Missouri. They were commanded by the youngest brigadier general in the Union army, twenty-five-year-old Brigadier General Francis J. Herron. On December 3, Herron received Blunt's summons to move to Fayetteville. His men gobbled rations and covered 110 miles in three days through a tree-covered countryside that had few farms and even fewer roads.

Like a beehive prodded too often, Hindman came out of the mountains on December 5, 1862, before Herron could reach Blunt. A fire-eating former congressman from Arkansas with the personality of a rattlesnake, Hindman had been wounded at Shiloh. Bad weather seemed only to anger him further. On muddy roads at Reed's Mountain his command ran into the pickets of the Sixth Kansas cavalry and four companies of Ewing's Eleventh Kansas regiment. The Kansas

46. Anderson, *Adjutant General,* 183; *O.R.* 22:1:36, 42, 45, 58; Ewing's report at Cane Hill, *O.R.* 22:1:52–54; "ended gallantly" from Monaghan, *Civil War,* 259; "puppy" from TEJr. to ECE, December 2, 1862, quoted in Scott, "Spoils of War," 212.

47. Monaghan, *Civil War,* 260; *O.R.* 22:1:41–43, 60, 827–28.

companies were personally led by Tom Ewing, and they fought a holding action in the trees and precipices along the base of the mountain road. Rebel cavalry charged the Eleventh's picket lines, and the old flintlock muskets roared a volley, the noise if not the lead throwing the enemy line into confusion. Skirmishing continued for two hours. Major Plumb came up with the remainder of the Eleventh regiment's companies, but the fighting petered out at dusk and the forces broke contact.[48]

Hindman's plan was to defeat the divided federal forces in detail. He boldly left his campfires burning, sidestepped Blunt's pickets, put his forces between Blunt and Herron, and marched hard up the Fayetteville Road, intending to smash into and destroy the newcomer, then double back on Blunt, who Hindman assumed was out of supplies and without reinforcement. It might have worked had the Confederate general had reliable men under him. But many were new recruits. Meanwhile, Herron's division reached Fayetteville on December 7. Assuming that Blunt had secured his communications lines southwest out to Prairie Grove, Herron sent his commissary wagons on ahead while the infantry rested. The wagons ran into Confederate cavalry and such a fierce cavalry skirmish that the surviving Union cavalry panicked back into Herron's lines six miles south of Fayetteville, sowing fear in the rest of Herron's command. Herron shot one of these cavalrymen in order to restore order.

Herron advanced on Hindman's positions on a ridge overlooking the Illinois Creek near the Prairie Grove Church. When Union forces contested a crossing of the Illinois Creek, rebel guns came up but superior Union artillery silenced them. The Twentieth Wisconsin and the Nineteenth Iowa assaulted the ridge and surged past rebel guns until meeting overwhelming numbers of advancing Confederates. The new Confederate regiments got the hang of volley fire, and several of Herron's assaults were repulsed. By midafternoon Herron's position was bleak. His lines were thin and holding on by sheer determination alone. Herron was in the same position as Wellington at Waterloo: he would wait for either nightfall or Blunt.[49]

As Blunt's force closed on the sounds of Herron's battle, Colonel Ewing's Eleventh Kansas was divided and formed in thick woods on the west of the Union line near the town of Prairie Grove. Ewing had assumed command of the right

48. Description of Hindman from Ronald H. Bailey, *The Civil War, Battles for Atlanta; Sherman Moves East,* 49; *O.R.* 22:1:9–10, 65–66, 69–71; Monaghan, *Civil War,* 262–63.

49. Ewing's Prairie Grove report at *O.R.* 22:1:98; Connelley, *Preston B. Plumb,* 120–24, *O.R.* 22:1:138–45, 148, 899–901.

side of the line and Moonlight the left, supporting Rabb's and Hopkins's batteries, which were arrayed across the Van Buren Road. Moonlight's wing advanced halfway up the slope and fixed bayonets for a charge at the crest. With bayonets they advanced in a line with the Thirteenth Kansas on Ewing's right and three dismounted companies of the Second Kansas cavalry on his left. All these units had moved forward when a rebel attack concealed in equally thick woods burst over the skirmishers of the Third Indian regiment and onto the Eleventh. The massed fire of the Eleventh's and Thirteenth's formations checked the rebel advance, but when the rebels settled into a standup slugfest with the outnumbered Union line, the day turned sour for the federals.[50]

Ewing's right wing was about to be overrun when he ordered his men back to a fence. Rebels pressured the Second Kansas until they broke. Cloud sent messengers forward to bring the Eleventh Kansas back to the fence line but Ewing had anticipated the need for the move. "My command held their ground, fired four rounds and, seeing the Second Kansas companies had withdrawn and the enemy was in our front, left and rear and near enough to surround us, I ordered my command to fall back." So intense was the Confederate attack, over half an hour in duration, that Ewing's portion of the regiment could not form on the fence line. He ordered them back to a road running through an orchard, where they remained nearly an hour, hotly engaged as the rebels swarmed his flank around a farmhouse. Cloud usually had few complimentary comments for Ewing's efforts, but he grudgingly wrote his superiors that Ewing's wing of 291 men was in the "thickest of the fight."[51]

Hindman was fighting an L-shaped battle. When Herron showed no signs of attacking, Hindman ordered his remaining forces to strike Blunt's command. The Arkansas conscripts refused to advance. Hindman ordered Marmaduke to use his cavalry as file closers, forcing the undisciplined rebels forward. Many were so ill-trained they bit off the ends of their powder charges and spat out the round, loading what amounted to blanks. Blunt's batteries were better manned and double-shotted with canister. "Our cannon mowed them down like weeds," Private William Haynes wrote his wife. When the Tenth and Thirteenth Kansas came up in support of the dog-tired Eleventh, they brought up Stevens's battery. Union infantry pressed Hindman's remaining men hard but were unable to take the ridge. "We fought desperately and hard until dark," Captain Alfred Pierce re-

50. Prairie Grove from Monaghan, *Civil War,* 265–71; Connelley, *Preston B. Plumb,* 115, 124–25; Anderson, *Adjutant General,* 185–86.

51. "My command" from Ewing's report, *O.R.* 22:1:97; Cloud's official report, *O.R.* 22:1:93.

ported. Veterans later said the noise of muskets and artillery was louder and more intense than at Wilson's Creek. Afterward, the battlefield resembled similar fields where desperate men had fought. Haynes wrote, "Some [Confederate dead] had that awful look . . . their heads blowed off and some with brains a running out of heads and still breathing." Ewing's regiment lost six dead and sixty-seven wounded; later it was clear it had been the poor marksmanship of Hindman's conscripts that kept Ewing's losses down. Blunt's cavalry followed Hindman's retreat and reported seeing dead and abandoned wounded as far as ten miles from the battlefield. Strategically, the battle at Prairie Grove ended Confederate thoughts of a strong presence in the Trans-Mississippi theater, and many troops were transferred east of the Mississippi River.[52]

For the first time Ewing had wounded men for whom he had to provide surgical help and round-the-clock care in the hospitals. Sam Worthington, who had fallen out of the line during the forced march, had come into the battle later and helped tend the wounded. Later he was made a permanent regimental nurse. "I do feel better when employed in relieving distress than I should in the common occupation of a soldier." His training was on the job. In spite of his best efforts, four of every five amputees left in his charge died of infection.[53]

Prairie Grove was just the beginning of Hindman's problems that December. Having learned that the federals were not so easy to drive off, over three thousand of his conscripts deserted over the next few weeks. His men had left five thousand muskets, three hundred thousand cartridges, and two artillery pieces on the Prairie Grove battlefield. The battle accomplished what Union departmental commanders wanted, a destruction of the Confederate war effort in northwest Arkansas. Captain Edmund Ross bragged that the rebel prisoners claimed they "would as soon fight the devil as to fight Kansas men." The irrepressible Blunt agreed and, rumor had it, was ready to push his army into Texas in the spring.[54]

Ewing's regiment, though still green, had fought well, and he received credit for it. Watching men die for abstract ideas moved Ewing. It was obvious in his field report. He was proud of his entire regiment. He recounted to his superiors the story of Private William Grigsby, who fell among the dead of the regiment.

52. "Mowed down like weeds" and "awful look" from William C. Haynes to Letia, December 10, 1862, Haynes Collection; "desperately and hard" from Captain A. C. Pierce to William Blakely, December 10, 1862, Josephine Blakely Martin Manuscript Collection, KSHS.

53. Sam Worthington to his sister, December 16, 1862, Worthington Collection; W. W. Denison, "The Battle of Prairie Grove," 586, 588n2.

54. Ross to his wife, December 12, 1862, Ross Collection.

Grigsby had done nothing extraordinary. He was a teamster, but he had found someone else to drive the team, grabbed a musket, and went forward to share the dangers of battle with the regiment. In his tribute to Grigsby, Ewing was in a way synopsizing his own military career thus far—men who did not have to enter battle but did so, and who fought well and sacrificed all.[55]

Ewing's surprising steadiness under fire had made a believer out of Blunt, and when it came to bickering with Cloud, Ewing had gained the upper hand. Even the men sensed it. "[Blunt] seems to have a great deal of confidence in this brigade, as he always puts us in the front in marching towards the enemy and in the rear in marching from him," wrote Edmund Ross. "I would just as soon he wouldn't take quite so much stock in us." In the camps of the Eleventh Kansas, Ewing's animosity toward army discipline returned. Blunt had issued safe conduct passes to local farmers whom he deemed loyal to the Union. Some of Ewing's men confiscated food from one of them, and Cloud held Ewing responsible. This time Ewing's men got into the fight. Ross and others lobbied Blunt to have Ewing replace Cloud as brigade commander. "Then we will have a general we shall be proud to follow and [the whole regiment] almost loves as a man." Ewing also made a direct effort to pressure Blunt, and via Blunt, Cloud. On December 14, he wrote an ill-advised letter to Jim Lane complaining that Blunt's brigadiers—Cloud and William Weer—were overly protective of rebel property. "Cloud is as high, as Colonel, as his capacity warrants. . . . Weer and Cloud both cling to the West Point policy of treating treason as respectful and the property of traitors as sacred. Under cover of a clamor against mean and detestable outrages rarely occurring and universally condemned, they would prohibit all use of secession property."[56]

As unreliable as Lane was with politically sensitive information, Ewing had to know this criticism of Cloud would get back to Blunt. The reference to plundering as "rarely occurring" was a bit disingenuous since plundering by Union troops in Arkansas, especially against Southern sympathizers, was the norm rather than otherwise. Even before Ewing's letter could have reached Lane, Blunt grew distrustful. Five days before Christmas, Cloud again reprimanded Ewing when his troops foraged without authorization. Ewing thought this reprimand preposterous since Cloud earlier had ordered seizure of any good mules found in the countryside. Ewing hated inconsistencies in a man. He decided that if Cloud was going to be a book man when seizing rebel-owned mules, then Ewing would bury Cloud in paperwork for routine camp items such as hospital food.

55. Ewing's report at *O.R.* 22:1:98.

56. "Stock" and "general" from Ross to his wife, December 12, 1862, Ross Collection; "as high as capacity warrants" from Scott, "Spoils of War," 214.

Blunt's enthusiasm to get at rebel armies did not extend to his care for his men. Food shortages were common. On the other hand the politician in Ewing ensured that his men had the best, even in the cold dampness of Fayetteville. For Christmas he managed to scavenge up an oyster supper for the men in the regimental hospital. Samuel Worthington wrote that, when the cooks brought in the oyster stew, Ewing's gesture could not have been better timed. Worthington gushed, "Never was a Colonel more beloved by his men than our Thomas Ewing Jr." Tom's natural leadership had come to the fore. His men had confidence in him, he could adapt to changing situations, and he could plan around obstacles, even obstinate and inflexible commanders. In an army with too few senior officers with those qualities, he was ripe for promotion.[57]

Hugh Ewing had had West Point experience. Although he had not graduated, his leadership was amply demonstrated at South Mountain and Antietam. Tom was a martial surprise to everyone, including Hugh and Cump Sherman, perhaps his senior officers, his men, and perhaps even to himself. From the summer of 1862 until the winter of 1862–1863, he wore the uniform, learned the tactics, relied on good young leaders such as Moonlight, Plumb, and Ross, and had excellent success on the battlefields at Cane Hill and Prairie Grove. He handled the strain of command with some aplomb, although he had the usual civilian problems with military martinets such as Cloud and Blunt. He had proved that he was no flash in the pan as a politician during Lecompton, and he was more than capable of commanding a regiment of infantry in a hot battle. It was an impressive six months' work. He was ready for new challenges, and highly placed men including the president of the United States had their eye on him.

57. Scott, "Spoils of War," 214–15; "more beloved" from Worthington to his wife, December 25, 1862, Worthington Collection.

7

EXTERMINATE THEM, ROOT AND BRANCH

No two men were less alike than Abraham Lincoln and James H. Lane. Lincoln was self-educated and had mastered the law enough to make a comfortable prewar living as a lawyer. He was a family man, erudite, virtuous, and at least among friends considered principled. On the other hand Lane was a self-proclaimed lawyer who made so little money he constantly borrowed funds from others. He claimed no redeeming virtues. Yet with Lincoln's backing, Jim Lane had become the equivalent of a warlord in Kansas and Missouri.

Generals James Blunt and Samuel Curtis were Lane's chief lieutenants. In Arkansas the previous autumn, during November 1862 Blunt and Tom Ewing had helped form a paramilitary organization of "Red Legs," named for the color of their dyed sheepskin leggings. The Red Legs were to operate on the Missouri border to protect Blunt's rear. If there ever was any chivalry of any kind in the American Civil War, very little was found in the Kansas, Missouri, or northern Arkansas theater. Warfare was not enough for some Red Legs, who could steal, murder, and loot with the best the South had to offer. The group included "Wild Bill" Hickock and Buffalo Bill Cody in their young days. Samuel Curtis warned Blunt that "Missourians fear the 'Red Legs' will have too much license under your command. That band of rascals must be checked." When Missouri loyalists retaliated by coming across into Kansas in search of missing livestock, Blunt's men compounded the problem by rounding up them up and hanging several as warnings not to interfere in Kansas. With Curtis and Lane on the one hand and Union Missouri governor Hamilton Gamble on the other, the feud grew to legendary proportions. Missouri politicians were outraged and took their case of Blunt's "reign of terror" to Lincoln.[1]

Lincoln became "tormented . . . beyond endurance . . . by both sides" in the Missouri controversy and felt he was "compelled to take hold." Lincoln used Blunt's unauthorized hangings as an excuse to remove Curtis and named Major General John Schofield to command the Missouri-Kansas Department. A Baptist preacher's son who later led the Army of the Ohio to Atlanta, Schofield oddly is most remembered in the postwar era as a secretary of war under Johnson after the impeachment and, later, for recommending Pearl Harbor in Hawaii as a primary Pacific naval base. A friend of the radicals in Congress, Schofield had commanded in Missouri in early 1862 and had warned Lincoln and Stanton that Kansans and Missourians should be kept apart, with force if necessary. In May 1863, upon Schofield's return appointment to Missouri, Lincoln instructed him to "do right for the public interest," repel Confederate forces if they appeared, and stay out of "pestilent factional quarrels." Lincoln suggested, "If both factions, or neither, shall abuse you, you will, probably, be about right. Beware of being assailed by one and praised by the other."[2]

Because Schofield was under obligation to provide troops to Grant's force at Vicksburg, his own available troop strength dwindled, making it harder for him to maintain the control in Missouri and Kansas that Lincoln had ordered. With fewer troops to cover the district, in June 1863 he divided the department of Kansas into two districts, shunting Blunt off to the inconsequential southern half to chase rebel-supported Indian tribes in the Indian territory and northwest Arkansas. Schofield needed cavalry more than infantry, and he provided men for his cavalry regiments by mounting some veteran infantry regiments like the farm boys in Ewing's old Eleventh Kansas. Then Schofield surprised everyone and appointed Thomas Ewing Jr. to command the new Kansas subdistrict of the border, which consisted of eastern Kansas and western Missouri, headquartered in Kansas City.[3]

1. Cody and Hickok as Red Legs, Starr, *Jennison's Jayhawkers,* 214; William E. Connelley, *Quantrill and the Border Wars,* 411–12; James G. Blunt, "General Blunt's Account of His Civil War Experiences," 239; Missourians protesting Red Legs at *O.R.* 22:2:5–6; "too much license" from Curtis to Blunt, *O.R.* 22:2:194; "reign of terror" at *O.R.* 22:2:5.

2. Lincoln's torment and compulsion to take hold at *O.R.* 22:2:281; Lincoln to Schofield, ibid., 293.

3. *O.R.* 22:1:14–16; Schofield's division of the district at ibid., 15.

The exact circumstances surrounding Ewing's promotion are obscure. No War Department district command had ever gone to a colonel. With Schofield's strong ties to the radicals, Ewing's new rank as brigadier general was quickly approved. After the Eleventh Kansas regiment was mounted and parsed out in various Kansas stations, Ewing was without an effective command. From Fort Scott, Ewing was ordered by General Francis Herron to command the First division of the Army of the Frontier and assist in garrisoning the area of southwest Missouri near Forsythe, east of present-day Branson. Indeed, on April 20, 1863, from Rolla, Missouri, Herron sent orders to Colonel Ewing at Fort Scott, and Ewing replied seven days later as brigadier general. There is no direct order in the *Official Reports* for his brigadiership, and several senior officers at the same time in the spring of 1863 refer to him as colonel while others refer to him as general.[4]

Regardless of its genesis, his appointment to the District of the Border and his elevation by Schofield over Blunt stunned Lane. Blunt was a major general and Ewing a newly minted brigadier. Blunt had handled troops well at Prairie Grove; Ewing was a competent leader in that battle but was not the strategic thinker that Blunt was. Yet Ewing got the plum assignment. Although they had gotten along well enough to raise the Eleventh Kansas Regiment, Lane had little practical influence with Ewing, who had proved long ago that graft was not an incentive. Lane had been able to discredit Governor Robinson enough that, in November 1862, Thomas Carney, a Lane supporter, was elected governor, whereupon Carney also came into conflict with Lane over who was going to control the naming of officers to the Kansas regiments. Furthermore Lane knew his control of who would get army contracts in Ewing's new district was unhinged when it became evident that Carney was courting Ewing.[5]

In reality Ewing's appointment over Blunt was a measure of the mischief that Lane, Blunt, and Curtis together had been causing the president of the United States. A warlord does not easily give up a profitable fiefdom, however, and Lane rushed back to Washington to get Halleck to countermand Schofield's actions. Lane supporters such as Major General Francis Herron and Brigadiers William Vandever and William W. Orme in Missouri threatened to resign if Schofield stayed. Orme was an Illinois lawyer before the war, familiar to the president, and fought at Prairie Grove with one of Herron's brigades. When Schofield sniffed out Lane's end run, he telegraphed Halleck that peace in the region required both sides of the Kansas–Missouri border be under a unified command. Ewing's political

4. Herron and Ewing, *O.R.* 22:2:229, 257, 285.
5. Carney-Ewing ties from Plummer, *Frontier Governor,* 20–21.

savvy was more valuable to Schofield than Blunt's military ability. Schofield wrote of Ewing that he had the "confidence of law-abiding citizens in Kansas," which, of course, also indicated an opinion that Kansas senator James H. Lane did not. For too long, malcontents on both sides had played one senior officer off against another. Halleck had seen this sort of bickering during his own stay in Missouri with Sherman early in the war. Halleck supported Schofield.[6]

As a last resort Lane went to Lincoln. The president had laid out his plan earlier to Schofield, and he was not about to undercut his specific directions to Schofield by second-guessing him. Lincoln was comfortable with Ewing, and in spite of Lane's concerns Ewing could not do a worse job than what had been done previously. Lincoln decided to ignore Lane's efforts, for now. Lane tried again—wanting to isolate Ewing and Schofield by getting Blunt an independent department of the frontier that would include Kansas. Again, Lincoln refused. Schofield's division of the District of Kansas into northern and southern divisions left Ewing in command in the north and Blunt in the south. So, whether he was chosen because of an anti-Lane-and-Blunt "plot" with Carney or on his own merit, Thomas Ewing Jr. took command of his Kansas district in mid-June 1863. He was by then sporting new stars on his shoulder boards and a close-clipped beard like Sherman.[7]

Even for soldiers lucky enough to avoid a bullet, a war can alter a career. Before August 1863 Ewing's career had been, like his life, in ascendancy. As a political leader he did not need to know how to play a bugle; he needed only to know how to stay in front of the band. Schofield had assigned him a truly grim command. Nowhere was the Civil War fought with more unremitting iron-fisted savagery than on the Kansas-Missouri border. Even senior officers were sending letters between the lines attempting to straighten out the rules as to whether civilian bridge burners could be executed. While Lincoln, Ewing, Blunt, Curtis, and Schofield sorted out pecking orders in these important Trans-Mississippi commands, guerrilla activities in Missouri escalated during the early summer of 1863. Almost from the beginning of his tenure, Ewing faced guerrilla marauding in eastern Kansas.

Guerrillas came in two different types—young Missouri farmers tired of

6. Pressure on Halleck by Lane over Schofield's appointment, see *O.R.* 22:2:285; "law-abiding citizens" from *O.R.* 22:2:351.

7. Lane's call for a department of the frontier see Castel, *Frontier State,* 111, and the Lane newspapers, the *Kansas Weekly Tribune (Lawrence),* May 23, 1863, *Kansas State Record (Topeka),* May 23, 1863, and *Leavenworth Daily Conservative,* May 6, 1863.

Kansas jayhawking raids, and "border ruffians" who were outlaws and castaways looking for loot. Cole Younger and Frank and Jesse James were representatives of the former, George Todd and Bill Anderson were in the second group. Confederate officers in Texas alleged that Quantrill's men "will not obey orders" and "regard the life of a man less than you would that of a sheep-killing dog."[8]

These guerrillas were not afraid of launching terror raids into Kansas. Yeager's band rode 130 miles west to strike the Santa Fe Trail near Council Grove. On the return trip to Westport, Missouri, they robbed stagecoaches and burned homes in Rock Springs, Black Jack, Gardner, and Shawnee. Prominent civilians were shot in their beds. One casualty struck by a stray bullet was a small girl. Kansans had had enough. Rural folks moved out of the border counties and into the cities as refugees. Governor Carney asked Stanton for a regiment of "home guards," even black regiments, to protect Kansas farms, homes, and shops. Stanton declined Carney's request for home guards, more out of political deference to Lane's ongoing feud with Carney than out of military need. Ewing agreed with Carney—men were needed. He wrote Schofield ten days after taking command in Kansas, asking for help to protect the Santa Fe Trail against predatory raids. "Until Governor Carney's new regiment is ready for the field," he wanted three cavalry regiments "whose men will hunt down the guerrillas without flagging or remorse." Ewing was new to the job but "stubbornly determined" to "blend adequately between Lane and conservative Schofield." William Clarke Quantrill shrugged it all off, supposedly telling Robert S. Stevens, "Ewing is in command of the district but I run the machine."[9]

Quantrill did indeed run the machine. Little in Quantrill's mild makeup would have led his friends to believe the ruthlessness he would assume during the war. He had come out to Kansas from Ohio before the war to work for Leavenworth's largest employer, Russell, Majors & Waddell, driving freight wagons. In 1860 he took up the duplicitous roles of both border ruffian and abolitionist, pretending to secure blacks for passage on the Underground Railroad in Lawrence, then reselling them back into bondage in Missouri.[10]

Nine months before his attack on Lawrence, a small guerrilla force under Quantrill had attacked Olathe, twenty miles from guerrilla strongholds around

8. For "bridge burners," see Sterling Price to Henry Halleck, *O.R.* 2:1:255–56; description of Missouri guerrillas from Castel, *Frontier State*, 104–5; "sheep-killing dog" from *O.R.* 34:2:942.

9. Yeager's attack on Santa Fe Trail in *Council Grove Press*, May 11, 1863; "without flagging or remorse," *O.R.* 22:2:328–29; "blend adequately" and "run the machine" from Monaghan, *Civil War*, 277.

10. Connelley, *Quantrill*, 152.

Westport (now a posh Kansas City suburb). Quantrill's men brought wagons with them to make the looting easier. They killed six men and fired the town. For defending against such raids and raids further into Kansas, such as at Council Grove, Ewing decided on a strategy to remain mobile with dispersed troop concentrations and respond to an attack quickly. But Ewing's mind was not only on guerrillas. Mobs of Union men continued their raids into Missouri, and these attacks had to stop if Ewing was ever going to show loyal Missourians that Kansans and the federal government could be fair to border state loyalists, in order to get Missourians to give allegiance to the government and deny sanctuary to the guerrillas.

To show Missourians he was serious, Ewing took on the Red Legs problem by employing only those Red Legs who were offering a service to their country and arresting the predators. Two weeks after taking command in Kansas, in a speech at Olathe, Ewing told his audience, "There are many men in Kansas who are stealing themselves rich in the name of liberty, arrogat[ing] to themselves and their sympathizers all the radical anti-slaveryism and genuine loyalty in Kansas. Under their aegis many of the worst men that ever vexed a civilized community have flocked and been protected." While there is disagreement among historians as to the specific date of Ewing's speech, his "stealing themselves rich in the name of liberty" was an indictment of Daniel R. Anthony and Jim Lane, while the "worst men that ever vexed a civilized community" appeared to attack the Red Legs themselves. Lane and Anthony, in turn, were not about to take this sort of broadside on their home turf without returning fire. Lane newspapers called Ewing naive. Anthony's *Leavenworth Conservative* accused Ewing of preferring to be a police officer than to protect Kansas from marauding guerrillas. Mostly, however, Kansans responded to Ewing's speech by declaring it open season on Red Legs. Missouri men as well as some Kansans assumed that any lawlessness fomented against Red Legs would be ignored by Ewing. Vigilante bands raided Red Legs' camps and scattered them.[11]

Having mastered Anthony's wing of the Red Legs and ultra-radicals and obtained control with martial law and help from loyal Missourians, Ewing turned to the guerrillas. He ordered routine patrols, but as July turned to August 1863, he had less than twenty-six hundred men available to garrison his towns and patrol his supply lines between Forts Leavenworth, Riley, and Scott, or forts west and south along the Santa Fe Trail. He set up listening posts—trip wires—on a line from Fort Leavenworth to Fort Scott. Small details passed constantly from post

11. "Stealing themselves rich" from Castel, *Frontier State,* 112; *Leavenworth Conservative,* August 16, 1863; Anti–Red Legs vigilantes from *Kansas State Journal (Lawrence),* August 6, 1863.

to post on hourly intervals, always on the move. But these men were no match for a determined guerrilla force. There simply were not enough men in the saddle at any one time. Quantrill was right. Ewing was in command. but Quantrill had the run of the sixty thousand square miles of the District of the Border.[12]

While Quantrill was planning his attacks on Kansas towns from sanctuaries in western Missouri, Ewing placed considerable faith in his spies within the guerrilla camps. Anyone could guess what Quantrill was going to do, but not exactly when. The day of an anticipated raid was of considerable importance. If the spies learned anything important, they would alert Union forces in time to muster the Union men and confront any attacker in Kansas with a combined force. If he tried to anticipate when the raid would come and by what route, Ewing might have an entire regiment confronting perhaps a dozen raiders, leaving other routes and towns undefended.

Ewing ordered Captain Henry Palmer's company of the Eleventh Kansas cavalry to shadow Quantrill wherever he might go within Kansas and Missouri. With Ewing's permission Palmer sent two of his officers to infiltrate Quantrill's band as spies. One of them was caught and executed in Quantrill's camp as he sat at a campfire. The other was not found out, yet he was unable to get any warning to Palmer about anything. Rumors flew. In late June, Lawrence mayor George Collamore began to hear from friends in Missouri that Quantrill was gathering a large force, and Lawrence was an obvious target. Collamore requested help from Ewing, but Ewing did not respond, apparently not crediting the source. Denied federal troops Collamore called out his own militia, set up pickets, and alerted outlying farm homes. Ewing did send a token force of twenty men to Lawrence in late July, and later a company of cavalry under Captain Edmund Ross. By August 10 no attack had occurred, and Ross's troops withdrew.[13]

In the weeks before the attack on Lawrence, Ewing was distracted by his new proposal to Schofield concerning how to handle local families who gave safe haven to guerrilla lawlessness. In early July Brigadier General Odon Guitar issued a general order in his Northern District of Missouri that any civilian who harbored guerrillas would be treated like a common soldier, subject to arrest and presumably made a POW. POWs could be imprisoned until the end of the war, without trial. Guitar's policy made sense to Ewing, as far as it went. However, imprisoning Confederate sympathizers was expensive. Ewing asked Schofield's

12. Lack of troops, Castel, *Whirlwind,* 121; Ewing's disposition of troops at *O.R.* 22:2:322–23, 416.
13. Castel, *Frontier State,* 125; Ewing's spies see *O.R.* 22:1:320.

permission to drive the worst of the rebel families out of his district and across the White River into northern Arkansas. That way the Confederacy could feed and house them. The hope was that bushwhackers would follow their families to Arkansas thus cleansing Missouri of guerrillas. Ewing had extended Guitar's POW analogy by effectively making Confederate sympathizers stateless people. It was a form of ethnic cleansing based on family ties but without considerations of ethnicity.

Schofield was occupied with troubles with Confederate raids into the boot heel of Missouri and with the impact of the national draft on his district. That summer draft riots had broken out in New York City, and Missouri was on the edge of anarchy over the same issue. Ewing's proposal went without a response for eleven days. Schofield finally agreed to the outline of Ewing's idea, but he was to limit the movement only to "families of the worst character." Uprooting anyone—even rebel sympathizers in fractured Missouri—created political problems. Schofield sent Ewing a proposal of his own for which he asked Ewing's guidance. It would need the cooperation of Missouri loyalists, and this required promises and actions designed to get and maintain loyalty, which meant Ewing had to control Kansas jayhawking.[14]

Some rebel families were already in federal custody. Several aunts, cousins, and sisters of Jim Vaughn, a notorious guerrilla, were under guard at Leavenworth. Ewing sent them under guard to a rundown Union hotel near Westport. George Bingham, the pro-Union Missouri state treasurer, complained to Ewing that the building was unsafe, and Ewing had received similar reports of its condition from his own provost officers. There was some indication that, in making room for the women, remodeling of the building weakened the center supports. Before the building could be repaired, it collapsed, killing four women and injuring the rest. The hotel incident was not a catalyst for Quantrill's raid on Lawrence since he was planning the raid before the building fell. However, it proved convenient for rebel sympathizers to justify what was to happen in Lawrence.[15]

In the weeks before Quantrill's Lawrence raid, pro-Ewing newspapers fought for his reputation against the howls of scorn from Bingham and other Missourians. "No general in command of the district has succeeded better," the *Leavenworth Daily Times* editorialized. "No one can adopt measures which suppress the evils which afflict the country without making enemies." The Leavenworth newspaper pointed out Ewing's remarks had lowered the incidence of bushwhacking

14. "Worst character" from *O.R.* 22:2:450; Schofield's proposed order, ibid., 471.

15. Collapse of the building from Connelley, *Preston B. Plumb,* 147–49.

and predations by Red Legs. "We believe the time is not far distant when everything will become quiet and peaceful on this border."[16]

Revenge for the fall of Vicksburg and the suffering of the town's civilians is one theory that historians believe prompted Quantrill's raid, but Vicksburg is a weak argument. All the civilians at Vicksburg—and most other Southern cities later bombarded by Union forces—had notice that a Union army was at hand with a siege in mind and Southern forces did not force any civilians to stay. The first Southern city bombarded in a systematic way was Fredericksburg in December 1862. Even there, however, the civilians had time to refugee out. Southerners remaining in Fredericksburg and Vicksburg did so voluntarily. Payback for the destruction of private property in a bombardment of a city under siege would hardly support the wanton slaughter of unarmed civilians in a small frontier town in Kansas. Nevertheless, in mid-August 1863 on the Blackwater River in Johnson County, Missouri, Quantrill gathered three hundred men for his raid.

On August 18, based on Schofield's input, Ewing issued General Order Number 10 from his Kansas City office. This was three days before Quantrill rode into Lawrence. It allowed federal officers to arrest and send outside the district any civilian willfully aiding rebels. A neutral magistrate would not determine who was caught "aiding" a rebel. That job fell to Ewing's cavalry, who had to sift through available evidence. Wives of known guerrillas were ordered out "forthwith," and those who disobeyed would be deported. It was a particularly tough law since the dead women from the Kansas City tragedy were only four days in their graves.[17]

Since the war began, guerrillas had slipped in and out of Missouri's civilian population to hide from pursuing federals, an eerie situation not unlike American military and Iraqi government problems in controlling insurgents in Iraq in the wake of the 2003 war. Ewing and other commanders in Missouri found it difficult to determine with certainty who were rebel sympathizers. In a post–Order Number 11 letter to his father, Ewing chafed at Schofield's requirement that "neutral" families be allowed to remain in the four affected Missouri counties. "No intelligence . . . can tell the neutral from the disloyal persons." Some neutral families also had members who were "willfully disloyal." He concluded that "the

16. "No general . . . succeeded better" from *Leavenworth Daily Times,* August 18, 1863; Ann Davis Niepman, "General Order Number 11 and Border Warfare during the Civil War," 198.

17. General Order Number 10, at *O.R.* 22:2:460–61.

removal of three fourths who are disloyal while leaving one fourth who are neutral would be impractical [to administer]."[18]

If he knew of Schofield's consideration of Order Number 10, it meant little to Quantrill. Lawrence's reputation as an abolitionist stronghold and haven for escaped Missouri slaves made it a prime political target. A day after Order Number 10 was issued, Quantrill laid out the final plans. They would attack bearing light arms and wearing no uniforms, which would allow them to split up and blend into the population if need be. There were no guidons or flags, no supportive wagons or cannon with limbers. This was business, not show. Quantrill had invited 104 recruits under guerrilla commander John Holt to tag along on the raid as a learning experience and get "christened." If anyone could not stomach what they were about to do, they could stand down. Quantrill's now 140 horsemen headed west, not in neat rows of four-abreast cavalry columns but as a mob, an apt description for those bent on committing what until September 11, 2001, was to be the largest mass murder of unarmed civilians in recorded American history.[19]

In the late afternoon of August 20, 1863, Quantrill crossed the Missouri border near Aubrey, Kansas, near where a careless junior Union officer named James Pike and his detachment of cavalry were stationed. Pike's orders were to report any movements by telegraph to his commanding officer and any community he guessed was in the path of the advance, then trail the Confederate column. For some reason, Pike did neither. Lawrence paid dearly for Pike's omission. One of Pike's telegrams came to Captain Charles Coleman of the Ninth Kansas cavalry at Little Santa Fe. Coleman sent a courier to alert Kansas City and other stations by telegraph, then started his column toward Aubrey. No one telegraphed Lawrence. By nine o'clock in the evening Coleman absorbed Pike's two companies, and 180 federal cavalry were moving in the dark toward Lawrence, but well behind Quantrill.[20]

Union forces all over eastern Kansas had access to telegraph stations all along the route—the Civil War technological equivalent of radar. Yet no telegraph had pinpointed Quantrill's whereabouts. Two Eleventh Kansas troopers on leave were

18. TEJr. to TESr., September 14, 1863, a letter provided to the author from Joseph H. Ewing Collection.

19. "Christened" from Castel, *Frontier State,* 126.

20. Henry E. Palmer, "The Lawrence Raid," 317–25; for Ewing's report see *O.R.* 22:1:579–85; for Pike's defense see Pike to Connelley, July 28, 1917, James A. Pike Manuscript Collection, KSHS; Coleman's report, *O.R.* 22:1:590–91.

surprised by Quantrill in the dark and were fired on. One was killed and the other, trooper William C. Haynes, fled. At midnight the large force had alerted a farmer named John Reed, who sped on horseback toward Lawrence. On a moonless night Reed's horse fell into a ravine and rolled onto Reed, mortally wounding the farmer. Reed was Lawrence's last chance to avoid total surprise. In the early morning darkness Quantrill became concerned that he was losing his way under a moonless night sky. At a farm he shanghaied a guide into his service to lead him to the outskirts of Lawrence. Once they were in position, the guide was shot, the first civilian to die by rebel gunfire in Quantrill's Raid.[21]

At dawn Quantrill's force paused on a small rise southeast of Lawrence and waited for trailing scouts to report on whether an active enemy was in pursuit. Quantrill sent two men into the town to reconnoiter. They rode to the river and back without waking anyone. There were no sentries. Quantrill had not sought a surprise, but he had achieved it. He drew up his men, had them check their weapons, and issued his last instructions. Burn whatever they could. Shoot the men and all the boys old enough to aim a rifle. Jim Lane and Charles Robinson were to be taken alive if possible. Quantrill would carry both men back to Missouri and publicly hang them. His men were warned that if they were captured, they could expect the same treatment. Females and children were off-limits, Quantrill ordered. After all Quantrill's men were not barbarians.[22]

What came out of the dawn from the east that morning in Lawrence was carnage both one-sided and devastating. Ewing described it as a "fiendish atrocity." Biographers point out that the "concentrated loathsomeness" of the Lawrence massacre was rivaled only by the massacre of black troops at Fort Pillow. Lawrence was worse. Yelling like demons Quantrill's men roared into Lawrence as "bearded, long-haired, wild-looking men" to those who saw them coming. Among the first to die was the Reverend S. S. Snyder, a prominent minister and a lieutenant in the Second Kansas colored regiment, shot as he stepped outside his house. His unarmed black recruits surrendered and then were shot down where they stood. Near a downtown hotel Quantrill's companies rode down a group of white recruits from the Fourteenth Kansas. Of the twenty-two men who came out of their

21. John Reed's death at *O.R.* 22:1:583; shooting the guide from Castel, *Frontier State,* 128. The Haynes story comes from Obituary, Haynes Collection.

22. Alec Miller, ed., *The Lawrence Massacre* (Lawrence, Kansas: J. S. Broughton Publisher, approx. 1864). The work has been made available by the Kansas Collection of Kenneth Spencer Research Library and the Department of History of the University of Kansas and is available on the Internet at <http://www.kancoll.org/books/cordley_massacre/quantrel.raid.html> last accessed April 2, 2008.

tents, seventeen died in the first pass. The remaining five unarmed men fled to the Kansas River, hiding in the cattails.[23]

Some tried to reason with the guerrillas. Ralph Dix, a carriage-maker, told Ed Thompson that if they just surrendered and did not resist, it would be all right. Thompson watched the guerrillas shoot Dix and throw him into a burning building. County clerk G. W. Bill was dragged from a building and asked for time to pray. His wish was granted, then four guerrillas shot him. Mayor Collamore had asked Ewing for army protection, but when he saw his neighbors gunned down, he frantically lowered himself into a cistern to escape. His burning house caved in, killing him. Next door Dr. Griswold, state senator Sam Thorp, newspaper editor J. C. Trask, and a lawyer named H. W. Baker were lured out of their houses with promises of being made prisoners of war and were shot down in front of their hysterical wives. Trask and Griswold died instantly, but Thorp and Baker feigned death. The women were not allowed to get to the bodies. A half-hour later a new group of guerrillas rode up to the scene, rolled Thorp and Baker over and shot them again. Thorp died the next day, but Baker miraculously survived the two wounds. Louis Carpenter, whom Tom Ewing appointed as the first reporter for the Kansas Supreme Court, was shot and wounded. His wife threw herself over his body. A third gunman calmly pulled her up with one hand and shot Carpenter in the head. Their house burned, taking with it part of the court's library.[24]

Not all the women were spared. When an attorney, Samuel A. Riggs, was shot at, he fled down an alley. Kate Riggs grabbed the bridle of the guerrilla trying to run him down and was dragged by the horse across a woodpile. When Riggs escaped, the guerrilla turned and in spite of Quantrill's orders swung his horse pistol at her, clubbing her.

Midmorning Quantrill's lookouts on the Oread Ridge reported dust columns to the east. Quantrill led his men south, out of the town. Then he turned southeast to evade pursuit.[25]

23. "Wild-looking" from Castel, *Frontier State,* 129; "fiendish atrocity" at *O.R.* 22:1:583; "concentrated loathsomeness" from Starr, *Jennison's Jayhawkers,* 254–55. I make the statement that Lawrence was worse than Fort Pillow because of Quantrill's premeditation. Quantrill's attack was a calculated and premeditated white-on-white ruthlessness against old men and boys. Fort Pillow in 1864, although gruesome and unnecessary, was carrying out the warnings the Confederate government had made against black troops and their white officers taken in combat.

24. Death of Dix from Statement of Ed Thompson, August 5, 1895, box 214, EFP/LC; Griswold's and Baker's deaths from John Speer, "The Burning of Osceola Mo. by Lane and the Quantrill Massacre Contrasted," 305–12.

25. Miller, *Lawrence Massacre,* on the Internet at <http://www.kancoll.org/books/cordley_massacre/quantrel.raid.html> last accessed April 2, 2008.

Upon entering Lawrence, federal troops found bodies everywhere—in gardens, on front porches, in bedrooms, and in the charred ruins of homes. Seventy buildings, homes, and businesses were burned. Lane had escaped by hiding in a cornfield, but his house was gone. Lawrence smelled like a giant barbeque. Quantrill left 180 dead, dozens more wounded, 80 widows and 250 orphaned children. Lawrence was among the more costly battles of the war except that no one was allowed to surrender in Lawrence, and most of the dead were unarmed civilians. The lack of men to build coffins required that fifty-three of the dead be buried in a mass grave. Reporters searching for metaphors went back to the 1857 Sepoy mutiny in India for comparisons.[26]

As the night of August 20–21 unfolded, Ewing was not in his Kansas City headquarters. He had taken "French leave" with Ellen at her room at the Planter's Hotel in Leavenworth. She had been ill much of the week, and he had taken some time to be with her because the telegraph wires had been quiet all week. Back at Ewing's headquarters, however, when the telegraphs began tapping out ominous messages, telegraphers in Kansas City could not find him.[27]

When Ewing went to his office that morning and the telegrams began detailing the loss of life in Lawrence, Ewing was "prostrate with grief." The list of the dead contained men Tom Ewing had known for years. He hurriedly gathered five companies of the Eleventh Ohio cavalry who had been at Fort Leavenworth outfitting themselves for duty in Wyoming; three hundred of them rode behind Ewing virtually unarmed except for pistols. He moved toward DeSoto and then Lanesfield, Kansas, south, to cut off Quantrill's retreat. But the guerrillas were long gone. Knowing that a stunned nation would want good news, when Lieutenant-Colonel Lazear, with his detachments of the First Missouri cavalry, encountered Quantrill at noon on August 21 at the Big Creek and broke up his force, commencing a running battle with different parts of the rebel leader's band, Ewing dutifully reported to St. Louis what his isolated commands were reporting to him; that between fifty and sixty guerrillas were killed during the retreat. "The most unremitting efforts are being made to hunt down the remainder of the band." The reports from his juniors were false, but he passed them along because he had no way of knowing the exact truth and he desperately wanted some good news for higher commands.[28]

26. Castel, *Frontier State,* 132; coffins from Elliott, "Grasshopper Falls Convention," 179–96; body count from Speer, "The Burning of Osceola," 305–12; Sepoy mutiny comparison in *Leavenworth Daily Times,* September 1, 1863.

27. "French leave" from Palmer, "Lawrence Raid," 321; Ewing reported at the Planter's Hotel in *Leavenworth Daily Times,* August 20–21, 1863.

28. "Prostrate with grief" from Palmer, "Lawrence Raid," 321; false Union reports at *O.R.* 22:2:477–78.

There was little the federal troops could do. Federal horses were fatigued. Quantrill's men on remounts pulled away in the 100-degree heat of August 21. Major Plumb's small force saw smoke from Lawrence, guessed at which direction the retreat would go, and turned to intercept them at Baldwin City, southeast of Lawrence. They struck Quantrill's rear at five o'clock in the afternoon near Paola. But before Plumb could press the attack, several horses had collapsed and two men died of sunstroke. Quantrill disappeared into the timber country along the Missouri–Kansas border.[29]

It surprised no one that James H. Lane was the first to use the bloodshed to his advantage. Lane telegraphed Lincoln that Kansans would have their revenge on Missouri even if Kansans had to fire on Union forces. He warned Lincoln in language calculated to be released in Missouri that he had organized the Kansas militia during Bleeding Kansas days and would do it again. He would have no recruiting problems. They would attack Missouri and search for Quantrill. If they found him, so much the better, but either way Missouri was going to pay heavily in lives and property for harboring guerrillas. He followed up his demands to Lincoln on August 27 with a call to all Kansans with guns to assemble in Paola on September 9 for a jayhawking raid that Missourians would never forget.[30]

Thirty-six hours after the attack and without having had much sleep, Lane borrowed a fresh horse and sent a telegram to Tom Ewing, demanding that Ewing meet him in Morristown, a border town in Cass County, Missouri. Lane had used the place as a jumping-off point for his brigade's jayhawking raids two years earlier, and his presence there once again was intended to give sharp-eyed rebel sympathizers information they could pass along to guerrilla leaders. In Morristown Lane immediately bawled out Ewing for the slipshod manner in which he had run the District of Kansas. He raged that he—not Ewing or Schofield—was going to set policy in the future, and that Ewing, as district commander, would carry out that policy. These were, of course, demands that Ewing could not obey. Ewing angrily reminded Lane that his Senate friends had pushed Lincoln into the Emancipation Proclamation, and the president and U.S. senators now would live by its limitations. Border state slaves were not to be emancipated. As for Kansas, Lane's political maneuvering had kept Governor Carney from raising a border regiment that might have defended Lawrence. As far as Ewing was concerned, the Lawrence massacre was as much Lane's doing as Quantrill's. If Lane continued to interfere, Ewing would go public with Lane's duplicity.

29. Plumb's last contact at Castel, *Frontier State,* 134; *O.R.* 22:1:580–81.
30. *O.R.* 22:1:583, 22:2:475.

Lane and Ewing had played this poker game before. Lane had no time to decide whose hand was better this time. The fact was that Kansans were enraged and far more loyal to Lane's retaliation calls than to either the governor or the commanding officer of federal troops. Lane told Ewing that he was not sure he could contain the rage in Kansas. Ewing had not been on the streets of Lawrence as Quantrill's goons came whirling through town with their guns blazing. Lane was right, but Ewing dared not admit it. Kansans were indeed in a stir. Samuel Adair of Fort Scott wrote in his diary on the day of the attack, "Arguments were made for organizing for defense and for going into the field if necessary. Very great blame (and probably justly) is attached to gen. Ewing." Anthony, still smarting from Ewing's martial law order, had ripped the general in print immediately after the raid: "The know-nothing, do-nothing policy of the general commanding this district has shown his utter incapacity. With 5,000 soldiers under his command and allowing a few hundred guerrillas to get 50 miles into the interior of our state and burn Lawrence, destroying two million in property, is ample proof that we must depend upon ourselves for the defense of our city and state." Anthony challenged Kansans wanting to avenge Lawrence to meet at a preset time with their mounts and he would provide the Sharps carbines.[31]

While such inflammatory language was expected of Anthony, Lawrence had ended the pretense of fairness, even on the part of moderate editors supportive of Ewing. They called for Missouri guerrillas to be "exterminated root and branch." Massacre survivor Sidney Clarke wrote his friend James Fry, who would ensure the letter got to Edwin Stanton, that the war on the border "promises to [become] one of extermination." Two thousand armed Kansans were going to defy "the policy of General Schofield and General Ewing." Clarke predicted the result would be "without parallel" in warfare.[32]

The Confederacy did not help itself in Missouri. Ignoring the high body count among Lawrence civilians, Southern newspapers gushed with stories about the "gallant" Quantrill, an adjective adopted by his Confederate superiors until Quantrill later began raiding Confederate sympathizers in Oklahoma and Texas. Even this structured encouragement did not result in Quantrill's ever filing an official report on his gallant Lawrence raid. How does one write a military after-action report on an atrocity?

31. Samuel Adair, "Diary," August 21, 1863, Adair Family Papers, KSHS; "know-nothing" policy from *Leavenworth Daily Times,* August 22, 1863.

32. "Root and branch" at *Leavenworth Daily Times,* August 24, 1863; for Lane's general attitude toward Schofield and Ewing, see Clarke to James Fry, *O.R.* 3:3:720.

At Morristown, Lane barked at Ewing that the federal government could no longer appease Missourians who were more interested in getting along with the Confederacy than fighting them. Jennison was raising a cavalry regiment that would carry its own oaths of allegiance to the Union so deep into Missouri that no order could recall them. Schofield, Lane argued, was "too sympathetic" to Missouri bushwhackers. "Just kill them!" he demanded of Ewing.[33]

Ewing seethed at Lane's dressing-down but knew he was not in a position of power at the moment. Ewing wanted something from Lane in return—he wanted time. He quickly explained to Lane the deportation plan he had been working on with Schofield. Ewing wanted Lane to keep the radicals in check long enough to give his new deportation policy a chance to work. Lane was astute enough to realize that, if he were patient, he might have it both ways—ending the scourge of guerrillas, for which he could take credit, while at the same time not risking the lives of his supporters. Some historians claim that Ewing was begging Lane to allow his policies—what became Order Number 11—to work before retaliating. Others believe Ewing was not the begging kind. Either way Lane thought it over and then agreed. He could let Ewing try his depopulation plan. But there would be no backsliding. "You are a dead dog if you fail to issue the order as agreed between us," Lane reputedly instructed Ewing. If it worked Lane would point out that he was present when it was hatched. If the order failed, Lane warned Ewing, he would still launch his jayhawking raid.[34]

What came out of the Morristown meeting was the most aggressive nonracial civilian relocation order in American history, and a lifetime of controversy for Thomas Ewing Jr. General Order Number 11, as the directive became known, was styled a military necessity and the logical extension of the policy already in place with Order Number 10. When Ewing first outlined how he was going to expand Order Number 10 into a harsher concept, Schofield balked. Federal authorities believed Quantrill's raid was, in part, retaliation to Ewing's Order Number 10, which removed a few bushwhacker families from the border. If the relocation order was expanded, Confederate retaliation might worsen. Ewing remained adamant. The army could not protect all Kansas towns. If federal officials left vital Union towns unprotected and did not effectively challenge the guerrillas, farms would be abandoned and the states of Kansas and Missouri would be isolated.

33. "Oaths of allegiance" from Starr, *Jennison's Jayhawkers,* 256–57; "gallant" Quantrill from L. A. McLean to W.C. Quantrill, November 2, 1863, at *O.R.* 53:908; "Just Kill Them" Lane speech in the *Leavenworth Daily Times,* August 27, 1863.

34. "Dead dog" from Castel, *Frontier State,* 144–45.

Kansas and Missouri stood on the brink of a civil war within a civil war, where loyalists might be killing other loyalists. Ewing informed Schofield that Missouri had to choose: give up its Southern sympathizers to Arkansas or endure Lane's wrath. Schofield reluctantly agreed to let Ewing issue Order Number 11, which he did on August 25, 1863.[35]

Order Number 11 was the most controversial action Ewing would ever take and was one of the more controversial actions of the war. Schofield made some changes before giving the plan his general approval. He wrote, "I am pretty much convinced that the mode of carrying on the war on the border during the past two years has produced such a state of feeling that nothing short of total devastation of the districts which are made the haunts of guerrillas will be sufficient to put a stop to the evil." The order combined relocation with the destruction of the private farms of known sympathizers. Within a fifteen-day period, whole towns and all the farms in Jackson, Cass, Bates, and parts of Vernon counties in Missouri were depopulated. Loyal Missourians could move off their farms to federal military posts or into towns such as Kansas City. Southern sympathizers were to keep moving south. All grain and hay found in the counties after September 9 would be confiscated or destroyed.[36]

Ewing's plan was to destroy the farms of those who refused to move. Schofield would have gone further, removing the disloyal and then destroying their farms regardless of whether they moved. Although the plan was in operation, Ewing was concerned whether Schofield could keep Halleck and Lincoln convinced such drastic measures were necessary to stop guerrilla predations. As it turned out Halleck's only concern was to suppress the press reaction. As for Missouri civilians, Halleck agreed with Lane's hardliners. "They seem to have lost all sense of the perils of the country and all sentiments of national patriotism." If Schofield could end virulent Missouri factionalism through Ewing's order, so be it.[37]

As Ewing put Order Number 11 into effect and while Kansans remained eager for a retaliation raid into Missouri, demands grew for a military inquiry into whose negligence had allowed the massacre to happen. Not needing this sort of diversion as they were trying to root out the guerrillas in western Missouri,

35. The forced relocation of numerous Indian tribes in the nineteenth century and of Japanese Americans during the Second World War involved more families but were racially motivated. Order Number 11 was ordered by whites and primarily affected whites.

36. Schofield to TEJr., August 25, 1865, *O.R.* 22:2:471.

37. Ewing to Schofield, August 25, 1863, *O.R.* 22:2:472; "lost all sense" from Halleck to Schofield, September 26, 1863, 22:2:574–75.

Schofield stalled. Such an inquiry, Schofield wrote Governor Carney, was appropriate only if Kansas officials first ensured that "the vengeance which they so justly demand" was left to federal troops to execute. The army was not going to conduct an inquiry while at the same time Kansans were rampaging through Missouri. Order Number 11 was providing solid information of immense value to the future of the district. One of Quantrill's men was captured at Spring Hill, Kansas, and taken to Olathe. Interrogation techniques were applied, and he gave up the names of fifty of Quantrill's band before what was left of him was summarily shot. Some of the names the tortured man gave up were Missouri Union men. While the names could have been provided to mislead Ewing, the obvious uncertainty in the list was evidence that few could be trusted in those four Missouri counties.[38]

After deportations began in early September, Schofield took the first boat from St. Louis to review the situation firsthand. He conferred with Ewing at Leavenworth and then with Carney and other political friends. Schofield's meeting with Carney angered Lane, so on September 3, Schofield met privately with the senator in an attempt to head off Lane's threatened Paola raid scheduled for September 8. Governor Carney had indicated that he would side with Schofield and Ewing rather than Lane on Lane's threatened raid. Lane did not care. "Mr. Lane explained" his belief "of making a large portion of western Missouri a desert waste in order that Kansas might be secure against future invasion and he proposed using the Kansas militia to aid this policy." Demanding that Kansans assembling at Paola should be allowed to enter Missouri, Lane claimed he could control their activities. "I assured Lane that nothing would afford me greater pleasure . . . but that the search [for Quantrill's guerillas] would be fruitless and . . . I had not the slightest faith in [Lane's] ability to control such a mass of people . . . when I, of course, would be held responsible for the murder and robbery which would ensue." Schofield insisted that Lane back off. Lane, who had tried repeatedly behind Schofield's back to get him removed, threatened to go to the president again if Schofield did not look the other way when Kansans invaded Missouri. This was defiance of martial law, and Schofield refused. He would not preside over a bloodbath and do nothing. He ordered Ewing to continue implementing Order Number 11 and to oppose any pretext used by Lane to stage a raid into Missouri.[39]

38. Schofield to Carney, August 29, 1863, *O.R.* 22:1:577; Castel, *Frontier State,* 147–48; for results of Order Number 11, see Lt. Col. R. T. Van Horn to TEJr., September 1, 1863, at *O.R* 2:6:245.

39. Lane's September meeting mentioned in Castel, *Frontier State,* 147–48; quotes from Schofield to the Secretary of War, September 14, 1863, *O.R.* 22:1:572.

Ewing's provost marshals had been at work since September 1, evicting Missourians along the border. His provosts indicated that a wide network of detectives had been watching suspected guerrilla sympathizers and knew exactly which families to oust. Lane wanted even harsher methods employed, and in a Leavenworth speech he urged that the targeted counties be burned into desolation. Ewing's reply went to Governor Carney, who, pressured by Lane, did nothing. Order Number 11 was working well. The threat of Missouri guerrillas' raiding Kansas in the future was small. Their families were being deported. There was, in short, no reason for Kansans to raid into Missouri, and if they tried for any reason, federal military units would resist. The irony that Ewing found himself in—that he was trying to prevent a retaliatory jayhawking raid into Missouri the same as Kansas territorial governors had tried and failed to contain in 1857—was not lost on him. "I have but little doubt I will be able to control matters so as to prevent any considerable acts of retaliation."[40]

Loyal Missourians sent their state treasurer, George Bingham, to demand that Ewing rescind the order altogether and arrest Lane as a seditionist. When Ewing refused the first request and would not discuss the second, the argument became heated. Bingham threatened to make Ewing "infamous with the pen and brush" if Ewing continued. Ewing held firm, and Bingham's painting "Order Number 11" would be trotted out against Ewing's political ambitions in later years. However, in 1863, it was clear that Ewing had far more on his mind than politics. He was the target of a dogfight. Ewing duly reported Bingham's and Lane's threats to Schofield, downplaying Lane's efforts as more bombast than threat. Perhaps working from their private understanding in Morristown, Ewing reported that Lane wanted to scare people out of the border counties and "into prompt compliance with my order."[41]

Others were not so sure Ewing could control anybody. The *Missouri Democrat* reported in special dispatches from Leavenworth that Ewing "was looked upon as a general without heart and brains," and that he could be bribed—that fifty noted Secesh of Platte County had contributed to a Lawrence relief fund hoping to escape the "anticipated devastation of Western Missouri." The *Leavenworth Daily Conservative* of September 1, 1863, heaped all sorts of "scathing invective" on Ewing, alleging that Ewing conspired with Quantrill for a share of the booty. Unlike scathing attacks earlier visited on Sherman, the family was unable to do

40. "Little doubt" at *O.R.* 22:2:490.

41. "Infamous" from Miller, "Thomas Ewing Jr.," 16; "prompt compliance" from TEJr. to Schofield, August 28, 1863, *O.R.* 22:2:490.

much for Tom during the attacks in Kansas. Ewing fired back on his own on August 26, when the *Leavenworth Daily Times* carried an unsigned printed chronology of what had happened before and after the raid. The information was taken in large part from Ewing's official report and probably was leaked by Ewing or Harrison Hannahs.[42]

The second thing Ewing did was retaliate for "political enemies" making him a "burnt offering to satisfy the just passion of the people." Accordingly, he asked for a court of inquiry into his role, but this was not an open-ended request. He preferred his old friend and Brigadier General George Deitzler to constitute the "impartial" court. Schofield disliked any sort of inquiry into this matter because he was unsure what it would stir up. Within days, as Order Number 11 caught on, the idea of an inquiry was dropped.[43]

As September 9 neared, it was clear that Lane had not called off his Paola rendezvous with his jayhawkers. On September 5, Ewing sent Weer's regiment to Coldwater Grove, near Paola. On September 8, detectives ended the Leavenworth agitation and kept a considerable portion of Lane's Paola contingent from arriving by arresting Daniel Anthony, dumping him into a carriage and driving him to Kansas City. Anthony's friends immediately telegraphed Lincoln for a release order. Ewing apparently had not known of this plot. As soon as he learned of the arrest, he immediately ordered Anthony's release. Anthony preferred to think it was all Ewing's doing and used the incident to rail about the excesses of martial law. Martial law had been used before Quantrill's attack and had not helped defend Kansas. Quantrill, not Anthony, was the enemy. Having lost the battle for public opinion, Ewing decided a quick retreat was appropriate. He revoked martial law, reluctantly, on September 11.[44]

On September 9, Lane's five hundred men, along with thousands of horses and wagons (the main implement for predacious jayhawkers), left Paola and marched east toward Westport, south of Kansas City. Westport and Independence were the first Missouri towns on Lane's list. Calling on the only troops he knew he could trust, his old Eleventh Kansas, Ewing sent Captain H. E. Palmer's company to the state line with 130 men and some artillery, where they drew up a battle line. Like Gaelic warlords in a Scottish pasture, Lane and Palmer conferred between the two lines. Palmer repeated Ewing's orders for the force to retreat and disband, and Lane snapped that the "Damn Ewing" was to "keep out of my way." Palmer restated

42. *Missouri Democrat* quoted in *O.R.* 22:2:487; *Leavenworth Daily Conservative,* September 1, 1863.
43. "Burnt offering" at *O.R.* 22:2:472; Martin, "Two Years of Kansas," 124–25.
44. Martial law from Castel, *Frontier State,* 149.

that Order Number 11 was doing what Lane wanted done, clearing out the border counties. Lane demanded to speak to Palmer's men, exhorting the Eleventh Kansas with the horrors of a massacre. Palmer then replied, "If there is a man in this line who on my command cannot fire on that mob and shoot to kill, let them ride ten paces to the front." The Eleventh Kansas was no mob. They did not like the prospects of seeing Kansans in a long line across from them, but Ewing's old outfit was as good a cavalry unit as any in the Union army. Horse heads nodded in excitement, but not one animal was allowed to move forward. Palmer ordered the cannon loaded with canister. When the gunners leaped to the muzzles of their weapons, Palmer suggested Lane should "reconsider his position." Lane did, returning to Leavenworth where he addressed ten thousand people and denounced Ewing as a "rebel, traitor, and coward." Anthony expanded on Lane's invectives, publicly calling Ewing a "liar, a puppy, a cur, a dog, and a coward." The great Paola raiding party, having verbally skewered Ewing in lieu of pursuing Quantrill, went back to their homes.[45]

The clash had been avoided, but Ewing remained extremely sensitive to the charges leveled against him. He saw his Kansas political career vanishing. While Schofield had felt enormous pressure to remove Ewing in Kansas, Schofield's support had not budged. Order Number 11 was proving popular, especially in Kansas, and if Ewing were removed then Lane would stir Kansans up into holy anger. Had Ewing been a less ambitious officer, Lane and Anthony would not have uttered a word against him. The only blot on his handling of the troops, Ewing said, was Captain Pike who "acted the idiot" for not reporting Quantrill's movement sooner. Lane and Anthony had "lied past all decency" against Ewing's reputation. In response Thomas Ewing Sr. wrote his son that Lane's demagoguery was having little political effect in Washington. This seemed to cool the situation.[46]

The guerrillas did not easily let go of western Missouri. In mid-September, guerrillas stopped the steamer *Marcella* on the Missouri River and shot three soldiers of the Fifth Missouri state militia. Ewing wrote Schofield in mid-September that "I have guerrillas here, convicted and unconvicted. Shall I retaliate?" Schofield said retaliation would be "just but unwise." Guerrillas should be executed for their own acts, not the acts of others. On September 22, Jo Shelby began one of his patented raids into central Missouri that lasted five weeks. Ewing was in the field much of the time, directing his five-hundred-man force. In far southeast Kansas, on October 4, Major General James Blunt and his staff were surprised a few hun-

45. Quotes from Palmer, "Lawrence Raid," 322–23; "cur and dog" invective from *Leavenworth Daily Times,* September 9, 1863.

46. TEJr. to TESr., September 11, 1863, Joseph H. Ewing Collection (photocopy in possession of the author); Lane's ranting with little effect is hinted in TEJr., to TESr., September 14, 1863, ibid.

dred yards from the cavalry camp at Baxter Springs, Kansas. Quantrill formed battle lines and sent Blunt's men reeling before attacking the Union camp. Elements of the Second Kansas colored infantry were among the significant Union casualties. Most bodies were shot multiple times through the head.[47]

However, the Shelby and Baxter Springs actions were distractions. Between implementing Order Number 11 and chasing Shelby, two-thirds of the population of four Missouri counties—including Jackson County (Kansas City)—had abandoned their farms. There was a certain amount of plundering, but Ewing's troops scattered the guerrillas south and east. A Presbyterian minister returning in 1865 reported "only stone and brick chimneys remained" and the place seemed "like a vast cemetery." That autumn twenty thousand Missourians were reported as forced to relocate. Modern scholars doubt so many were driven out, since county census documents do not show so many civilians living in those counties.[48]

Clearly, the movement in the four counties caused hardships for friend and foe alike, and it was hard to determine who was who. One of the semiloyal Jackson County Missourians affected by the new order was Solomon Young, whose young daughter Martha Ellen took part in the 1863 evacuation. In 1886 she would give birth to John Truman's second son, Harry, who grew up with legends of that era and, after his own presidency, told friends that "Old Gen. Ewing was a bad egg and Bingham surely showed him up." The former president's memory was perhaps slightly jaded because two of his uncles rode with Shelby. However, Order Number 11 did not use a sweeping net by large bodies of troops to remove the Missouri residents. Provost reports of the operation indicate that Ewing employed a large detective force watching suspects, but not the forcible removal implied in Bingham's painting. Ewing's order worked as intended. Brigadier General Clinton Fisk observed, "Depopulation and devastation are extreme measures but if this infernal warfare continues it will be humane and economic of human life to adopt and vigorously enforce such measures . . . when bushwhackers have more friends than the government."[49]

By late fall the pressures of the work were affecting Ewing, confirming the opin-

47. Marcella incident and quotes, *O.R.* 22:2:541; guerrilla and anti-guerrilla operations at this time, see *O.R.* 22:1:379, 610–12; action at Baxter Springs, *O.R.* 22:1:693–701.

48. "Vast cemetery" from Miller, "Thomas Ewing Jr.," 17; the twenty thousand estimate from Austin King to Rosecrans, *O.R.* 34:2:243. The curator of the Fort Davidson Historical Site in Pilot Knob, Missouri, Walter Busch, in his masters thesis on Ewing and Order Number 11 and in private emails with the author, estimates a lower figure of ten thousand civilians. Walter Busch, "General, You Have Made the Mistake of Your Life."

49. Truman's negativity is discussed in a letter to the author from David Schafer of the Truman National Historic Site, Independence, Missouri, folder 1, Post Presidential Correspondence, Truman Library. Provost marshal report Van Horn to Ewing, September 1, 1863, *O.R.* 2:6:245; "Depopulation" from Fisk report to Rosecrans, *O.R.* 41:4:454; also *O.R.* 22:2:566–68, 610–12, 41:3:454.

ion of those who alleged immediately after the Lawrence attack that he was out of sorts. He battled a fever much of that autumn. Chills and stress left him "unfit for business" for long periods. The saving grace for Tom was that his efforts implementing the order were going well. Almost all "rebels and neutrals, are glad to leave." He had predicted earlier to his father that "The neutrals all [are] going to the towns to await permission next spring to return with the Missouri refugees. When return is permitted by a strict enforcement of orders against disloyalists returning, a peaceable and loyal population will fill in the Missouri border, and the old wound will cauterize."[50]

Lane made one last attempt to get Lincoln to dump both Ewing and Schofield. He faked a telegram to Lincoln that Missouri guerrillas were still in the Park City and Platte City areas. Although Ewing and Schofield confirmed the rumor was false, Lane pursued another tactic. He alleged Ewing could not cut the mustard along the Kansas-Missouri border and should be replaced with one of Lane's men. Ewing knew that nothing angered Lincoln more than allegations of corruption. Ewing had previously ordered his officers to keep wary eyes on Lane's and Blunt's machinations, and the detectives soon were able to report to Schofield that Blunt's henchmen in Fort Scott had filled two hundred wagons with sutler merchandise and sold $100,000 worth of goods to desperate Union sympathizers in Fort Smith, Arkansas. It was "commonly understood that General Blunt is interested in the prospective profits" of the enterprise, Ewing alleged. All this reached Lincoln's attention during his conversations with Lane. Lincoln had had enough of the Missouri-Kansas nonsense. Ewing might have lost the newspaper war with Lane, but Lincoln came down solidly on Ewing's side. On October 5, 1863, Lincoln told Lane that Schofield, not Lane, was in charge in Kansas and Missouri. In the decision was a silent warning. Mass murder of civilians during wartime would not be tolerated, and whoever did that or made war on Schofield and Ewing was making an enemy of the president of the United States.[51]

Ewing's high profile that fall led many to keep an eye out for his safety. There were concerns that Missourians—even Lane's radicals—might try to assassinate him. One incident almost cost him his life. A drunken Union army scout fired a

50. "Unfit for business" from TEJr. to Schofield, November 10, 1863, *O.R.* 22:2:702; other quotes from TEJr. to TESr., September 14, 1863, Joseph H. Ewing Collection (photocopy in possession of the author).

51. "Commonly understood" from Ewing to Schofield, *O.R.* 22:1:693. Missouri dislike of Schofield and Lincoln's reaction found in A. A. King to Lincoln, reported in *O.R.* 22:2:472–73, 487–88, 581–84, 591, 595, 604, 692–93.

pistol at Ewing at a dance hall in Leavenworth over some grievance, and one of Ewing's lieutenants shot the would-be killer. The War Department decided the incident was the result of Order Number 11, and Halleck began urging Schofield to suspend the order for a time. Even Lincoln was concerned about a possible massive retaliation from Kansas and "indiscriminate slaughter on the Missouri border." Missouri congressman Austin King agreed, roasting the administration with his opinion that Missouri's only problem was that it lay next to Kansas, a district that was "commanded by a Kansas general and a Kansas politician with Kansas troops at his command." Schofield ignored most of the criticism, but the problem was growing. He passed along Halleck's concerns but agreed with Ewing not to issue the modification order until November 20.[52]

Meanwhile, returning Missouri loyalists were required to turn in any suspected rebel "and give every possible aid and information to [the government]," a course of action that, if followed, could earn a civilian a quick bullet in the night. Those that returned to their property did not find much left. In early December, Colonel Edward Lynde of the Ninth Kansas cavalry reported to Ewing that Mother Nature was having her way in Cass County: "The country is very much devastated by prairie fires, many good farms being destroyed, and the loss seems to have fallen heavier on the loyal than [on the] disloyal."[53]

Lane's political violence toward Ewing was irrepressible. While Governor Carney preferred working with Ewing rather than Lane, Lane had never given up on wrestling control of Kansas from all his enemies, real or imaginary. Lane kept pressuring Lincoln to re-create the District of Kansas to get rid of Ewing. He promoted the astounding rumor that Ewing had prior knowledge of Quantrill's plans, and he made sure the administration understood that Ewing was a pea from the same pod as Sherman when it came to using Negro troops or abolitionist sympathies. Missouri loyalists were eager to believe such about Ewing.

Anti-Lane men in Kansas helped Ewing fight back, sometimes with mindless accusations of their own. Robinson wrote Amos Lawrence that "Lane and his element were in collusion through third persons with Quantrill," since Hoyt and his Red Legs were conveniently out of Lawrence during the raid, and Lane escaped so easily when 180 other Lawrence citizens did not. Castel points out that Robinson's views have "very little logical basis" given Quantrill's intentions if Lane

52. Attempted shooting from Robert LaForte, "Cyrus Leland Jr. and the Lawrence Massacre: A Note and Document," 181; "indiscriminate slaughter" from *O.R.* 22:2:488; "Kansas general" from *O.R.* 34:2:243.

53. General Order 20, issued by TEJr., November 20, 1863, at *O.R.* 22:2:713; Lynde's report at *O.R.* 22:2:732–33.

were captured in the raid, and that his men robbed and murdered pro-Southern people too. Ewing demanded a court of inquiry to expose all of Lane's corruption in the state.[54]

Lincoln neither removed Ewing nor granted him a court of inquiry about Lane, at least not immediately. While Lincoln hated to admit Lane's ideas had merit, Lane's suggestion of enlarging the District of Kansas made sense. And although Lincoln's respect for Ewing never flagged, as Lane, Carney, Curtis, and Blunt hotly attested, not all Kansans were high on the general after the Lawrence massacre. From Washington, Lincoln simply saw more pro-Lane inquiries than support for Ewing and, unlike the family's efforts in the press when Sherman was maligned earlier in the war, there was no such effort for Tom after Lawrence. Essentially, the president did not think any single man could govern the contentious districts of Kansas and western Missouri at the same time. Lincoln sent Ewing a good news–bad news cable. He was enlarging the District of Kansas to include all of Kansas and two other states plus the Indian territories, but he wanted a new commander. It was a measure of what a man loses when his command is buffeted by a disaster such as Quantrill's raid on Lawrence.

The change of command took place without much ceremony. Ewing's only regrets were private, that Curtis's reemergence would allow Lane's rats back into the granary, which it did. When Curtis was restored to command of the newly constituted District of Kansas, he was met with the same swarm of contract seekers that Ewing had purposefully banished. Lane immediately saw the opportunity to bury Schofield and Ewing under charges of mismanagement. In January 1864 Lane's victory was complete. Schofield was ordered to command the Department of the Ohio, and a month later Curtis ordered Ewing exiled to command of the cactus, rocks, pine trees, and occasional wild Indian raids in the Colorado Territory. Ewing was not going to go quietly to a dull Colorado assignment without a fight. Within two weeks, his connection to Sherman and direct lobbying with Schofield got him assigned to a staff position in Washington. Eventually he was reassigned to the District of St. Louis as deputy to William Rosecrans. Rosecrans had replaced Schofield and was new to Missouri and wanted an experienced staff who knew the political minefields. Curtis grumpily wrote Rosecrans that, while he disliked giving up Ewing, so long as it helped the border situation, he would approve.

54. Robinson to Amos Lawrence, published in the *Council Grove Press,* September 14, 1863; Castel, *Frontier State,* 138; Ewing-Schofield retaliation on guerrillas at *O.R.* 22:1:541; court of inquiry at *O.R.* 22:2:488–89.

Ewing presided in Kansas over its most tempestuous moment in the war. General Order Number 11 had its desired effect, however. By November 20, 1863, the border district was so quiet that Ewing issued Order Number 20, which partially rescinded Order Number 11. While the onset of winter might have slowed guerrilla warfare, Schofield knew the value of Ewing's work and wrote in his official report, "The [Order Number 11] adopted seems a very harsh one, but after the fullest examination and consideration . . . I am satisfied it is wise and humane." Schofield's report also took Ewing off the hook for Lawrence, at least for Union sympathizers in Kansas and western Missouri. "It is possible that General Ewing might have done more than he did do to guard against such a calamity as that at Lawrence; but I believe he is entitled to great credit for the energy, wisdom, and zeal displayed while in command of that district." For as much criticism as he took from both sides after the raid on Lawrence and after issuing his controversial order, and for the fact that Order Number 11 would continue somewhat to cloud his later political aspirations, Ewing's only consolation was that Lawrence was the last Kansas town to be raided by Missouri guerrillas.[55]

55. Schofield to the War Department, September 14, 1863, at *O.R.* 22:1:572. Contrast Schofield's report about the aftermath of the Lawrence attack with his pre-raid view of problems in Kansas and Missouri; see *O.R.* 22:1:573–75, 22:2:6–7, 692–93, 703, 713–14, 732.

8

THE VISIBLE INTERPOSITION OF GOD

After Antietam, having had as much of Eliakim P. Scammon and Jacob Cox as he could stomach, Hugh Ewing asked for a transfer to the Western theater. Having met success in the East but also frustration with the psychology McClellan had instilled in the higher commands of the Potomac Army, Hugh asked for duty with Sherman's under-strength corps in January 1863, at the beginning of the Vicksburg campaign. In fact, after the name he had made for himself at Antietam, Hugh came out to Sherman's corps with his rebuilt Kanawha brigade and unofficial orders from Grant to give his brigade to Morgan Smith's division and take over command of Brigadier General David Stuart's division. Stuart had commanded the First brigade of Sherman's division at Shiloh, where he was wounded. Sherman had a soft spot for such men, keeping the division spot open for Stuart until later, when Congress did not approve Stuart's bid to become a general and Stuart resigned. Charles Ewing, who had been assigned to Sherman's headquarters but without any official title, warned Hugh when he arrived that he had, as he put it, "brought my pigs to a bad market," meaning that Hugh would never achieve the promotion he desired under Sherman.[1]

Hugh threw his brigade into the campaign, realizing that while the Potomac

1. Ewing, "Autobiography," 282.

Army was fighting Lee and attempting to best a rebel army, Grant was after strategic territory. Hugh was fascinated with the different thinking in Grant's Western command. Grant went about his military goals differently than McClellan, including the abortive effort to build a canal around Vicksburg for the navy's transports. He spent evenings watching the riverboat navy brave the Vicksburg defenses, the dark ships moving through a black night like monsters, lighted eerily by fires on the shores. With Grant's army across the Mississippi River at Port Gibson, the Jackson, Mississippi, portion of the campaign began. Grant would attack toward Jackson to hold off Joe Johnston, then double back to the west, smashing into any force Pemberton sent out from Vicksburg. On May 18, 1863, Grant's army had encircled Vicksburg and made a tentative attack. On May 22 Ewing's brigade, behind 150 volunteers dubbed the "Forlorn Hope" after Wellington's storming parties, fought their way up the "graveyard road" toward a rebel redoubt. Youngest brother, Captain Charley Ewing, part of Sherman's original Thirteenth regiment of regulars attached to Hugh's brigade, led a second wave of assaults in perhaps the most gutsy and fearless attack led by any Ewing on any field during the war. When Charley's commanding officer went down, Charley took over, carrying the colors to the parapet after three color bearers of the Thirteenth had fallen. Enfilading fire came "crashing through the ranks" while the same regiments caught direct fire from the rebel entrenchments in their front.[2]

The dead and wounded men from Hugh's four regiments were stacked in a defile and blocked additional reinforcements at a critical moment in the assault. As Hugh watched, mumbling a prayer under his breath, Charley pushed the flag forward to the base of the redoubt before his men were driven back. Sherman's forces lost more than 1,000 men in the attack; 77 of the 250 in Charley Ewing's Thirteenth regulars were casualties. General Frank Blair made sure that all 150 men in the storming party, including friends from Hugh Ewing's earlier days commanding the Thirtieth Ohio, were awarded the Medal of Honor.[3]

After the nearly six-week siege, twenty-seven thousand men of the western Confederate armies surrendered at Vicksburg. It was another triumph for Grant, and it put Sherman at the forefront, too. After Vicksburg, in the short chase of Johnston's forces near Jackson, Mississippi, to the east, Hugh was given command of the Fourth division in Sherman's Fifteenth Corps.[4]

At the time that Tom Ewing was dealing with the aftermath of Quantrill's raid and General Order Number 11, many of the rebel prisoners from Vicksburg had

2. Report of M. Gen. Frank Blair, *O.R.* 24:2:257, 258.

3. *O.R.* 24:2:260.

4. Hugh Ewing's division command from *O.R.* 24:3:537.

been paroled and had rejoined the rebel army in time to fight at Chickamauga, the war's second-bloodiest battle, south of Chattanooga in mid-September. William Rosecrans's army had held its own until a mishap in obeying an order left a division-sized gap in his line, where Longstreet's corps, on loan from the Army of Northern Virginia, then hammered a breach in Rosecrans's line. A disorganized Army of the Cumberland fled the battlefield toward Chattanooga, protected by the stoic rearguard action of George "Pap" Thomas and what was left of his command. In the battle's aftermath, and while Rosecrans dithered, Grant was sent to Chattanooga to take command. If Bragg was able to drive Union armies from Chattanooga, the gains of the previous siege at Vicksburg and taking Tennessee from the Confederates would vanish. Grant took with him to Chattanooga all of Sherman's corps, which now included Brigadier General Hugh Ewing as a division commander and Colonel Dan McCook, leading a brigade in Jefferson C. Davis's division.

Sherman's family had been with him several weeks at Vicksburg, and the orders for Chattanooga made him hurriedly send them home. En route to Memphis on navy ships and from where his corps would strike out overland for Chattanooga, Sherman suffered his most grievous loss of the war. Nine-year-old Willie, Sherman's first-born California son and favorite, died on October 3 from a bloody dysentery. Sherman could not stop even to mourn. He had to press on behind his divisions that were working their way through difficult Tennessee terrain toward Chattanooga, leaving it to Ellen to bury their boy in St. Louis. Willie Sherman died of an illness he had caught while playing soldier in Mississippi, an end to his young life that gave him more in common with the regular soldiers of the Civil War than anyone else in Ewingville.[5]

Missionary Ridge formed the south and east crescent of hills above Chattanooga. Rebels had spent nearly two months working on fortifications by the time Sherman's corps arrived in mid-November. In the mists of November 24, Sherman's corps began moving south across the Tennessee River east of the town, landing on both sides of the mouth of the South Chickamauga Creek. Hugh Ewing's old Kanawha brigade, led now by Brigadier General Joseph Lightburn, moved forward a few hundred yards and dug in. When daylight appeared Hugh saw there was another ridge five hundred yards east of the one they had fortified. Ewing's division went forward to the new ridge, meeting surprisingly little resistance along the extreme right of Bragg's line. With a landing site secure, a

5. Willie's loss to Sherman, *O.R.* 30:4:73.

thirteen-hundred-foot bridge allowed the remainder of Sherman's corps to cross in a fog.

Ewing pulled his three brigadiers together and told Lightburn, John Corse, and John M. Loomis that the hill assigned them in the upcoming battle for the flank of Missionary Ridge was important and there would be "no retrograde step" in their attack. What they were to attack was Missionary Ridge's right flank, a scraggly rock- and tree-strewn hill with a railroad cut through it aptly called Tunnel Hill. Ewing ordered his brigadiers to carry the summit or die on it.[6]

What lay before his brigadiers was formidable. While Sherman's divisions were digging rifle positions on the wrong hill, Hooker's divisions assaulted Lookout Mountain. The Yankee "Huzzaaah!" reverberated and magnified in the thick fog. Hooker's three divisions drove a rebel division and supporting artillery off the mountain, and sent two thousand Confederate prisoners down the mountain into captivity. However, this stellar work by Hooker had not assisted Sherman's understanding of the terrain on the Confederate right. "I had inferred that Missionary Ridge was a continuous hill, but we found ourselves on two high points, with a deep depression between us and the one immediately over the tunnel, which was my chief objective point."[7]

On the morning of November 25, Hugh Ewing's men in wet woolen uniforms faced a raw, cold wind. On the backside of the ridge occupied by Sherman's corps, pack mules and whole companies spent the predawn stumbling around, replenishing their ammunition and rations supply. The haze gave way to a cloudless morning. Grant and Thomas moved their headquarters to Orchard Knob where they could better see the expected fighting for the north end of Missionary Ridge.[8]

Among those in and around Chattanooga surveying the gloomy morning were three of the four law partners from Kansas. Watching Ewing's preparations was a nervous Dan McCook, whose brigade was part of Major General Jefferson C. Davis's division, on loan from Howard's corps to Sherman as a reserve that would exploit any breakthrough Hugh's division made at Tunnel Hill. Sherman claimed in his postwar memoirs that his attack at Tunnel Hill was designed to panic Bragg into sending reinforcements to the Confederate right flank so Thomas could break the center. This claim was contrary to the orders Grant issued but is supported by what occurred. Although he had four divisions and parts of a fifth on his ridge, Sherman used only two brigades from Ewing's division in the attack at Tunnel Hill, which is more in line with a reconnaissance in force than a frontal

6. "No retrograde step" from Ewing, "Autobiography," 313; Sherman's report, *O.R.* 31:2:572–82.
7. Sherman's report, *O.R.* 331:2:573.
8. Peter Cozzens, *The Shipwreck of Their Hopes*, 202.

attack. The previous night Sherman had cabled Grant that the attack on the left (not a reconnaissance or diversion) had been postponed long enough and he would "put all our strength." Thomas was instructed to "start a strong reconnaissance" at daylight, not the type of order you expect to result in a charge against fortified heights. That morning Sherman told his brother-in-law, "I guess, Ewing, if you are ready you might as well go ahead," as if he feared the results of what he was ordering. Hugh was to keep his formations until their attack reached the base of the Tunnel Hill and not call for help "until you need it." There are few more ambiguous orders in the *Official Reports.* Either Ewing underestimated how many Confederates controlled Tunnel Hill, or it was his understanding that when his first brigade got into trouble, Sherman would attack elsewhere on the line and overwhelm the defenders. It is perhaps commentary on Hugh Ewing's desperation for the glory of commanding a decisive engagement and to cement his position in the postwar army that he did not fully assess what Sherman had ordered.[9]

McCook watched through glasses as Ewing's brigades went forward. By ten o'clock, Corse's brigade was still mired at the base of the hill in his initial attack. More regiments were poured into the attack when signal corps messages indicated that Grant wanted action. Sherman sent word to Corse and Lightburn, bypassing Ewing, to get their brigades going. In addition Corse was now calling for reinforcements. A fierce fight for the top of Tunnel Hill roared to life. Corse went down with a leg wound, and he being Ewing's best combat commander, the vinegar went out of Ewing's attack. By noon all that had been accomplished on Tunnel Hill was heavy losses in Union infantry.[10]

In the midst of the failure of Ewing's attack came the most breathtaking sight of the war. Late in the day and to draw some Confederates away from Sherman's end of the ridge, Grant ordered Thomas to make a diversionary attack on the rifle pits at the base of the ridge. The men of the Cumberland Army, snubbed by Grant in favor of Sherman for the main attack on the Union left, were not about to take rifle pits in the center and leave it at that.[11]

No rational commander would order an assault on Missionary Ridge. Bragg knew it. So did Grant. If Pickett could not take the low open ridge at Cemetery Ridge at Gettysburg, the Yankees could not take the steeper tree- and stone-

9. McCook's position, *O.R.* 31:2:504; "put all our strength" from *O.R.* 31:2:41; "strong reconnaissance" from *O.R.* 31:2:45; Sherman to Hugh from Cozzens, *Shipwreck,* 203; for the Confederate perspective, see *O.R.* 31:2:45–53.

10. Battle reports, *O.R.* 31:2:633–34, 768–70; Ewing, "Autobiography," 313–14; James Lee McDonough, *Chattanooga: A Death Grip on the Confederacy,* 149.

11. *O.R.* 31:2:128–32, 189, 264–65.

covered ground of Missionary Ridge. Even when the Confederates saw Thomas's four divisions form their lines, they guessed it was but a diversion. Bragg watched the movement without fear; Missionary Ridge could be held by a skirmish line.[12]

When the attack began, Colonel John Martin's Eighth Kansas stepped off toward Orchard's Knob, "through the branches of leafless trees we saw bright flames leap out and dull gray smoke curl up all along the summit of the ridge." The ridge where the Kansans advanced was a crescent. Private Henry McElroy in the Thirty-Sixth Ohio, a veteran of Antietam and Chickamauga, went with the regiment as it surged toward the northeast end of the Ridge, in Baird's division. A "loud, hearty, ringing cheer" from four attacking divisions swept the field. They went up and over Missionary Ridge in a single wild assault. No one gave the order. The four divisions reached the base of the ridge and just kept going, four divisions, four giant mobs, companies mixing with other regiments as men pulled themselves up the ridge, from tree to tree and from outcropping to boulder. There was no visible leader but each man was his own leader, and each man had his own objective. These were Cumberland Army boys, the goats of Chickamauga. They had something to prove to Grant, to Sherman, to everyone. To stop them, the Confederates would have to kill them all.[13]

Ten minutes after the Union regiments reached the ridge, the Confederate army fell apart. Nearly half the artillery of the western Confederate army and much of its transport was abandoned. An army in disarray can feed on panic and produce blind unreasoning terror, and Bragg's army was just such a body. The Confederates fled toward Atlanta, but they did not get all the way and instead slowly reformed several miles south of Missionary Ridge. The attack had been a probe that produced spectacular results, what Charles Dana effusively described to Stanton as "the greatest [of] miracles in military history" brought on by "a visible interposition of God." Union general Thomas Wood predicted history could be "ransacked in vain for a parallel" to it. Except for storming Chapultepec in Mexico, Grant had seen nothing like it and, literally, did not know how to explain his success.[14]

In the afternoon, before the full attack by Thomas broke Bragg's army on Missionary Ridge, Ewing renewed his own attack, but in spite of his men's crawling up the hill in the mud, there was no meaningful advance. Rocks rained down on

12. "Skirmish line" from *O.R.* 31:2:666.

13. Anderson, *Adjutant General,* 136.

14. Cozzens, *Shipwreck,* 308; Dana's "visible interposition of God" from *O.R.* 31:2:69; "ransacked in vain" from Wood's report at *O.R.* 31:2:259; see also *O.R.* 31:2:130–36, 191–92, 208, 257, 264, 273–74, 277–78, 301, 517, 522–23, 525–26, 752–53, 31:3:615.

Lightburn's brigade from Confederate positions. At the end of the day the attack just petered out. General Patrick Cleburne's defenders had to form up and withdraw from their positions since the rest of the Confederates had already withdrawn. Sherman watched Ewing's division attack all day and watched Thomas's successful assault, and he still had no idea whether there was a rebel rearguard on Tunnel Hill. That night Ewing reported in his journal that, at a council of war with senior officers present, he proposed to move "to the enemy's rear, turning his flank" and that he was supported in that view only by McCook. Sherman and the rest of the division commanders "proposed to plant batteries in the open fields and shell out the enemy, and fight on the same plan as today." Hugh later wrote that "Whilst the Council was sitting, I pushed a line forward to feel the enemy and found him in retreat." It is hard to believe Ewing's account, since it would have been hard not to know, long before Sherman met with his council of war, that Thomas's attack that afternoon had been total and complete and that Bragg and Cleburne were in retreat. Further, much of Ewing's journal was completed from diaries, after the war, at a time when the two comrades in arms were alienated from each other.[15]

Peter Cozzens called Tunnel Hill "one of the sorriest episodes in this or any other battle of the war" and blamed Sherman's "egregious lack of imagination" for the failure of the attack. Stephen Sears would probably agree with Cozzens, having pronounced Sherman the "most overrated" general of the war. Like Cozzens, Sears cites Tunnel Hill as an example. They have a point. Sherman could have flanked the entire Tunnel Hill position with far less cost in life than sending Ewing's division straight at the position. He had all day on November 25 and three divisions to probe south and east along Cleburne's flank for a weak point. In such an important battle, if Sherman somehow misunderstood his role, he should have clarified his orders with Grant before the attack. Sherman simply piecemealed his attack to a deplorable degree and spent much time in his memoirs trying to justify the results.[16]

While the consensus of these historians is accurate concerning Sherman's actions, there is another explanation. As Hugh's account indicates, Sherman was out of it—understanding neither how badly Ewing's division had been whipped nor the great success the Army of the Cumberland had engineered a few miles away at Missionary Ridge. Cump Sherman was still mourning the death of Willie Sherman. His anguish was barely below the surface the day after Willie's death, when

15. Ewing, "Autobiography," 314–15.
16. Cozzens, *Shipwreck,* 248; Stephen W. Sears, "Civil War General," 1.

in a letter to Halleck Sherman wrote, "his loss to me is more than words can express but I would not let it divert my mind from the duty I owe my country." To refuse to mourn the death of a beloved child is not manliness but, rather, self-deception. At Tunnel Hill Sherman, the grieving father, was a mediocre general. After a bitterly cold day of fighting, with nearly twelve hundred dead and wounded, the soldiers of Hugh Ewing's division paid the price of that deception.[17]

After the bloody triumphs and setbacks of 1863, the miracle at Missionary Ridge was seen by some, Abraham Lincoln among them, as a sign that the war could be won in 1864. Lincoln faced the daunting task of getting reelected in the middle of a bloody war when the voters had been nearly uniform in their unhappiness with his administration. The Republicans were strong in the North but still a minority party; the Democrats still had strength in the Northern states, especially along the border where Lincoln's policies were most opposed. The country was weary from the war and its cost in human lives. He had to show significant progress in destroying the South before November 1864 or his reelection would be in doubt.[18]

The Army of the Tennessee took winter quarters at Scottsborough, Alabama. The winter was hard on Hugh's gout and his aspirations concerning an army career. He spent much of his court-martial time with repetitive squabbles among his senior officers and trying junior officers for, among other things, "discouraging reenlistment" among white regiments, who were being asked to reenlist as veteran volunteers. Colonel John Loomis wanted the winter to be used to court-martial junior officers who had "behaved badly" at Tunnel Hill. The request of the coldly formal Loomis picked at the scab that Tunnel Hill had left on Ewing, and he was not inclined to grant this request. Ewing may have been having second thoughts about the planning of the undersized attack, and he did not want junior officers bringing this up as a defense in a court-martial. Furthermore, he was not going to court-martial men for being unable to engineer on the battlefield what Ewing had failed to protest at the time.[19]

On February 2, 1864, at a time when he was seriously considering resigning, Hugh received a telegraph from his father calling him home due to his mother's

17. For Sherman's depression prior to Tunnel Hill, see WTS to Phil Ewing, October 24, 1863, quoted in Joseph H. Ewing, "Sherman Bashes the Press," 37; "duty I owe" from Sherman to Halleck, *O.R.* 30:4:73.

18. For Lincoln's political concerns for 1864, see Paludan, *Abraham Lincoln,* 226; Richard Curry, *Radicalism, Racism, and Party Realignment: The Border States during Reconstruction,* 162.

19. Ewing, "Autobiography," 319.

lingering illness. He left immediately. At Nashville he spent an evening with Grant discussing his future in the army. The senior officers in the postwar army would be those with experience as corps commanders. After Missionary Ridge, Grant had been ordered east by Lincoln to assume command of all the armies, and Sherman had made no decision on whether Hugh could command a corps in the Western Army. Hugh sensed Sherman was dealing with the issue by ignoring it. Ewing asked Grant about a corps command in the Army of the Potomac. Even if Grant were so inclined, he had more such requests than corps to bestow. The real problem, Grant bluntly reminded Hugh, was his political allegiance to Douglas Democrats. Having fought the fight against McClellan's clique, radical Republicans were unwilling to place more Democrats in charge of a corps and take the chance that a military success would produce political candidates for the opposition political party. Grant did indicate that the command of the District of Louisville was open, and it was the vital backdoor command for protecting Sherman's planned movement south into Georgia. Louisville was also close to Lancaster. Was Ewing interested? Hugh would think it over.[20]

In Lancaster, February chills brought the family to the realization that Maria Boyle Ewing was in her last illness. The grief-stricken Thomas Ewing Sr. faced the loss of his wife of forty-five years by writing long unhelpful letters to Stanton about potential military disasters that might arise if Lee skirted the Army of the Potomac and stormed Washington. His children spent intermittent time with their failing mother. Every time Hugh saw her, Maria recognized him, but by the time Charley arrived home on February 10, the archbishop of Ohio had already given her last rites. On February 20, 1864, Maria Ewing passed quietly away. The children were most concerned about their father. They had never seen this big austere man so overcome with grief.[21]

Maria Boyle Ewing's passing allowed latent recriminations within the family to boil to the surface. Cump and Tom Ewing were not able to get away for her funeral, and Ellen expressed to Charley and Hugh her anger at being left alone during her bereavement of Willie. Tom had written many letters to his father over the five months since Willie's death, covering a variety of topics. He had neglected to mention the boy even once to Cump or to Ellen. This slight and the silence behind it Ellen mistook as indifference. She raged that Ellen Cox had made Tom Ewing a "supremely selfish man," that he cared nothing about the rest of his family. "I hope to see them but seldom again in my life," she raged. She demanded

20. Ibid., 321.
21. Ibid., 321–22.

that Cump never allow Tom to handle any of her affairs, and that Cump was not to discuss any more family business with Tom. To do otherwise, she insisted, would be to betray her! Her mother "has joined our darling Willie now," she wrote Sherman. "*They* [will] watch over us." If Sherman was concerned at this growing irrationality in his wife, he had a great place to hide out—staff meetings and planning sessions for the Atlanta campaign were in high gear.[22]

On March 16, 1864, Tom Ewing was ordered to St. Louis on Rosecrans's staff, and Hugh received orders to the Department of Kentucky in Louisville, which had a reputation for quality quarters and good food, the type of thing that made serving there more pleasurable than the sparse haunts of Louisiana, Tennessee, or Georgia. Grant had described Louisville to John Schofield, the new commander of the Department of Kentucky, as full of senior officers who "desired to make a luxury of their position" instead of "serv[ing] the government." Grant clearly wanted this to change, and he expected Hugh to change it. Ewing's department was to guard the line of the Louisville & Nashville Railroad and points west, but he was given only one under-strength division for the work.[23]

Stanton preferred Brigadier General Steven Burbridge for overall command in Kentucky. Burbridge, a rabid War Democrat, Kentucky planter, and slave owner, had remained loyal, one of Stanton's few perfect Southerners. Grant felt Burbridge was more interested in Lane-like internal one-upmanship against old political rivals than following military orders, and Grant had had enough of generals with political connections. He resisted Burbridge's appointment as long as he could. However, Burbridge called in all his political chits, even getting Governor Thomas Bramlette to petition Lincoln on his behalf. Stanton forced the issue by cabling that he would rather leave Burbridge in command in Kentucky, unless Grant saw some reason for not doing so. For Grant to block Burbridge's appointment in favor of Hugh Ewing required Grant openly to cross a local commander and a popular war governor. On February 15, 1864, Grant ordered Burbridge to command the District of Kentucky until relieved of command by Brigadier General Jacob Ammen. Ewing was reassigned to command the Louisville post but as Burbridge's subordinate.[24]

Hugh Ewing had left a combat command in the best-known corps in the West-

22. "Selfish" and "but seldom" from EES to WTS, February 22, "watch over us" from EES to WTS, February 26, 1864, SFP/ND, in Fellman, *Citizen Sherman,* 345, 205.

23. *O.R.* 34:2:632; Grant to Schofield at *O.R.* 32:3:14–15.

24. Burbridge's internal Kentucky political machinations causing internal War Department investigation, *O.R.* 39:2:212; for Stanton's box-in question to Grant, *O.R.* 32:3:384.

ern Army for a promised department command that now was undercut and subdivided by politics. He was a brigadier general whose chances of commanding a corps were going nowhere. The gloom in his Louisville apartment was palpable.

In mid-February 1864, Sherman led a corps from Vicksburg to Meridian, Mississippi, and back, suffering just over a hundred dead and wounded men from skirmishes but wrecking a hundred miles of railroads and public buildings along the way. He had purposefully cut loose from his supply lines during this march, measuring what his men had to do to survive without supply lines. Obviously, he had other operations in mind requiring similar marching. However, Sherman was not the only former Leavenworth law partner planning grandiose raids that spring.

William Rosecrans was assigned to the overall command of the Department of Missouri where Tom Ewing commanded the St. Louis subdistrict. Perhaps as a means of upgrading his toughness quotient in the senior ranks, Tom Ewing suggested to Rosecrans a jayhawking campaign through Louisiana, Arkansas, and Texas. Between Rosecrans's pushing rebel armies toward Banks in northern Louisiana, and vice versa, the two armies would sweep the Trans-Mississippi clear of remaining Confederates. What Ewing proposed was little different from Lane's old 1862 plan. However, the timing and scope of the project was better. The sweep would be aimed at three states in the Confederacy, not at any border states. Union armies were also much larger and more capable in 1864 than they had been in 1862. At the least the campaign would pin down significant concentrations of Confederate troops west of the Mississippi River.

During the Chickamauga campaign, Rosecrans had allowed Dan McCook some license regarding outside-the-chain-of-command messages to and from the army headquarters. Rosecrans's friendship with Hugh Ewing went back to West Point, and it was natural that Rosecrans would at least hear Tom Ewing's plan. Rosecrans was impressed with Ewing's strategic vision. However, since Grant's and Sherman's campaigns that spring were to have every available regiment from all other theaters, the plan would require that the Trans-Mississippi retain troop levels that could be authorized only by Sherman and, ultimately, Grant. Rosecrans knew few people better placed to obtain Sherman's approval for such a plan than Tom Ewing. Rosecrans asked Sherman's staff to notify him when Sherman came near St. Louis in the near future.[25]

25. Rosecrans's request for a Ewing-Sherman meeting at *O.R.* 34:2:619, 633. Rosecrans's reference to a Trans-Mississippi attack at *O.R.* 34:2:633. Rosecrans refers to "a plan" rather than "my plan," which indicates that the plan's author was someone other than Rosecrans. The Meridian expedition is at *O.R.* 32:1:173–79.

Late in the evening of March 18 the telegram came. Ewing was ordered to meet Sherman's train at Pana, Illinois. Caught by surprise Ewing grabbed a coat and left, telling his aide Lieutenant Harrison Hannahs to alert Ellen as to where he was going. At Pana, a railroad town one hundred miles northeast of St. Louis that sits atop regional coal mines, Tom Ewing found himself in Grant's private car as the command train edged its way through a gaggle of stalled commercial freight trains on sidings. Ewing later indicated to Hannahs that the tables were covered with maps of the terrain between Chattanooga and Atlanta. The discussion taking place between Grant and Sherman in front of Ewing was not only Sherman's Atlanta campaign but also a strike overland from Atlanta to Savannah, similar to Sherman's Meridian march.

Grant disliked the logistics of both plans. Meade's relative inactivity after Gettysburg had allowed Lee to send Longstreet's battered corps to Chickamauga and caused the federal setback that Grant remedied only at Missionary Ridge. Grant and Sherman were determined that never again would the Confederates have time to use their internal lines of communications. Only coordinated attacks in Georgia and Virginia could keep the Confederacy from reinforcing its armies in both theaters. While Grant's campaign in the East could be supported with sustained supplies from the North that Lee could not cut, Sherman's railroad between Chattanooga and Atlanta was a precarious lifeline, subject to damage by raiding Confederate cavalry. Sherman was going to need energetic cavalry commanders and plenty of horsemen.

After Sherman's energetic review, Grant agreed to approve Sherman's plans for the Atlanta campaign, but Lincoln's approval would be needed for any March to the Sea—and only after Atlanta was secured. Neither Sherman's nor Grant's memoirs indicate Ewing's presence at the meeting, but according to Hannahs he was there. Further, later correspondence from Sherman to Rosecrans hints at Ewing's presence. The demanding nature of Sherman's telegram indicates that Ewing may have been Sherman's unofficial reporter of the planning for the March to the Sea in case something later went wrong. Other commentators believe that while Sherman trusted Grant and Grant's chief of staff, John Rawlins, everyone knew that when Grant got to Washington he would necessarily have to work through Meade and other Potomac Army subordinates, who might have agendas of their own. Sherman wanted authority to attack Atlanta, not just keep Joe Johnston's forces tied down while the Army of the Potomac moved on Richmond. Sherman needed Tom Ewing as an unimpeachable witness if Sherman later needed Lincoln to override a balky War Department.[26]

26. For Sherman's distrust of the War Department, *O.R.* 32:3:92; compare with Hannahs, "Thomas Ewing Jr.," 278–79. While no reference is directly made in the *Official Records*, reports indicate that

Ewing rode on Grant's train with Sherman from Pana to Cincinnati. There, at the Burnett House, the two foster brothers discussed their own futures. Sherman was to command the largest army in the West, a command he had not imagined when he offered himself to Lincoln as an out-of-work army captain in 1861. Ewing told Sherman of the breakdown in his political career in Kansas, thanks to Lane's, Blunt's, and Curtis's constant post-Quantrill sniping. He duly relayed the idea for Rosecrans's Trans-Mississippi campaign but knew instinctively that the nation's armies could not launch five simultaneous attacks on the Confederacy at one time. There would be insufficient supplies and manpower to make a simultaneous Trans-Mississippi campaign alongside the army's attacking Atlanta. The official answer for Rosecrans was no. However, Sherman knew how to silence Ewing's critics in Kansas. Sherman offered the former chief justice a division command in the Atlanta campaign. The offer was a sign that Sherman wanted men around him he could trust. Several staff officers, including his chief quartermaster, were acting under "special orders" of Stanton, and Stanton's assistant Charles Dana was always hovering nearby, reporting everything noteworthy to Stanton. In the swirl of battle if a subordinate failed, Sherman did not want to consult with Dana before making a change. Besides, he had learned in the Vicksburg campaign that illness could idle division commanders as well as privates.[27]

To Sherman's surprising offer, Ewing brought up the obvious. He was a junior brigadier to many major generals in the Western Army with divisional command experience, including his brother, Hugh. Why seniority did not matter to Sherman when the subject was Tom Ewing rather than Hugh is a mystery known only to the three of them, but it would appear that Sherman was plugged into the political battles of Senate confirmation more than he let on. Unlike Hugh, Tom Ewing was a well-respected Republican whose toughness in western Missouri the previous autumn would win easy approvals from a radical Congress. As a major general Tom Ewing's reputation for cruelty in Missouri might be useful to provoke fear in Georgia at the right time. "I am going to Atlanta as sure as the sun shines," Sherman explained ebulliently to Ewing. The South was as "hollow as an eggshell," and Ewing could help Sherman prove it. Although Sherman had

---

Grant was en route to an Illinois meeting with Sherman on March 19, 1864, when he got his War Department telegrams in Louisville or Nashville. Sherman's messages on that date are from Nashville.

27. Stanton's spies at *O.R.* 32:3:135–36; Hannahs, "Thomas Ewing Jr.," 278–80; McGonigle, "First Kansas Infantry", 292n3. "Five" campaigns because Grant authorized three military campaigns for May 1864 (Grant's, Sherman's, and George Crook's Shenandoah Valley campaign); Banks's ongoing campaign on the Red River is the fourth. Sherman's "no" to Rosecrans's fifth campaign at *O.R.* 34:2:656. Sherman's division command offer to Ewing from Monaghan, *Civil War,* 298–99.

disapproved of the jayhawking campaign through Arkansas and Louisiana, his March to the Sea was simply "jayhawking across Georgia." Would Tom Ewing like that opportunity?[28]

Curiously, Ewing declined Sherman's offer. Perhaps Sherman's offer had hit him without sufficient time to consider it. Ewing had his future mapped out. Events had conspired against his ever being a Kansas senator, but he had made some plans with Browning and his father. Those plans would put him squarely in the middle of postwar Washington, where he would directly participate in the growth of the nation and, he hoped, his own fortune. If for any reason he were captured, there was no telling what Southerners might do to the author of General Order Number 11. Tom Ewing was not afraid of the assignment; he had risked his life leading troops before; however, he was not a glory seeker. He had learned in his battles with Blunt and Curtis that they had been political dunderheads before the war and their general's stars had not made them any better politicians. Perhaps he felt confident that, even without the glory of a Georgia campaign, his political career somewhere was possible, even with what Quantrill and Order No. 11 had done to his reputation. If Sherman was disappointed at Tom's decision, it was not mentioned in his memoirs. Sherman and Ewing parted on good terms, each toward his destiny.

When Ewing returned to St. Louis and told Hannahs, the adjutant was astonished, saying, "General, you've made the biggest mistake of your life." He bet Ewing that Sherman not only would take Atlanta but would "go to the sea just as sure as there is a God in Israel." That sort of romantic campaign could turn any man into Senate material in any number of states.[29]

Kansas historian Mary Scott Rowland in an unpublished work suggests Sherman's offer came when Ewing was still recuperating from a bout with recurring illnesses, including malaria from his teenage years in Washington. Further, his fights with Lane and Quantrill made him "insecure." Ewing reportedly replied to Hannahs' prediction, "If I were as sure of it as you are, I would go," and he offered to get Hannahs a staff position with Sherman if that was what Hannahs wanted. Obviously, he had some doubts about what was going to happen in the campaign—perhaps because he was not as acquainted with strength reports on enemy positions and manpower as Sherman was privy to, and Sherman had not shared these with Ewing during their brief meeting in Pana. If Ellen was con-

28. "Sun shines" and "eggshell" from Hannahs, "Thomas Ewing Jr.," 278; "jayhawking across Georgia" from Monaghan, *Civil War,* 298.

29. Hannahs, "Thomas Ewing Jr.," 279.

cerned about his physical safety, she did not show it. She, too, thought it was a mistake to reject Sherman's offer.[30]

The choice also might have had some family concerns involved in it. For all the problems Hugh had with Sherman, Tom was not anxious to make problems for Hugh. His older brother hungered for another division command and he was a West Pointer of sorts. If Hugh wanted back into the war in Sherman's army, and Tom got the appointment to one of the few division commands, it could cause considerable friction within the family, especially with Ellen Sherman. Further, from Hugh's vantage point, for Sherman to reach down into the junior brigadier ranks and pluck his brother out to command a division in an important campaign would be the ultimate breach in the family. Hugh's eye was on a possible postwar military career, whereas Tom had no attraction for that career. If he was concerned about his political career, Tom Ewing's snap decision did taint his future; but he was content that his political star, such as it was, would rise or fall on his merits and not according to the stars on his shoulder. What is unusual is that Sherman should have foreseen the same family problems before offering the post to Tom Ewing, but he did not. However, the decision left Tom gloomy. "From that time on [Ewing] seemed to gradually lose his interest in the war," Hannahs later reported. Tom's illnesses—neuralgia and boils—returned. He became irritable, complaining of Ellen's spending habits and her tendency toward hypochondria. For the first time Tom's marriage showed some strain.[31]

The Pana trip resulted in a lost opportunity for military glory, but it was clear that military glory did not interest Tom Ewing. He had seen battlefields and listened to the cries of the wounded. He had seen the devastation of Lawrence, the widows' staring eyes, the burned homes and businesses without men to run them. He had seen the desolate farms of western Missouri where Missourians had been forced to move south under Order Number 11. He had done his share. Yet, six months later, his mundane staff position in Missouri would soon bring more excitement for Tom Ewing than he had ever desired and would prove most fortunate for the reelection of Abraham Lincoln.

30. Ewing's insecurity, see Rowland, "Thomas Ewing Jr.," 22; Hannahs, "Thomas Ewing Jr.," 280–82.

31. Hannahs, "Thomas Ewing Jr.," 280.

9

THERMOPYLAE OF THE WEST

The morning of Sunday, June 26, 1864, dawned quietly. In northern Georgia, two armies were catching their breath near Kennesaw Mountain, sensing that something big awaited them in the morning's sweltering heat. Sergeant Nixon Stewart of the Fifty-Second Ohio had spent the previous night at a campfire with his Bible, where he read over and over the Ninety-First Psalm, the Soldier's Psalm: "A thousand shall fall at thy side and ten thousand at thy right hand, but it shall not come nigh thee." He took the promise to heart and commended his life to God but still had slept fitfully.[1]

Before the end of the next day, June 27, Daniel McCook Jr., the youngest lawyer in the firm of Sherman, Ewing & McCook, led his brigade in the van of a two-division frontal assault at the center of the Confederate lines. McCook led his men forcefully into the Dead Angle, a killing zone where withering Confederate musket volleys cut down hundreds in his brigade. As he was going over a parapet McCook fell, a bullet in his chest. Miraculously he was carried off the field by flag bearers, his wound was stabilized, and he was sent home to Steubenville. But his health worsened, and on July 17, surrounded by family, McCook died. Later Sherman would admit this attack was a mistake, and he never again ordered a frontal attack in the Atlanta campaign.[2]

1. Soldier's Psalm from Stewart, *McCook's Regiment,* 113–14.

2. The frontal assault at Kennesaw Mountain, Sherman, *Memoirs,* 2:58–59. "Nixon Stewart, a participant in the assault, claims the pre-war law firm association between Sherman and McCook

Given the difficulty of communication during the war, it is unclear when Tom Ewing learned of the mortal wounding of his former partner. His writings do not refer to McCook's death. And Ewing was busy. As Sherman was moving his army on Atlanta, Brigadier General Tom Ewing was making war on Confederate guerrilla bands in southeast Missouri. The boundaries of Ewing's new St. Louis district were formed by the Missouri, Mississippi, and Meramec rivers and Rolla, Missouri. The new command was much like that in Kansas, small units of cavalry and a few forts in small towns defended by companies of infantry. The nearly flat Kansas prairie was replaced by tree-studded gnarled ravines and small mountains. Roads were narrow, winding, and made of mud. Traveling the region by wagon or on foot was torturous. Lieutenant Colonel John Burris of the Tenth Kansas cavalry was one of the Kansas units that Ewing brought with him from Kansas. Burris's report on his unit's actions in August 1864 describes the terrain of southeast Missouri:

> We were engaged in scouting the counties of New Madrid, Mississippi, and Stoddard . . . burned a distillery and a grocery at which [three men] were accustomed to meet . . . crossed the Saint Francis River just below Chalk Bluff, . . . marched north to the Chicasawba Settlement, crossed Pemiscot Bayou, and encamped in Cowskin Settlement. . . . We pursued the enemy six miles across Dogskin Swamp, when we found him in line of battle in a dense forest, two miles south of Elk Chute, in Pemiscot County, Mo. . . . A running fight was kept up for two miles, through the swamp, among the trees, and over logs. . . . [They] fled precipitately, many of them rushing, panic-stricken, into the stream, some attempting to swim their horses across, . . . while the rebel colonel, . . . hid in the dense forest and almost impenetrable swamps of that region.[3]

Ewing took over the St. Louis District on March 21, 1864, replacing Brigadier General Clinton B. Fisk, a Curtis protégé from the regular army. Fisk's constantly demanding style of leadership required subordinates to keep him informed, but

prompted McCook to ask Sherman to lead the charge." Stewart, *Dan McCook's Regiment,* 113. This may have been an assumption on Stewart's part, he being a sergeant at the time of the assault and not a high-ranking officer. A McCook biographer, Charles Whalen, Jr., indicates in correspondence with the author dated November 26, 1996, that Sherman ordered the attack three days before it was executed, and that Generals Thomas and McPherson chose the assault divisions. General Jefferson C. Davis, McCook's commanding general, chose his assault brigade for what he later called "conspicuous duty."

3. Burris's report, *O.R.* 41:1:81–82.

otherwise he was a martinet who issued orders to subordinates to "Try the bushwhacker by drumhead court-martial to-night, and let every soldier in Macon shoot him if guilty, as he doubtless is. Don't allow such prisoners to be brought in." Although Ewing's measures were to be as harsh as Fisk's, he did it without all the flowery rhetoric.[4]

Ewing also brought Kansas regiments with him to the area, which proved extremely valuable to loyalist citizens, who knew that the Kansas boys, unlike those in Missouri militia regiments, would not have relatives among the guerrillas and thus would not pull their punches. "[The] Tenth Kansas Regiment on the southwest branch also tends to mollify the warlike propensities of our rebels, because they have a very distinct sensation in what peculiar manner these Kansas boys are wont to settle accounts with bushwhackers. [A store was] robbed by four bushwhackers. It has since been reported that four men have been found in the woods, each with a hole in his head, but as I have been unable to trace this report to any reliable source, I just give it for what it is worth."[5]

To the curious who met Tom Ewing and wondered if he was of a lesser mindset than his brother-in-law, he quickly dispelled such notions. He was a hands-on, hard-nosed leader, not content to push pins around a map at headquarters. Dealing first with Lane and then Quantrill had changed his attitude. Ewing's guerrilla hunters were stretched from Cape Girardeau to Rolla and back to St. Louis, fighting on a shoestring. In June Colonel John Rogers of the Second Missouri state militia cavalry and Ewing's chief lieutenant reported, "Our men got in pursuit of the guerrillas . . . and ran them into Mingo Swamp, where they scattered. . . . Three men who had been harboring them were taken, and, attempting to escape, were shot and killed." A later report by Rogers describes the no-quarter black-flag fighting. "One had the oath of allegiance in his pocket but the bullet missed the pocket and thus the oath failed to protect him."[6]

Guerrilla families found no sympathy from Ewing. He appreciated good subordinates with initiative, since he felt he had been ill-served in Kansas by key lieutenants before the Lawrence massacre. Nor was he about to squash Rogers or J. N. Herder's efforts. Herder, who commanded the Cape Girardeau subdistrict, was ordered to continue to break up the copperhead camps in southeast Missouri and Illinois and that Ewing wanted none of the thieves taken prisoner. "Such trials, however, only result, where the prisoner is convicted, in putting the Government

4. "Every soldier in Macon" from *O.R.* 34:3:216.
5. Missouri State Senator Gert Goebel to TEJr., June 10, 1864, at *O.R.* 34:4:297.
6. "Mingo Swamp" from *O.R.* 34:4:234–35; "oath failed to protect" from *O.R.* 34:3:482–83.

to the expense of boarding and lodging him during the war. As the President rarely approves a sentence of death, it is therefore best to take few prisoners."[7]

Guerrilla bands in eastern Missouri began to feel this new steel from the command determination in St. Louis. Ewing had learned at Lawrence that a proactive defense was vital to the safety of local populations. In the style of the Leavenworth Red Legs, Ewing tried to organize a band of Missouri mercenaries to carry on individualized warfare against the guerrillas, essentially a force of counterinsurgents. Ewing's staff officers argued against this policy. Rogers reported, "A few guerrillas can go around and in one night disarm a company." Colonel John Tyler, commanding at Fort Davidson, agreed with Rogers. A brutal warfare was needed, with no quarter asked or given, but not with a quasi-civilian force. "It will serve only as a means of supply[ing] arms to the rebels." This no-quarter warfare in the shadows continued most of the spring and summer of 1864 while the conventional armies fought set-piece battles in Virginia and Georgia. A report to Ewing from the Tenth Kansas cavalry operating along the southwest branch of the White River showed no hesitancy to settle scores with the bushwhackers for the Lawrence massacre.[8]

Ewing's law training and belief in the presumption of innocence was by necessity subordinated to the suppression of a lawless and vicious rebellion where the murder of Kansas and Missouri civilians was promoted by choice of the Confederate government. He had tried fairness and dignity in Kansas, and Quantrill had butchered the men and boys of Lawrence. Ewing, and even Sherman, had given the Confederacy the option between honorable conventional warfare and the ruthless suppression of guerrillas. Sherman would write Halleck later in 1864 that he did not care if Atlanta civilians "howl against my barbarity and cruelty. I will answer that war is war, and not popularity-seeking." By 1864, Tom Ewing agreed with that general sentiment. Carrying warfare to the civilians became necessary when it proved the only form of fighting that would break the spirit of the enemy population, especially the spirit of a population that made heroes out of men such as Quantrill. When Ewing's subordinates in southeast Missouri captured Confederate recruiting officers who then claimed POW status, Rogers tested Ewing's resolve by wiring, "I can't see the prisoner of war in it." Ewing did not persuade Rogers differently. Slowly and inexorably, dealing with guerrillas in a ruthless manner increased their casualties and diminished their enthusiasm.[9]

7. "Putting the Government to the expense" at *O.R.* 34:4:260–61.
8. Rogers's report at *O.R.* 34:4:268, 296–97; Tyler's agreement "it will serve" at *O.R.* 34:4:430.
9. WTS to Halleck, September 4, 1864, *O.R.* 38:5:794; "can't see" at *O.R.* 34:4:261.

Rosecrans and Ewing adopted a get-tough attitude with guerrilla operations in eastern and southeastern Missouri. Their harsh actions carried at least the implication that another Order Number 11 in eastern Missouri would clear the region of problems as it had in western Missouri. Confederate officials could not see guerrilla operations handing Missouri over to the Confederacy. They had to try something else. That "something else" revolved around a former governor of Missouri and a Mexican War veteran, Sterling Price.

In August 1864 every Confederate commander, including Price, knew the two main Confederate armies outside Atlanta and Richmond were to keep Grant and Sherman from capturing those cities before November's elections made George McClellan president. Longstreet had written A. R. Lawton, the Confederacy's quartermaster general on March 5, 1864, "if we can break up the enemy's arrangements early and throw him back, he will not be able to recover his position nor his *morale* until the Presidential election is over, and we shall then have a new President to treat with." Lee and Longstreet had carried out their portion of the plan, keeping Grant bogged down before Petersburg. But Joseph E. Johnston, in Jefferson Davis's view, had failed to keep Sherman from surrounding Atlanta. On July 17, Davis relieved Johnston of command and inserted Major General John B. Hood as overall commander of the Army of Tennessee.[10]

Kirby Smith had fought a successful defensive campaign in northern Louisiana along the Red River, but a defensive campaign was not going to convince the North to give up the war at the ballot box. Price commanded the last mobile army in the Confederacy capable of attacking anything of significance. Rosecrans advised Lincoln later that one of Price's objectives had been to "turn the election in [Missouri] for McClellan." With McClellan already pledged to make peace, success on the battlefield was no longer required for the Confederacy to survive, only the illusion of success needed to be shown an anxious American populace. The administration could not abandon Missouri and Kansas to a Confederate army whose raids through Missouri and Kansas before the election would leave dozens of towns like Lawrence smoldering in its wake. Northern spirits were sagging under the weight of the casualties in Virginia, especially. A hell-fire-and-brimstone campaign through Missouri would excite local OAKs lodges and other secret societies, and Confederate enlistments would force Sherman to send men from his Atlanta army to stem the tide.

If Price's small army was going to invade federal territory, take St. Louis, and destroy Lincoln's chances of reelection by knocking Missouri out of the war, Price

10. Longstreet to Lawton at *O.R.* 32:3:588; also Rosecrans to Lincoln, *O.R.* 41:4:576.

had to get going before autumn rains mired down his wagons and cannon. After St. Louis, he would turn on Kansas City, brush aside any Kansas militia sent to fight him, destroy the Leavenworth fort and arsenal, turn south and burn Lawrence, Topeka, even get as far west as Fort Riley. Such a campaign would net him at least twenty thousand new recruits and throw the entire Trans-Mississippi into a panic. Richmond reluctantly approved the plan. A third of Price's men were recruits who marched into Missouri unarmed. Price's hungry soldiers would have to campaign further than any Confederate army in the war, but there were new weapons for them in the St. Louis arsenal, and new horses and foodstuffs on the Missouri farms in their path. It was a desperate gamble engineered by officers in an overly optimistic government who secretly knew the end was upon them but dared not admit it.[11]

Fort Davidson lay at the end of the railroad and telegraph lines between St. Louis and the Ironton-Arcadia depot. The area was ninety miles southwest of St. Louis and a major iron ore smelting region for Missouri. The railroad allowed Union reinforcements rapid movement up and down the line if the Confederates chose an invasion route that menaced either Rolla or St. Louis. A marauding enemy coming north out of Arkansas aimed at St. Louis had to march north either between the first set of Ozark Mountains and the narrow plain next to the Mississippi River or through the Arcadia valley past the fort.

Davidson was a dowdy octagon-shaped earthen structure nine feet high and ten feet thick situated near a creek and on a slight rise in a one-thousand-acre saucer encircled by four small mountains—Cedar and Rock mountains on the north, Pilot Knob on the east, and Shepherd's Mountain to the southwest. So-called mountains in the Arcadia valley were between five and six hundred feet high, rising from the valley like typical Ozark mountains, each gully covered with rocks, gnarled oaks, and undergrowth. Like a castle, Fort Davidson included a dry moat with steep sides. Behind its walls were four thirty-two-pound howitzers and three twenty-four pounders. Its defenders could shoehorn six more field guns into the place when pressed. Two rifle pits were dug outside the fort, one running southwest to the dry creek bed and the other north toward the Potosi road.

The weakness of the fort was that the defenders tried to cram a thousand men, guns, horses, ammunition, and food into a place less than sixty yards across. If

11. Price's men unarmed, Monaghan, *Civil War,* 311; Paludan, *Abraham Lincoln,* 284; Cyrus Peterson and Joseph Hanson, *Pilot Knob: The Thermopylae of the West,* 24–25. Price's objectives from Henry E. Palmer, "The Black Flag Character of the War on the Border," 432. Price's orders at *O.R.* 41:1:728–29.

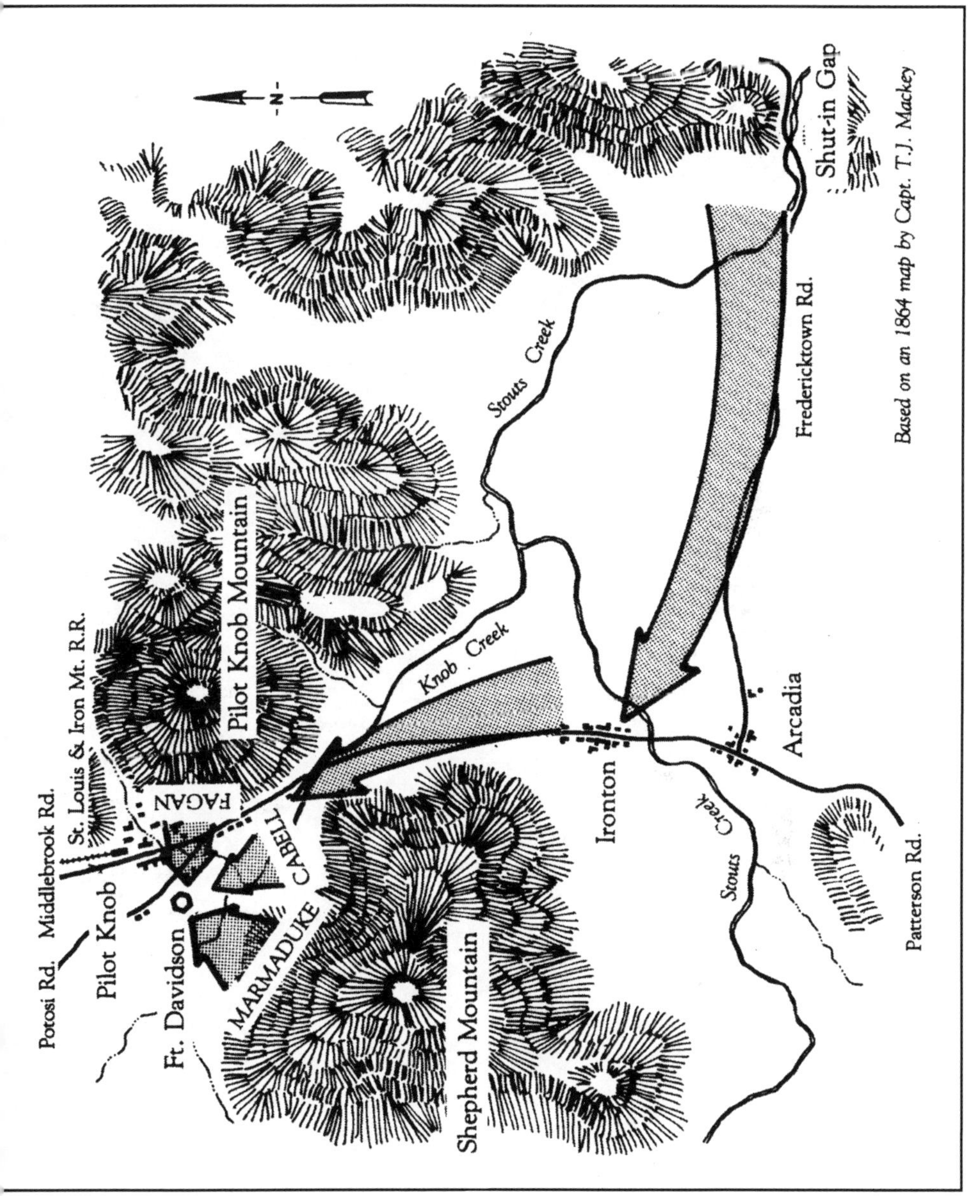

Price's invasion and the battle at Pilot Knob, Missouri, on September 27, 1864. Courtesy of the Missouri Department of Natural Resources.

sharpshooters could get within eight hundred yards of the fort, they could scarcely miss hitting something. Furthermore, if they could get cannons up through the gnarled undergrowth, artillery on Pilot Knob and Shepherd's Mountain could pound the place into submission. While it stood, however, Confederates marching that direction could not go around the fort without danger.

Nothing about Fort Davidson concerned Sterling Price on August 28, 1864, when he ordered tents struck and marched his men out of Camden, Arkansas, into southeast Missouri. His army included eight thousand mostly mounted infantry in three divisions led by Major Generals James Fagan and John Marmaduke and Brigadier General William Cabell. The mounted infantry was joined en route by Jo Shelby's large cavalry division of about six thousand, giving Price about fifteen thousand men under arms. His ultimate goal might have been a secret among his own men, but federal officials assumed St. Louis was the prize.[12]

Marauding guerrillas north of the Missouri River tried to confuse the federals as to Price's ultimate objective. Seven hundred guerrillas and their sympathizers took Parkville and Platte City, just across the river from Leavenworth, in western Missouri. A year after Ewing's Order Number 11 had stripped the Missouri countryside of guerrilla supporters, the guerrillas were back. Among the most notorious was Bloody Bill Anderson. Operating ahead of Price's vanguard, his terrorists attacked a train north of the Missouri River, took unarmed Union soldiers off the train, and shot them down near the tracks, ran over the bodies with the locomotive, and burned the train. Later, when Anderson was killed in a cavalry skirmish, Price's invasion orders were found on Anderson's body. When Union commanders cabled Rosecrans that Price had given federal forces the slip in Arkansas, the federal commanders implemented their defensive plans. Brigadier General Clinton Fisk quipped to a subordinate, "Hot times are upon us."[13]

Hot times, indeed. Not since the war's first summer had St. Louis seen a threat like Price's invasion. Rosecrans had little to work with in order to meet it. He had determined that there were three possible main invasion routes in central and eastern Missouri. He ordered Springfield and Rolla defended at all costs, with heavy infantry regiments, and he placed a mobile force in the Arcadia valley with which to slow Price if he came that way. Rosecrans's later report indicated "The safety of Saint Louis was vital to us." There were only sixty-five hundred troops scattered

12. Confederate estimated force, Clement A. Evans, ed., *The Confederate Military History,* 9:179–82; original Confederate plan at *O.R.* 41:2:1023.

13. Bloody Bill Anderson from Eldridge, *Early Days,* 198n78; Fisk at *O.R.* 41:3:422.

between Price's army and St. Louis. False civilian sightings began to report that the invading army exceeded twenty thousand men. Rosecrans scrounged every available regular or militia regiment in northeastern Missouri and central Illinois for assistance, including some hundred-days men whose enlistments had already expired. "The enrolled militia of Saint Louis, though but skeleton regiments, were called out and the citizens also requested to organize and arm. General Ewing was sent to Pilot Knob, with directions to use his utmost exertions to find out whether any more than Shelby's division was in Southeast Missouri, and to that end to hold Pilot Knob until he was certain."[14]

Realizing that Rosecrans could not fight with what he had against Price's Confederate army, the War Department acted swiftly. Major General A. J. Smith's division, en route from Louisiana to Sherman in Georgia, was rerouted to St. Louis and deployed southwest of St. Louis on the Iron Mountain Railroad. When Price's spies learned of Smith's deployment and that Rosecrans had whipped St. Louis civilians into a fever, while on the march from Camden Price casually changed his initial plan. He decided to overwhelm the garrison at Fort Davidson, confiscate the fort's arsenal, and destroy the Iron Mountain Railroad between the fort and St. Louis, then turn west to plunder central and western Missouri and eastern Kansas without striking St. Louis.[15]

Union commanders continued to believe St. Louis was the target. Ewing's commander at Fort Davidson, Major James Wilson, was the lone holdout, who suggested that St. Louis ignore civilians' reports of Price's movements. All the signs he could see pointed to Price's moving toward central Missouri. Even when new reports came in that Price was consolidating his army at Fredericktown, it still was not clear to Rosecrans that Fort Davidson was the point at which the Confederate columns would converge. As late as September 25, Ewing's subordinates wired Rosecrans that Price's force was headed toward Cape Girardeau, yet Colonel Rogers from that city was reporting Price's objective to be Jefferson City to the northwest. Confusion reigned. Rosecrans needed reliable eyes and ears in the field. He ordered Ewing to take the train to Pilot Knob and report what he saw, hold the fort against any detachment of rebels if he could, but to destroy Fort Davidson and retreat if Price's whole army threatened.[16]

Ewing's train reached Pilot Knob on September 26, just as Price was consolidating his forces at Fredericktown. What Ewing found was disturbing. The orig-

14. For Rosecrans's report and Ewing, *O.R.* 41:1:309.

15. St. Louis fever, *Leavenworth Daily Conservative,* October 1, 1864.

16. Ewing's report at *O.R.* 41:1:446–52; also *O.R.* 41:3:214, 322–23, 342, 360, 361, 954; Peterson and Hanson, *Thermopylae,* 95.

inal garrison was made up of men who were primarily guerrilla fighters, unskilled in stand-up warfare. More experienced infantry were needed if the federals were going to defend anything. On September 27, Smith sent two hundred veterans of the Fourteenth Iowa under Captain William J. Campbell on the night train to Fort Davidson. The Iowans were Shiloh veterans and had been captured at the Hornet's Nest. Paroled, they had fought at Vicksburg and along the Red River. Ewing could not have been given more stubborn infantry, and he would need all of their mettle.[17]

Instead of attacking Fort Davidson with the troops he had at hand, for two days Price consolidated his columns at Fredericktown, twenty miles east of the fort. He sent Shelby's cavalry to destroy parts of the Iron Mountain Railroad north of the fort as a brigade of Fagan's division moved directly on Pilot Knob via the Fredericktown road. The rest of the Confederate army would follow. Ironton was only a mile south of the fort. As Ewing was arriving at the fort, Fagan's men advanced on Ironton from the southwest, skirmishing throughout the day of September 26 until a Union cavalry vidette pushed them back toward Shut-Ins Gap. The Fourteenth Iowa's two hundred men and some armed civilians fought tree to tree, captured some of Price's advance guard, and retreated slowly. Confederate prisoners taken by the Iowans reported Price's force at fifteen thousand. Fort Davidson began to look evermore like another Alamo.

Late on September 26 Ewing met with a friend, Dr. Seymour Carpenter, and Colonel Thomas Fletcher who commanded the local Missouri infantry. Fletcher had been wounded at Chickasaw Bayou and served under Sherman in the Atlanta campaign until rumors of Price's raid brought him back to Missouri. Should we abandon the fort or fight? Ewing asked them. Fletcher wanted to stay. He was second in command, but he was also a candidate for Missouri governor that fall and, like Ewing, expected harsh treatment if captured. Carpenter appealed to Ewing's ambition—that no candidate for high office could win an election if he ran away from a battle. Still, Ewing was uncertain. That night he sent all the quartermaster supplies he could by rail to St. Louis. At midnight he wired Smith not only for "a full regiment" but for advice from the more experienced commander whether to "fight it out or leave." He advised Smith he could hold out for a day but that this might mean Price would cut off his retreat.[18]

17. *O.R.* 41:1:325.

18. Three-way discussion from Bryce A. Suderow, *Thunder in Arcadia Valley: Price's Defeat, September 27, 1864*, 77; quotes from *O.R.* 41:3:385–86.

Through the morning hours of September 27, the Confederate forces trudged through the valley until Fagan's entire division was up. Marmaduke's division was camped less than ten miles from Pilot Knob. Ewing sent a frantic message to Rosecrans advising that Price's objective was Fort Davidson, and the central-route invasion was on. He estimated the rebel force at between three and five thousand in the immediate vicinity and fifteen thousand more on the way. Ewing's last message to Rosecrans was "A considerable body is upon me." He claimed he could hold the fort against five thousand cavalry, implying that if Price used his mounted infantry effectively, Ewing did not know what would happen. Smith reported to Rosecrans that communication with Pilot Knob was intermittent, but Ewing was still there. Smith would organize a relief force if this was what Rosecrans wanted. Rosecrans cautioned Smith against going to Ewing's aid if it meant Price might get between Smith's infantry and St. Louis. Ewing had stepped into a situation not of his own making but, like other junior officers, was now committed to the defense of the fort and would have to fight it out as best he could.[19]

At daylight on September 27, Ewing sent Major Wilson's cavalry and Campbell's Fourteenth Iowa companies to the cool misty gap between Shepherd's Mountain and Ironton, their sniping slowing the Confederate advance through Ironton and around the new courthouse. After an hour of fighting, at about ten in the morning, the mist evaporated. Wilson's detachment fell back toward Fort Davidson, where by now dozens of civilians and freed slaves had gathered.[20]

At noon on September 27 Price got his first look at the Union redoubt. He hesitated, deciding whether to lay siege to the fort or overwhelm it with an immediate attack. What he saw did not impress him. With Marmaduke's and Fagan's divisions now at Ironton, he conferred with his general staff about the size of the force needed to take the little fort. Shelby urged Price to bypass the place altogether. The Union force was mostly infantry and could not pursue Price's mounted forces. They would have to march around the fort, but it was only a little out of the way. Hysteria in federal enclaves in Missouri was better aroused by attacking St. Louis, not some earthen fort in the middle of nowhere. Marmaduke and Fagan disagreed with Shelby and urged Price to blow Fort Davidson apart as an example. Price's preferences were with those who urged an attack. Price gave Fagan a self-fulfilling prophecy, "If you can carry the place without much loss, do so."[21]

19. "Considerable body" TEJr. to Rosecrans, September 26, 1864, at *O.R.* 41:3:385.

20. *O.R.* 41:1:447.

21. Shelby's bypass from John N. Edwards, *Shelby and His Men, The War in the West,* 396; "carry the place" *O.R.* 41:3:959.

While Marmaduke's division deployed, stretching from the entire front of Shepherd's Mountain to Pilot Knob, couriers reported to Ewing that Price was displaying a flag of truce. With Marmaduke's division as a backdrop, Price sent his chief of staff, Lauchlan MacLean, forward to negotiate a surrender. MacLean and Ewing had not seen each other since the infamous candle-box affair in 1858. They had parted enemies at that time, and nothing had changed. Ewing spurned the offer and MacLean took the message back to Price, who ordered Marmaduke's and Cabell's lines closer and then halted. MacLean came out again, telling Ewing the Confederates could not be responsible for the consequences if Ewing did not surrender. Concerned about the black civilians in the fort, Ewing consulted with his officers. If there had not been blacks in his fort Ewing might have considered a surrender. "They will play no Fort Pillow on me," Ewing said. He sent the flag back. The Fourteenth Iowa's men gripped their muskets.[22]

The rebel attack was planned to converge from all four sides with covering fire from cannon on Shepherd Mountain. Unimpressed by his commanding general's tactics, Jo Shelby watched the preparations. Well-entrenched infantry would give the Confederates hell. "And hell we did get," he wrote later.[23]

The Confederates put two guns on the summit of Shepherd's Mountain to begin bombarding the fort. Before the Confederate attack, Ewing suggested to First Lieutenant David Murphy of the Forty-Seventh Missouri that he try suppression fire on the Confederate artillery on the mountain. Ewing was adamant about keeping the Confederates from getting guns into position because the recognized weakness of Fort Davidson was its vulnerability to Confederate artillery from the heights. When the first Confederate round came arching over the fort, exploding long, he had no real idea whether Murphy could do anything to assist. Murphy sighted his guns, fired, and hit the rebel caisson, the explosion obliterating the gun crew. Ewing knew it was luck but had no more reason to doubt the abilities of his young artillery commander.[24]

Colonel Thomas McCray's and Colonel W. F. Selmons's brigades of Fagan's Arkansas division, mostly dismounted cavalry, deployed and came over Pilot Knob, overwhelming the remainder of Wilson's small detachment. Wilson was last seen skirmishing with his cavalry east of the fort. Ewing could see Marmaduke's four lines of dismounted infantry moving forward from the southwest,

22. "No Fort Pillow" from Peterson and Hanson, *Thermopylae,* 155.

23. Confederate preparation, *O.R.* 41:3:959; "Hell we did get" from Shelby to C. C. Rainwater, January 5, 1888, quoted in Peterson and Hanson, *Thermopylae,* 100.

24. Murphy's accuracy from Peterson and Hanson, *Thermopylae,* 149.

descending the mountain through the line of cleared timber. Murphy trained his guns on the advancing infantry and opened fire, and the butternut ranks began to fall, staggering the Confederates. Clark's brigade of Marmaduke's division charged and got all the way into the moat before federal fire turned on them. Many of them remained pinned down in the ditch until dark, hugging the earthen sides. Infantry volleys from the rifle pits to the south broke up the remainder of the attack, and the survivors regrouped along shelter in a creek bed.

Fagan's and Cabell's divisions advanced steadily from Pilot Knob. Every mounted infantryman with a musket left his horse with handlers and was in the attack. The Confederates had to stop and reform their lines. Fagan's attack from the east was slowed by Ewing's cannon facing that direction. The uncoordinated attack fell back into hiding behind a railroad cut. At this time Colonel Archibald Dobbin's dismounted cavalry brigade threatened from the north but was beaten back with another blast of Murphy's cannon and timely musket volleys.

Confederate divisions "vying with each other" to take the fort, charged "nearly into the muzzles of the enemy cannon," Price wrote later, self-righteously. In fact all they charged into was withering grapeshot and musket volleys from desperate men. The butternut infantry came on, bayonets gleaming. During the raging battle, Sergeant H. C. Wilkinson later wrote, "the stately . . . General Ewing, . . . his mouth tightly closed and face slightly pale was as 'firm as a stone wall,' walking side to side, head erect, watching the struggling mass around the fort."[25] The Eleventh Kansas had given Ewing the nickname "Jesuit Tom," and with this mulish manner, he strode the parapets of Fort Davidson amid the roar of his artillery and muskets. Later Ewing wrote,

> [Rebel] lines were greatly broken by the houses and fences of the skirt of the town [Pilot Knob], but were hastily reformed . . . and swept upon the plain in handsome style, yelling and on the double-quick. We opened on them when at 600 yards from the fort with musketry from the ramparts and from the long line of the north rifle-pits, and with canister from seven pieces of artillery. They rushed on most gallantly, but were broken, confused, and swept down by our rapid and well-directed fire until the advance reached the

25. Price's report, *O.R.* 41:1:629. The Wilkinson description of Ewing on the parapets is from "General Thomas Ewing's Great Military Feat Fifty Years Ago," a public domain advertising piece thought to have been written by Cyrus Peterson or John Hansen to tout their book *Pilot Knob: Thermopylae of the West*. The document is found on the Internet at <http://www.mostateparks.com/ftdavidson/ewingmilitaryfeat.pdf> last accessed on May 11, 2008.

> ditch, when the attacking forces fled in dismay, leaving apparently almost half their comrades dead or wounded on the plain.[26]

Ewing had left little to chance. The walls were lined with his Iowa infantry in ranks two deep, firing so quickly the barrels grew hot. Older men in the fort's pit loaded muskets and passed them up to the Shiloh veterans on the ramparts. Likewise, Murphy had organized ammunition lines to get canister and shot up to the cannon. The hail of fire broke Fagan's division and scattered them "like wheat chaff." Ewing cheered his artillerymen's efforts with the rest of his command.[27]

Ewing walked the parapets amid the whistle of incoming shells and the answering blasts of his four thirty-two pounders double-shotted with canister aimed at the solid Confederate lines. MacLean's words with Price must have been weighing on his mind. Every man in the advancing Confederate ranks had to know that the man who had destroyed the opportunity for a slavery government in Kansas before the war, and who had issued Order Number 11 after Lawrence, was commanding the rabble in the fort. If he was taken alive, Ewing knew he would not live. MacLean had said as much. The only question would be the nature of his death.

Cabell ordered his men to form their line of battle in the lee of Shepherd's Mountain and advance slowly on the fort. Unlike Fagan's division, Cabell came forward in what Ewing described as "handsome style," behind the rebel yell. Union cannon threw canister at the rebels at six hundred yards. Cabell's lines came on behind the Arkansas secretary of the treasury, now sword-waving Lieutenant Colonel Olinver Basham, who drove them forward until their commander fell mortally wounded near the moat. Other key officers were down, and rifle volleys from the north rifle pits punched more holes in the lines. Cabell rallied the charge in person, and his horse went down in a bloody mess forty yards from the moat. His tumble left him stunned. Cabell's men pressed into the ditch under Ewing's guns, but again the steepness of the sides stopped them. To advance or retreat was to die, and the fort's sides were too steep to climb without ladders.[28]

Cabell's division retreated, leaving bodies all over the ground, and then incredibly they formed and came again. The rebel yell was drowned by the roar of big cannon that Captain Murphy directed into their lines. Men began to die in the fort, too. C. W. Purcell, a former army captain, was a civilian crewing a can-

26. Nickname "Jesuit Tom" from Busch, "Mistake of Your Life," quoting private emails from Robert S. LaForte concerning LaForte's unpublished notations circa 1990. Ewing's description of the battle from *O.R.* 41:1:448.

27. Monaghan, *Civil War,* 312.

28. Ewing's description of Cabell's charge at *O.R.* 41:1,448.

non manned by former slaves who had never been under fire. Sharpshooters on the mountain killed Purcell and several others. Several of the untrained civilians huddled behind the parapet, scared to fire, claiming their weapons did not work. Murphy pressed the men into the parapet and, grabbing a musket, fired the weapon. He swore, "If you turn your back again, I'll shoot you down where you stand!" When Cabell's men reached the moat, Murphy leaped onto the parapet and swore abusively at the Southerners, urging the federals to double their fire, throwing rocks at the retreating Confederates. Ewing had to drag Murphy bodily off the parapet. Again Cabell's men reformed and fought forward desperately, and Ewing's cannon knocked down whole rows. Civilians like the father of George Hammock of the Forty-Seventh Missouri moved along the parapets, biting open cartridges. Another civilian, Reverend D. A. Wilson, chaplain of the Eighth Missouri state militia regiment, brought his only weapon, a shotgun. During a lull between attacks, Ewing saw him behind the parapets. "Why aren't you up there?" he asked Wilson. The only enemy soldier was a cavalry scout, three hundred yards distant. Holding out his shotgun, Wilson replied, "Will this reach 'em?" Ewing smiled and moved on.[29]

A final attack came before sundown. Three long lines came on, four ranks deep, from two directions. Price remembered Cerro Gordo, and he expected his men to sweep the federals from the valley like the Mexicans had fled seventeen years earlier. Campbell's brigade got to the steep moats. Ewing's muskets and cannon made short work of the front ranks. A color-bearer fell dead, next to his flag. When rebels entered the moat, crude hand grenades were tossed into the ditch by Campbell's Fourteenth Iowa. The grenades were a godsend, since they allowed the defenders to keep attackers at bay in the moats without exposing themselves on the top. Cannon smoke hung over them. "Davidson was like a mighty burning tar-kiln as our smoke rose heavenward," one man wrote. The smoke was so dense Confederate sharpshooters on the mountains could not tell blue from grey. After the last attack, back on Pilot Knob Mountain, Fagan pleaded with Price to allow another charge before dusk. Price had had enough. A "damned wise decision," Cabell later wrote. St. Louis reporters claimed over fourteen hundred Confederates lay dead and wounded, the most experienced men in Price's small army.[30]

29. Peterson and Hanson, *Thermopylae,* 170, 197.

30. "Tar-kiln" from ibid., 167; "wise decision" from Albert Castel, *General Sterling Price and the Civil War in the West,* 215. Price's court of inquiry (*O.R.* 41:1:715) began in March 1865 and was not completed until after Lee surrendered. Casualties (from *St. Louis Democrat,* October 3, 1864) may be inaccurate.

That night the groaning and keening of the wounded echoed throughout the hollow valley and the houses and churches at Pilot Knob. The Confederates torched the charcoal piles in the smelting furnace in Pilot Knob, and stretcher bearers used the light of the fire to retrieve their wounded. The fire complicated Ewing's efforts to engineer an escape. Ewing sent some of his men out to gather up arms and ammunition from nearby rebels. The wounded had crawled together in piles, resembling huddled pigs against a cold night. Both groups went about their work without bothering each other. Ewing could smell the "courage" the rebels had summoned; the smell of applejack permeated the bodies near the fort "like an overcrowded grog-shop."[31]

Inside the fort Ewing met with his officers. To Campbell, Ewing joked that he had been in big political fights—but nothing like this. Ewing had lost about two hundred killed and wounded. Campbell replied that, given the size of the Union force, Pilot Knob was the hottest battle he was ever in. Considering Campbell's combat pedigree, it was perhaps the best praise Ewing would ever get.

Ewing knew he had been lucky. Dozens of his men had never made it to the fort and had been captured in the valleys and nooks of the mountains around Fort Davidson. He had lost a fourth of his effective strength in the fight that afternoon. The Confederates would spend the night pushing artillery up the slopes of Shepherd's Mountain and Pilot Knob itself. Price would take his time the next day and then bombard the fort from the mountains. Ewing's options included flight to the rugged land near Mineral Point or Potosi, another day's march to the north, where even more of Smith's veterans could link up with the Fort Davidson men and block Price once more with a formidable force. If Ewing remained at Fort Davidson he must eventually capitulate. He decided they would evacuate.

Just before the evacuation began, Ewing got some unexpected help. A woman came into the fort bearing a message for Ewing from Confederate colonel Alonzo Slayback. A veteran of Pea Ridge, Slayback was a Missouri lawyer described as "kind-hearted and noble." Slayback and Ewing had been friends and fellow attorneys before the war. Slayback's note suggested that, if Ewing was resisting surrender because of Order Number 11, Slayback would guarantee Ewing's personal safety. Had Ewing not already decided to evacuate, he might have taken Slayback up on the offer. But Slayback could guarantee nothing for the black civilians in his command who had helped kill Confederates that afternoon. Ewing sent the woman back to the Confederates with word that the garrison would fight on.[32]

31. Pigs from Peterson and Hanson, *Thermopylae,* 210; "grog-shop" from Castel, *Sterling Price,* 216.
32. Slayback description from Peterson and Hanson, *Thermopylae,* 218.

At three in the morning the assault column sallied out of the fort, rifles at shoulder arms, trying to look like a Confederate regiment changing its position. The drawbridge had been muffled with tents, and the cavalry and a battery of field guns crept outside with the infantry. Ewing's men walked quietly, hearts in their mouths, every eye and ear keenly tuned for any sound of any kind. The groaning from federal wounded was not taken as anything out of the ordinary by the rebels; all Confederate units had walking wounded. The cries of the Confederate wounded still on the fields covered much of Ewing's movement. They marched right by A. S. Dobbin's brigade, who were sleeping in shifts and working on assault ladders to bridge the fort's moat. The federals marched up the Caledonia road, north, through the Confederate campfires and idle pickets. It is utterly incredible that, in this fog of war, no one challenged them.

Back at the fort Sergeant Daniel Flood supervised laying the Union dead alongside the magazine while Colonel Fletcher wired the magazine to blow. Lieutenant Henry Milks of the Third Missouri lit the fuse. Then Fletcher led his rear guard out of Fort Davidson through the north rifle pit. When twenty tons of powder blew up, Fletcher wrote, "The heavens were lighted by a grand column of fire . . . hundreds of feet in the air. . . . The whole region reverberated as if a thunderbolt had driven Pilot Knob from its base to its peak."[33]

The best measure of how much Ewing's force had hurt Price's divisions was that Price assumed the explosion had killed the entire garrison. Either there had been a terrible accident or Ewing's men had made a Masada-like end to their own lives. Price felt immense relief, but he did not send a patrol to investigate until daylight. Then, when he saw no signs that Ewing's force had died in the explosion, Price realized he had been hoodwinked. Price issued hurry-up instructions to Marmaduke to "pursue [Ewing] with your command as soon as you can rest and feed the horses!" Price ordered Shelby into motion, too, despite protests by both generals that their men needed rest. Even with Price's insistence, Marmaduke's sluggishness in getting his troops under way was testimony to the havoc the battle had caused his division, and it is not unreasonable to believe the other Confederate divisions were in the same shape.[34]

Ewing's infantry struck Shelby's videttes north of Caledonia. There was a sharp skirmish in the morning light. With his escape to Caledonia blocked, Ewing

33. *O.R.* 41:1:446–51. Evans, *Confederate Military History,* 9:179–82, claims that Ewing abandoned his wounded in the fort when it blew, which is untrue. "Grand column of fire" from Peterson and Hanson, *Thermopylae,* 219–20.

34. "Feed the horses" at *O.R.* 41:3:961–62.

turned west. Led by local guides he struck out toward Harrison and Rolla, Missouri, through some of the most densely wooded rolling hills in the country. The single-track roads were not much wider than a gun carriage. Marmaduke and Shelby had linked at Caledonia and were in pursuit, but the terrain included wooded sheer-walled canyons that slowed cavalry movement. Rebel cavalry that took the wrong road required hours to double back. Ewing's choice was fortuitous. The wooded countryside and the winding roads favored rearguard actions. Ewing used this strength. A *New York Times* correspondent, writing after Ewing's force was safe, opined, "Exposed in the open field to an experienced and overwhelmingly superior foe, nothing could have saved the entire force from utter demolition but the unflagging energy, coolness and courage of Gen. Ewing and the battery of Rodman guns." Indeed, Ewing did not have to fear being flanked most of the way along the road. From behind this well-crewed mobile battery, his Iowa sharpshooters blunted Shelby's aggressiveness with sharp ambushes in the narrow defiles.[35]

By sundown on September 28, Ewing's scruffy command reached Webster, Missouri, thirty-one miles from Pilot Knob, after an exhausting sixteen-hour forced march without sleep. Captain Charles Hill's Tenth Kansas cavalry sent men to Harrison Station on the railroad. Once there they wired Rosecrans that, by midnight, Ewing should be at Harrison with his entire force, and to send rations. It was Rosecrans's first word that Ewing's command had survived.[36]

Ewing had his men marching toward Harrison in the pitch dark of a Missouri September storm. He worked his column to keep them together. Stragglers were pushed into line and groped forward, following the man in front across wild uncharted streams, moving slowly but knowing that Shelby was out there on their flanks and Marmaduke was worked Ewing's rearguard. In that rear, however, were the Fourteenth Iowa boys along with a blast of canister from the Second Missouri light artillery. Rebel probes hung back. The final four miles to Harrison was an ongoing running fight, fought on the rear and sides of the column, fought amid fleeing refugees that had plagued the column all day. Ewing halted his forced march on September 29, at Harrison (present-day Leasburg), where he had counted on there being a militia company to help defend the town. The militia was gone. Ewing reluctantly ordered his bone-weary men to dig trenches behind a railroad cut. Shelby, citing Ewing's luck, wrote later, "Night alone saved Ewing from capture."[37]

35. *New York Times,* October 10, 1864, 1; rearguard actions from Castel, *Sterling Price,* 217.

36. Hill's message, *O.R.* 41:3:482.

37. The running fight to Harrison from Peterson and Hanson, *Thermopylae,* 280; Shelby from *O.R.* 41:1:653.

With the Iowa flags and sharpshooters prominently displayed along the federal works, Shelby and Marmaduke had postured in long lines as if they were going to charge. Ewing's Rodmans unloaded, "killing more horses than men." After twice trying to re-form, eventually the rebels fell back into the woods to rethink a frontal assault. Shelby made a decision he thought Price should have made at Ironton. He was not going to bleed his men further by attacking a force that was no longer significant in the campaign. Shelby turned his brigades north. However, under a white flag, General Marmaduke sent in a threat that Ewing's force would be slaughtered if they did not surrender. Ewing shouted back, loud enough for the men to hear, that there was nothing to surrender to. "If you couldn't take us on the road, we are not going to surrender behind breastworks!" Marmaduke sent a heavy skirmish line at the Union line, but federal volleys sent the rebels back into the woods. And at that moment five hundred men and horses under the command of Colonel John Beveridge of the Seventeenth Illinois cavalry rode onto the field to join Ewing's men in the garrison. A chilly rain at dawn cooled any remaining Confederate ardor for avenging the Pilot Knob fiasco. Thinking the cavalry was the van of a larger relief force, Marmaduke withdrew his cavalry under cover of the rain.[38]

Dispatch riders came and went from Harrison while Ewing's men made coffee and ate hardtack and raw bacon, their first food in thirty hours. Word of the little command's exploits, like those of the Greeks who delayed the Persians, was sweeping the country. With the Seventeenth Illinois, Ewing now commanded a strong brigade. On September 30, Ewing marched his new force into Rolla, sixty-six miles in thirty-nine hours over an abysmal road system, with Confederate pickets sniping at his fifteen-hundred-man column the entire way. At Rolla dispatches greeted Ewing with the news that he was a new father. Ellen Cox Ewing wrote her husband from Lancaster, ebulliently praising God his life had been spared. "Your career is now onward and upward," she predicted proudly.[39]

Three days after leaving his remnants to help garrison Rolla, Ewing took the railroad back to St. Louis, where he was greeted with a hero's welcome. The mayor led the parade of dignitaries. Given the sort of threats Marmaduke had made on his men at Harrison, and the news that Major James Wilson's small detachment had been found executed like criminals, he very much believed his men would have been murdered had he surrendered the Fort Davidson garrison. "Nev-

38. "More horses than men" from *New York Times,* October 10, 1864, 1; "take us on the road," from Peterson and Hanson, *Thermopylae,* 296.

39. "Onward and upward," from Monaghan, *Civil War,* 314–15.

er while I had voice or sword to raise should it be surrendered," he told a cheering crowd. As excited as Ewing was at this triumph, he never wrote about the battle in later years. Price apparently asked after the war if Ewing was a West Pointer. Even Southern biographers praised Ewing's "indomitable pluck and endurance" and that his fighting abilities and leadership "deserved to escape."[40]

Price was not so lucky. After Ewing's escape, Price turned his battered army north and west of Rolla. On his march toward Kansas City, quite inexplicably he halted for two weeks, giving his Missouri soldiers time to scatter and visit their homes. This pause gave Rosecrans time to put Pleasonton's new twelve-thousand-strong cavalry detachment from Tennessee into the field near St. Louis and turn it west, and it gave Samuel Curtis time to call out the Kansas militia. When Price resumed his march, along the Big Blue River on hilly ground that now is the upscale Plaza area of Kansas City, Missouri, forty thousand rebels, Kansas militia, and federal troops fought for two days with unexpected fierceness at the Battle of Westport. The ferocity of the charges by the untrained Kansas militia and the absence of two thousand of his most veteran soldiers who now lay in cemeteries or in hospitals near Pilot Knob forced Price to retreat south into eastern Kansas.[41]

On October 26, federal cavalry under Pleasonton finally cornered the Confederates at Mine Creek, a few miles northwest of Fort Scott, Kansas. The thunder of two brigades of horses one mile wide and two rows deep, the largest cavalry charge of the war, came over a low rise in undulating ground and bore down on Price's rebels whose backs were to a creek. Ewing's old Eleventh Kansas cavalry was part of Pleasonton's attack, and Samuel Worthington was able to report, "My horse was so hard mouthed I could do nothing with him. I had emptied my revolvers before I got to the rebel line of battle and with three other horses [mine] charged clear through the lines. The rebs are completely whipped." "Whipped" was an understatement. In twenty minutes Price lost three hundred dead and wounded, nine cannon, and nine hundred prisoners, including two generals and four colonels. His common soldiers had had enough. Abandoned equipment was scattered along the roads for miles. Huge numbers of Price's men deserted before he reached the Arkansas River. What was left of the Confederacy's last active military campaign suffered 50 percent casualties in four months. The Trans-

40. "Voice or sword" from Peterson and Hanson, *Thermopylae,* 314; Southern biographers from Edwards, *Shelby and His Men,* 389.

41. Anderson, *Adjutant General,* 207, 217; Price's pause in the campaign from Palmer, "Eleventh Kansas," 433, 437, 443; also *O.R.* 41:1:335, 337, 352, 372, 480–82, 493–94, 637, 41:3:822, 41:4:16–17, 145, 209, 727–29.

Mississippi war was over, six months before Lee surrendered; there just was nobody to surrender the broken Confederate army.[42]

At that time Tom Ewing received little recognition for his stand at Fort Davidson and subsequent fighting withdrawal to Rolla. Lane's editors indicated erroneously that Ewing's command had been lost in battle. Upon Ewing's report of the safe retreat of his command, Rosecrans wired Curtis, "I notice in the Leavenworth papers a dispatch to you from Gen. Brown saying that 'the rebels captured four guns from Ewing and at last accounts nearly his whole command.' I am happy to inform you that General Ewing made good his retreat to Rolla with all his guns and his entire command. Please publish this."[43]

Other mistaken accounts were not corrected, however. Horace Greeley's postwar history of the war indicated that Fort Davidson was commanded by Hugh Ewing. Union officials kept referring to Price's movements as a raid rather than an invasion, and Grant, who ever since Chickamauga had little use for Rosecrans, was critical of Rosecrans's handling of Price's invasion. Clearly, however, while Sherman had taken Atlanta, as official correspondence shows, if any sort of "military disaster to the Federal arms occurred about the same time, we might have had a different state of things." The siege or destruction of St. Louis would have been just the sort of disaster federal officials feared.[44]

Albert Castel argues that Ewing wanted to use Pilot Knob for glory hunting. While his pre-battle conversation with Carpenter and Fletcher would support this thesis, a more pragmatic view would indicate that if Ewing had wanted glory, he could have accepted Sherman's offer to command a division in the Atlanta campaign. Ewing was sent to Fort Davidson on a reconnaissance. When Shelby cut the railroad north of him, he was stranded, and he made do with what he had—amazingly so, but his heroics were a by-product of the moment. He had orders not to risk his command unnecessarily, but luckily he commanded stubborn troops. It is hard to believe that anyone could view these actions—commanding an open-air fort in southeast Missouri against a much larger force of Confederate veterans while carrying a price on one's head—as the stuff from which brilliant exploits spring. When fighting a war in hopes of political advancement, there is but one rule: dead heroes do not go to the U.S. Senate.[45]

42. Mine Creek from Samuel Worthington to his father, October 27, 1864, Worthington Collection; Starr, *Jennison's Jayhawkers,* 340; desertions from Monaghan, *Civil War,* 341, 343.

43. Rosecrans publication demand of Curtis at *O.R.* 41:3:762.

44. Horace Greeley, *The American Conflict: A History of the Great Rebellion in the United States of America, 1860–1864,* 2:557; for Grant's critical remarks of the Rosecrans-Ewing-Price campaign, see *O.R.* 46:1:35; "different state of things" from J. W. Perit Huntington to General Benjamin Alvord, November 12, 1864, *O.R.* 50:1:1056.

45. Castel, *Sterling Price,* 211, 219.

Whether the effort was calculated or not, one man was very much aware of the service Tom Ewing's actions at Fort Davidson had done for him. In 1862 Abraham Lincoln had sent Tom Ewing's name to Congress as a brigadier general entirely on his own initiative. He knew Thomas Ewing Sr.'s namesake was the least likely of the Ewing boys to be of military material. The old Whig had scornfully asked Lincoln, "What did you appoint the brat a Brigadier General for?" After Fort Davidson, with that remarkable memory Abraham Lincoln had for the families of people to whom he was close, he saw the elder Ewing at a social function and asked, "What do you think of your brat now?"[46]

With Price's raid just a memory when the November election rolled around, Kansas turned to politics as usual. Tom Ewing was on the receiving end of some nasty political sniping. While military events in Atlanta and the Trans-Mississippi with Price's invasion had now given the administration better footing for the final weeks of the election of 1864, Tom Ewing expected the aftermath of Lawrence and Order Number 11 to work its way into state politics. Even though Ewing was not running as a candidate for any post, the political paranoia of the time meant that Lane saw challengers to his Senate position at every turn. Ewing's new popularity after Fort Davidson might lead to a Senate campaign and candidacy, so Lane's supportive newspapers began a concerted effort to tarnish Ewing's reputation at the same time praising "General" Lane's leadership of Kansas militia at the Battle of Westport. Daniel Anthony's *Leavenworth Daily Conservative* did not even mention Ewing's role at Pilot Knob. The one-sided attacks infuriated Ewing, who remembered the organized lies and falsehoods by Lane's newspapers after Quantrill's raid a year earlier. His mistrust of Lane was now complete. Ewing uncustomarily wrote an angry letter to Ellen, warning her against reading what could come in the Lane newspapers: "Look out for outrageous lying dispatches from Lane, Blunt, Carney and Co. They have each a pack of most disagreeable and scoundrelly liars that ever filtered filth through a goose quill." He was right. The blasts by Republican supporters were especially harsh in Kansas.[47]

What had made Lane's people so paranoid was a belief that perhaps Tom Ewing was involved in Carney's efforts to salt the 1865 Kansas legislature with men supportive of Carney, who was trying an end run around Lane's reelection chances to the Senate. The pro-Lane *Leavenworth Daily Conservative* wrote sarcastically

46. "Brat" remarks noted in papers of Thomas Ewing III, February 26, 1896, found in box 214, Thomas Ewing Collection, LC.

47. "Filtered filth" from TEJr. to ECE, October 18, 1864, EFP/LC; for examples of criticism, see *Leavenworth Daily Conservative,* October 16, 1864, see also Castel, *Frontier State,* 182.

after the election that Kansans did not want "a rotten hulk of a man [Carney], half the brains of Gen. Lane, who was trying to steal into office by the same arts Gen. Lane had so often used. If people are to be humbugged, they prefer that it should be done by a master hand, not by a botch at the trade. If they cannot have an honest man in the Senate, they prefer that the rascal who represents them, should be a man of brains."[48]

Fresh from leading desperate men in a bloody fight, Tom Ewing found that his newer and more mundane duties in St. Louis included building prisons for POWs and convincing reluctant Union men to reenlist. Even as Pleasonton's cavalry was chasing down Price's remnant force in Kansas and southwest Missouri, several companies of the Fourteenth Iowa were among three-year regiments scheduled to muster out of service on November 5, 1864. Rosecrans's staff were doing all they could to shame the Iowans into reenlisting in order to reduce the severe manpower shortages in Missouri and Kansas. Ewing was torn. He remembered how the proud Iowans had saved his bacon at Fort Davidson, and he took their side in this dispute. They had enlisted for three years, survived the hell of the Hornet's Nest and their capture at Shiloh, had fought at Corinth and at Vicksburg, Mississippi, and in the Red River campaign. They had proved themselves the decisive unit at Fort Davidson. Rosecrans's adjutant John Du Bois finally relented. "Let the sore-headed exempts go home two days after the receipt of this order. The enrolled Missouri Militia will be enough to hold Franklin Co." Several companies of Iowa men who had nothing to go home to remained on active duty and, as luck would have it, formed a guard of honor at Lincoln's burial in Springfield six months later. That these Iowans would survive the war was of great comfort to Ewing, who began to think that perhaps Fort Davidson should be his last fight too.[49]

Winding up his military career so that he could join the lobbying firm with his father and Orville Browning took up more of his time. No matter how well he did in the army, he sensed a successful political career was remote. His boredom after Fort Davidson made him increasingly critical of the army's routine and mindless orders. Among his last duties in St. Louis was to oversee the execution of rebel soldiers in retaliation for the murder of Major Wilson. Tim Reeves, a notorious Baptist preacher and bushwhacker traveling with Price's army, had executed Wilson and six of his men. Retaliation executions of six captured Confederate soldiers chosen at random were scheduled. Ewing had gone from fighting

48. *Leavenworth Daily Conservative,* November 24, 1864.
49. Du Bois from *O.R.* 41:4:78.

Quantrill, a general commanding a successful defensive operation in a politically important campaign, to being an executioner of common soldiers who had done nothing but follow orders in a difficult cause. It was time to go.[50]

Having completed his March to the Sea in just over one month (the "glorious old expedition," as it was commonly known, meeting little resistance and proving that the South in 1864 was indeed as hollow as an egg), Sherman was resting with his men in Savannah. Meanwhile, Tom Ewing had gone back to Topeka in early January 1865. The Kansas legislature met to decide whether to send Jim Lane back to the Senate. Ewing decided to attend the political fight brewing in Topeka, and to see one more time an effort to get the state rid of the man who had tormented Ewing most in his times in Kansas. It was also a chance to learn directly whether Order Number 11 and his Fort Davidson command had hurt him with Kansans.

The legislature met under a cloud. The Union Pacific had received its congressional allocation of $640,000 in bonds. John Perry had managed to get his fledgling railroad built from Kansas City to Lawrence, which prompted his competitors to suggest that a congressional investigation would show federal bonds were about to purchase a poorly constructed and substandard railroad. This set off a howl of protest among state officials, especially Governor Sam Crawford who loudly defended the quality of the Kansas road. To charges by inspectors that the Kansas road was using fewer ties per mile than Eastern railroads, Crawford called the charge a "technicality." Crawford was a Lane man, and his support of the railroad had been rewarded with a section of land along the main line. When this exchange was uncovered three years later, in 1868, it brought demands by anti-Crawford advocates for an investigation. The *Leavenworth Conservative* rolled its editorial eyes and opined that, for the work he had done and value he had given the growth of Kansas, Governor Crawford had been truly patriotic, since such work was easily worth two sections of land and he only asked for one.[51]

The tense Crawford railroad fight bled over into the senatorial election. Lane followers leased the Topeka House Hotel and worked on the sensibilities of their colleagues with plenty of liquor and most of Topeka's available prostitutes. Tom Ewing came back from St. Louis to see old friends and lobby quietly against Lane, and he ended up as Lane's opposition. Ewing's supporters tested Lane's solidarity by passing the word that it was really Ewing's defense of Fort Davidson, not the

50. Reeves retaliation executions at *O.R.* 41:3:658.
51. Plummer, *Frontier Governor,* 94.

Kansas militia actions at Westport, that had saved Kansas from Price's invasion force. Kansas legislators were not strategic thinkers, however, nor were they about to give credit for anything to the Missouri militia and Iowans who defended Fort Davidson, even if the commanding officer was a Kansan. Lane was the warrior chief with the better press.

When patriotism did not work, Ewing's supporters offered $1,000 to legislators known to support Lane if they would vote for Ewing. Lane, of course, did the same thing in reverse. If these bribes were offered on the floor of the legislature by one legislator to another, it would invoke the sometimes murky law of whether bribes offered in support of government business are immunized by the speech and debate clause of the 1859 Kansas Constitution. That vagueness extends even unto modern Kansas lawmakers who extort votes from each other all the time, with privileges to do so. In the end Lane's support, when bought, stayed bought. With no movement possible in Lane's ranks and his blue uniform with single stars on the shoulders making no impact on the patriots within the Kansas legislature, Ewing quietly pulled his name from consideration. Lane went back to the Senate at the peak of his career, a pompous pain in the behind to most Kansans but ready to support Lincoln's efforts to finish pacifying the South.[52]

After Lane's reelection Ewing had time to think as he rode the trains back to Washington. In his mind were the words his wife had spoken to him when he took the command in St. Louis. He had indeed lived to regret not taking the division command under Sherman. While there was not much he could do now about missed opportunities, he did set about planning the law partnership with his father and Orville Browning. The new startup was complicated by his father's ailing health. In January 1865, during oral argument in the Supreme Court, Thomas Ewing Sr. had almost collapsed. He had later admitted to Browning that his days for the stress of making oral arguments were over. Part of his stress was a contentious partnership with Edgar Cowan and Britton Hill, which had recently dissolved into a heated argument over fees that sapped not only Thomas Ewing's patience but his physical strength. He could still affect things behind the scenes for Browning & Ewing, and for the time being this was to be his role, with Tom taking on the more active law work. The firm of Browning & Ewing would spe-

52. Edwin Manning, "The Kansas State Senate of 1865 and 1866," 364; Taylor, "Business and Political Career," 154; Tom Ewing's Senate election from Phil Ewing to WTS, December 31, 1864, in Ewing, *Sherman at War,* 149–50. Lane's bribery of Ewing supporters in John Cone letter, March 7, 1865, box 1, Sidney Clarke Collection, Carl Albert Center, University of Oklahoma, Norman, Oklahoma. For modern use of the Speech & Debate Clause to protect legislative chicanery on the House floor, see *State v. Neufeld,* 260 Kan. 930 (1996).

cialize in clients who needed influence within Lincoln's administration. Every form of rebellion spawns post-rebellion amnesty for some and not for others. Amnesty brokering was something they discussed, and they thought that two former senators and a Union general could provide Southerners needing such advice with vital services. The key was whether those Southerners would have any money left to pay for the services.[53]

While in Washington Tom Ewing went to the White House to present his resignation from the army to his friend and commander in chief. Before he could meet with Lincoln, Hugh persuaded Tom to help make one last effort at convincing Grant to give Hugh a better command. They headed for City Point, Virginia. Grant hosted the Ewings on February 18, 1865, for a lengthy period and "treated us in fine style." Grant was interested in Tom's details of Fort Davidson, and both Ewings were given tours of the battle-scarred trenches around the Confederacy's base of operations. After dinner on February 19, Tom Ewing made his case to Grant that Hugh should have one more combat assignment.[54]

Hugh had sought help from Sherman after the March to the Sea. Sherman had recommended he apply to Lorenzo Thomas in the War Department for a field command. He warned Hugh that a coastal command in South or North Carolina would require him to command mostly black regiments, but such commands would not hurt his career. To Hugh it may have looked like Sherman was avoiding the issue again, but in fact the advice was sound. Command of a black division, even for only a few months, would have erased from his Douglas Democrat credentials any taint the radicals could create. Hugh did not see it this way, however, and ignored the advice. He was asking a favor from his last hope, Sam Grant.

Grant listened and took stock of what he knew. Hugh had finished a lackluster stint in Kentucky as a department subcommander. It was clear he had not impressed Grant. Sherman was not saying much to the commanding general on Hugh's behalf, and Grant could read that silence well. When Grant had finally obtained permission to rid himself of Steven Burbridge in Kentucky, Grant had finagled the Kentucky command for George Stoneman, not Ewing. Part of Grant's reluctance to appoint Hugh to anything in Kentucky was Hugh's ill health. His gout had grown worse and painful enough that he had begun to self-medicate with opium. Hugh tried to mask his condition, but the facts were that, when others in Kentucky had been in the field dealing with Confederate cavalry raids, Hugh had

53. Father Ewing's declining health, Taylor, "Business and Political Career," 198–99; also Orville H. Browning, *The Diary of Orville Hickman Browning,* 2:2.

54. "Treated us in fine style," Ewing, "Autobiography," 340.

been in bed. Grant pointed out there were no more field commands; all he had left was command of a provisional division along the coast. Hugh was down to the wire. There was nothing left to command in any of the armies that mattered. He did not want an obscure Western assignment and would take any command in the East. According to Hugh, Grant agreed to give Hugh the command of the "largest and best division in the two armies." It was, in fact, a far lesser command.[55]

On February 20, 1865, the Ewings left City Point with the best news possible under the circumstances. Grant inquired of Washington later that day whether Hugh Ewing could be assigned to lead North Carolina forces in the place of General Thomas Meagher, the former commander of the Potomac Army's Irish brigade whose favor in Washington was waning because of his Democratic ties to Seymour and McClellan in 1864. Grant's nomination of Hugh Ewing obviously carried weight with Halleck and Stanton, but it was impossible to know if the assignment would reinvolve Hugh in the war effort.[56]

His errand complete, on February 23, 1865, Tom Ewing went to the White House and tendered his resignation to Lincoln. It was the first time they had met since the battle for Fort Davidson. Lincoln asked Ewing to reconsider and promised a posting as major general if Tom would stay on. Perhaps he could join Sherman in the Carolinas? Ewing declined. They discussed Kansas politics and Ewing's disgust with the whole situation there. Lincoln reminded Ewing that Pomeroy, not Lane, was the real thorn in the side of the administration. Pomeroy's reelection was coming up in two years. Perhaps Ewing could use Lincoln's help then? And perhaps Lincoln would have the time then to get more involved for his friends. Ewing told Lincoln of his plans to join forces with his father and Browning, and that he felt the administration's postwar civilian friends in Washington were just as important as a new senator in Kansas, which had yet to choose county seat towns in half its territory. With their solid national contacts, a Washington firm could be enormously helpful to Lincoln's administration. Tom Ewing preferred the role of a Lincoln confidant to being one of his generals. Lincoln appreciated Ewing's views but nevertheless told Ewing he intended to hold the resignation in his office in case Ewing changed his mind. It was their last meeting. Afterward, Tom Ewing wired his resignation to Grenville Dodge, who had taken command of the Department of Kansas. The border's military problems were now someone else's headache.[57]

55. *O.R.* 45:2:54, 68, 154, 194–95; gout treatments, Ewing, "Autobiography," 336.

56. Ewing, "Autobiography," 338–40; *O.R.* 46:3:847, 47:2:415–16, 501.

57. Hannahs, "Thomas Ewing Jr.," 280; Browning, *Diary,* 1:xxii; Tom Ewing's resignation, *O.R.* 48:1:998.

On March 4, 1865, Hugh and Ri attended Lincoln's second inaugural as guests of the vice president. Andrew Johnson had been ill most of the winter with typhoid fever and fought the lingering illness with liquor. He garbled his oath badly. Lincoln, too, appeared tired. The Ewings listened as the unpopular president gave his powerful glimpse into the depth of the nation's compassionate soul, and the promise to its soldiers and their posterity of "malice towards none, and with charity for all." Hugh missed the significance of the message, as it was not mentioned in his diary. He simply noted the day was an "interesting spectacle." Then he left for his new duties in Wilmington, in North Carolina, which Grant had secured for him.[58]

The Confederacy had come to its darkest moment. Sherman's columns had left Savannah in January and continued unchecked into the South Carolina midlands. After the last battle at Bentonville, North Carolina, and with his army resting near Raleigh, Sherman was summoned by Grant to City Point via the faster overland route of the New Berne railroad. Their meeting was set for March 27. Two days prior to that meeting, Sherman met with Hugh and claimed he had told Schofield Hugh wanted a division, but Schofield had none available at that time. Hugh was angry with his brother-in-law. Sherman had written a letter to Philemon Ewing in January, acknowledging Hugh's anger to Ewingville but explaining why he could not brush aside one of his own officers for command of a division, even though Hugh was senior in rank to them:

> I have no doubt Hugh is offended with me. He wrote me for a command in this army. I offered him a division at Nashville but he declined and now to give him a place I would have to remove some other General who has stood by his command through both the Atlanta and Savannah campaigns. I foresaw it at Nashville and told him so, but he knew better and now I cannot remedy it. . . . A man in war must go with events. If he steps to one side for a moment, he is drifted into an eddy and can never recover the channel. In the same way Charley should not hope for a general's commission unless he gets a regiment and takes the time necessary.

What had angered Hugh was that in early March, Charley Ewing had been serving on Sherman's staff and was commissioned a brigadier general in charge of a brigade without ever serving as a regimental commander in Sherman's army. Hugh

58. Lincoln's second inaugural speech is on the Internet at <http://www.bartleby.com/124/pres32.html> last accessed April 5, 2008; "spectacle" from Ewing, "Autobiography," 340.

demanded to know why the discrimination? When Sherman's response was tepid, Hugh stormed out of their meeting. "I left him when he entered the car and he followed me out and renewed the conversation. He talked of giving me command of a joint naval and military expedition up the river." Sherman no doubt reminded Hugh that he had offered Hugh a command before the Atlanta campaign and had suggested a command of black troops, but Hugh had not even contacted Lorenzo Thomas about the possibility. And Hugh could rightly feel discrimination in those remarks. If Sherman would not use black troops in combat, why should Hugh have to command Negro troops in order to bolster his career?[59]

From this meeting, the brothers-in-law parted in anger. It was the beginning of the final breach between Hugh Ewing and Sherman that family ties could not mend. Sherman was on his way to fame in the country's military history. Hugh was not. When John Sherman visited the North Carolina theater, he and Cump called socially on Hugh. Hugh officiated as military courtesy required, but he had little to say to either of the Sherman brothers. A few days later Lee met Grant at Appomattox Courthouse, and the American Civil War was over.[60]

The family's accomplishments were spectacular. Sherman was a hero of the war. Three other Ewing sons—Tom, Hugh, and Charley—had achieved general officer rank in the army. For the three Ewings the war had not ended in a blaze of glory, but they had done their duty and helped bring it to its conclusion. Charley had commanded a brigade in the last days of the Carolinas campaign, which entitled him to brevet brigadier general status in the postwar period.

Much had happened since Cump Sherman first tramped a dusty Virginia road leading a green brigade toward Bull Run and his first combat. On May 23, 1865, not quite four years later, Sherman's Western Army numbered eighty thousand men and marched in the Grand Review by a huge banner on the Capitol that read, "The Only Debt We Can Never Repay: What We Owe To Our Gallant Defenders." Charley Ewing in dress uniform marched at the head of his brigade, and Hugh accompanied his old Fourth Division, tramping past the reviewing stand where President Andrew Johnson, his cabinet, and all of official Washington stood to attention. Also on that reviewing stand was Thomas Ewing Sr. As the foster father of Sherman and the patriarch of a remarkable family, his pride that day must have known no boundaries.[61]

59. WTS to Phil Ewing, January 29, 1865, quoted in Ewing, *Sherman at War,* 153–57; Charley's promotion is at *O.R.* 47:3:75; Ewing, "Autobiography," 341–42.

60. Ewing, "Autobiography," 341–45.

61. Steve Meyer, *Iowa Valor,* 481; Reid Mitchell, *Civil War Soldiers,* 207.

Part Three

THE POLITICS OF MONEY

10

DR. MUDD'S TRIAL AND WIDOW ADIE'S COTTON

On April 14, 1865, Good Friday, four years to the day after the war began, the flamboyant John Wilkes Booth accomplished what the mercurial William Quantrill had only schemed to do. At Ford's Theater the actor entered the president's box while the president and Mary Lincoln were watching a play and fired his pistol into the back of Lincoln's skull. In the screams and confusion, Booth leapt onto the stage, broke his leg, and limped out the backdoor. Within the hour he had vanished, riding a horse into Maryland.

The nation was stunned. After all the bloodletting of the Civil War, Lincoln's death made no sense at all. One Confederate army had capitulated; the other was in camps with its arms stacked, hungry, demoralized, and waiting for terms of surrender. Confederate government officials had disappeared into the countryside. Northern radicals were already planning a harsh peace for the South. While history notes that Lincoln might not have been as forgiving to the South as postwar legend might make out, nobody profited from Lincoln's death, least of all the South. Lincoln's death left the country in Andrew Johnson's hands, and Johnson had neither a vision for Reconstruction nor any plan on how to handle the radicals. Orville Browning wrote to his diary the night Lincoln was assassinated, "I have never feared what the rebels could do to us—I do fear what we may do to ourselves."[1]

Stanton took charge of the investigation and resulting manhunt almost immediately. Treachery would be met with the full weight of federal might. However, news of the murder itself and the identity of the murderer were not released for several days. At the Maryland farm of Doctor Samuel Mudd, two men appeared at his door and asked the doctor to set a broken leg. Neither man identified himself. The doctor's wife noticed that one of the men was wearing fake whiskers, as an actor might wear onstage. Booth spent a day with Mudd under an alias, then he left.

Rewards for knowledge of Booth's whereabouts were posted on April 20. The next day, after the discovery of a boot belonging to Booth, Mudd was taken to Bryantown and was asked to give a written statement. In his statement he indicated that neither man had given him any clue to suggest he might have been part of an assassination. Booth gave his name as Tyser or Tyson. The younger man, David Herold, gave his name as Henson. Without knowledge of who his patient was, Mudd could not logically be tied to the conspiracy. As a result of information from other sources, Mudd and other conspirators were questioned vigorously and then formally arrested on May 7, 1865. Booth was cornered and shot dead by federal cavalry nineteen days later. Herold was captured.[2]

A jury pool from Washington would undoubtedly contain many Southern sympathizers, and Stanton was not going to tolerate any sort of jury nullification. Booth was dead, but the conspirators would be court-martialed. While General Hugh Ewing's last days of military service were spent in trials in military courts, the entire Ewing family was not radical enough for Stanton, thus Hugh never made the short list of officers for the conspiracy court. Eight generals and two colonels were named to the panel, with Major General David Hunter presiding.[3]

Private defense counsel did not line up for assignments in this high-profile case. John Ford, the owner of the theater and an old Whig friend of Thomas Ewing Sr., had agreed to pay the legal fees for his employees Samuel Arnold and Edward

1. Browning, *Diary*, 2:19. For Southern reaction, see *O.R.* 46:3:787.

2. Mudd's statements from Elden C. Weckesser, *His Name Was Mudd: The Life of Dr. Samuel A. Mudd, Who Treated the Fleeing John Wilkes Booth*, 63–73. See also Laurie Verge, ed., "From War Department Files. Statements Made By The Alleged Lincoln Conspirators Under Examination 1865," *Clinton: Surratt Society* (1980): 29–38.

3. Ewing, "Autobiography," 343.

Spangler. Spangler was charged with aiding Booth in gaining entrance to the presidential box at Ford's Theater and aiding his escape from the theater after Booth jumped to the stage. Arnold had provided transportation for what turned out to be Booth's escape from the theater. Ford asked Tom Ewing to represent his employees. Through a priest friend, Hugh Ewing had gotten word to the Mudd family and suggested that Browning represent Dr. Mudd. Browning was contacted but declined, having other matters on his plate at that moment, not the least of which was the grief from having just lost one of his best friends to an assassin. When Browning declined, Frances Mudd persuaded Tom Ewing to add her husband to his list of codefendants. He agreed, on the day before the trial began.

The conspiracy trial came to a head during the flap between Sherman and Stanton over Johnston's surrender terms. Sherman had offered secret terms to his old friend Joseph Johnston to surrender the Army of Tennessee. His terms were more liberal than Grant's had been to Lee. At Sherman's last meeting with Lincoln, in March, the president had left the impression with the general that the military could offer Johnston any terms that would end the war without guerrilla operations continuing to plague the country for years to come. Chief among Sherman's gaffes were terms that kept existing Southern state governments in place with the voting rights of its citizens unaffected.

When the president and the cabinet read the proposed terms, most were speechless. Stanton was apoplectic. He took out his anger on Sherman, almost cashiering him on the spot but instead resolving to publicly humiliate Sherman—even though the surrender terms were secret and could have been altered by the War Department in secret. From the war's end through Sherman's public humiliation as the armies marched back to Washington for the Grand Review, the country had been treated to a soap opera. All of Ewingville was upset with Stanton for the way he treated Sherman. When Stanton took over such direct control of the conspiracy investigation, it was obvious he would direct the trial, too.

Representing the three men in Stanton's kangaroo court was an exercise in mental gymnastics that Tom Ewing secretly relished and there were no naysayers in Ewingville. However, representing three alleged conspirators in an emotional show trial with virtually no time for preparation was highly unusual under modern rules of procedure. This immense job was made more difficult because the defense lawyers had no copy of the indictment, no list of the specific charges, and no list of witnesses the government planned to call, which prevented defense attorneys from interviewing the witnesses and gauging their credibility before they testified. The rules of evidence were less strict in military tribunals. Field officers were the jury, and under the law at that time defendants in military trials could not take the stand in their own defense. Joseph Holt, the prosecutor, could sit with the commission when it deliberated.

The idea that the defense might know most of the prosecution's evidence and have pretrial access to it was foreign to the Lincoln conspiracy trial. The hearings were an old-fashioned trial by ambush, each side keeping secret their important witnesses until they testified. In 1932 the U.S. Supreme Court held in *Powell v. Alabama* that a defendant is denied effective assistance of counsel when one lawyer represents multiple defendants in a capital trial, but such rulings were decades away from Washington that hot May and June of 1865. Historian Theodore Roscoe wrote, "It is doubtful if the history of American jurisprudence contains a trial where the defendants and their counsel entered court under similar handicaps."[4]

The trial began on May 10, 1865, at the Old Arsenal Penitentiary, less than a month after the assassination and while Sherman's army was still marching from North Carolina for the upcoming Grand Review. When the trial began, all defendants except Mary Surratt were manacled, and their heads were hooded as during the Spanish Inquisition. The restraints remained on them throughout the proceedings even though the court was stifling in the summer heat. The government's excuse for this sensory deprivation was that before the trial one of the men had sought to kill himself. Ewing represented three of the eight defendants. The other five were represented by Frederick Stone, Reverdy Johnson, and William Doster. Johnson was the better-known of the three lawyers, a pro-emancipation radical and Zachary Taylor's attorney general who had lost faith in Lincoln's policies and supported McClellan in 1864.

As the trial opened, Ewing moved to dismiss the entire case because the commission had no lawful jurisdiction. None of his three accused had ever served in any military unit, he argued, and the federal courts were available for prosecution. Judge Advocate Joseph Holt had anticipated this motion. The attorney general had been asked by Stanton for a legal opinion on the legality of the court-martial of the civilian conspirators. The attorney general's argument was weak, and a year later would not prevail in front of the Supreme Court in *Ex parte Milligan,* but in that hot May of 1865, the tribunal was a group of army officers, and the cabinet and the president had made a decision. Lincoln was the former com-

4. Specifications and charges against Mudd and the others at *O.R.* 2:8:696–97; the Sherman-Stanton flap over surrender found at Marszalek, *Soldier's Passion,* 348–54, and Fellman, *Citizen Sherman,* 246–49; Theodore Roscoe, *Web of Conspiracy,* 439.

mander in chief of the army, thus a "military" figure. The tribunal was lawful, Holt said.[5]

When his motion was denied, Ewing tried to get the court to strike the conspiracy count against his clients. The only evidence against Mudd was that he had not reported his medical services to federal authorities. Holt was a humorless dour Kentuckian and former Democratic secretary of war in Buchanan's administration who suffered from recurring tuberculosis. He would make a name for himself more for prosecuting Henry Wirz, the Andersonville commandant, and traitorous congressmen than for prosecuting the Lincoln conspirators. In this way he imitated his immediate superior, Edwin Stanton, who also took a keen interest in the daily trial developments. For now Holt was concentrating on those who had conspired to kill the man who had appointed him judge advocate general. Holt countered that the government would prove its case against Mudd, and the court should not drop any part of the prosecution against any defendant until it had heard all the evidence. The commission agreed with Holt.[6]

The indictment against the seven men and one woman was for the crime of "traitorously murdering Abraham Lincoln." Since no federal law had defined what act constituted "traitorous murder," the commission had to make up their own definition. Much of the initial damning testimony came from Charles Dunham, who also went by the name of Sanford Conover. Dunham can most charitably be described as a paid liar. A House investigative committee in 1866 indicted the Bureau of Military Justice for paying Conover and others for work not performed, except for the thousand dollars paid for his testimony in the conspiracy trial. Obviously paying a fact witness for testimony is contrary to the rules of modern litigation. Dunham testified that his friends had sat in bars and overheard conversations between Booth and high Confederate officials. It was rank hearsay testimony, but it was allowed into evidence because of the tribunal's evidentiary rules, which basically held that whatever the tribunal wanted admitted was admitted. Dunham's testimony brought Jefferson Davis's name into the courtroom.[7]

In addition to Dunham, Marcus Norton testified that just before Lincoln's second inaugural, Norton saw Booth talking to George Atzerodt in the lobby of the

5. Weckesser, *His Name Was Mudd,* 101; *Ex parte Milligan,* 71 U.S. (4 Wall.) 2 (1866).

6. Ezra Warner, *Generals in Blue: Lives of the Union Commanders,* 233.

7. Weckesser, *His Name Was Mudd,* 109, 110, 111; fabricated testimony, Milton Lomask, *Andrew Johnson: President on Trial,* 72–73. Expert witnesses are, of course, paid witnesses, but paying a fact witness to be available and testify constitutes witness tampering—unless you are the government, and after the trial, in return for his or her testimony, the witness needs a government protection program.

National Hotel when Mudd came in looking for Booth. To bolster Norton, William Evans testified that Mudd stayed at Mrs. Surratt's boarding house on H Street, around the first days of March. Daniel Thomas swore that Mudd had criticized Lincoln and his administration about two months before the assassination and had predicted Lincoln's death. This was devastating testimony if it stood.

As the government's testimony unfolded, Hugh was driving Tom to the court each day and spending some of his days tracking down and interviewing witnesses for the prosecution. Tom Ewing was able to find witnesses that showed Mudd was not in town the days Norton said he was, and eight witnesses who discredited Thomas—including Thomas's own brother, a doctor, who testified that Daniel Thomas was mentally unstable. With the testimony of every rebuttal witness, Ewing painted the picture that Stanton was persecuting ordinary citizens and laid out the premise that the government lawyers' case was so weak they had to secure convictions on paid testimony.[8]

Ewing's arguments had a factual foundation, especially when it came to the role Stanton was playing. Stanton was autocratic and knew very well his reputation of being a Cromwell, a description he privately enjoyed. He was hated by many and viewed such hatred as high praise, depending on who leveled the charge. The only person who had any sway over him was his wife. Over thirteen thousand people had been detained by the War Department during the war on suspicion of traitorous activities. This required a good number of clerks just to process the paperwork for this part of the department's activities. What Stanton had instigated against the conspirators was just another piece in this ever-expanding puzzle. Stanton and other radicals felt that the power of the federal government, if not used to crush its opponents, was useless and would render the country impotent when instead it needed to be vengeful.[9]

However, not all innocent men are so innocent, and this was the case with Mudd. Some witnesses against the doctor were indeed credible. Louis Weichmann swore that he and John Surratt were walking along Seventh Street and met Booth and Mudd coming from the opposite direction. The four retired to Booth's room in the National Hotel where Booth reviewed a plot to kidnap Lincoln. Weichmann's testimony pinned Mudd into the original conspiracy. Ewing vigorously attacked Weichmann's testimony as being a means to avoid Weichmann's own culpability as conspirator himself. On this point history is murky. When Mudd was en route to Florida to serve his sentence, it is alleged that he confirmed to a guard

8. Weckesser, *His Name Was Mudd,* 110; Ewing, "Autobiography," 344–45.
9. The "thirteen thousand" from Whalen and Whalen, *Fighting McCooks,* 299.

his previous meetings with Booth and Weichmann. At the very least it seems Mudd misled Ewing, or if Ewing was indeed informed, he was unable to do the necessary background investigation to uncover the truth because of the telescoped trial schedule.

In June 1865, the weather turned hot and humid. The crowded trial room became an oven, and only three small windows allowed any air into the penitentiary. Where Mudd was concerned, the prosecution proved he was a Confederate sympathizer but that he had taken the loyalty oath and had voted in the 1864 national election. Mudd had made derogatory statements about the president, but Ewing deftly pointed out that so had many Democratic congressmen. As for meeting Booth in 1864, many Americans could lay claim to having met the famous actor. Mudd had not immediately reported the visit of the two strangers on April 15; indeed, he had treated an injured stranger. The prosecution proved that, when questioned, he appeared nervous and evasive. Only Weichmann's testimony indicated that Mudd was part of any conspiracy.

The prosecution's rebuttal witnesses began testifying on June 12 and promptly victimized Mudd with some of the era's "junk science." Hunter allowed Brigadier General Thomas M. Harris to testify that he had studied phrenology and that Mudd had a "bump of secrecy" on his head. Ewing furiously objected to the testimony. How could he ever hope to cross-examine such idiotic hearsay? About all Ewing could do was mock Harris's lack of credentials and the prosecution's "head bump" case against Mudd.[10]

By June 23, the other attorneys presented their defense of the major conspirators, and Ewing began his formal defense of the others. The assistance Tom Ewing received from Browning, Hugh, and his father was without peer in Washington at that time. None of the three attended the trial, but the interviewing of witnesses and outlines of questions and discussion points helped immensely. Originally, Browning did not want to be involved. He changed his mind when one of his old clients was arrested and kept in Stanton's military jail on bread and water for two months with no explanation. Ewing's defense for Spangler was that he was a drunken "drudge" and that holding horses for riders was not a crime. Giving Booth a horse did not automatically reveal why Booth needed a horse in the back alley of the Ford Theater, and not knowing this fact did not make Spangler a conspirator. As for the allegation that Arnold was a wagon-maker and provided transportation for the plot, Ewing argued that being asked to make a wagon for a fu-

10. Harris testimony from Thomas R. Turner, *Beware the People Weeping: Public Opinion and the Assassination of Abraham Lincoln*, 187.

ture kidnapping that was never carried out was not a crime unless wagon-making itself was a crime.[11]

Ewing had significant factual hurdles to jump in order to defend the doctor, however. Mudd's family did have a checkered history on loyalty. James Mudd, a relative of Samuel's, had run munitions from Baltimore to Virginia in order to aid the Confederacy, and there was certainly considerable doubt as to Mudd's personal loyalty. Even so, as part of the defense, Ewing tried to bootleg into the record testimony of Mudd's brother George. Dr. Mudd had suggested George contact the authorities when he realized that Booth and Herold had given false names. When Dr. Mudd did take Booth's boot to the authorities, he was taken to Bryantown, Maryland, to make a statement. A conspirator would never have done those things, Ewing argued. Judge Advocate Joseph Holt objected to the line of examination. Mudd was not charged with disloyalty but, rather, with receiving, entertaining, and setting the broken leg of a co-conspirator. The crime was completed at four o'clock in the afternoon of April 15, and what Mudd did after that was irrelevant. Ewing snapped back, if his crime was setting a broken leg, where in the criminal code was this act made into a capital offense?[12]

Ewing then took the government investigation to task. Mudd claimed never to have met either of the two men who showed up on his doorstep. In a later statement Mudd indicated that neither man had done anything to make him think they were part of a crime. He had met Booth one time before but had not recognized Booth at his farm in April, since Booth had used an alias. The War Department did not name Booth as the assassin until April 20, well after Booth had left Mudd's place. Mudd was charged with the crime of conspiracy merely because he did not notify federal authorities about a crime he did not yet know had happened.[13]

In summation, Ewing reopened his argument that military courts were improper to try and judge civilians, and that only grand juries can order a citizen to answer for a capital crime. Stanton declared on April 20, 1865, that it was a crime to give assistance to Booth, Herold, or Atzerodt, but Congress never enacted this law. If setting the broken leg of an assassin who is not known to the doctor as an assassin is to be made a crime, Ewing snapped, Congress should make this law, not the secretary of war! Mudd could not be charged with violating the laws of war because he was not a soldier. If he was not a soldier, the military courts had

11. Taylor, "Business and Political Career," 194; *New York Tribune,* June 21, 1865.
12. Weckesser, *His Name Was Mudd,* 117.
13. Ibid.

no jurisdiction. "The term is unknown in our language, a quiddity, wholly undefined and incapable of definition. It is what the Judge Advocate chooses to make it. Therein lies the danger," Ewing warned.[14] Ewing patiently went through the only direct evidence given against Mudd:

> Mudd did not participate in the conspiracy. He was not an accessory before the fact. Can he be held for an accessory after the fact? Booth arrived at daybreak not to a doctor on watch for him as a guilty accomplice, but to a household in profound sleep. An accessory after the fact occurs when a person knowing a felony to have been committed receives, comforts, or assists him whom he knows to be a felon. He must know the felon is guilty to be an accessory. Mudd sets Booth's leg, allows him to rest that day at the house, while Mudd goes to his tobacco fields to work.
>
> Even if he had supplied a felon with food or professionally assists him when sick or wounded, though he *knows* him to be a felon, these acts are not sufficient to make him an accessory after the fact.
>
> Yet the evidence does not show Mudd knew Booth was a fugitive murderer. The worst that can be said is that Mudd learned from his wife that Booth was wearing false stage whiskers, which aroused his interest. But Mudd did not do anything Saturday night, he delayed until Sunday noon to communicate with authorities.

Could Mudd be convicted on these facts? "If this tribunal is governed in its findings by the just and time-honored rules of law," Ewing reminded them, "he cannot. If by some edict higher than constitutions and laws [of Congress], I know not what to anticipate or how to defend him."[15]

After seven weeks, on June 29, the commission retired to deliberate. They did not take long. By six o'clock in the evening, they announced that all but Spangler were guilty of the charge of conspiracy. When deciding penalties, the commission needed a two-thirds vote to impose a death penalty. Herold, Mary Surratt, Atzerodt, and Lewis Payne were sentenced to die. Originally, the vote for Surratt was 5–4. Somehow the vote was changed to 6–3, for death, unless the president granted clemency. Mudd and Arnold got life in prison as conspirators. Spangler received life, even though he was not convicted of any conspiracy or murder, only holding

14. *Washington Daily Morning Chronicle,* June 21, 1865; "quiddity" in Roscoe, *Web of Conspiracy,* 446.

15. *New York Tribune,* June 24, 1865, quoted in Weckesser, *His Name Was Mudd,* 119–20.

Booth's horse outside the theater. There was later controversy as to whether Johnson was even aware of the clemency possibility for Surratt; he claimed Holt never informed him. Throughout the trial, furthermore, Booth's diary was kept in Holt's safe, away from any defense attorneys. The diary would have cleared Mrs. Surratt of any wrongdoing. Access to a federal appeals court was blocked by the government. The executions were scheduled for July 7 and swiftly carried out.[16]

Eighteen years later and after Mudd's death, Frederick Stone told a newspaperman that Mudd's "prevarications" were "painful" for the lawyers. Edward Steers Jr. indicates that, after Mudd was serving his time at Fort Jefferson, he confessed to having met with Booth on a prior occasion contrary to what he maintained (with Ewing's assistance) at trial. Furthermore, George Atzerodt gave a statement on May 1 to a Baltimore provost marshal after his capture and before trial. Notes were made of the interview by Atzerodt's brother-in-law, who happened to work on the provost marshal's staff. Atzerodt gave investigators a convoluted statement that "Mudd knew all about it," because Booth had told Atzerodt that Booth had sent "liquors and provisions for the trip with the President to Richmond two weeks before the murder to Dr. Mudd's." The information never came up at the trial because William Doster, Atzerodt's attorney, objected to the hearsay statements and the jailhouse interview. This was a time before Miranda warnings, and this author is surprised the notes were not allowed into evidence. They would have devastated Ewing's defense by tying a more active Mudd to the kidnapping plot and hence the resulting assassination. Whether Holt could have extended that information from conspiracy to murder is problematic now. It was clear that the doctor in fact knew Booth well, and Mudd did not help Ewing prepare a defense with the truth. Mudd was at least an accessory to a kidnapping that never occurred.[17]

Ewing's defense of Mudd made sense to at least one officer on the tribunal. Major General Lew Wallace told Browning's wife at a social event that, if Booth had not broken his leg, the world would never have heard of Samuel Mudd, but "The deed is done. Somebody must suffer for it. And he may as well suffer as anybody else." Ironically, the main character in a novel Wallace was to publish in 1880, Judah Ben-Hur, suffers the same innocent indignities of wrongful accusation and

16. Hal Higdon, *The Union vs. Dr. Mudd,* 208. The death warrants are at *O.R.* 2:8:699.

17. "Prevarications" from Edward Steers, "The Deceptive Doctor," *Columbiad* 2 (1988): 114. For "Mudd knew all about it," Atzerodt's lost interview is on the Internet, see <http://home.att.net/~rjnorton/Lincoln82.html> last accessed April 7, 2008. Mudd's deceptions explained in Benn Pitmann, *The Assassination of President Lincoln and the Trial of the Conspirators,* 421.

summary punishment at the hands of Roman officers that the House of Mudd suffered under Stanton.[18]

Originally, Mudd was sentenced to the federal prison at Albany, New York. Thomas Ewing Sr. suggested the firm seek a habeas corpus action in Democratic New York and retry Mudd to a jury. Browning wrote Tom that Stanton had caught wind of their snooping and changed Mudd's destination to the federal prison at the Dry Tortugas. With War Department appointees running the federal offices in former Confederate Florida, Mudd was beyond the reach of a writ, and thereby beyond the reach of law.[19]

Although the nation moved on from that hot summer when it forgot its own rule of law, in the backrooms of the War Department army clerks were still ginning up praise for the tribunal system even into November 1865. In a report to Stanton, Joseph Holt tried again to summarize their façade of fairness. He lauded the work of the commission in heroic terms, for posterity if nothing else. Lincoln, he noted, "unhesitatingly employed this tribunal [system]" throughout the war years. The Congress continued it as "indispensable during the war." In spite of the "shallow and disloyal clamors raised against it," Holt was proud of the tribunal's value "as an arm of the military administration evidenced alike by the fairness of its judgments and by its enlightened and vigorous action." Holt's document simply restates Ewing's thesis. What was never used in peacetime but might be indispensible in war became unnecessary once peace returned.[20]

Mudd was indeed lucky he had Ewing's vigorous defense. "I feel profoundly thankful to have saved my clients from the gallows built for them before the trial," Ewing wrote his father the day after the executions. The court had voted 5–4 for hanging Mudd, one vote short of the minimum. "If they had been convicted they would be in their graves tonight." He also wrote that all but Surratt were guilty.[21]

The trial was not financially rewarding for Ewing. He was to have received a fee of $2,500 for Mudd's defense and $1,500 from Ford for Spangler, and he had trouble collecting the fees from Mrs. Mudd. However, he had established himself as a first-class lawyer who was unafraid to take on the government, and as it later turned out, the radicals. Late in 1865, he wrote a friend that his practice was potentially "lucrative" if he could swear off politics.[22]

18. Turner, *People Weeping,* 187.

19. Dry Tortugas warning in Browning to TEJr., July 19, 1865, in ibid., 189; Mudd's transfer order to the Dry Tortugas at *O.R.* 2:8:700.

20. Holt's tribunal report to the War Department at *O.R.* 3:5:490–94.

21. TEJr. to TESr., July 7, August 22, 1865, EFP/LC.

22. "Lucrative" from TEJr. to Ed Russell, July 28, 1865, EFP/LC, quoted in Taylor, "Business and Political Career," 199.

The conspiracy trial was an example of American justice at its worst, but it was not surprising, given the passions that run high in the aftermath of civil war. Often the losers share a traitor's noose in high-profile executions. Certainly the thought had to cross the minds of Lee, Longstreet, and especially Jefferson Davis that, notwithstanding the terms of surrender from Grant and Sherman, the end of the war would mean an ignominious end of their stellar lives. The five conspirators who were hung after the conspiracy trial provided a symbolic expiation for the leaders of the defeated Confederacy, whose existence spawned both Lincoln's murder and the punishment of the conspirators.

Even in its best light (that is to say, the need for expedient action to overcome the horror of a country left leaderless), the conspiracy tribunal was an example of rampant despotism carried out by men wearing the uniform of army officers who had sworn to uphold the Constitution of the United States. While the condemned were not innocents, they deserved a better brand of justice. That some of the targets of his malice had escaped the hangman's noose Stanton would view forever as a failure for the government. Ewing's own words indicate his view that the trial was a star chamber, but he had to admit grudgingly that it was in fact efficient. His best efforts had not resulted in acquittals, but men of the South now had a new champion in Washington, Jesuit Tom, a former enemy who was not afraid to take on the radicals.

Several months after the uproar had subsided after the conspiracy trial, Orville Hickman Browning called on Edwin Stanton on behalf of a client, Joseph R. Anderson, who had owned the Tredegar Iron Works in Richmond before the war. The Tredegar works had become a major munitions and cannon factory for the Confederacy during the war. Anderson had been a brigadier general in the Confederate army, commanding coastal troops in North Carolina. A Pennsylvania company had bought railroad maintenance equipment from Tredegar in early 1861. The war broke out before the equipment could be delivered, and the Confederate government confiscated the ironworks and converted the inventory for its own use. On the fall of Richmond the factory fell into Union hands. Anderson wanted to file with the government to reclaim his property.

Stanton did not care a whit about the Pennsylvania claim or Anderson. Tredegar and its inventory were spoils of war. No one in a Confederate state, even loyal Unionists, could create contracts that would stand in a federal court of law during a rebellion. Browning argued that, absent congressional laws not operating ex post facto, a Southern rebellion did not dissolve normal legal relations between parties. Stanton told Browning that the secretary of war would rather suspend

Anderson's pardon and send him to prison than recognize the validity of an 1861 contract made in Virginia. Furthermore, Stanton was not in any mood to accommodate Browning, an open ally of the Ewings.[23]

Stanton was being disingenuous that day. Both men were premier lawyers of their time and they both knew the federal government had on occasion honored prewar contracts made by Northern businessmen with parties in what became Confederate states. Federal courts during Reconstruction would later reject Stanton's 1865 position on a variety of contract law conclusions. The postwar federal confiscation policies posed immediate problems for Southerners such as Anderson and threatened to become obstacles to sectional reconciliation. Southerners felt such policies were a Yankee means of continuing to lord it over the fallen Confederacy. Radical confiscation policy was in fact just that. In 1863, as a means of paying for the war and integrating blacks into the national fabric after the war, Congress had enacted the Captured and Abandoned Property Act, which authorized the Treasury Department to collect Confederate property—primarily its cotton—and forward it north for resale.[24]

Not unlike thousands of others the Ewings were interested in taking advantage of business conditions and helping rebuild the South in some small but profitable way. Cotton wholesaling had held their family interest for some time. Late in the war Sherman was inundated with demands from civilians wanting the army's blessing to their entrée into some lucrative cotton business. Hugh and Charley, in conjunction with Phil, had made initial plans for cotton wholesaling as a fallback business enterprise, and at one point before the war was over, Charley mentioned leaving the army in order to build just such a business. Hugh ran into the cotton issue in the last weeks of the war, when Hugh learned from John Schofield that General Curtis made a fortune out of sending his men out to gather cotton as plunder.

Cotton turned over to the Treasury agents required a detailed accounting of its ownership, value, and description. Government agents would obtain the cotton and move it to a market to sell it. Loyal citizens with valid claims on cotton wrongfully taken from them by the government could look later to the government for the proceeds, but not for the cotton itself. The burden was on the owner, however, to show a chain of ownership into and remaining in federal hands. To entice agents to get the product to federal warehouses, a 25 percent bounty was paid to

23. Browning, *Diary,* 2:52–53; confiscation policies at war's end, Dana to Stanton, *O.R.* 46:3:683–84, 1265.

24. Captured and Abandoned Property Act mentioned *O.R.* 3:4:721.

those agents, and some of Lincoln's special agents received a 75 percent fee for special dangers faced. In such a system making money was easy. It was up to Tom and Hugh to figure out what opportunities were out there and the details of the transactions. Confiscation policies made it risky to work with confiscated Confederate cotton, but Ewingville in general felt that fortunes might be made in finding, moving, and selling cotton owned by loyalists living in the Mississippi River valley who remained faithful to the Union. Their belief as to the proper hands-off role of government led the Ewings to view continued confiscation after the war as unconstitutional. They believed that government surely had no right, either before or after the war, to confiscate cotton produced by loyal planters who were victimized solely by geography.[25]

Among the loyalists wanting to prove their claims and net their cotton proceeds was Adie Douglas, the widow of Stephen Douglas. The senator had died early in the war, and Adie had spent the war years in Illinois, but she, a former Arkansas belle, owned her father's old plantation along the Arkansas River near Pine Bluff. She inherited slaves when her father died, and during the war her plantation continued to prosper in Confederate hands. The property was deep enough in southern Arkansas that Union forces did not get near it until late in the war, when Adie bought twenty-five hundred bales of cotton from neighboring Arkansas plantations. A month before his death, Lincoln authorized a certain James Andrews to deliver the cotton to her agent, Tom Ewing. Ewing's well-known activities in the prewar fight over the Lecompton Constitution and Stephen Douglas's affiliation with Orville Browning made them instant Douglas allies. Whatever Ewing could arrange as a price was to be given over to Mrs. Douglas as a small fortune on which she could live out her days. Lincoln went out of his way to help Mrs. Douglas, even authorizing the sale of her cotton, which went counter to the 1863 Confiscation Act. When Lincoln was assassinated, Andrew Johnson followed through on Lincoln's plan and approved Grant's authority to involve the army in assisting the enterprise. James Andrews failed during the war to get Mrs. Douglas's cotton "out" and sold so that she had the proceeds to live on. The Ewings stepped into this role after the war.[26]

25. Cotton policies at *O.R.* 38:5:648, 39:2:863–64, 41:3:265, 49:2:1099–1100; *O.R.* 2:7:1063, 1072–73; cotton accounting mechanism and 25–75 percent division, from Taylor, "Business and Political Career," 201; Schofield's cotton story from Ewing, "Autobiography," 341; Sherman, *Memoirs,* 2:234, 252, 264–67.

26. Grant's initial efforts to get Stephen Douglas's cotton out of Arkansas found in Steele to Grant, April 10, 1863, *O.R.* 24:1:502; additional reports by General Frederick Steele to WTS, at *O.R.* 24:3:173; Steele's effort thwarted by Nathaniel P. Banks in Banks to Col. Chandler, *O.R.* 34:3:515.

The Adie Douglas project was just part of a larger postwar cotton-farming plan. The second and third parts of the business involved bringing out the cotton of other loyal planters, which could be sold at market prices, and also confiscated Southern planter cotton, which would be sold to the government for a bounty. The weakness of what otherwise was a solid money-making enterprise was that the old Confederacy was full of men—former rebels and Yankee carpetbaggers—who had similar money-making ideas.

Later in the war, while the cotton plantations kept churning out product, most of the transportation infrastructure in the Red River area on either side of the river through Arkansas and Louisiana was destroyed. The military controlled most of the available transportation. Military transportation or private freight-haulers worked for the military, and government rules prevented such transportation from carrying any freight of private individuals. In power in the federal government in the defeated South there were men such as W. W. Orme, a former brigadier at the Battle of Prairie Grove with Ewing. Orme's tuberculosis had assigned him rear echelon duty, and later he resigned as a controversial commandant of the Camp Douglas POW camp outside Chicago. He was caught, as a special treasury officer in Memphis, for allowing persons in that area to collect Confederate cotton and giving them a 25 percent "in kind" bounty (every fourth bale of cotton brought out), which the agent then sold privately for higher prices than were paid by the government. For some reason Orme was never cashiered from his government job and was available to extend similar courtesies to the Ewing consortium.[27]

One of the problems with the Ewing cotton project was to find enough local agents to go out and acquire cotton in certain regions. Local planters liked to work with local men whom they knew, not with transplanted Yankees. At Vicksburg Hugh befriended a former Confederate colonel and Arkansas slave owner named John W. Polk, who offered to broker the effort, with grandiose claims he could find enough quality men from the ranks of the former Confederacy to get title to fourteen thousand bales of cotton piled high and rotting away on landings in the Washita River in northeastern Louisiana. Two weeks before Lee's surrender, Polk and some others had already bought ten thousand bales from the Confederate government at 50 cents per pound, competing directly against federal officers who were already buying bales in the area and at the same time giving the dying Southern government an infusion of cash. In mid-September 1865 Polk predicted most

27. Disallowing private freight, N. P. Banks to Col. Chandler, May 9, 1864, *O.R.* 34:3:515; Orme's methods, *O.R.* 48:2:835.

of the private cotton west of the Mississippi could be sold for at least 25 cents per pound and, because the country was swamped in the product, purchased for half that price. There was never a better opportunity for an "association of capital" to buy a scarce commodity low and sell it high, Polk reasoned. Even Stanton's radical government would recognize former Confederate officers who were working with respected Northern businessmen and former generals in the Union army. Polk knew this and agreed to divide the profit with the Ewings if the consortium could provide transport. Hugh agreed to Polk's offer with a handshake, noting in his journal, however, "Will use all means lawful to secure success in the cotton venture as the golden opportunity may never return." Polk began making the rounds of Southern cotton owners along the Washita River, to talk them into transferring their remaining interests to the Ewing consortium, which he claimed to represent.[28]

Categorizing the "good" and "bad" cotton proved difficult. Examining Confederate confiscation records to track loyalist bales was often a waste of time. Many records were destroyed in the waning days of the war. Polk contracted with Southern planters where he could, using contingent fee arrangements. His argument was simple: if the Ewing consortium could realize a profit from the Confederate cotton they brought out to the government, the Southern men would get something. Otherwise, cotton was simply confiscated, and the owners who could not prove wartime loyalty would receive nothing.

While some might term the cotton idea a scheme, the Ewings thought of it as a business plan. One of the strong themes of nineteenth-century America—both North and South—was opposition to the government's taking of private property, everything from land, cotton, other crops, or slaves. In a true democracy men were paid for the "free labor" of their hands and bodies, and any thought of taking that property from a man after he had sweated for it was anathema to most citizens. It was more important to get the sections back into mutual economic commerce than to adhere slavishly to a radical view of vengeance against the South. This new vision by the Ewings would manifest itself in more than just the cotton projects.[29]

Tom Ewing initially had misgivings over the "cotton matter," as he called it. Too many shortcuts would have to be employed to make it work, and he was clear-

28. Polk to TEJr., September 9, 1865, "association of capital" from Polk to TEJr., September 17, 1865, TEJr./KSHS; "all means lawful" from Ewing, "Autobiography," 347.

29. Ewing, "Autobiography," 352.

ly uncomfortable with that aspect of the project. Hugh was not so worried—or if he was he kept it hidden. He met Tom in Memphis to map a new approach to seek Grant's help for the Louisiana cotton. Hugh's enthusiasm prevailed over Tom's skepticism, and the brothers alerted Browning to stand to help if help was needed with senior officials in Washington.[30]

Hugh put more agents into the work, offering them $5.00 per bale to go with Tom and supervise the shipment and sale of the cotton. Included as a new agent was their brother Phil Ewing and John D. Martin, Phil's boss in the Lancaster bank. On September 24, 1865, Hugh empowered Tom "[t]o dispose of such portion of the gross or net proceeds . . . necessary in negotiating the business." Hugh began his work on the project while still on active duty with the army, and his characteristic optimism in the project led him to consider "leaving the [military] service" to give the project his personal attention. On September 28, his instructions to Tom concluded, "If *any* obstacle occurs in your path, remove it, or take high bold ground and vault over it. Cut the knot if it will not untie! Possession is ten-tenths of the law!"[31]

With Browning's help, Tom eventually received initial authorization from the Treasury Department to seek out the Douglas cotton. This, along with Grant's help, would give "Mrs. Douglas" a paper "to make good to them their losses during the war." What they were doing was getting permission to move the Douglas cotton to market without being forced to sell to the government. The venture remained private but now had the respectability of a government agency behind it. As of early October, however, Tom viewed the prospects of success only as fair.[32]

The Ewings sweetened the pot by volunteering to have the cartel reimburse the government any of its transportation expenses out of cartel profits. By October 10, 1865, the coveted permit from Grant had been received, which allowed the Ewings to use government transportation facilities, if such were available. By mid-October the plan was that Ewing would obtain the cotton from the federal government and pay all expenses of transportation out of the proceeds. The government got something for its efforts, but the lion's share of the risk was Ewing's. New Orleans banker Hugh McDonald helped finance the deal. Gill & Able, well-

30. Ibid., 353.

31. HBE to TEJr., September 24, TEJr./KSHS, quoted in Taylor, "Business and Political Career," 204; HBE to TEJr., September 28, 1865, TEJr./KSHS.

32. HBE to TEJr., October 2, 1865, TEJr./KSHS.

respected Memphis cotton brokers, would sell the cotton, and the cartel would get the rest. The affair was now "tolerably promising," Tom wired Hugh. "Tell Browning."[33]

Hugh had another project requiring him to be off for Memphis, this being the creation of a twenty-thousand-acre cotton farm in Arkansas. Impoverished white families owned three-fourths of Southern cotton plantations, and many of these plantations were for sale because there was no available labor. Speculators such as the Ewings felt that this idleness of the land and a lack of cotton as a commodity would drive up the price of cotton. If they could not buy existing bales of cotton without running afoul of federal authorities, they could buy the land and begin growing a crop and turn a profit. The multiregional partnership was important for the Ewings' efforts. The partners included Thomas T. January, James H. Hammond, John W. Polk, John Lee, and Lancaster banker John D. Martin. Others involved in the farming venture included J. Madison Cutts (Douglas's father-in-law whose son had served as an aide to Ambrose Burnside), James M. Brooks (a former officer in the Seventh Louisiana), and banker Hugh McDonald (a captain in the First Pennsylvania cavalry). The most prominent Southern investor was Hammond, the former South Carolina senator whose "King Cotton" speech in the U.S. Senate in 1858 steered the country toward war.[34]

Labor costs were crucial to the success of the farm and proved the Achilles heel for the management. Unlike plantations that fed and housed the slaves all year, Polk suggested that cotton farms could hire black labor for only the months during the year needed to plant, tend, and harvest the crop. He was confident the blacks would return to the plantations to work the cotton and eke out subsistence living, regardless of the siren songs of the Northern abolitionists: "They must work and will work. No people however fanatical will be satisfied to work themselves to support an inferior race in idleness [and] the state will soon pass laws, deferring and settling the question." However, Polk argued, "I have no philanthropic views. I pity the nigger and think he has got the worst of it." That idleness, however, would force blacks to spend the rest of the year sharecropping, which is what happened later in much of the old Cotton South. Polk's was a remarkably cynical view of how black slave labor should be utilized in a free labor

33. TEJr. meeting with Hugh McDonald found in Taylor, "Business and Political Career," 206; quote from Ewing, "Autobiography," 353.

34. "Cotton Is King," from Stampp, *America in 1857,* 326.

environment. The new Ewing cotton-farming enterprise in southern Arkansas got off to a slow start but, within ten years, was doing well.[35]

By mid-October 1865 Tom had concluded that Adie Douglas's cotton had been either stolen or destroyed and that a reliable accounting from Confederate records was impossible. During the last year of the war, her Confederate neighbors had taken over a thousand bales to Shreveport and sold her cotton as their own, probably to share the proceeds with her as a former Southern girl and to avoid confiscation of her crop by Confederate authorities. As Ewing investigated deeper, he met local resistance. While the papers Tom carried from Grant directed military authority to render lawful assistance, either this lawful assistance was interpreted by local officers as insufficient to commandeer military transport for civilian enterprises or the transportation was given a low priority. Hugh asked Mrs. Douglas to use her influence to get Grant to clarify that the transportation services available to the Ewings included army wagons. "Otherwise," he wrote, "further efforts on the matter are useless."[36]

From an office in New Orleans, Tom Ewing considered filing a lawsuit to recover the proceeds of Mrs. Douglas's cotton. However, the defendants were newly impoverished Southern planters—turnips from which blood would not pour. With national policy continuing to confiscate Southern plantations and with carpetbagging bureaucrats invading the South, any judgment against Southern real estate was worthless. Also, with cotton prices climbing, Hugh wanted Tom to buy all the cotton he could, not sit around dreaming up litigation.[37]

The grease came from a determined Adie Douglas. Through Browning she obtained from Grant special authority asking B. F. Flanders, the supervising Treasury agent in New Orleans, to cooperate. Grant ordered as much government transportation "as can be spared" to be made available to the Ewings. They now had authority from the army and an inroad to the Treasury Department—essentially to ignore Treasury Department regulations. Hugh was ecstatic. Grant was essentially asking government agents to bypass Treasury regulations on Adie Douglas's behalf. Army officers in Little Rock were ordered to furnish transportation to the Ewing enterprise. Hugh Ewing's notes of the meeting indicated that, in relation to Grant's efforts on their behalf, "Honors were easy." This was a

35. Polk to TEJr., September 9, 1865, TEJr./KSHS.

36. Tom Ewing's discovery of status of Adie Douglas's cotton from unsigned letter, possibly draft, TEJr. to Mrs Douglas, October 10, 1865; quote from HBE to TEJr, October 2, 1865, TEJr./KSHS.

37. HBE to TEJr, November 16, 1865, found in Taylor, "Business and Political Career," 207.

kind of code between Hugh and Tom meaning that Grant's special efforts would be considered by the consortium for an unstated reward if the venture had future success. It would be wrong to view this as a bribe of Grant. He was motivated by simply wanting to help Adie Douglas because of his strong friendship with her late husband.[38]

Adie Douglas, with Browning in tow, met with the president. They wanted Johnson to make any raised eyebrows in either the War Department or the Treasury Department disappear. Johnson had been a friend and an ally of Stephen Douglas, but he asked them to first check with Hugh McCulloch, the secretary of the treasury appointed by Lincoln. When Browning and Mrs. Douglas called on McCulloch, Browning's considerable negotiating skills ran into a brick wall. No one but the government could obtain title to Southern cotton, and McCulloch reminded them there were ways of making a legitimate claim on the government for reimbursement. The cotton belonged to the government until proved otherwise. Browning asked the president to overrule McCulloch, but McCulloch anticipated this move and had alerted Stanton. Since Sherman's confrontation with Stanton at the Grand Review and Tom Ewing's defense of Mudd, Stanton took a personal interest in anything in which the Ewings had an interest. Stanton overrode Grant's transportation order. Further, in mid-November, someone in McCulloch's Treasury Department leaked the cotton venture and the involvement of government officials to the *New York Herald.* Johnson was trapped. Johnson was no fan of Stanton's, but he was not going to put pressure on the views of either Stanton or McCulloch. Nobody in Washington was going to wink either officially or unofficially at the national confiscation laws.[39]

The resourceful Browning had one more idea. Hugh would draw a letter for Adie Douglas to sign that would promise the Treasury Department a voluntary 25 percent tax on the sale of her cotton in return for government transportation assistance. Nobody paid taxes that high. Her gesture would overcome any negatives associated with the scheme, since the purpose of the cotton confiscation was to pay the war debt. By November 15, Tom was in Washington to promote this last idea. However, new voices in the administration became concerned that, if Douglas's venture was allowed and not others, it could be seen as influential people buying their entrée to a fortune with a 25 percent premium. The administra-

38. "As can be spared" from paraphrase of government letter in HBE to TEJr., October 19, 1865, TEJR./KSHS; "Honors were easy" from notes in Ewing, "Autobiography," 354.

39. Browning, *Diary,* 2:47.

tion's answer remained no. The cotton farm would continue in operation, but Ewingville officially declared the cotton-buying venture dead.[40]

The conspiracy trial and the aftermath of the cotton venture cemented Tom Ewing's presence in Washington for the next few years. He sensed that important matters were coming to a head in the city. He was certainly known to Andrew Johnson before Lincoln's assassination, so no introductions were needed. His work against Stanton at the trials was all the entrée he needed into Johnson's inner circle of advisors. He found a comfortable fit there, among men who wanted reconciliation not retribution between former enemies. For the time being Tom Ewing would pitch his tent along the Potomac.

40. Ewing, "Autobiography," 355.

11

THE GATHERING OF EVIL BIRDS

At the center of any discussion of Reconstruction are the questions posed by Frederick Douglass. Was the enormous war fought so heroically by so many Americans to have no value to liberty or civilization? Would those who fought to preserve slavery in the South be given status in the region's future as if nothing had happened? In peace, Douglass predicted, "the nation must fall or flourish with the Negro":

> Custom, manners, morals, religion, are all on its side everywhere in the South; and when you add the ignorance and servility of the ex-slave to the intelligence and accustomed authority of the master, you have the conditions, not out of which slavery will again grow, but under which it is impossible for the Federal government to wholly destroy it, unless the Federal government be armed with despotic power, to blot out State authority, and to station a Federal officer at every crossroad. This, of course, cannot be done, and ought not even if it could. The true way and the easiest way is to make our government entirely consistent with itself, and give to every loyal citizen the elective franchise a right and power which will be ever-present, and will form a wall of fire for his protection.[1]

While Douglass was writing of the liberty and civilization of free blacks, others saw Reconstruction as a means of reforming Southern white political and fi-

1. Douglass, "Reconstruction," *Atlantic Monthly* 18 (1866): 762.

nancial customs. Reconstruction began as a political reformation but was expanded by radicals to include a last—and in some ways, desperate—chance to change the social and economic policy of the entire country. The federal government had spent nearly $3 billion fighting the war. This spending had completed the mechanization of the industrial North. Reconstruction sought change of Southern social and political institutions, but also change of the nation's priorities—from those of imported capital fueling an agrarian society to those of a nation building its own financial resources in order to feed the visions of the new industries of John D. Rockefeller, Andrew Carnegie, Jay Cooke, and the thousands of entrepreneurs with their own aspirations in the wake of the super-rich. So long as they could influence government, these entrepreneurs were not about to let America slide back into a system of small shops and farms. Since all change becomes political at some point, the fight over how to regulate capital expansion ushered in a Gilded Age for American entrepreneurs. The Ewings' postwar cotton venture was but a small example. But this change also created stark political differences between America's very rich and very poor. To some congressional leaders, reform of Southern capital formation and American banking dependence on Great Britain had to occur simultaneously even at the risk of despotism. Ewingville would figure significantly in this political debate.[2]

Within a week of the Grand Review in 1865, Andrew Johnson began his own vision of Reconstruction by granting amnesty to all Southerners except the senior officials, on condition they sign and file a written loyalty oath with the government. When he later ordered that the Sea Islands of Georgia and South Carolina be returned to their white owners and vetoed the Freedmen's Act, he declared war on Republican radicalism. It was clear that Lincoln no longer was in the White House. Hugh Ewing later wrote that the Freedmen's veto was a "good" one.[3]

The radicals were aghast. The blood spilled in Northern regiments during the war was being squandered by that Tennessean in the White House. Stanton was especially unnerved and turned his vitriol on the man in whose cabinet he served. Postwar policies of the defeated Southern states would not be made by slave owners while Stanton had any say in Washington.[4]

Perhaps the most unusual of Johnson's allies was Kansas senator Jim Lane. The

2. Foner, *Reconstruction,* 19–20.

3. Ewing, "Autobiography," 361; contrast the work of the Freedman's Bureau, *O.R.* 3:3:73, 3:4:382, with Johnson's amnesty policy at *O.R.* 3:5:38.

4. Curry, *Radicalism,* iv.

consummate radical abolitionist saw in the Freedmen's Act both a loss of federalism and social integration of the races, both concepts he opposed. Lane's support for Johnson's veto of the Freedmen's Act was extremely unpopular among radicals in the Kansas legislature, where his primary antagonist was Edmund G. Ross, an editor and close confidant of radical governor Samuel Crawford. Tom Ewing had to shake his head at how bitter the rancor had turned between the various factions in Topeka. To local criticism of his votes Lane argued that he was not obligated to the president. He came back to Kansas to explain himself by claiming that Johnson's veto was sound policy, which brought only more denunciations. Lane tried to meet with key Kansas radicals and strike an understanding. However, his supporters stated that his backsliding gave Kansas Democrats the idea that Republicans were fracturing over Reconstruction. If Lane did not change his views, a massive catastrophe of the first order would fall on Kansas—Democrats would take over and oust Republican officeholders and their patronage. Radical publishers such as Daniel Anthony poured on the editorial pressure. Southern property owners should be impoverished, not appeased.[5]

Rejection was a new feeling for Lane and drove him to despondency. On July 1, 1866, in Leavenworth he put a pistol in his mouth and pulled the trigger. Hugh Ewing was in Leavenworth settling old business debts when the headlines captured every Kansan's attention. Hugh went out to the fort to "see the remains," perhaps to make sure the devil Lane was truly dead and to pass the hat in case they had to pay pallbearers to get him buried.[6]

Filling a power vacuum is not easy. Rumors circulated that the governor favored Edmund Ross, a newspaperman and a newly retired captain of the Eleventh Kansas cavalry. Tom Ewing was as delighted at these rumors as Kansas radicals were appalled. Although a great many Lane men supported Ross, he was not radical enough for some others. C. W. Adams telegraphed Crawford, "If you appoint Major Ross, you will go to hell in this county." Crawford ignored the warnings and his critics. Ross was a former combat veteran and comrade. "We need a man with backbone in the Senate," he wrote, calling Ross an "honest and straightforward" soldier of "unflinching courage." Crawford predicted there was no waffle in Ross's view of how the South should be reconstructed. Newspaperman George Anthony was incredulous. Good radicals, like good Christians, do not consort with sinners. Ross's sin was his friendship with moderates such as Tom Ewing surrounding the president. Anthony warned his readers, "The ball that went through

5. Lane's problems from Plummer, *Frontier Governor,* 51, 56.

6. Ewing, "Autobiography," 367; Plummer, *Frontier Governor,* 63; Davis, *Bicentennial History,* 88.

Lane's head took from the Governor all his brains." Ross's appointment to the U.S. Senate would have spectacular national consequences.[7]

Radicals were understandably jealous of Johnson's status in 1866. They might have been more prepared for a president such as Johnson if Lincoln had lost to McClellan in 1864. McClellan's platform had at least been set forth squarely before the nation. Johnson, however, was repapering the White House with appeasements. Radical Reconstruction would have to be engineered in Congress, and Congress would have to roll over the president to accomplish the goal. This meant the radicals needed a veto-proof Congress from the 1866 midterm elections.

With the radicals divided over Reconstruction and the Democrat base in the South rebuilding, the National Union Party (NUP), the compromise party of 1864, was the only viable medium through which Johnson could seek reelection. For the NUP to be a force in the 1868 presidential campaign, it had to do well in 1866. The NUP attracted conservative Republicans and Democrats such as Orville Browning, senators Edgar Cowan of Pennsylvania (a former partner of Thomas Ewing Sr.) and James Doolittle of Wisconsin, and Alexander Randall, the postmaster general. The young turks of the new party now included Tom Ewing Jr. The general feeling of NUP men was that Southerners had usurped power, but the Union had remained intact, thus Southern civil rights were unimpaired by the war and their rights of citizenship should be "reinstated" rather than "restored," a subtle distinction but one that carried marked consequences during Reconstruction. Tom wrote his father about the formation of the party. The NUP felt the new equal protection amendments (later the Fourteenth Amendment) were good for the country because they were "in favor of liberty," but some felt they were unworkable so long as the radicals also supported confiscation of property, which NUP officials labeled "an act of revolution [itself]."[8]

The NUP was Tom Ewing's first venture into politics outside the Republican Party. And at first blush there was not much difference between the party he was joining and the one he was leaving, especially on views as to whether blacks should be "elevated" to some sort of citizenship. The view is best summed up by Judge James Shackelford, who addressed an 1865 Republican convention:

7. "Go to hell" from *Crawford Telegram,* July 19, 1866; "unflinching courage" from Plummer, *Frontier Governor,* 67–69; "brains" from *Leavenworth Evening Bulletin,* July 21, 1866.

8. NUP outline from Taylor, "Business and Political Career," 176; TEJr. to TESr., June 26, 1866, EFP/LC.

> You are told by the enemies of the Government the federal authorities . . . will make the Negro your equal, giving him social and political rights. Those who make such statements know them to be false. . . . [The Negro] is inferior to the white man and will be controlled and governed by him subject to such laws as may be proposed for his government. . . . The God of nature has placed His fiat on it, and no power on earth can make him the equal of the Anglo-Saxon; but as Christian men we can elevate them in the scale of human beings . . . it is our duty as the superior race to control, govern and elevate them from the degraded situation in which they are.[9]

Frederick Douglass and other intellectuals of this era might have wondered just which party was the black man's champion.

In early August 1866 Tom joined his brother Hugh and Orville Browning for the NUP convention in Philadelphia. Johnson supporters, former copperheads, and Union Democrats dominated the convention. The speeches and resolutions blamed radicalism for all that was wrong with postwar America, including recent race riots in Memphis and New Orleans. Tom Ewing liked what he heard and wrote cousin James G. Blaine a letter seeking to justify Tom's willingness to ally himself with former rebels since Blaine's Republican Party was in no position to speak to national unity. "I am entirely satisfied with the course of the rebels and copperheads in the Phila. Convention—and am willing to vote with them to restore the Union now that my [Republican] party has failed [at unity]." Tom volunteered to organize the Soldiers' and Sailors' National Convention to blunt the growing political strength of the Grand Army of the Republic. Blaine did not bite at Tom's invitation to cross over to the NUP. Although recognizing Stanton's political excesses, Blaine still preferred the radicals to Andrew Johnson.[10]

Ewing's organizing efforts began at the Willard Hotel during the NUP convention and continued at the Soldiers' and Sailors' National Convention in Philadelphia. Former soldiers approving of Johnson's Restoration policies were encouraged to attend this satellite meeting. Among the prominent federal officers attending were George Custer, Irvin McDowell, and Dan McCook's brother Alex. Some, like Custer, were still on active duty. Former general James Blair Steedman was elected president and Hugh Ewing was named secretary of the convention. Those attending the convention also witnessed numerous blunders. Tom Ewing gave the major address of the convention and tried to focus attention on Recon-

9. Shackelford cited in Curry, *Radicalism,* 55.

10. For Browning's convention view, Browning, *Diary,* 2:88–89; "rebels and copperheads" from TEJr. to Blaine, August 31, 1866, EFP/LC, quoted in Taylor, "Business and Political Career," 178; Blaine's reaction from Hamilton, *James G. Blaine,* 213.

struction policies of the Congress. While he had once accepted the idea of the Fourteenth Amendment, he castigated it now if it meant that blacks could vote. His rhetoric got the better of him as he alluded to the New Orleans race riots as the natural reaction of "good citizens" who feared a "government of Negroes." Restoring the Union had been the only true basis for fighting the Civil War, and the war's outcome had decided the issue of whether states could secede. The war was fought, Ewing felt, to restore the national government, not allow that government to decide state issues concerning civil governments. Only the National Union Party, Ewing thundered, could preserve federalism, the Union, and the protections of the Constitution.[11]

Not everyone agreed. So strong were the pro-Southern statements at the convention that even Nathan Bedford Forrest endorsed the convention's goals. It is a measure of Ewingville's ongoing transformation in postwar politics that the family would take part in a convention that even tolerated Forrest's presence. It was clear that the Ewings were not radicalized enough to survive the postwar political pressures among Stanton's supporters. A political base for them, without going back to a discredited Democrat Party, meant pushing the NUP ticket as high and as far as it could go. Forrest's endorsement of the NUP, however, struck a blow at the entire Johnson campaign, and the radicals could not believe their good fortune. After the NUP convention, the president's support slipped rapidly. Never a good speech-maker, when he took his views on the road Johnson could not explain his vision of Reconstruction. He attacked Congress in words he could not retract, challenging them as the "real traitors" to American ideals, not the South. This infuriated Union war veterans. Senator James Doolittle wrote Browning that Johnson's trip had been a "fatal mistake." John Sherman realized that Tom Ewing was too involved with Johnson to be turned, but he sternly advised Cump to "stay away" from Johnson or risk losing all credibility.[12]

If nothing else, Andrew Johnson was stubborn. He fought on against the growing odds in the congressional campaigns. Over cabinet objections Johnson unilaterally restored full citizenship to Southerners through a simple oath of allegiance to the executive branch. Congress retaliated by passing laws excluding all landowners, senior officers in the Confederacy, and former government officials

11. Ewing, "Autobiography," 368–71; "government of Negroes" from Taylor, "Business and Political Career," 180; Curry, *Radicalism,* 122.

12. Johnson's barnstorming disaster, *Louisville Journal,* September 10, 12, 1866; "real traitors" from Marszalek, *Soldier's Passion,* 369; "fatal mistake" from Browning, *Diary,* 2:93n; John Sherman to WTS, September 25, 1866, from Marszalek, *Soldier's Passion,* 369.

with a net worth of more than $20,000 from any consideration for amnesty. Johnson finessed Congress by issuing presidential pardons, which Congress could not control. This pardon activity—a major drain on the president's time—spawned a new Washington industry of "amnesty brokers." Johnson's mass pardons slowed confiscation efforts. If a man's treason were pardoned, he could own property again and, as a citizen, could not have his property taken by the government without compensation. In the next few years Browning and Ewing became among the best brokers in town. Their first client was George Pickett. In Johnson's first two years, fifteen thousand applications for a general pardon were received, including one from Hugh Ewing's father-in-law, who needed his civil rights restored in order to press claims for damages for when his plantation was used as a Union cavalry depot and his croplands laid to ruin under tons of manure.[13]

With a president as a close friend and a growing network of friends who represented a considerable financial presence in the South, Tom Ewing's Republican credentials from prewar Kansas days put Browning and Ewing in good standing with Johnson's war against the radicals. Browning and Ewing advised Johnson to reject his earlier statements labeling Confederates as traitors worthy of impoverishment, and to consider reinstalling the Southern states into the Union with full political rights. As for enfranchising former slaves, Thomas Ewing Sr.'s influence on Johnson was evident. Whether the Ewings were falling back into an intolerant racism or simply adhering to that policy as a natural outgrowth of their growing list of pro-Southern activities is not clear. However, Tom Ewing told crowds that the Negro did not need "a ballot he doesn't want, can't read, and is notoriously unfit to use." Whether this represented Tom's true feelings about the newest American citizens is unknown, given the fact that he owed his life to a few dozen untrained black civilians who had stood beside him on the ramparts of Fort Davidson loading cannons and fighting off the assault troops of Sterling Price. It was, however, what he felt in the high tensions building in Washington in those days.[14]

In a meeting with the president on February 23, 1866, Browning, the new secretary of the Interior, suggested that the first shot at the radicals would be a change in the War Department and that General Tom Ewing should replace Stanton. A "fierce war" was going to be made upon Johnson by the radicals, and he would need good advisors. Hugh later claimed that Browning was going to suggest

13. Johnson's finesse from Lomask, *Andrew Johnson,* 111–13; "amnesty broker" from Browning, *Diary,* 2:32.

14. "Unfit" from undated speech to the Soldiers' and Sailors' National Convention, quoted in Taylor, "Business and Political Career," 175.

Hugh's father as Stanton's replacement, and it was Hugh who talked Browning into suggesting Tom, who was younger and, because of his Order Number 11, would be more likely to pass the radicals' hard scrutiny. Although either Ewing would have been acceptable to Johnson, he discounted even Tom's ability to withstand a confirmation fight over the removal of Stanton.[15]

In early November 1866 radical newspapers called on Americans to remember the sacrifices of the "spirits of the martyred dead," and in overwhelming numbers they did, repudiating Johnson's policies and electing a veto-proof Congress. Horace Greeley's *New York Tribune* chirped triumphantly that the people had spoken and the president should stop the "useless fights with loyal people." The normally serene Browning saw something more sinister in Johnson's loss. He believed the new Congress would impeach Johnson and "depose him."[16]

After the pivotal 1866 election gave Republican radicals overwhelming numbers in Congress, they planned their assault on the presidency to come from four angles. Stanton continued to solidify his power within the administration, in a cabinet led by a president he personally detested. Stanton was a minister without portfolio, who neither talked with the president nor supported him, and he came to few cabinet meetings. During the election he had grown suspicious that Johnson would install a pro-South Congress by fixing elections in Southern states. To ensure that the army would not assist this effort, Stanton persuaded Thaddeus Stevens to attach a proviso to an army appropriation bill prohibiting any army officer from following an order not signed by the general in chief, Ulysses S. Grant. Since a commander in chief should be able to work with military subordinates without going through the general in chief, Johnson asked his attorney general for an opinion on the constitutionality of this proviso. Henry Stanbery dubbed the "military despotism" portion of the bill a nullity and then spoke to the second part of the bill—that military district commanders in the South did not have authority under the act to write new laws for those areas but must work with local civil governments. The latter view would thwart the plans of the radicals who wanted key military commanders to usurp the state laws when it came to civil rights. From a practical view the despotism portion of the law did not limit much. Johnson could order Grant to sign an order and dismiss him if he disobeyed, if he wanted to endure the firestorm that would follow. Even with Stanbery's opin-

15. "Fierce war" from Browning, *Diary,* 2:63–64; Tom Ewing as secretary of war, in Blaine, *Twenty Years,* 2:363; also see Ewing, "Autobiography", 362.

16. "Martyred dead" from *New York Tribune,* November 6, 1866; "useless fights" from ibid., November 11, 1866; "depose" from Browning, *Diary,* 109.

ion, Johnson decided to sign the bill, but he reminded Congress, however, that he felt the despotism proviso was unconstitutional and he would ignore it.[17]

A second round of fire came when two Supreme Court justices died unexpectedly in December 1866. The 1866 Senate warning to the president was direct. By resolution, and before ever seeing his nominees, the Senate let Johnson know that not one of them would be considered favorably.[18]

A third effort was launched not so much at Johnson as at Great Britain. Thaddeus Stevens, the Speaker of the House, viewed the Southern states as despotic aristocracies. "If the South is ever to be made a safe republic, her land had to be cultivated by the toil of its owners and free labor of intelligent citizens. This must be done even if it drives the nobility into exile." Since British and New York banking interests owned most of the $3.5 billion in Southern plantation mortgages, confiscation would strike the greatest blow at the haughty British Empire through the soft underbelly of its financial institutions. It would also dethrone New York City as the national commercial center.[19]

The final act in the play that spring was when the new veto-proof Congress enacted the Tenure in Office Act in March 1867. By this law, once the Senate confirmed the appointment of any government official, then Senate approval was needed to remove that official. The legislation was applied retroactively to past appointees, which protected Stanton. While everyone but Stanton in the cabinet discussion of the act felt a veto was proper, the Senate overrode Johnson's veto quicker than he could get the veto to them. Violation was a "high misdemeanor," the trigger language of the Constitution's impeachment clause. The president was the only man in the country who could violate this law.[20]

Tom Ewing had no concerns about being labeled a Johnson supporter against these congressional encroachments on executive power. He sought affiliation with Johnson partly because he disliked radicalism but also because he was growing closer to Browning's line of thinking and conservative Democratic causes. It was clear that Southerners with money and prominence would not join the Republican Party banner, and he wanted such men to hire the influence his Washington law firm could provide. He was urbane, witty, handsome, and influential, a potent combination. His extended family (Thomas Ewing Sr., James Blaine, Cump

17. Lomask, *Andrew Johnson,* 239; "despotism" from Browning, *Diary,* 2:150n.

18. Lomask, *Andrew Johnson,* 240.

19. Ibid.; "nobility into exile," Stevens letter to Samuel May, quoted in Frederic W. Henderson, "Reconstruction: The Civil War Battle Yet to Be Won," 9, on the Internet at <http://american_almanac.tripod.com/fwhrecon.htm> last accessed April 8, 2008.

20. Cabinet solidarity from Browning, *Diary,* 2:132–33; "high misdemeanor" from Barrows, *William M. Evarts,* 139.

Sherman, and John Sherman) and his friends and colleagues such as Orville Browning and Henry Stanbery, along with dozens of bankers and industrialists throughout the East, formed a formidable power base.

With Tom's help, Johnson nominated Hugh Ewing in late 1866 to a posting in Johnson's State Department, representing the United States as the minister to The Hague. Without waiting on confirmation, Hugh left for Europe, taking his family with him to The Hague in the Netherlands until the seaside air drove him to more comfortable quarters in Paris. While Hugh faced a nasty confirmation fight, the family was confident that John Sherman and Edmund Ross could muscle Hugh through the process.

At this time, just before the impeachment hearings, Tom Ewing began to flirt with greenback ideas, a fact all the more interesting because of his Whig heritage. Coined money was specifically adopted by the constitutional convention as the means by which debts would be paid in the United States. States were prohibited from coining their own money or preparing scrip. As policy, paper money—bills of credit—were tolerated by the moneyed interests but only during times of national peril. However, almost immediately, the states flouted federal law, providing for their own means of paying debts and as mediums of exchange within their own boundaries. Strict adherence to gold and silver exchanges, greenback rhetoric claimed, might be a religion to the gold bugs but it limited the country's ability to expand its economy. Although nothing indicates that Ewing was aware of the data, the American economy grew from $3.8 billion in 1860 to $4.0 billion in 1864, in spite of a monumental war effort and the loss of the Southern states from the pie. While a gold standard and supply could perhaps handle a prewar economy, it was creaking at the hinges at rapid postwar developments.[21]

Greenback theory divided opinions in the country not only among political theorists but also among hostile classes. Monopolies, the argument went, eventually had enough power to confiscate private property through price-fixing and by keeping money scarce. Add to this high interest rates, also to be paid in gold, and the result was an enormous transfer of wealth from the middle class back to the money-lending sector. Keeping money scarce, an effort applauded by the rich, was accomplished by requiring that contracts be paid in specie rather than inflatable currency.

The irony in Johnson's earlier thoughts to nominate Tom Ewing to the cabinet was that Ewing's monetary views had more in common with those of Thad-

21. Ali Kahn, "The Evolution of Money: A Story of Constitutional Nullification," 404–6, 418–19; growth of economy, Paludan, *Abraham Lincoln,* 211.

deus Stevens, Ben Wade, and economist Henry Carey, who were Johnson's archenemies. Lincoln's and Johnson's Treasury departments were tied to the gold standard bankers that Ewing later derisively named "swallow tails." The radicals' aim was the destruction of English banking influence in America by seizing its Southern collateral, which Ewing outwardly opposed. Johnson recognized this schism between Tom Ewing's political and financial theories, even if Ewing had subordinated them to his general political disapproval of radicals and Edwin Stanton. When Johnson later considered changing the government's monetary policies to attract anti-impeachment support from key radicals, he privately discussed appointing Tom Ewing secretary of the treasury in place of Hugh McCulloch, a clear signal for a 180-degree directional turn in monetary policy. Although Johnson did not nominate Ewing, his even considering such a nomination was a measure of the attractiveness of the greenback cause to Southern interests.[22]

Ewing spent this portion of his life strengthening his law firm's involvement in developing railroad interests and employing his influence for friends and clients. In 1865 he was still a primary investor in the Missouri River Railroad, and the firm served as counsel for the Leavenworth, Lawrence & Galveston Railroad. After fighting the Kansas City concerns for so many years in Leavenworth, in 1868 Tom partnered with a variety of other men to form a town company that formed the heart of what became Kansas City, Kansas.

Ewing's influence in Washington and business circles was growing rapidly. In 1866 James McDowell sought his help in getting the postmaster position in Leavenworth. It was an easy choice for Johnson, as the ultra-radical publisher Daniel Anthony was the postmaster at the time. Pomeroy and Congressman Sidney Clarke struck back on Anthony's behalf, promising a better working relationship with the president if they controlled patronage in Kansas. Pomeroy was intensely disliked by the Ewings. Tom labeled him a "sanctimonious Radical spoilsman" in a letter to Thomas Carney and termed Anthony a "wretch." Anthony accused McDowell of taking a bribe to relocate the local post office in Leavenworth. Ewing asked Blaine to shepherd McDowell's nomination through the Senate, and McDowell was one of the few Johnson Democrat nominees to achieve confirmation.[23]

Ewing's economic visions were now international. Along with Henry de la Reintrie, former Pierce cabinet official Caleb Cushing, and Pittsburgh capitalist

22. "Swallow tails" from TEJr. to HBE, September 17, 1875, EFP/LC.

23. "Sanctimonious" from TEJr. to Thomas Carney, March 21, 1867, EFP/LC; "wretch" from TEJr. to McDowell, January 26, 1866, TEJr./KSHS; bribe allegation from TEJr. to McDowell, July 17, 1867, James L. McDowell Manuscript Collection, KSHS.

and cannon-maker Charles Knap, Ewing tried to secure a contract to build a railroad and telegraph across the isthmus of Tehuantepec. The deal collapsed when the Mexican government required the Yankee investors to absorb a previous contractor's debt in gold. Tom Ewing tried a similar deal in China, fronting for a New York corporation that wanted to construct a telegraph from Canton to Shanghai. However, unrest in China in 1867 made the venture too hazardous. His preference for the telegraph industry as the major transcontinental communication device was long-standing. Later, in 1883, he would begin a series of lawsuits against the Bell Company on behalf of Western Union Telegraph concerning Bell Labs inventions, including an objection to Alexander Graham Bell's patent of the telephone. Hindsight being what it is, clearly the more consumer-friendly technology was the telephone, and Ewing's blindness to changes in this technology cost him the ground-floor investment of a lifetime.[24]

As Americans approached the 1868 election, the more intense the battles became between Congress and Andrew Johnson. The possibility of impeachment was great. Within six months after the 1866 election, the radicals had sent him a series of bills that humiliated him, attempted to take away his constitutional powers, and threatened criminal prosecution if he changed the makeup of his cabinet. Johnson was an unlikely champion to defend the tripartite system of government and whether it would survive in America as envisioned by the Founding Fathers, but he did. Johnson was no Lincoln or Jackson, but he would declare war on Congress by testing the tenure act. He knew Congress would retaliate with impeachment, and he needed a good defense team. Ewingville friend and mentor Henry Stanbery was the first to resign his post as attorney general in order to head up the president's impeachment defense. Browning took over the duties of both the attorney general's office and secretary of the Interior until July 20, 1868, when a distant relative of Sherman's, William Evarts, became Johnson's new attorney general. If Tom Ewing was tempted to join the active defenders of Johnson, someone talked him into remaining in the background.[25]

The Ewings recommended that Johnson strike first by filling all open appointed positions with men personally loyal to the president. Johnson was in a procedural box, however. As president he had no means of forcibly removing his own secretary of war. As a means to bypass Stanton, Johnson appointed Grant as temporary secretary of war; however, Johnson then required Grant to agree that,

24. Overseas investments from Taylor, "Business and Political Career," 213–15; blind to telephone investment from conversation with Ewing scholar Walter Busch.

25. Browning, *Diary,* 2:187n.

as general in chief, he would not execute any request or order unless fully satisfied it came from Johnson. This prompted an exchange of letters that went public, which angered Grant and cemented his break with the Johnson administration. He resigned his temporary secretary of war posting. On January 13, 1868, the Senate formally rejected Johnson's suspension of Stanton, which, as far as Congress was concerned, restored him to the cabinet.

On February 20, 1868, the same day the House voted overwhelmingly to impeach the president, he no longer had any reason to hold back his true feelings about Stanton. For a second time Johnson considered sending Tom Ewing's name to the Senate as secretary of war. This time the Old Salt Boiler was adamantly against it. His son Tom was not going to be cannon fodder for the U.S. Senate, not so long as he had an opportunity in 1868 or 1872 as a Democratic candidate for higher office. Thomas Ewing also had another reason, however. Ben Wade was one of few men whom Thomas Ewing Sr. considered a mortal enemy. As Senate Majority Leader, Wade stood to be president if Johnston were impeached. If this happened the Ewings and Browning would have no influence left anywhere in Washington. Any civil servant who spoke to the Ewings would be cashiered and no client would have entrée anywhere in Washington. Thomas Ewing Sr.'s name was sent up as the replacement for Stanton.[26]

Ewing Sr.'s appointment presented the Senate with a clear breach of the Tenure in Office Act. The House adopted thirteen articles of impeachment, separated into four main accusations, focusing primarily on the allegation that Johnson attempted to remove Stanton without Senate permission. The lesser charges were that Johnson influenced the army improperly, refused to cooperate with Congress by not enforcing civil rights legislation in the South, and had criticized the Congress. None of the charges hinted at corruption, just differences of political opinion on postwar policy. Unlike impeachments of other presidents that were based at least in part on criminal activity, Johnson's impeachment was based on politics alone.[27]

Eventually the focus was on Washington, however. State governments filtered constituent feelings and sent demanding letters to their senators on how to vote. Both the friends of impeachment and Johnson's followers brought their long-

26. Second effort for Tom Ewing as secretary of war and vice presidential discussions from Castel, *Frontier State,* 228.

27. Although historians may disagree about whether there was any valid basis to President Clinton's impeachment, the author believes that lying under oath in a deposition meets the "high crime or misdemeanor" standard.

winded street harangues to rally support. The mall became a sort of Hyde's Park, speakers hailing passersby and, within rock-throwing distance of each other, thundering their views in long-winded speeches separated by a scattered line of police. Tom Ewing was among the anti-impeachment speakers and once debated General William Stokes, a former commander of loyalist Tennessee cavalry. Ewing began his speech "uncharacteristically swayed by the most intense excitement." With a face darkened by passion and a voice that could be heard above all the noise of the crowd, he argued that men such as Stokes intended to destroy the government, and there would be all kinds of disasters if a president was impeached. If Americans did not like Johnson's policies, they should vote him out. Impeachment was illegal under such circumstances. Benjamin Simpson left the square after the speech with General James Blunt, who remarked that he had "never liked Ewing, never thought he was sincere. But that is the most tragic and impassioned speech I ever heard." Simpson was incredulous that Ewing's speech had not sparked a riot.[28]

At the White House the pressure grew. Tom Ewing helped Andrew Johnson behind the scenes with undecided senators. The defense team decided early that the article of impeachment on Stanton and the Tenure in Office Act was Congress's strongest point. If two-thirds of the senators would not impeach on that article, all other accusations would fall. It was a technical defense requiring analysis of constitutional law, and it was risky. Johnson's defense had to peel away the anti-Johnson votes one at a time. They went to work.

It is ironic that Tom Ewing's argument for Johnson's position on the tenure act was actually contrary to the position his father had taken as a sitting senator against the removals exercised by Andrew Jackson in 1836. At that time then-senator Thomas Ewing Sr. argued the Whig doctrine that incoming presidents' practice of removing public officers for any reason other than malfeasance in office was hostile to the spirit of the Constitution and dangerous to the liberties of the people. Ewing Sr. was fighting the nation's first attempt by a president to provide the "spoils" of a successful campaign to his supporters. It was an anti-patronage view bordering on what later would find its way into debates over a new federal civil service. It applied, of course, to all appointed officers, including cabinet members. Ewing Sr. had argued that since the power to remove was neither a specifically delegated power nor inherent in the executive powers, Congress could regulate how and when removal occurred. While the Whig reading of the removal powers was

28. "Swayed" from Martin, *Proceedings and Debates,* 659; "never liked Ewing" from Monaghan, *Civil War,* 349.

contrary to Madison's detailed notes of the 1789 convention, the Whigs simply argued Madison was wrong. Such language from Whigs concerning a Democratic president's power was powerful justification for the 1867 tenure act.[29]

Tom was trapped by his father's previous work and needed a counterargument. In this he got help from the original author. Ewing Sr. suggested his old anti-Jackson arguments did not apply because the Whigs had not advocated that removal be made a crime. The fight between the Whigs and the Democrats had been to outline the contours of political patronage, not a pretext for impeaching Andrew Jackson. The Tenure in Office Act was unconstitutional, Thomas Ewing confided, on that thought alone; but if it were indeed constitutional it could not apply to Stanton since Stanton was appointed by Lincoln, not Johnson. As the Old Salt Boiler knew well, new presidents needed their own cabinet members. If a tenure law were to make any sense, it had to limit the president who made the original appointment.[30]

Since the Senate had charged the president with defying Congress, the president's handlers urged a secondary defense strategy coinciding nicely with Tom Ewing's monetary views. While the nation could survive the political impeachment of Johnson, the country's financial situation would "go to ruin" under president pro tem Benjamin Wade. Without a vice president in office, the president pro tem of the Senate would succeed Johnson to the presidency. The only thing a president could truly do wrong in office, cotton financier Edward Atkinson wrote his friends, was to "tamper with the currency." As an indication of the unusual support Johnson received from men who ordinarily were his enemies, Atkinson wrote Hugh McCulloch, "I am endeavoring with some others who are known as extreme radicals to give such direction to the reorganization of the South as shall prevent the creation of an exclusive black men's party and also to kill the scheme of confiscation." Atkinson also reported he was attempting to elect Southern delegations "not under Thad Stevens's lead on tariff and currency questions, but of this I am not hopeful." Wade would remove McCulloch from the cabinet (with the blessing of some radicals, of course), and this change would bring greenback legitimacy and ruin to larger banks. Johnson, the argument went, intended no such change in McCulloch's position and was, therefore, the preferred among evil choices.[31]

29. "Hostile to the spirit" from Leonard White, *The Jacksonians,* 40–41.

30. Exception to Whig theory from ibid.

31. Both quotes Atkinson to McCulloch, August 7, 1867, in Letterbook, vol. 3 (July 26, 1867, to December 2, 1869), Edward Atkinson Papers, Massachusetts Historical Society.

This financial argument was a powerful one to a few senators who looked beyond the petty nonsense of the tenure act. James Garfield speculated that, if impeachment came, Wade intended to appoint E. B. Ward to the Treasury Department. Ward was a leading greenback man described as a man of "violent passions, extreme opinions and narrow views with a grossly profane coarse nature who was surrounded by the worst and most violent elements in the Republican Party." Editor Horace White wrote Representative E. B. Washburn that "the gathering of evil birds around Wade leads me to think a worse calamity might befall the Republican Party than the acquittal of Johnson." Slowly a hard-money anti-impeachment coalition was building, and Republican senators began privately to splinter along financial persuasions before the impeachment proceedings even opened.[32]

With the elite of Washington society in the Senate galleries, the "Great American Farce" began on March 13, 1868. Ben Butler's opening speech on behalf of the Senate managers labored on for more than three hours, and he concluded the U.S. Senate could oust the president of the United States whenever the House of Representatives brought bills of impeachment to the Senate and any two-thirds of them had the votes to do so. It was an argument with a dangerous precedent, but Butler and the radicals did not care.[33]

A month of testimony, charges, and countercharges carried the trial into early April. The defense opened its case on April 9, 1868. Benjamin Curtis's opening statement was a course in basic civics. And while Curtis was stage-managing the live testimony, Tom Ewing and William Evarts were lining up political favors for no votes. William Fessenden and Lyman Trumbull were obtaining assurances that, if acquitted, the president would not make reprisals. Senators such as Edmund Ross of Kansas let Johnson know through intermediaries that if Johnson would approve pro-radical state constitutions submitted by carpetbagging governments in South Carolina and Arkansas, such activity would have a "salutary influence" on the views of some senators concerning impeachment. Johnson could take a hint, and he signed the bills.[34]

Tom Ewing wrote Hugh in Brussels that, although the case was going well for the House managers, he predicted the radicals were not above shenanigans. Indeed Butler boasted after the impeachment that he had sent spies to break into Evarts's room at the Willard Hotel and search for information that might benefit

32. Garfield speculation about Ward and "gathering of evil birds" from Henderson, "Reconstruction."

33. "Farce" from Barrows, *William M. Evarts,* 144.

34. Curtis's statement from ibid., 149; Ross's overture by Browning, *Diary,* 2:195.

the House, a nineteenth-century second-rate burglary. Tom predicted that Hancock would be the Democrat nominee in 1868 and would carry the white states, but the "impeachers are revolutionists" and would use "fraud and force in the elections." Both parties, he predicted, would arm and settle the election with the sword.[35]

On April 21, 1868, final arguments began. Evarts suggested the president send up General John Schofield as the nominee to replace Stanton. Schofield was identified with the radicals, which allowed Evarts to pose the question in the Senate: Why, if Johnson were anti-radical, would he be willing to appoint a radical to his cabinet? Schofield's nomination did not stop the Senate's proceedings. When Evarts finished his summation, the prosecution had the last rebuttal. Stevens, frail and tired, virtually confessed the weakness in the House's case when he said, "No corrupt or wicked motive need instigate the acts for which impeachment is brought." Then the managers sat down. Behind the scenes Thomas Ewing Sr. had been charting the doubtful senators. With Johnson's fate now up to the U.S. Senate, a dozen Republicans held his fate in their hands. Thomas Ewing Sr. wrote Tom that "tall men" must be found who were not "overawed and driven to judicial perjury by threats or party clamor."[36]

Before the impeachment vote, Kansans began to hear alarming rumors that Edmund Ross's friendship with a known associate of the president, Tom Ewing, might cause Ross to reconsider his vote. When Governor Samuel Crawford first heard the rumors, he termed them "fabrications." However, Ewing had indeed spoken with Ross, just as the Senate managers and radicals within the Republican Party had also worked each wavering senator. West Virginia senators were told the wild tale that, if Johnson was not impeached, he and the copperheads would become stronger and would sweep to victory in 1868, upsetting Grant as well as undoing the war's gains, which would send West Virginia back into the Old Dominion of Virginia! The president's men then had to convince the senators otherwise.[37]

Tom Ewing's relationship with Edmund Ross had been forged in Kansas politics and in the dusty bivouacs of the Eleventh Kansas infantry. Each man respected the other, and there was nothing they would not do for each other. Ross

35. "Spies" from Barrows, *William M. Evarts,* 149; TEJr. to HBE, April 17, 1868, EFP/LC.

36. Stevens from Barrows, *William M. Evarts,* 152; TESr. to TEJr., around mid-April 1868, quoted in Lomask, *Andrew Johnson,* 317.

37. "Fabrications" from Plummer, *Frontier Governor,* 107; West Virginia argument from Curry, *Radicalism,* 97.

had come to Topeka in 1856 and then moved west into Wabaunsee County. As a newspaper editor he helped construct the state's Wyandotte Constitution. Of slight build, he was "mild and shrinking in manner," but he made up for his stature with boundless energy and courage. He had two horses shot out from under him at the Battle of the Little Blue, near Westport.[38]

This was a different war, however, requiring different courage. In their discussions Ewing told Ross that the impeachment was designed to make Wade the president, in order to control the entire government. This was a usurpation that no man who fought for the Union should support. The fight had turned into a political battle of will between coequal branches of government. Ewing knew what Ross needed as a senator—the power of patronage. Jobs for political supporters were the stuff upon which nineteenth-century politics was built. Patronage gave a public servant influence in the city and county politics beneath him, and power up the chain of authority, too. Since those with the jobs were often voluntarily assessed a portion of their salary for assisting the success of the patron, large numbers of patronage jobs became a tax-supported form of campaign financing. With the friends of state legislators holding federal positions, the implication was that if the appointing senator was not returned to office by the state legislature, the jobs for their friends would disappear, too. This gave politicians a hard-working base of support in their districts, which translated to reelection. With Johnson in office, Pomeroy, an ultra-radical, had little chance of getting anyone he championed into federal positions in Kansas. If Johnson was ousted, however, Wade would favor Pomeroy's appointments in Kansas, and not Ross's. Ewing suggested that Ross vote for impeachment if his vote did not matter. However, his vote would come well on down the alphabetical roll call. If his vote was decisive, he had to do the right thing—not only for the president but also for himself.[39]

Before the first crucial vote the Republican national committee chair, Hugh Ewing's old commanding officer Robert Schenck, sent scores of telegrams to radical newspaper editors in the states with wavering senators urgently encouraging grassroots campaigns to pressure those senators such as Ross. Ross's continued silence only increased the pressure from Kansas. Daniel Anthony wired Ross on May 16, "Kansas has heard the evidence and demands the conviction of the President." Ross telegraphed Anthony, "I do not recognize your right that I shall vote either for or against conviction. I have taken an oath to do impartial justice . . .

38. "Manner" from Lomask, *Andrew Johnson,* 319; Ross at the Battle of the Little Blue, *O.R.* 41:1:593; also Martin, *Proceedings and Debates,* 661.

39. Ewing's discussion with Ross from Eugene Berwanger, "Ross and the Impeachment: A New Look at a Critical Vote," 236–38.

for the highest good of my country." Ross's reply poked at the old political maxim: never argue with anyone who buys ink by the barrel. Anthony reprinted Ross's telegraph in the newspaper and fired off his public response: "Your telegram received. Your vote is dictated by Tom Ewing, not by your oath. Your motives are Indian contracts and greenbacks. Kansas repudiates you as she does all perjurers and skunks!" When more word came that Ross was backsliding, Pomeroy met him at the Senate door before the 10:30 vote. Pomeroy snapped that a vote for acquittal would be political suicide and that Pomeroy would ask personally for an investigation of bribery.[40]

The voting began with high drama. Senator James Grimes was recovering from a stroke but was determined to participate. Roll call was taken alphabetically. To each senator Chase put the question "How say you, is the respondent, Andrew Johnson, President of the United States, guilty or not guilty of a high misdemeanor, as charged in this article of impeachment?" By the time Ross was called upon to vote, there were fourteen not-guilty votes. Four more expected no votes would come from the Democrats whose names were behind him. That would give the President eighteen votes, but there were no more undecided Republican votes behind Ross. His vote would either impeach or acquit the president of the United States. Nervously Ross played with a paper on his desk, tearing it to strips. When the chief justice asked the question of Edmund Ross, the short man from Kansas put down the paper, stood next to his desk, and said to the hushed Senate, "Not Guilty."[41]

The galleries exploded. Newspapermen ran for the telegraph office. The voting went on, icily and quickly, to its ordained conclusion. Johnson supporters were jubilant. Hugh Ewing chortled all the way from Europe, "Seven have returned, not lost, out of the many fallen [heroes]," although he wrote Browning that since the radicals took office, "it would take years to air the Senate Chamber and make it fit once more for occupation."[42]

Tom Ewing's efforts with Ross did indeed prove fateful. One can argue that radical Reconstruction was completely on target and on schedule until Ross's vote derailed the effort. While the vote did not slow the advance of radicalism toward electing a new president in 1868, Johnson's impeachment victory gave Democrats new heart and fight, and above all, the notion that hard work by Democrats might just pay off even against Stanton and the enormously popular Grant. Ross's vote

40. All telegrams printed in the *Leavenworth Daily Conservative,* May 17, 1868.
41. Lomask, *Andrew Johnson,* 329, 332, 344.
42. "Seven have returned" from Ewing, "Autobiography," 415.

bought Democrats a year without the influences of Benjamin Wade, who would have been the interim president of the United States. What roads to radicalism might have been forged then are now speculative. When news of the victory reached the White House, Browning wrote that Johnson "received the congratulations of the cabinet with the same serenity and self-possession which have characterized him throughout this terrible ordeal." Within a few weeks Stanton resigned as secretary of war and faded out of sight, Schofield was named to replace Stanton, and life went on.[43]

Tom Ewing's postwar efforts to build a law practice in Washington were intensified by his defense of Mudd and by his efforts for Johnson during the impeachment crisis. His efforts also reached back into Kansas once more. This time instead of land speculation or Free State politics, he was involved in helping various railroads acquire key routes. The rapid onset of war after Kansas statehood had not given the Department of the Interior time to solidify its land acquisition policies in the newest state. This malaise lingered on throughout the war. If land policy was abused by Buchanan, the Lincoln, Johnson, and Grant administrations did not remedy the overall situation in any way. Indian lands remained open to barter, and Ewing helped set the price. After the war, however, he worked not only for the railroads but also for the tribes. Ewing no longer owned stock in the LP&W (now known as the Union Pacific, Eastern Division). The sale of his stock is a story unto itself.[44]

Construction began on the LP&W in November 1862, just as Ewing was leading the Eleventh Kansas in northwest Arkansas. In six months, only one mile of roadbed had been graded and track laid. The company was in severe debt, and fresh infusions of cash were desperately needed. True to the times, because money for trackage was so hard to come by, the key for the acquiring entity was to buy a controlling interest of stock with as little cash as possible. In May 1863 John Fremont and Sam Hallett proved the best at this game. Fremont had resigned from the army and had done well in business with his father-in-law, Thomas Hart Ben-

43. Browning, *Diary,* 2:199–200. There is no paper trail concerning Tom Ewing's direct influence on Ross's key impeachment vote. The circumstantial evidence is there, however. Walt Busch notes in his thesis on Ewing that in 1894 Ross asked Ewing's help in finding a publisher for a book on the impeachment. Much can be made from the following statement by Ross: "Your habitually candid, conservative judgment and strong common sense, upon which I have so many times implicitly relied in the past, peculiarly fits you to advise me & I shall rely very much upon what you may suggest." Ross to TEJr., July 10, 1894, EFP/LC, from Busch, "Mistake of Your Life."

44. For information in the next few paragraphs, I am indebted in large part to Taylor, "Origins of the Kansas Pacific."

ton. Hallett was a scrappy financial agent for the successful Atlantic & Great Western railroad.

Fremont and Hallett approached Tom Ewing about buying him out. Ewing sold three-fourths of his holdings in the railroad as part of the overall sale price for the road, $200,000. But before the conclusion of the deal, corporate infighting broke out between Fremont and Hallett, with each man trying to buy the allegiance of LP&W stockholders. Fremont paid Tom Ewing and the other stockholders about a tenth of the cash that was obligated under their agreement. The remainder was deposited in trust with Washington Hunt, a New York banker, to be paid when the LP&W's incorporators completed their list of terms in the contract by July 12, 1863.

The Fremont-Hallett consortium was well aware that they were buying into an important piece of the transcontinental railroad. Fremont was to be the president of the new railroad, but Hallett was the brains and muscle. Fremont had political connections, but Hallett's extensive network of European bankers and wealthy friends was in the end more important. In their business dealings they resembled two veterans squaring off with fixed bayonets. Hallett's concern was with the "quality" of the roadbed. The new purchase contract required Ewing and LP&W stockholder James Stone to issue new mortgages covering the railroad's rolling stock. The contract also stated that they would be paid after the railroad began receiving government entitlements once the track was laid. Since this might never happen, there was considerable risk that Ewing and Stone would never be paid. Since the rolling stock of the line was previously mortgaged to Ross, Steele & Company as security for that company's construction of what track was already laid, these second mortgages impaired title to the railroad and guaranteed that lawsuits would be necessary to clear them up.[45]

Stockholders James Stone, Andrew Isaacs, and Tom Ewing remained with Hallett for a while, but when Isaacs and Stone followed James McDowell and sold out their stock for a lesser sum than what he was entitled to, Ewing agreed to sell before he lost everything. He received a reduced sum in return for signing over his directorship and was out of the railroad business in Kansas.[46]

However, after the war Tom Ewing was willing to lend his skills to benefit railroad expansion. He owned short portions of what became the Ohio Central Railroad, which catered primarily to the West Virginia coal fields until it went bank-

45. Details in James C. Stone to TESr., June 18, 1863, quoted in Taylor, "Origins of the Kansas Pacific," 174.

46. TEJr. to TESr., January 4, 1864, quoted in Taylor, "Business and Political Career," 148.

rupt during Reconstruction. Ewing's postwar interest in greenback monetary systems for the common man dovetailed nicely into his representation of railroads. Railroad tycoons wanted farmers and merchants to repay debts to the railroads with gold, but the tycoons themselves were not wedded to the idea of repaying their own bank loans in gold specie. Ewing's positions were a bit convoluted at this point. While he eagerly represented railroad interests, he also took some time off to help draft a new Ohio constitution, which had a provision in it that prevented Ohio elected officials from accepting any gratuitous service from a railroad, such as free rides on the railroad to Columbus to legislative sessions.[47]

For his abilities to engineer favorable results for an underdog president, Tom Ewing's influence on Democrats was growing. This made Ewing a force to be reckoned with and a stern, hard-bitten lobbyist. The remaining Indian lands were essential to the transcontinental railroad and the expansion of the West. This time the tribes hired Ewing and made him an advocate for their own railroad interests. Working on behalf of the tribes now, he did not like what he saw brewing in the Department of the Interior.

Lincoln had appointed James Harlan as secretary of the Interior, but Harlan was a man who was never happy unless he was manipulating events, all the while demonstrating as few scruples as possible. He worked a secret deal to sell eight hundred thousand acres of the Cherokee reserve in southeast Kansas to the American Emigrant Company (AEC), a large speculation company that wanted to build a railroad from Kansas City to Fort Scott, the beginning link of a major north–south artery of commerce from Arkansas, the Indian Territories, and eastern Texas to the transcontinental road, connecting in Kansas City. This tract of Indian land was commonly called the Neutral Tract, and there were thousands of squatters already on the land. Harlan's deal with the AEC made sure the company could oust squatters and resell the land for operating capital. In a swindle of national proportions, Harlan's deal did not require the AEC to buy the land with cash. It just had to pay 5 percent simple interest rate on the government's paper value of the land in the Neutral Tract. The AEC was getting the land for next to nothing.

In 1866 Johnson's relationship with Harlan soured, and Browning was named to replace him. Harlan wanted to stay in office to clear his desk of some last-minute items, one of which was the AEC sale. Ewing took offense at Harlan's shenanigans and wrote Harlan that his backroom sale was coming from a "pious

47. Ewing's railroad efforts in Ohio from *The Official Report of the Proceedings and Debates of the Third Constitutional Convention of Ohio, 1873–1874* (Cleveland, Ohio: W. S. Robinson and Co., 1873), 68.

swindler" and an "enormous corruption." Ewing made sure his attack was printed in several national newspapers. One Kansas newspaper summed up Harlan's career with a cryptic notation that Kansas, like Iowa, sent "pickpockets [as its] Senators." This charge was leveled at Harlan because, although he resigned, it was only to take an Iowa gubernatorial appointment to the U.S. Senate where, in 1868, he worked for the impeachment of his former boss.[48]

The AEC deal left a bitter aftertaste from Harlan's ventures. When the details of the contract were leaked, it became a major scandal of the Johnson administration. To control the damage Johnson asked Tom Ewing to explain what was happening. During his cotton negotiations in Arkansas for Adie Douglas, Ewing had negotiated the 1866 Cherokee Treaty as the tribe's agent and, indirectly, for the tribe's creditors. Ewing had argued that what was good for the tribe was good for their creditors, thus aligning their potentially conflicting positions. Ewing's postwar reputation was growing. He had become such a "go-to" person on railroad issues that it was known in Washington any businessman wanting to be successful need only hire Ewing. Ewing had no problem nixing the AEC deal—he only needed to conference with his former law partner, Orville Browning, whose interest in skewering any idea of Harlan's was acute. The cancellation helped Ewing with his other clients, the tribes.[49]

However, Johnson did not want to cancel the sale of these Indian lands entirely. He still wanted to see the transcontinental railroad completed, although it was clear this would not happen during his second term. While the main line was to be from Omaha, west through Wyoming, Utah, Nevada, and into northern California, there was still a scramble to build feeder lines to the national road. Approval of a new treaty using Indian lands for trunk lines depended on its terms. Johnson felt he could avoid public and congressional criticism if he forced a cash sale of the land to a railroad. He relayed this suggestion to Browning, who agreed. The Tebo & Neosho Railroad offered a deal similar to the AEC's, but with more cash available. Browning rejected the proposal because not all of it was in cash. The UP-Southern Branch also made an offer, as did a third road, John Fremont's Atlantic & Pacific. Fremont's offer was a total of $1 million for the tract, with $150,000 up front, $150,000 in two years, and the balance in five years. Fremont's

48. TEJr. to James Harlan, August 29, 1866, in ibid., 156–57; "pickpockets" from the *Fort Scott Monitor,* January 12, 1872. For the information in the next few paragraphs I am indebted in large part to the late Professor Paul Gates's seminal work on Kansas land speculation, *Fifty Million Acres,* 157–84.

49. Gates, *Fifty Million Acres,* 158.

offer was not cash, but it was the best non-cash offer of all. Fremont persuaded Browning to allow him to negotiate a treaty on those terms. Browning and Johnson agreed to the proposal and sent it to Congress for approval.[50]

With Ewing representing the tribe, with his closeness to Browning, and even his grudging respect of Fremont the tycoon, it is hard to believe he was not involved in getting Browning's favorable reception to Fremont's offer. The tribes were losing their land anyway, and they wanted to be paid as much as possible for the tract. This was in the tribe's best interests—and in the best interests of their creditors. Like the AEC deal, the Fremont deal also allowed the railroad to jettison the nearly twenty thousand Kansans living in the tract and to resell the land. This term, when made public, caused among settlers an uproar against the "land sharks." Although the tribes did not care, every white politician in Kansas rallied to their aid, urging Congress and the president to kill this sale too.[51]

At this moment, a third element entered the fray. Ewing's old Leavenworth competitor James F. Joy owned the Chicago, Burlington & Quincy and the Hannibal & St. Joseph railroads. As ruthless as he was crafty, Joy's intentions with Fremont's ideas would bring to mind the image of a mongoose stalking a cobra. Joy intended to expand his longitudinal routes, acquiring the St. Joseph & Council Bluffs road and chartering a southern Kansas route through Fort Scott. He raised $750,000 from cities along the Fort Scott route and obtained a significant concession from the Kansas state government. Joy informed the federal government he would pay the same $1 million as pledged by Fremont, but on better terms for the government. The price of Joy's involvement, however, was that Ewing's pro-Cherokee treaty with Fremont's road had to be repudiated. Considerable sums of money were used by both Joy's and Fremont's supporters in lobbying the U.S. Senate. Using prewar tactics Joy tried to prove to Browning that dissident Cherokees felt the treaty was unfair and that Fremont was trying to "soak the Senate floor" with cash to swindle the Indians. Joy's tactics created enough doubt that Fremont's deal was rejected, including the treaty Ewing had negotiated. The late historian Paul W. Gates, whose life works studied these events closely, concluded that Joy's forces simply "outbid" Fremont's on the Senate floor.[52]

Browning's vacillation puzzled Tom Ewing. The administration was under enormous pressure from Kansas politicians over these Neutral Tracts. The secretary kept pushing for a cash sale, but none was offered. The tight-fisted and unscrupulous

50. Ibid., 159.
51. Ibid., 160.
52. Ibid.

Joy was still finagling. Now that Fremont's offer was off the table, Joy's deal required a lot of cash, and Joy was bent on getting as much of the Neutral Tract for as much credit as he could manage. However, Browning held firm. On October 9, 1867, with talk of impeachment filling Washington, Browning agreed to let Joy buy the reserve for one dollar an acre, cash up front, but without ejecting the settlers. The settlers could buy their existing lands for the same price. Whether the funds came from Joy or the settlers, Joy would get use of the funds to build his road. When the AEC threatened to sue the government and Joy for specific performance on their old contract, Joy bought out their interests. When the deal with Joy was announced, accusations came that Browning had been corrupted. Nobody could prove anything. And this time Johnson did not cancel the sale.[53]

While Washington was distracted with impeachment talk, all hell broke loose in Kansas. Under Joy's deal settlers in the Neutral Tract who had already paid for their claims had to pay again. When they balked, they were summarily thrown off their land by a mixture of railroad thugs and quiet title lawsuits. The storm produced by the deal in southeast Kansas was part of the Kansas pressure on Ross and Pomeroy to support impeachment.

Bleeding Kansas erupted again in southeast Kansas. This time the antislavery element was replaced by the anti-railroad efforts of the Cherokee Neutral Land League. A squatter association of sorts, they held mass meetings where the speakers reviled Joy, Ross, and Pomeroy for their support of the treaty change. Many of the settlers were former Union soldiers, which brought into the equation the growing power of the Grand Army of the Republic. Many had settled in the Neutral Tracts on the theory that the Cherokee had helped the Confederacy during the war and so they had forfeited their rights to the land just like the Southern plantation owners. Violence grew. Land offices in Baxter Springs were raided, records were destroyed, and railroad survey parties and construction crews were attacked. The land league was alleged to be in league with Joy's competitors. Their threats, however, were real enough. Anyone buying the railroad's land was warned they would not live to sell their property to others. Two men died that way, in the night. The sheriff who tried to arrest the suspects was declared insane by a local judge. As well as perpetrating local intimidation, the land league heavily influenced the legislature in Topeka, arguing that "The west was smothered with land monopolies" and something had to be done.[54]

Ewing's thoughts during all this unexpected unrest are hard to determine. He

53. Ibid., 167.
54. "Land monopolies," ibid., 174.

was not a man who tolerated anarchy, and anarchy was what he saw across southeast Kansas. It was anarchy with considerable credibility in the Kansas legislature. The land league was too quick to cause mayhem, and thus no different from the old war wing of the Free State party. He was on first-name terms with important industrialists, not the squatters on Kansas's Indian lands. Ewing watched Joy try to slow the growing public outrage. Joy started newspapers to get out his message, or he bought large ads in other papers. He bribed land league leaders with lifetime railroad passes. He sent private detectives to league meetings looking for any signs of criminal conspiracies he could report to federal authorities. Nothing worked. The violence escalated. Eventually Governor Thomas Carney asked that four companies of federal cavalry be sent to the Neutral Tract to keep order.

Attempts to get Congress to reject the new deal fell flat. The Kansas legislature tried to enact "squatters first" rights to any of the Indian lands scheduled to be sold to the railroad. However, state legislation could not override a federal treaty. Members of the land league placed their final faith in a direct appeal to Johnson to squelch the deal. Their faith was ill-placed. Johnson's advisors were men of property who disliked squatters.

This railroad controversy continued throughout the Johnson administration and into Grant's. Ewing was unable to assist Joy within the Grant administration, but he did have influence with James Blaine, a Ewing cousin and Speaker of the House. Eventually, the small landowners of Kansas pooled their funds and hired lawyers for the U.S. Supreme Court, where, in 1872, they argued the tribe did not have the right to sell their tracts to Joy. Although Joy prevailed at the national level, the carping about the deal continued in Kansas. In the 1873 Panic Joy's railroad aspirations in the Neutral Tract came to a halt, then his railroad faced receivership.[55]

President Johnson became increasingly isolated as the nation awaited his successor. Tom Ewing felt he had to try at least to keep sanity in Washington if only for the sake of his own future. Having helped organized the National Union Party in 1866, he used the NUP spin-off group, the Soldiers' and Sailors' National Convention, to give Democrats respectability. On July 4, 1868, Ewing gave a keynote speech at the convention. His views against radicals and radicalism had hardened since 1866 and moved toward a growing racial bias, which appeared in this speech. He argued that any integration had to be gradual and supervised, and that suffrage was not a right blacks should acquire overnight. His references to

55. Ibid., 183–84; *Holden v. Joy*, 84 U.S. (17 Wall.) 211.

blacks as "boorish field hands" and only "half-civilized" showed that his thinking put him inside the mainstream of Democrat theory at the time.[56]

The difference between radicalism and the form of social experimentation embraced by Tom Ewing was that Ewing believed three hundred years of slavery could not be changed overnight. Change had to be individualized, and implemented state by state. This was the essence of the Union they had fought to save. Control was not turned over to a national government without thought. Looking at the same history of the same three centuries, the radicals on the other hand mistrusted state governments and preferred a central authority to control the change. Ewing's view was the weaker, given the history of antebellum America and Reconstruction. The states had acted as the chief impediments to change during the past fifty years, and there was no indication that the Southern states especially would initiate bold action. What good was freedom or equal rights, the radicals argued, if the strong retained a continuing license to oppress the weak?

In stump speeches Ewing railed against the radical vision of Reconstruction. "It is unmanly and inhuman to subjugate [the South] to a race so inferior to them—a race in the history of mankind that has never given any evidence of capacity of self government. It is madness, and frenzy and fanaticism to do so." In another remarkable discussion, Ewing commented that he was "most unwilling to have a black daughter-in-law." This sort of narrow assumption—that Ewing's sons would choose black wives—had widespread appeal in a fearful postwar white America facing integration.[57]

Although he had fought Southern secession on the battlefield and led troops whose national purpose was to free slaves, that had been war, and business was business. While Ewing was not afraid to associate with Southerners such as James Hammond, this did not mean he would associate himself with the violence brought on blacks in the South after Reconstruction. A great many public men openly assisted freedmen to better themselves and their families while at the same time harboring racist views—men such as Jim Lane, Ben Wade, and Thaddeus Stevens. Lane once crassly told admirers that he would "rather own a nigger than a mule." He had changed rapidly into a self-proclaimed abolitionist and during the war was creating black combat regiments long before Lincoln issued the Emancipation Proclamation and before Hollywood's preferred black regiment

56. Ewing speech at the Soldiers' and Sailors' National Convention, July 4, 1868, quoted in Rowland, "Thomas Ewing Jr.," 12.

57. "Unmanly and inhuman" from a speech in Portland, Maine, quoted in the *New York World*, September 8, 1868, and referenced in Taylor, "Business and Political Career," 173; "daughter-in-law" from Lawanda Cox and John H. Cox, *Politics, Principle and Prejudice, 1865–1866*, 217.

charged on Fort Fisher. Ewing may have remained indifferent to integration as a business response, but he always preferred moderate and conservative politicians to wild-eyed true believers on any topic, whether abolitionists or segregationists. While his views were not politically correct from the aspect of men and women in the post–civil rights era of twentieth-century America, Tom Ewing's definition of normalcy was always the middle.[58]

Ewing's vision of what greenback changes would mean to the expansion of industry was taken much further when radical populism arrived in the Midwest. Just as government should not control the accumulation of wealth, government should not allow those with wealth to dictate redemption policies. Otherwise government became a shill for the wealthy. Ewing was a man who had sought wealth all his life, but he understood intrinsically that if the gap between the Haves and the Have Nots continued to widen, it would spark revolution. Concentrated wealth and democracy did not necessarily go together.[59]

Ewing had learned during the presidential impeachment fight that the right monetary policy could change minds. Because his monetary views were new and his tough war record was well-known, the Democrats briefly considered Ewing as a vice-presidential candidate. Democrats from mainstream money centers like New York City were appalled. Lincoln's Democrat, Gideon Welles, wrote that paper money "is a fiction, sustained by public confidence in part because there is a belief that it will ultimately bring gold. Irredeemable paper is a lie; gold is truth." But Ewing began to make a name for himself on a national stage. He was allowed to address the Soldiers' and Sailors' National Convention, which convened just before the Democratic convention, where the delegates heard this former Union general, to great applause, say of certain white politicians, "We earnestly wish to accomplish the purposes of the war as we understand them . . . the truly cordial, unconditional restoration of this Union. . . . We have no sympathy for those purposes that have been falsely and dishonestly substituted by the Republican Party for the avowed objective of the war. . . . We care not for their dogma of negro suffrage; we abhor their measures of white disenfranchise-

58. "Nigger than a mule" from Robinson, "Topeka and Her Constitution," 291–300. Lane's First Kansas colored regiment was part of a mixed infantry-cavalry unit that fought Stand Waite's regiments on June 30 and July 1, 1863, eighteen days before the Fifty-Fourth Massachusetts assaulted Fort Wagner in South Carolina. See *O.R.* 22:1:381, 450.

59. Louis Brandeis is quoted as saying, "We can have a democratic society or we can have great concentrated wealth in the hands of a few. We cannot have both." The quote may be apocryphal, according to Brandeis Law School librarian Scott Campbell in Louisville, Kentucky, who indicates that Brandeis scholars and biographers have never found the source. Email, February 15, 2007, to the author.

ment. . . . We look upon [these issues] as enemies of the Republic . . . [and] the settled foundations of our Government."[60]

Although his name was placed in nomination from Kansas for Democratic Party vice president, in order to balance the ticket if an Eastern man was nominated for president, this was not a serious effort. Ewing's opponents brought up his Order Number 11. He would be a problem in the key states of Missouri and Arkansas and throughout the old Confederacy. His candidacy was shelved in favor of the less controversial Frank Blair.[61]

Then the convention got down to nominating someone to run against Grant. From the polyglot of names two front-runners emerged. They were Winfield Scott Hancock and McClellan's vice-presidential candidate in 1864, George Pendleton. The convention remained deadlocked after twenty-two ballots, and delegates then swung toward a third candidate. Horatio Seymour had been New York's war governor. His work with federal authorities during the draft riots of 1863 was hardly stellar, prompting Colonel Robert Nugent in command of the famed Irish brigade to question Seymour's loyalty. Seymour certainly was not the War Democrat that Western Democrats wanted to offset Grant's popularity. Andrew Johnson had a better war record than Seymour. Things then got worse. Within weeks of the election Tom Ewing mentioned to Browning that there was movement afoot in New York to substitute Salmon Chase and William Franklin for the Seymour-Blair ticket. Browning predicted it was too late. The convention had not considered Chase as a nominee, and a change now would destroy party activists and make the looming defeat a farce.[62]

Seymour was taking on Grant, the man whom Robert E. Lee could not handle. If he was to have any chance against Grant, Seymour had to offer something new and distinct to the American people. Ewing sent a monetary issue paper to Johnson outlining that the Democrat monetary policy should be different from that of the Republicans and that Johnson should get Seymour to embrace a new policy if Democrats wanted to overcome Grant's juggernaut. Tom Ewing's speeches on monetary policy in the 1868 campaign discarded tariffs, where the small farmer and shopkeeper were being sacrificed on the altar of the gold standard. Inflating the money supply was the only way to repay the war debt while growing the economy.

60. Welles from Smith, *Trial by Fire,* 794; Ewing at the convention from the *New York Times,* July 7, 1868. The speech is published at Thomas Ewing, *Speech of Maj. Gen. Thomas Ewing, Jr., of Kansas, at the Soldiers' and Sailors' National Convention, at Cooper Institute, July 4, 1868: reported and published by order of the convention.*

61. Convention concerns about Order Number 11, from Browning, *Diary,* 2:220.

62. Chase substitution from ibid. 221.

Seymour had to embrace this idea in order to gain critical Western support, even if it meant losing his party's influential Manhattan Club bankers. Johnson sent Ewing's paper on to Seymour for consideration, but the Democratic candidate for president was not a man ready to chart new national monetary policy.[63]

The venom of impeachment politics spilled into the 1868 presidential campaign. Welles noted that "speakers are overrunning the country with their hateful harangues and excitable trash." An October parade by Republicans in Philadelphia included wagonloads of wounded war veterans and former Andersonville prisoners.[64]

On election night Tom Ewing and Orville Browning dined with the president at the White House. The gloom in Washington's Democratic headquarters was mirrored in their dinner conversation. Radicals carried Pennsylvania, Ohio, and Indiana, which settled the electoral college numbers as well. Browning, always the pessimist, predicted "darker days and afflictions" than the country had yet endured. Armies would fill the South to prop up despotic radical state governments. Johnson disclosed that he had given up all hope of victory when the Democratic convention nominated Seymour. Even as before the war Democrats suffered from myopia; elements within their tent were too tied to the past to determine a new course for the good of the country. In 1868 as in the past, they had "sacrificed the country on the altar of the party."[65]

While Tom Ewing and Orville Browning were soberly watching the election results, on New Year's Day 1869 Hugh B. Ewing put on the dress uniform of a major general for his audience with the king of Holland. The king suggested he was glad that the "vile impeachment of the President was dead," and that America could now get on to other, more important matters. To a king who had never had to consider removal from office, Hugh suggested that American politics was not quite so simple. He sensed now, in his audiences with the king, that the monarch was more standoffish, assuming that the new administration would bring a new ambassador to Holland. Since Hugh had served under Grant during the war, the king naturally inquired as to Grant's mannerisms and military skill, and there were long conversations in the palace on military campaigns in America.[66]

Hugh Ewing had tracked the 1868 election developments in the English newspapers brought to The Hague's legation. With Grant's election, Hugh's diplomatic

63. "Manhattan Club" from Smith, *Trial by Fire,* 794.
64. Ibid., 798.
65. Browning, *Diary,* 2:220.
66. Ewing, "Autobiography," 402.

career now had a time limit, unless someone could prevail on his old mentor. He spent time corresponding with Orville Browning, John Sherman, and the others who had helped him obtain his appointment. If some means could be found to change Grant's mind on a reappointment, Hugh would be grateful. Browning, who was finishing his public life before Grant took over, vowed he had served his last president. He now loathed his former colleagues. As far as Browning was concerned, Thomas Jefferson's prediction was prophetic: "Congress is by far the most corrupt and most dangerous power in the government."[67]

Hugh now sought the "pleasure of independence and quiet" back home. Europe's lingering bad memories left Paris without its usual luster. Diplomats were advised to carry personal pistols and avoid certain neighborhoods. Parisians were eating dogs and rats and "all manner of garbage," the social deterioration brought on because the Second Republic continued its enormous spending on military preparations. The arms race was Napoleon III's method to convince Bismarck that war would be futile. Hugh's sense was that the French people wanted a war with Germany, although his prediction that the French would win easily proved faulty.[68]

Earlier at The Hague, on January 9, 1869, Thomas Fenwick Ewing was born. Within days he was baptized at the old Cathedral of Charlemagne. It was a heady time for Hugh's wing of the clan. While he awaited better word from Washington as to his future, he resolved to spend his remaining diplomatic days in grand style with his family. Ri deserved to be spoiled. Perhaps it would relieve her of the funk she had been in since little Henrietta's death. The daughter, always frail, had died from a summer fever in the south of France. To avoid her melancholy, Hugh moved the family to the coast of Holland, into a country house with gardens and grounds, leaving behind the damp, salty air of The Hague. His gout was nearly unmanageable. His knees were stiff and swollen with pain, and he resumed taking morphine mixtures with water, all the while fearful he was becoming an invalid. During the impeachment months, when it appeared the radicals might prevail, he had written home that if recalled he and Ri would retire to the lower Potomac near Westmoreland, Virginia, and "become a model farmer and look down with lofty indifference on the gilded flies, the Sumners and Wades, that infest the capital." Although there might be war in the future of Europe, he wrote Mary Denman that he had seen his war and longed for "the sun of America," even if it meant living under radical Republicanism. Ellen Sherman had written him

67. Jefferson to James Madison, March 15, 1789, quoted in Browning, *Diary,* 2:237.

68. Ewing, "Autobiography," 403, 406.

describing the horrid campaign venom between Grant and Seymour's forces. "Honor appears pretty much to have fled the land," he replied.[69]

By the summer of 1869 Hugh Ewing had not been formally recalled from The Hague, but his father wrote in April 1870 that it was only a matter of time. The family was pulling all the strings they could to keep him in Europe, but it was a losing proposition. Tom Ewing had asked his old regular army friend Tom Moonlight of the Eleventh Kansas to contact his friend Sidney Clarke to influence Senator Pomeroy. At the same time Clarke was being pressured by radical editor Daniel R. Anthony of Leavenworth for help in getting Pomeroy's sponsorship for Clarke to replace Ewing in Brussels. Although even Sherman tried to see Grant on Hugh's behalf, Hugh continued to believe his political problems with Grant were due to Sherman's "graceless" vacillation on the task. Of Grant he wrote, "Some President should be shot if these removals are kept up." He wrote Phil to sell his remaining Leavenworth and St. Louis properties in order to provide funds to buy the Potomac farm, hoping to raise the $36,000 needed to pay Ri's share of her father's estate at Geisborough, his residence of choice.[70]

Politics was still a strong part of Hugh's life. He was overjoyed to hear from old friends such as William Roelfson and from the newspapers that Tom had been given an early nod as a proposed Conservative Democratic candidate for governor of Ohio in 1870. From there Tom would be in a good position to succeed John Sherman in the Senate and even consider a presidential run by 1875. Hugh spent a week of angst in November concerned over more news of his father's failing health, and this apparently became the final straw for Hugh. He no longer wanted the reappointment. The children, he reported home in a long letter, were praying for their grandfather. As for his own situation he suggested that the family do nothing more to "stay the uplifted ax" over his position. He was not yet removed but had no authority from Grant's State Department to do anything.[71]

Hugh and his family began their trip home on July 6, 1870. His first stop was to hire a guided tour of the Waterloo battlefield, wondering at the end of the day if his feelings at the end of a career were the same as Napoleon had felt on that field when the French Imperial Guard streamed back from their failed attack as-

69. HBE to TESr., March 17, to Mary Denman, March 5, to EES, April 13, 1868, in ibid., 410, 408, 413.

70. Tom Moonlight to Sidney Clarke, December 30, 1869, February 7, 1870, also Daniel R. Anthony to Clarke, December 29, 1869, boxes 3, 4, Sidney Clarke Collection; "graceless" Sherman, "removals," and selling Leavenworth property from Ewing, "Autobiography," 444, 442, 407.

71. Ewing, "Autobiography," 455.

saulting Wellington's center. A week later, while Hugh was finishing a stopover in Paris, France declared war on Prussia. Hugh watched the troops moving through the city, with despair that he would miss the action that was sure to come. Frenchmen were optimistic of victory, he telegraphed Washington. He stayed a few extra days in Paris to pen a longer paper regarding the "Position of Holland in the Coming War." It was here that Roelfson found him. Roelfson's wife had been vacationing in Germany and she needed "rescuing" from behind the Prussian lines. Incredibly, Hugh dropped everything and set out to find her.[72]

He took the trains and crossed the lines at Liege. In Hamburg he was accosted by a squad of Germans who took him into custody as a spy. No one in Prussia wanted any incident that would sour relations with the Americans, especially the outgoing American ambassador who found more in common with Prussian pride and virtue than with the French. After his release, Ewing easily located Roelfson's wife, and they returned to Paris, where he reported to Washington that travel was becoming dangerous for foreigners in Europe. French soldiers, he noted, appeared more cheerful and happy than their German counterparts along the Rhine. It was a different continent but similar to 1861 again—one side ill-prepared and the other mobilizing for war. By mid-August fighting was reported near Metz and a great excitement took control of Paris, the *Marseillaise* being sung everywhere. The Franco-Prussian War, Hugh noted privately, was fought because of the egos of Napoleon and Bismarck. The patriotism seemed contrived.[73]

On June 24, 1870, Grant formally nominated Michigan's Charles Gorham to replace Hugh Ewing as minister to The Hague. In December, nine months later than originally planned, Hugh and Ri set sail from London on a new coal steamer. His return home from Europe led him to lament to his journal not only the passing of the era of wooden ships but also the slower pace of life represented by them. "All the new ships are of iron, and sails are being driven from the sea." Hugh, a man of a sail, longed for earlier days.[74]

On their return to Washington they were met by most of Ewingville and Ri's father. Tragedy almost struck the family during this homecoming. The family was on board a Baltimore & Ohio Railroad sleeping car. As the train descended a mountain pass near Bellaire, their car, the last one on the train, left the tracks and slammed onto its side. The debris was dragged twice the length of the car before

72. Ibid., 470.
73. Ibid., 472.
74. Ibid., 479.

it came to a stop. The wreck terrified Ri, who "screamed repeatedly" for several minutes until Hugh could calm her. "Young Tom" (Thomas Fenwick Ewing) and Hugh were "bruised a little" but a Mrs. Smith in the same car was left "quite bloody and faint." The lack of injuries was because there were few people in the car at the time and the car had spun away from the others without dislodging the whole train. After railroad officials showed their concerns for the Ewings' injuries, Hugh reported, "we took seats in [the other cars] and we were soon underway again." They reached Lancaster later in the evening. "Father is looking better than he did four years ago, and he says I do not look a day older."[75]

For several years after his return from Europe, Hugh Ewing tried to find solace for wanderlust that had first led him to strike out with the Lancaster Mining Company for the California gold fields when he was a young man, and which had never truly been satiated. His old infatuation with horses came back, and he tried to buy several herds near San Antonio, Texas. Although he longed for part of the Youngs' Maryland plantation, this wish never materialized. He had learned that his old Kansas blood was still with him. "I long to get out on a prairie with the boys, and have with them a few years on horseback."[76]

Perhaps impressed with his sister's efforts at an autobiography of their father, in 1871 he distilled his lifetime of diaries and journals into "An Autobiography of a Tramp." His growing health problems slowed him down for his later years and certainly did not permit more years in Kansas. His gout made him more of an invalid every day. Within a few years he bought into some saltworks, several railroads, and even a business or two with William Roelfson at a tidy savings, perhaps in part as thanks to Ewing's work saving Mrs. Roelfson from imprisonment in Germany during the Franco-Prussian War. Hugh Ewing moved into what Americans now call "early retirement." He declared that central Ohio would be his home indefinitely. For thirty-eight more years on a small estate near Lancaster he raised horses, managed the family businesses, and wrote unsuccessful novels.

75. Ibid., 480.
76. HBE to TEJr., November 21, 1875, SFP/Yonkers.

12

THE CRÉDIT MOBILIER AND "HIS FRAUDULENCY"

At precisely noon on March 4, 1869, the greatest American soldier of the century stepped forward on the east portico of the Capitol and repeated the presidential oath of office. Ulysses S. Grant was about to begin a job he had been thrust into, not one he had pursued (always a bad combination). His predecessor had begun his term the same way. As a former general, used to having his orders obeyed instantly, Grant felt a measure of concern about the presidency and its executive branch. Unlike the case of an army in the field where success could be measured by the ground taken in battle, measuring the success of bureaucracy was harder. Since Grant did not pal around or make small talk with men he disliked, he went against tradition and sent word to the White House that he preferred to ride to the inaugural ceremony by himself. It was a snub to tradition that Andrew Johnson took personally. Johnson did not attend Grant's inaugural and ordered his cabinet to stay away, too.[1]

Among Johnson's last-minute pardons was that of Dr. Samuel Mudd, which made sense, just before the radicals took office. Tom Ewing was quick to file the request. The radicals even overlooked Johnson's late shenanigans, preferring the joy of Grant's moment. Claiming Grant would soon establish himself as the new Washington or Lincoln, James Blaine forgot his cousin's role in Mudd's pardon and ex-

1. Grant and Johnson, Smith, *Trial by Fire,* 802.

coriated Johnson's legacy: "With the election of General Grant comes a higher standard of American citizenship, with dignity and character." Blaine's support would later wane. But at this moment the new Speaker of the House was ecstatic.[2]

However, the man of the hour with the messianic vision was no Lincoln with words. From the inaugural audience, Tom Ewing shuddered at the glimpse at Grant's monetary policy. "Every dollar of government indebtedness should be paid in gold," and "no repudiator of one farthing of our public debt will be trusted in public office." Grant was tucked safely in the pockets of the swallowtail city bankers.[3]

After the tense mercurial days he had spent defending Johnson, the first years of the Grant administration were a vacation of sorts for Tom Ewing. The bug was still in him, and he knew he would not fight a political self-exile for very long. With Seymour's debacle in 1868, the National Union Party had faded away, leaving only the radical Republicans and the rebuilding Democrats. Several Ohio newspapers owned by friends advanced the idea that Ewing might run for governor as a Democrat. He was reluctant. Ellen had been ill much of the time since the nerve-wracking year of 1864, when she thought she might lose her husband to a vengeful Confederacy at Fort Davidson. Six years later, she had become a devotee of "the baths," a young woman grown old before her time.[4]

There was no denying, however, that Tom Ewing was moving forcefully into the Democratic camp. He began making speeches and working on the party's behalf. How could one of the leaders of Republicanism in Kansas make the change? First, his venue for politics had changed. Kansas was now out of the picture. He was living in Washington but spent a great deal of time in Ohio. He was torn because of his allegiance to the old Republican Party he had helped create, yet he had come to the realization that ultra radicals such as Sumner and Wade controlled Grant, and the Republican platform he had long supported no longer had any real vision. He had not supported radical abolitionism before the war, but at least there had been a moderate wing of the Republicans. Now even moderates were in decline. He had always been a centrist, especially in politics, but the centrist party of his frontier days had abandoned him. He could not support a party whose main agenda was Negro suffrage and the destruction of Southern sovereignty.

2. Hamilton, *James G. Blaine,* 214. The pardon freed Mudd. There have also been recent efforts to clear his name. See *Richard D. Mudd v. Louis Caldera, Secretary of the Army, et al.*, 134 F.Supp 2d 138 (D.C. 2001).

3. William S. McFeely, *Grant: A Biography,* 288.

4. Ellen at the baths from Taylor, "Business and Political Career," 294–95.

By this time, this Lincoln party man and former Republican chief justice of Kansas was now an Ohio Democrat of the first stripe, however reluctantly the Ohio Democrats might be to accept him. Furthermore, for all its support of Lincoln during the war, Ohio was a mostly Democratic state (it had nominated isolationist Clement Vallandigham as its Democratic gubernatorial nominee in 1863) and Ewing wanted to succeed in his home state. Earlier views of Ohio Democrats on most other issues of the day except monetary issues were much like those of the state's Republicans, yet in 1867 behind Congressman George Pendleton, the birth of the "Ohio Idea" came about, which was to repay the war debt with greenbacks, not gold. This was the crux of Ewing's beliefs. Ohio Democrats gave Ewing a logical forum to advance his soft-money causes, and a tent large enough for both the peace-at-any-price Democrats such as Pendleton and the restore-the-Union-by-force men such as Ewing. Completing his switch to the Democratic Party was not easy, however. Cousin James Blaine, a consummate Republican insider, later wrote "In supporting the policy of President Johnson [Tom Ewing] made a large sacrifice—large enough certainly to free his action from the slightest suspicion of any motive other than conviction of duty."[5]

In June 1870 at the Ohio Democratic convention, Ewing began his official quest for high office as a soft-money advocate. He predicted that any hard-money policy constricting the money supply would be "ruinous to the masses" and only benefit creditors. Ironically, his prediction found its way into a later U.S. Supreme Court case, *Knox v. Lee,* where the Court reversed itself and held that greenbacks were constitutional and legal tender for prior and subsequent contracts. Justice William Strong echoed the growing soft-money concerns: "If now, by our decision, it be established that these debts and obligations can be discharged only by gold coin; . . . the government has become an instrument of the grossest injustice . . . [and] a large percentage is added to every debt and such must become the demand for gold to satisfy contracts, that ruinous sacrifices, general distress and bankruptcy may be expected."[6]

Ewing's views were received tepidly at first. Being the namesake of an old Ohio Whig and a former confidant of Abraham Lincoln made party men puzzled and nervous. The 1870 convention was run by Dan McCook's brother George whose good-old-boy network had kept him in power for a decade and whose eyes were on the gubernatorial nomination for himself. McCook had seen the editorials.

5. "Ohio Idea" discussed in Foner, *Reconstruction,* 311; "Large sacrifice" from Blaine, *Twenty Years,* 2:222.

6. "Ruinous to the masses" from Taylor, "Business and Political Career," 296; Strong's opinion from *Knox v. Lee,* 79 U.S. (12 Wall.) 457 (1871) 529–530.

The Democratic Party also included bankers and creditors. McCook argued that Ewing was too new to the party to carry its standards into battle.[7]

The "Ohio Idea" demanded that greenbacks be made convertible at the holder's option into 3 percent bonds redeemable in more greenbacks. However, while he could easily sell his monetary policies in Ohio, Ewing had other problems. His former Catholicism hurt him among Protestants, Republicans, and strong-money advocates such as John Sherman, whose financial views were going in the opposite way from Ewing's and who labeled his old friend a repudiationist. To strengthen himself with the Protestant Democrats, Tom lost his Catholicism. Ellen, a practicing Presbyterian, had made him realize there were far more Methodists and Presbyterians in high political office than Catholics. Still, the professional Democrats maintained a dislike of his Republican background even though his appearance and rhetoric had changed. Now Ewing, broad-shouldered and full-bearded, was a frequent stump speaker. Instead of the old deliberative thinker with a deep voice and slow cadence, he had become a maverick orator with a faster delivery, who championed causes designed to unify Democrats with discontented labor and entrepreneurs against the Old Money Republicans whom he viewed (much as he had viewed antebellum planters) as backward and leading the country to ruin. Ewing wanted Democrats, greenbackers, and labor as the backbone of a new party to appeal to the disenchanted.

The old pols lined up behind McCook but not before a considerable floor fight by Ewing's young turks. When Ewing lost, he closed ranks and stumped for McCook and solidified a following within the party that stood for a "New Departure" on monetary policy. It did not work in 1870. The ravages of war were still fresh. Ohio had too many of its soldiers buried all over the South. It was fairly easy for Republicans to convince voters not to vote for Democrats unless they wanted Southern politicians to dominate Congress again.[8]

When newspapers do not have a war to report, scandals are worthy substitutes. In May 1872 the *New York Tribune* published a list of public figures in a memo that listed those who had been bribed by persons associated both with the Union Pacific and with its predecessor, Tom Ewing's old railroad the Leavenworth, Pawnee, & Western. The memorandum had been written six years before, in 1866, by fellow stockholder and director J. C. Stone, and it listed the probable disbursement of 64,450 shares of stock with a face value of $4.2 million to persons

7. Taylor, "Business and Political Career," 296.
8. Ibid., 288.

such as Edmund Ross, Cyrus Holliday, and former Missouri governor Thomas Fletcher. "Hold over them in terror" was Stone's notation. Even newspaper owners, such as the influential Wallis family of the *New York Herald,* had received $20,000, presumably for favorable editorials. U.S. Senator Samuel Pomeroy "friends" Junction City, Kansas, editor Robert McBratney and Pomeroy's son-in-law, Willis Gaylord, received shares for their indirect help. One entry for LP&W lobbyist Benjamin Cheever of Washington, D.C., indicated that if Cheever could deliver a railroad bill, he would get twenty-five thousand acres of land, $65,000 in company stock, and $10,000 in cash. This article was the beginning of the Crédit Mobilier scandal.[9]

The Crédit Mobilier was a holding company for the UP. The railroad received government bonds worth $27 million and could mortgage its properties up to that amount. The stock of Crédit Mobilier was divided among the managers of the UP, who proceeded to mortgage the UP rolling stock for the full sums and to mortgage the road's land grants for additional millions. Then they gave the contract to build the UP's track to Crédit Mobilier. The cost equaled the company's assets. The proceeds were divided among Crédit Mobilier managers as dividends. Before the first mile was laid, the UP was mortgaged to the hilt but without funds to begin construction, a brazen swindle of the other investors in the railroad.[10]

Some of the wealthiest and most notable men in America were involved in the expanding reach of the corporation. In March 1866 Hamilton G. Fant, Thomas Ewing's old Leavenworth banker friend, agreed to purchase 250 shares through a third party named Henry McComb, but when Fant did not complete the buy, McComb kept the right to the shares. It was McComb's later attempt to get actual possession of the stock itself—through Oakes Ames, a Massachusetts congressman whose brother Oliver was the third president of the UP—that caused McComb to sue, and the compromising letters to reach the front pages of newspapers.

Expanding the loot involved allowing friends of the UP to invest in railroad lands at favorable rates. Even Cump Sherman was approached in 1869 by Oscar Davis with the news that the general's family now owned a section of land a hundred miles west of Omaha if he could pay $2.50 per acre for the land that was appraised at $8.00. Sherman refused. Ames had placed the stock with key lawmak-

9. TEJr. to Devereaux, Washington, on March 30, 1866, EFP/LC; "Hold over them" cited in Taylor, "Origins of the Kansas Pacific," 179; *New York Tribune* article quoted in Taylor, "Business and Political Career," 134. U.S. Senator Samuel Pomeroy found posthumous and lasting infamy as the model for the corrupt Senator Dilworthy in Mark Twain and Charles Dudley Warner's *The Gilded Age.*

10. Athearn, *Union Pacific Country,* 125.

ers all over Congress. The list of officials who were offered the stock included James Blaine, Henry Wilson, Schuyler Colfax, James Brooks, Henry Dawes, James Garfield, Roscoe Conkling, and John Logan.[11]

Blaine's role as Speaker of the House was to protect the UP from hostile legislation. This is not necessarily either illegal or bad politics. Modern lawmakers look after business constituencies all the time, and some of those constituencies are headquartered in other states. In the 1870s there were no elements of the UP running through Maine, but this did not mean Blaine was not interested in a transcontinental railroad. Greeley's newspaper alleged that Crédit Mobilier was how Blaine grew wealthy on congressional pay.[12]

In October 1872 Blaine sent the *Tribune* stories to Tom Ewing, pointing out that the original bribery activity allegedly came from a list of contracts made by J. C. Stone and Ewing as agents of the LP&W: "I write to you for some solution of the mystery. As I was not a member of Congress at the time the act referred to was passed, . . . the *Tribune's* charge is, of course, absurd. . . . The political line that separates us will not, I am sure, prevent your recognizing the claim I have upon your friendly candor, nor will it forbid my making public use of your reply should I deem it needful."[13]

Ewing's response was of considerable help to Blaine:

> Your brother, J.E. Blaine, at the time Clerk of the District Court in Leavenworth and one of the early settlers of Kansas, was the owner of $10,000 of the stock of the Leavenworth, Pawnee and Western railroad company, which indeed was held very generally among influential men of all parties along the line of the road in Kansas.
>
> I know nothing whatever of the list alleged to have been furnished by General Stone. It purports to have been prepared nearly a year after the act was passed and long after I had entered the military service and more than six months before you took your seat in Congress.
>
> My general knowledge of the business of the company, and especially my intimacy with you, make it certain that you could not have had any contract

11. For a general review of the scandal, Smith, *Trial by Fire,* 881–82. Sherman's involvement in a letter from Oscar Davis to Oliver Ames, August 20, 1869, cited by Athearn in *Union Pacific Country,* 153.

12. The *Tribune's* article is quoted in Hamilton, *James G. Blaine,* 276. Greeley's rival, the *New York Times,* noted the *Tribune's* article and Tom Ewing's response to Blaine on October 11, 1872. The allegations that he profited from improper railroad investments dogged Blaine's later campaigns for the Republican presidential nomination. See a sample at *New York Times,* May 2, June 8, 1876, and "Mr. Blaine's Record," on June 13, 1884.

13. Blaine to Ewing, October 1, 1872, in Hamilton, *James G. Blaine,* 281. For a contrary view, that Blaine was indeed involved, see Smith, *Trial by Fire,* 884.

> with the company without my knowing the fact; and I unhesitatingly declare that you were not in any manner, or at any time, directly or indirectly, employed by the company, or in any way interested in its affairs as stockholder, agent or otherwise, in any capacity whatever.

Ewing denied knowledge of Stone's list and indicated in the letter that the LP&W never "by any of its officers, agents, or attorneys, made any contract, the proceeds of which there was good reason to believe were to be in an manner participated in by any member of Congress or other public officer." The *Tribune* took Ewing's word and retracted its allegations against Blaine.[14]

His answer begs a larger question, however. The fact that Blaine's brother did own stock in the LP&W is interesting but irrelevant. It is true that Blaine's name could not have been associated with any 1862 irregularities. Whether Blaine obtained Crédit Mobilier stock for its magical 100 percent dividend when he was Speaker of the House is another matter.

Without a public stock monitoring system, the private trading of stock by lobbyists or other congressmen to public officials was legal, if no special dividend or discounted purchase rate was given them that was not given to other stockholders. When the storm broke and investigations began, those congressmen who confessed to taking the stock suffered no indignities whatever. There were no prosecutions. Even Ames went unpunished. One result of the scandal was the outlawing of most contingent fee lobbying in Congress and state legislatures, and a greater use by congressmen of blind investment trusts upon entering office.[15]

Railroad scandals kept congressional investigative committees active for nearly thirty years after the war. In 1887, two decades after Ewing sold out to Fremont, various persons were still making demands on the UP to honor the LP&W's "contracts." Nearly two decades earlier, Ewing had been asked by Thomas Scott, the president of the UP, to explain a list of persons with claims against the old LP&W since, if their claims and contracts were valid, it constituted a liability to the profit sheet of the road. Admittedly, Ewing wrote, the "nature of the transactions" would prevent those men listed from going to court to enforce compensation, but they had "acted in good faith," and in his opinion the UP was "strongly obligat-

14. TEJr. to James G. Blaine, March 20, 1876, EFP/LC. In 1876, Blaine was spoken of as a candidate for president, and the adversary press began drumming up the 1872 railroad controversy. Blaine contacted Ewing, and in the *New York Times,* May 2, 1876, Ewing explained Blaine's non-involvement for a second time.

15. Hamilton, *James G. Blaine,* 283–85.

ed to pay equitably for the services through which [the railroad] became so richly endowed."[16]

In 1887 Ewing, Stone, and John Usher were subpoenaed by the Pacific Railroad Commission investigating whether members of Congress were unduly influenced to get the railroad built. At a Kansas City meeting of the commission, all three men denied they had bribed anyone into supporting the bill, but each admitted he had heard the rumors that bribery had occurred. In deference to his former position as chief justice and brigadier general in the army, Ewing was allowed to present a written statement without cross examination. He explained what he knew about contracts made by the company but denied being more than a figurehead director of the LP&W. He had helped hire lobbyists, and perhaps his lobbyists had crossed the line. Then his candid assessment of the excesses of the Gilded Age was laid bare: "[However,] without such lobbying activities," he told the commission, "no measure of mixed public and private interest is ever enacted in Congress or any State Legislature." It was a remarkable testimonial—that, in Ewing's world, competent corporate society would take care of management decisions and bring about a public good so long as government did little more than offer strategic guidance and set goals.[17]

The late Professor David Taylor indicates that Ewing's statement may have misled a congressional committee. He claimed he had been nothing more than a figurehead in the LP&W, which was accurate for the time after he sold out to Hallett but not for the time while he still owned stock. No figurehead sits on an executive committee of a corporation. Some of Cheever's stock was destined for public officials in Rhode Island when there had been resistance in 1862 to using Eastern capital to build a Western railroad. In 1866 Ewing had written J. P. Devereaux, a UP director, "I cannot tell exactly what [Cheevers] did though he . . . gave considerable time and effort to procure the passage of the Pacific bill." A Rhode Island official was making a discounted claim on the UP for late compensation for some work performed in obtaining the legislation. "I think he is entitled," Ewing wrote. The timing problem is that Ewing indicated under oath to the commission what he said in his letter of support to Blaine, that he was not aware of Stone's memorandum until the 1870s; but it seems he was quoting from it to Devereaux in 1866.[18]

Since the congressional investigation never linked Stone's memorandums and

16. TEJr. to Thomas Scott, February 7, 1866, EFP/LC.
17. Ewing's statement to Congress quoted in Taylor, "Origins of the Kansas Pacific," 170–71.
18. TEJr. to Devereaux, Washington, March 30, 1866, cited in ibid., 171.

Ewing's discussions with Blaine, Devereaux, and Scott, Ewing was never charged with any wrongdoing. What he had done before his postwar congressional career was nothing more than utilize the form of soft-money campaign finance used during the Gilded Age. Modern campaign contributions are the legal form of bribery that is available to citizens and corporations in every state to support campaigns for public office and to influence public policy, and the ones who determine what constitutes a legal bribe are the same ones who are receiving the money.[19]

A second Grant election should have been a cakewalk. It was not. Grant was buffeted by scandal and in political trouble until the 1872 Democrat convention nominated the editor Horace Greeley to lead their ticket. The editor had spent a lifetime blaming Democrats in print for everything bad in the country, and he had to eat so much crow he had little time to take on Grant. There were Republicans who went with Greeley, having had enough of Grant's inconsistencies. One such was Charles Sumner of Massachusetts, whom Blaine attacked for disloyalty. But it was not enough. Voters picked up on the major policy shifts by the Democratic presidential ticket and preferred an honest but hapless former general to a holier-than-thou prig. Grant buried Greeley in electoral college votes after Greeley had conveniently buried himself. Hugh Ewing wrote James Doolittle a morose letter, "I think the curtain has fallen on the Democratic Party, and its part of the play ended."[20]

The 1872 election completed not only the country's postwar transformation but also the political transformation of Tom Ewing. In 1873 at the Democratic convention in Allen County, Ohio, the party was continuing its struggle to chart a new direction. Ewing told a party rally that the Republicans were "corrupt" and the Democrats "powerless," a statement he would later regret. The *New York Times* noted that Ewing "was a gentleman who had an itching to [the U.S. Senate] if the country could frighten enough Democrats into succumbing to Ewing's new party movement."[21]

The off-year congressional elections of 1874 set up the 1876 presidential campaign. Hugh Ewing's views on the demise of the Democratic Party were prema-

19. *Kansas Statutes Annotated,* 2006 supplement version, chapter 25, article 4153a, prohibits contributions during the legislative session by Kansas lobbyists, corporations, or other "persons," but not by individuals. While Kansas has regulated lobbying since 1909, only in the 1990s did members of the legislature impose such limits on themselves.

20. Blaine's anger at Sumner in Blaine to Sumner, July 31, 1872, quoted in Hamilton, *James G. Blaine,* 270; HBE to James Doolittle, November 29, 1872, EFP/LC.

21. Ewing to party rally, *Cincinnati Enquirer,* August 3, 1873; "itching" to the Senate, *New York Times,* August 1, 1873.

ture. In 1874 Democrats rode the aftermath of the Panic of 1873 to wipe out two decades of congressional minority party status and climb to a sixty-seat margin in the House of Representatives. The House tsunami almost led to a Senate majority. So much of a blow was dealt to radical Republicanism that among the newly elected senators was ex-president Andrew Johnson of Tennessee.

If economic policy was to drive the new party's direction, Tom Ewing was reading more into the national disenchantment with financial issues than was there. He worked hard for the party but began to lose what he had always maintained as a Republican, national perspective. Among his speeches was the following:

> The business of the country generally, and the business of the West, is carried on, to a large extent, by borrowed capital. The men who have accumulated wealth are generally the elderly men who, to a large extent, are done with the active business of life. It is the young, energetic men of the community, who combine their talent with the money of nonproducers to carry on the works of production and exchange—they are the men that do the business of the country in the main.

While Ewing's analysis was correct, no bank was required to make loans on favorable terms because the borrower was young and had fought a war.[22]

After the 1874 Democratic gains a reenergized Tom Ewing convinced Ohio Democrats to test the appeal of the greenback wing of the party by nominating an "ultra inflationist," William Allen, and Samuel Cary, as the party's governor and lieutenant governor. Ewing had by this time moved his law practice back to Ohio, realizing that his monetary policies and a Washington business address did not mix. He was heavily involved in Ohio politics. Allen had been a protégé of Douglas in the prewar U.S. Senate and a supporter of the Kansas-Nebraska Act. He and Senator Allen Thurman were related and had controlled much of the party machinery in central Ohio for years. The Republican candidate for governor was Rutherford B. Hayes. Instead of focusing on money issues, Hayes exploited the Democratic Party's "Catholic" problems—Ewing's influence in the party and an ill-disguised pandering to German Protestants. Those who did speak on money issues came with a different monetary vision. They worked to get voters concerned with other issues, playing on middle-class fears that Ewing's views would bring confiscation of property. The *Cincinnati Gazette* invoked a form of nineteenth-century McCarthyism to attack the greenbackers: "When such men as Cary, Ew-

22. Taylor, "Business and Political Career," 316.

ing, Pendleton and Kelly rose to the surface . . . appealing to the masses against property and capital," a Democratic vote would be for "communist revolution."[23]

The anti-greenback strategy allowed Hayes to eke out a narrow victory over Allen when heavy rains kept down the farm vote in central Ohio. Hayes now had a platform and a stage for further discussion on financing the country's development in 1876. As architect for the Democratic platform, Ewing was blamed for the party's defeat by Eastern liberals such as Samuel Tilden. Ewing wrote Hugh his prediction of "hard times" for the economy in the Midwest and West. "Eastern Democrats and Republicans are blind to the real drift of events and feeling through the west and south—and will find the rag baby [greenback philosophies] out of its swaddling clothes next year, and much stouter notwithstanding the spanking [at the 1875 Ohio polls]."[24]

Others viewing Ohio politics were not so sure. Two years later, behind the back of the leadership, Tom Ewing maneuvered to introduce a platform plank on monetary policy that included repeal of the resumption law. "The majority platform on hard money," Ewing shouted in a convention speech, "is more dangerous than the Republican policy it supplants. We can win the Presidency only if we fight the hydra-headed financial measures of the Republican Party. Great God! Has the Democratic Party lost its animating purpose? Is its mighty spirit fled? Never! Never! It is the friend of the people and the foe of all schemes . . . for their enslavement." Ewing's emotional speech caught party leaders off-guard. The convention stampeded and adopted Ewing's viewpoint by a narrow vote, and he was named an at-large delegate to the national Democratic convention.[25]

Samuel J. Tilden used his Tammany Hall connections and the 1874 Democratic surprises in Congress to forge a huge margin over a New York Republican incumbent governor, which catapulted him into front-runner presidential status at the national Democratic convention. Tom Ewing disliked this development because Tilden's backers had little vision, especially on how monetary policy could set the Democrats apart from the Republicans. So Ewing did his best at the convention to swing the Western states away from Tilden and preferably to General Winfield Scott Hancock, a rising star in the party who could articulate a new economic policy.

23. "Catholic problems" from TEJr. to HBE, September 17, 1875, EFP/LC; "communist" from *Cincinnati Gazette,* August 4, October 5, 1875.

24. TEJr. to HBE, October 17, 1875, EFP/LC.

25. Speech quote in *Cincinnati Enquirer,* May 18, 1876. See also Taylor, "Business and Political Career," 319.

In the preliminary sparring Ewing and Daniel Voorhees of Indiana fought Tilden's language approving the Republican Resumption Act. Ewing's minority report condemned the national banks as "a monopoly thoroughly hated" by ordinary citizens. When he brought the fight to the floor, Tildenites ordered Ewing to shut up and sit down. Pandemonium broke out. The *Cincinnati Enquirer* reported, "When the tall form of Voorhees came forward, the audience rose and cheered; at least half the Delegates rose too. Breckinridge was screaming for the previous question. Eaton, of Kansas, was yelling until his upper teeth dropped loose and confused his voice. Davis of Kansas, wanted the galleries cleared; everybody shouted and the chairman broke his gavel in two." In the chaos Tilden's forces asserted their strength and crushed the minority plank, and Democrats once again were badly divided as they left St. Louis to do battle for the presidency.[26]

Ewing was a Democrat but he was having a hard time with the party's message. He had been unable to support Greeley four years earlier, and he went back to Ohio not knowing whether he would support Tilden. His monetary policies had been blamed for Allen's loss in the 1875 gubernatorial campaign. Tilden plainly was a hard-money man, and if Ewing supported Tilden he could be accused by his friends of abandoning greenback policies and the New Departure (the Ohio Idea). Americans in general were better prepared for new directions than were the Democrats. The seed was there to isolate the Eastern money center banks. Tilden was a pawn of the New York Democratic establishment and hardly in a position to make that sort of change.[27]

To exploit this development Ewing needed a personal platform. In March 1874, before Tilden's selection, he made it known that he was interested in the nomination to Ohio's twelfth congressional district, and he would have won, except that, at the convention, his opponents read back to him his 1873 Allen County remarks about powerless Ohio Democrats. The 1874 nomination went to Ansel Walling instead. In 1876 Ewing wrestled the primary nomination away from Walling's reelection effort. At the convention in mid-June, a rejuvenated Ewing power base took control when he gave the keynote address on the need for an inflationary money system, and his views were met with a "storm of applause." He helped write the party platform, which charged that "a currency indispensable to the welfare of the country should be regulated by the necessities of business," not government favors to the banking class. Ewing called for abolishing the national banking system, a position entirely contrary to his father's efforts as Tyler's secre-

26. The Resumption floor fight from *Cincinnati Enquirer,* June 29, 1876.

27. Taylor, "Business and Political Career," 311–12, 324.

tary of the treasury to create one. A bland campaigner, Walling had nothing in his arsenal to thwart Ewing's magnetic greenback oratory, which made repeal of the Resumption Act the central campaign issue. Ewing's long-standing abilities to wheel and deal behind the scenes with key supporters proved profitable. In 1876 Ewing was nominated easily.[28]

He was a candidate for Congress. The sniping between Charcoals (wartime radical Democrats) and Claybanks (the moderates and conservatives within the Democratic party) resurfaced during the campaign, however. The buzz was over Ewing's Order Number 11. How could Ewing be a man of the people when during the "late unpleasantness" he made war on common folks? Although the issue was more of an irritant than a problem, Ewing tried to get Schofield involved to clear up the issue of why hard war was necessary in Missouri in 1863. Schofield confirmed that, while it was Ewing's order, it had received his support as department commander, and Lincoln's. Publication of the letter quieted the issue this time and strengthened Ewing's congressional campaign.[29]

The only bright spot for Ewingville in this disputed 1876 election was that Ohioans in his district sent Tom Ewing to Congress, where he was joined a few months later by freshman senator and former captain of the Eleventh Kansas cavalry Preston Plumb. Also in his congressional class were future presidents William McKinley and James Garfield. More than once Tom Ewing must have felt better about the makeup of the Congress as he looked across the seats at the familiar faces of Joe Johnston of Virginia, Alexander Stephens of Georgia, and John Reagan of Texas. Across the rotunda in the Senate with Plumb were John B. Gordon and Wade Hampton of South Carolina. The former sworn enemies were now making laws for the general good.

Not all Americans agreed with Ewing on Southern influence. Johnston never succeeded in besting Sherman on the Civil War's battlefields, but he would do so in the Congress. Appointed to the Armed Services Committee, Johnston found himself making the laws that Cump Sherman, as general in chief, had to carry out. When the army was withdrawn from the South, many congressmen from those states began to wonder why its top generals such as Sherman were paid the huge sums. Former major general John Logan was one of the reformers, and he found Joseph Johnston a good ally. Reductions in pay and the size of the army itself became major issues, at which Sherman later blustered, "The

28. Ibid., 311.

29. Schofield quoted in "Gen. Ewing's Missouri Order," *St. Louis Missouri Republican,* February 21, 1877, 5.

southern element is so strong [in the Congress] that we find ourselves governed by the very men whom we fought as enemies." Tom Ewing probably thought such concerns a natural progression to a peacetime army and a new and reunited Union.[30]

For 124 years the presidential campaign of 1876 held the singular distinction of being the closest election in American history. The campaign that bridged the end of Reconstruction and the beginning of the Gilded Age laid bare the excesses of Grant's administration. Election returns in four states were disputed, and the outcome of the election hinged on the recount. In all four states, the army was accused of intimidating voters in key locations.[31]

Congress created a joint commission of five senators, five representatives, and five Supreme Court justices to decide the victor. When the commission decided all four states in favor of Hayes, a renewed civil war seemed likely. Southern Democrats realized that another war would be a second disaster, however, so they brokered a deal. The Democrats had swept to power in Congress, and the Republicans would get nothing if Hayes did not play ball. The price for Democrats to declare a Republican victory was the withdrawal of federal troops from the Southern states, and thus to enforce the ending of radical Reconstruction.

Hayes ordered the army out of the South within a few months of taking office. Freshman Ohio congressman Tom Ewing approved of and voted for the withdrawal. Hayes consulted General Sherman on whether to shift Joseph Johnston out of the House and appoint him secretary of war, fulfilling the promise made in the brokered compromise to appoint a Southerner in the cabinet. While Sherman personally liked the idea, he told Hayes the country would not stand for it. Hayes appointed David Key as postmaster general. Key was a former colonel in the Confederacy. While Tom Ewing was pleasantly surprised that Hayes kept this part of the agreement, the compromise shattered an already bitterly divided Republican Congress. Within months of taking office, Hayes offered a plan for civil service reform, which, if enacted, would have shot his shaky Republican administration in the foot. John Sherman, the new secretary of the treasury, convinced Hayes to resume gold specie payments for greenbacks, which proved unpopular with constituents even though Secretary Sherman thought highly of the

30. New Southern influence found in WTS to Tommy Sherman, undated (May 1877), in Joseph T. Durkin, *General Sherman's Son: The Life of Thomas Ewing Sherman,* 49–51; "southern element" from WTS to Willard Warner, December 6, 1877, Willard Warner Papers, Illinois State Library, quoted in Fellman, *Citizen Sherman,* 293.

31. Marszalek, *Soldier's Passion,* 431.

move. Ewing heard even Republican congressmen begin to refer to Hayes as "His Fraudulency."[32]

Without the military presence in the South, a Southern apartheid both social and economic blanketed the region. A struggling people had been anointed by one government with the meaningless word "free," but the American Southern apartheid created an underclass that continued to help build—and defend—America without being allowed to participate in its governance. While the major parties spent their time discussing arcane issues such as civil service reform, greenback policies, Indian resettlement policy, and whether to return captured Civil War battle flags to the various states, black Americans now were adrift in an inhospitable land where white legislatures were determined to keep them enslaved.

32. Johnston appointment from Gilbert Govan and James Livingwood, *A Different Valor: General Joseph E. Johnston, C.S.A.*, 388; "His Fraudulency," *New York Times*, June 22, 1879.

13

SWEATY OLD COINS AND LAST HURRAHS

During the early 1870s, in addition to his progression from moderate Republican to greenback Democrat, Tom Ewing tried to find his stride as an investor. Doing well in business had several advantages other than just making money. He had built a modest fortune from a collage of mining properties in New Mexico and Alabama along with farms in Kansas, Iowa, and Illinois. He purchased a bank in New Orleans, and he still owned an interest in the cotton farm in Arkansas. Behind his New York banker and investor Hamilton Fant and with a former Confederate staff officer and postwar power in West Virginia politics, R. H. Catlett, Ewing acquired coal and iron reserves near Anthony Creek in the Kanawha River valley and began all-out promotion of the area as he had done in Leavenworth before the war. There were rumors that Cornelius Vanderbilt and the Pennsylvania Central Railroad were interested in developing the region. The Ewing group would link their properties with the Penn Central. With his share of the family saltworks in Lancaster Tom's private fortune was nearly $180,000.[1]

To the nineteenth-century American male, success in political endeavors usually first required success in a trade or business. The Gilded Age embodied the epitome of avarice, but it was from such materialism that leaders were molded.

1. Ewing's holdings from Taylor, "Business and Political Career," 224; Catlett to TEJr., October 15, 1870, EFP/LC.

The 1870s did not spawn political candidates from the lower classes. It was the ethos of the times that a tested business leader would gravitate to politics and public service. With the exception of men such as James Blaine and John Sherman, whom the presidential bug had bitten hard, few men considered holding public office to be a career. Candidates in the middle class might campaign for office just for the paycheck, but men of substance never thought that way. Obviously there were exceptions, but the Gilded Age ethos was that some gentlemen were to give public service, leave the country better than when they took office, then devote their years of wealth to their doting families and grandchildren.

Tom Ewing wanted these things, too. The recession of 1873 turned into a mini depression, however, and all of Ewingville was affected. Western states labeled the panic "the Crime of '73." For two years the country stagnated. Iron prices dropped sharply, furnaces closed, and thousands lost their jobs. Coal lands valued at $10 million in 1872 deflated to $6 million in 1877. Cash was so rare that state scrip reemerged. While Ewing, Fant, and Catlett were each clairvoyant in the importance of the Kanawha to their fortunes, the recession limited the area's growth until later in the century, after Ewing and Fant had been forced to sell their interests. By the political summer of 1876 the railroad that Ewing controlled—the Atlantic & Lake Erie, later the Ohio Central—was on the verge of failure. He sought help abroad for the railroad, but new investors were scarce. On June 12, 1877, he resigned as head of the railroad, deeply in debt. The family was hoarding funds, too, riding out the Panic of 1873.[2]

Tom Ewing reached the summit of his career as a politician in the late 1870s in the Congress. He found ready allies for greenback politics in Preston Plumb in the Senate and a fellow congressman from Kansas, former governor Sam Crawford. They advocated that the 1877 Congress use the money earmarked for repayment of war bonds to build the transportation system in the West, so that immigration would expand the total economy, end the lingering recession, and more than repay the government's investment. Congressman Tom Ewing served on the banking and currency committee during his first term, the "soft-money" committee of the Congress at that time. Additionally, Ewing felt it only proper that Eastern banking interests, steeped in hard-money policies of debt repayment, bear the burden of paying for the war through inflated money, since these same East-

2. Effect of the 1873 Panic and his resignation from the railroad from David G. Taylor, "Hocking Valley Railroad Promotion in the 1870s: The Atlantic and Lake Erie Railway," 270, 276.

ern banks had also fueled the slave economy in the South that had brought on the war.

Monetary fights in Congress were watched also by the Supreme Court. Salmon Chase had argued in the legal tender cases earlier in the decade that Congress could create temporary greenbacks if these could then be redeemed later in gold. He never argued for permanent greenbacks. Legitimacy in the nation's monetary policy required a gold standard. Greenback advocates were appalled by Chase's 4–3 majority opinion in *Hepburn v. Griswold,* which held that prewar contracts demanding repayment in gold had to be honored. Although Grant appeared (at least from his inaugural address) to be a monometalist, after his inauguration the Court with two new Grant appointees had another go at the issue, and *Knox v. Lee* overturned *Hepburn,* 5–4. Chase wrote in his diary, "It is a sad day for the cause of constitutional government." However, every silk purse has a sow's ear, and *Knox* was the precedent for taking the majority at its word. If Congress could choose between monetary systems without constitutional constraints, it could reimpose the gold standard by statute. Furthermore, one party could use monetary policy for political advantage over the other. The wealthy owned most of the nation's war debt, having been induced to invest in the war bonds by high tax-free interest and a promise of repayment of the principal in gold. Democrats argued that if the debt was repaid with inflated paper money, the national debt could be reduced on the backs of the wealthy who had profited most from the war while younger men fought it. Specie thus became synonymous with patriotism and religion, while greenbacks became the tools of the unpatriotic, immoral, and ungodly. Greenbacks in the Gilded Age became all-out economic war in an ancient American political art form—the Haves against the Have Nots.[3]

With the different varieties of give and take on financial matters that had festered throughout Reconstruction before 1876, Ewing leaped into the fray and quickly established his name on the topic. His position led him into a series of debates in Ohio during the presidential campaign with hard-money champions such as Governor Stewart Woodford of New York. Woodford, having argued a simplistic position in favor of the Resumption Act, particularly caught Ewing's ire. "The gentleman [claims] that sweaty old coins could be put through the fire and would come out bright and pure; whereas the sweaty greenback might be put

3. *Hepburn v. Griswold,* 75 U.S. (8 Wall.) 603 (1869), overturned in *Knox v. Lee,* 79 U.S. (12 Wall.) 457 (1871); "sad day" from Chase's diary cited in Kahn, "Evolution of Money," 427. Western buildup from Plummer, *Frontier Governor,* 149; reducing national debt on wealthy from Kevin Phillips, *Boiling Point: Republicans, Democrats and the Decline of Middle Class Prosperity,* 102.

in the fire and would be entirely consumed. True—but if the sweaty greenback were put into the fire and consumed, you could get another from the treasury in its place. Besides, what under the heavens should the people want to put their money in the fire for?"[4]

The greenback position as the source of monetary power in the United States was in the van of twentieth-century government policy, which would finally end the national reliance on the gold standard. Greenback strength reached its nineteenth-century zenith during the Hayes administration. On November 23, 1877, Tom Ewing as a new congressman and Representative Aylett Buckner of Missouri pushed H.R. 805 through the House of Representatives, repealing the Resumption Law. In committee hearings Ewing grilled the new secretary of the treasury, John Sherman, about Hayes's views on monetary policy. Sherman indicated that Tom Ewing was a member of Congress and "a friend . . . a Member of ability and influence" but that his monetary policy was wrongheaded. Former secretary of the treasury under Andrew Johnson, Hugh McCulloch later wrote in the *North American Review* that there was a "higher law which makes gold the standard in all large commercial transactions . . . [and] will prevail among enlightened nations" and that those who believe "cheap money" essential to prosperity were "eminently dangerous."[5]

During congressional hearings Ewing pulled from John Sherman a reluctant admission that the Resumption Law was solely a means of destroying greenback currency, not a means of solidifying the economy or reducing the national debt. Ewing asserted that the Treasury did not have enough specie available to redeem all the greenbacks by January 1, 1879, as required by the Resumption Law. Sherman disclosed that he was negotiating a loan with European banks in order to complete the process, a disclosure that had congressmen scratching their heads. Would this debt not make the U.S. government beholden again to English capital resources in order to avoid a paper currency over here?[6]

In a series of written debates in the *North American Review,* Ewing and others took on the allegation by metal men that anything short of a gold or silver standard was unconstitutional. Instead of going in hock with England, Ewing sug-

4. The Ewing-Woodford debates were held October 2, 4, 8, 9, 1875. See J. V. Lee, ed., "Joint Discussions between Gen. Thomas Ewing, of Ohio, and Gov. Stewart L. Woodford, of New York, on the Finance Question," 100 (quote).

5. John Sherman, *Recollections of Forty Years in the House, Senate, and Cabinet,* 2:630; McCulloch's remarks from Hugh McCulloch, "Resumption of Specie Payments," *North American Review* 125.259 (November 1877): 404.

6. John Sherman before TEJr.'s committee and admission of foreign debt financing, from Taylor, "Business and Political Career," 325–26.

gested, a "patriot's syndicate" could buy back the paper currency with 5 percent bonds. For Ewing anything was preferable to sending American gold assets to England for loans to Washington to redeem its wartime paper currency. In the *Review,* Ewing claimed that of the $285 million in gold coin in 1860, and after American mines had provided an additional $700 million in gold through 1877, there was only $150 million in gold left in the system. "It has nearly all been shipped abroad to pay coin debts and expenditures." Ewing predicted that the Borrow-from-the-Brits scheme would "starve the workers and fatten the drones [of capitalism]," and wreck small town economies throughout America. Our use of paper money was not excessive in 1877, he wrote. It was $17.50 per capita, whereas the wealthiest nation, France, allowed circulation of $45 of paper money per capita, and England allowed $34 per capita. At the same time, Ewing pointed out that Americans were taxed more heavily per capita than France, England, or Germany. In the years after the end of Reconstruction, thousands of American land parcels were being forfeited for high taxes. Debtors were the chief workers of the land, but also the class on which American debt was foisted when only gold could pay off contracts. Debtors lived "on the ragged edge of the chasm," he wrote.[7] "Resumption policies" would bring on a greater "general destruction of business" than did the Civil War itself, he predicted. William "Pig Iron" Kelley, congressman from Philadelphia and another radical greenbacker, added fuel to Ewing's pro-labor argument. "It is labor that supports society and provides revenues to government," he wrote in the *Review,* urging Americans to resist the temptation to look to England for help. "The proudest nation, if unduly indebted to foreigners, is the slave of its creditor."[8]

Greenbackers were concerned that the continued tendency in American banking circles to follow London's lead too closely in monetary policy would have a negative effect on our national self-respect and independence. As the cornerstone of greenback policy, Ewing's bill had taken on the flag of labor against capital, but it had more than enough votes in rural and Western states to prevail over the administration's attempts to block it. The bill passed the House. John Sherman's supporters then stalled Ewing's bill in the Senate committee by threatening a filibuster.[9]

Ewing remained skeptical of Republican motives. In 1878 he supported the Bland-Allison Act, the greenback high-water mark, which remonetized silver on a limited basis, at one-sixteenth that of gold. Silver was considered by the mono-

7. Thomas Ewing Jr., "Resumption of Specie Payments," 413, 414, 415.
8. William D. Kelley, "Resumption of Specie Payments," 405, 406.
9. Connelley, *Preston B. Plumb,* 251.

metalists as a sop to the greenbackers. Blaine engineered a Republican compromise to bridge the gap between "free silver radicals" and the gold bugs in order to aid national liquidity. The monometalists (including John Sherman) convinced Hayes to veto the bill, however. Blaine, Bland, and others (including Ewing) enthusiastically overrode the veto. With a strict gold standard fading as national policy, Hayes's allies and banking lobbyists pushed through Congress a system that allowed a legal tender limit at $350 million, which included an increase of $46 million in greenbacks, in part to stall greenback momentum. Ewing's own legislation had failed, but the increase in the money supply of silver and greenbacks under Bland-Allison was a major concession. Greenbackers, not Hayes, got the credit. Between the veto of the silver act and opposition to repeal of the Resumption Act, the Hayes administration had burned bridges with laborers and businessmen in the Western states. Ewing and Congressman Richard Bland from Missouri, on the other hand, became the West's new darlings.[10]

What slowed greenback momentum in 1878 and 1880 to a crawl was the economy. The return to national prosperity eased pressure for monetary reform in rural and Western areas. Specie advocates argued that good times had come to America in spite of the allegations of men such as Ewing that all manner of calamity would fall on a nation linked to the gold standard. By late 1878 Ewing sensed that his effectiveness on monetary policy was about over. He let friends know he was interested in being governor of Ohio. Hayes had used the gubernatorial route to pull enough national spotlight on himself to impact the Republican convention in 1876. Ewing hoped similar lightning would strike among Democrats in 1880.[11]

Ewing had used his four years in Congress well, gaining support in Ohio for his gubernatorial campaign. He faced minefields of his own making, however. He now had an imposing appearance, was a first-rate stump speaker, and provided the press with good quotes and background. This attractiveness caused the Ohio Democratic Party gubernatorial convention in Columbus to nominate him on the second ballot. But the June 1879 meeting grew raucous. Allen Thurman's followers widely believed that the campaign would determine whether Thurman or Ewing would lead the Ohio Democratic Party. There were two other leading candidates for governor, one of them incumbent governor Richard Bishop. Ewing and Thurman were the dark horses. Bishop faded and threw his support in the convention to Ewing. General Americus V. Rice ended up the lieutenant governor on

10. Taylor, "Business and Political Career," 327–28.
11. Ibid.

the ticket. Correspondents covering the convention opined that Ewing and Rice were nominated by a "drunken crowd of delegates" and the place was filled with "disgraceful scenes." Thurman chose his own political survival over party success in the election and decided to work against Ewing's interests.[12]

Although local issues were important to Ohioans, it was Ewing's attacks on White House monetary policy that galvanized President Hayes. This turned into a strategic mistake for Ewing. While he was trying to show that he had a mind for national issues, and although Hayes was enough of a family friend to serve as a pallbearer for Thomas Ewing Sr., Ewing's attacks made Hayes want the younger Ewing hung out to dry. Ewing was an "upstart" whose beliefs were built on an "ancient Bourbon faith" of a northern Kentucky aristocracy in deference to the wealthy. Hayes's men were good with words. Ewing was labeled a "dangerous repudiationist" and "the high priest of exploded financial vagaries." Voters were reminded of Ewing's "crooked and dirty road of Johnsonism" and his "unbounded greed for office."[13]

This was the up-front position. Hayes predicted in his diary that Ewing's nomination would be formidable, and his victory could be "disastrous to the Republicans." The Ewing name in Ohio was something around which Democrats and greenbackers could rally, or at least so the candidates hoped. Ohio Democrats and greenback party members collectively outnumbered Ohio Republicans. Hayes's diary indicates his concern that the Republicans must find a way to divide the Democrats by exploiting Ewing's congressional votes on greenback issues with Democrat hard-money men; otherwise, Ewing was a man of few fixed principles and would pander to those allies.[14]

As president Hayes had deeper concerns. If Congress adopted a paper monetary system, Hayes would be blamed. He suggested that Republicans should stand firm for the gold standard, which, he argued, was fueling the national recovery. It was clear that Hayes did not fear Ewing's views; it was Ewing's popularity that had him concerned. With these interesting hooks and Thurman working behind the scenes against his own nominee, the campaign began to draw national newspaper interest.[15]

The campaign for governor included torchlight parades and a slogan never de-

12. The 1879 Ohio gubernatorial convention from *New York Times,* June 5, 1879.

13. Hayes, *Diary,* 3:557, cited on the Internet at <http://www.ohiohistory.org/onlinedoc/hayes/Volume03/Chapter37/June7.txt> last accessed on April 14, 2008; "upstart" and Hayes's men from *New York Tribune,* June 11, 1879.

14. Hayes, *Diary,* 3:557.

15. *New York Tribune,* June 18, 1879.

signed for bumper stickers, "Free Ballots, Impartial Juries and Money Issued by the People Through Their Government." The campaign also became nasty. Although Ewing and Rice were former Union generals they were labeled as "Confederates" by Republican newspapers. Charles Foster, the Republican nominee who had no war record at all, was named "Citizen Foster." Ewing's greenback views got him labeled "Tissue Thomas." His votes in Congress were scrutinized, along with alleged sweetheart deals between Tilden and Ewing. Questions were raised about his religion, but these were deftly turned aside when it was pointed out that Sherman and Sheridan were both rumored to be Catholic and Congress had put them in charge of the postwar army. As the campaign wore on, Thurman finally came around to support Ewing, but only when it appeared Ewing might win. There were rumors that Missouri Democrats were making war on Ohio's Democratic nominee over Order Number 11. George Bingham had died before the Ohio campaign began, but his son campaigned against Ewing in Ohio with replicas of the painting. A congressman from Missouri wrote to Lancaster newspapers that the attack on Ewing was "Republican propaganda" and "mindless partisan clamor." Although Ewing never carried out the order in person, many later historians bought into Bingham's depiction.[16]

In fact Bingham's attack had little impact on the campaign, in spite of the romantic aura given the painting. Hayes, especially, urged Republicans in Ohio not to mention Order Number 11. The last thing Hayes wanted was the public to be reminded that Democrats had strong war records, too. Instead, Republicans attacked Ewing's business acumen, and this Ewing had a more difficult time defending. If Ewing could not run the Ohio Central Railroad, the theme went, how could he run government? His fuzzy-headed soft-money positions encouraged "irresponsible and careless business projects and stock gambling." This assault was led by John Sherman, who was the administration's point man in Ohio. The irony of this campaign was that Ewing's two most difficult opponents were family friends—President Hayes and Senator John Sherman.[17]

Charles Foster, the Republican gubernatorial nominee who had been associated with Ewing in the management of the failed Ohio Central Railroad, was able to sell Ohio voters a strange argument—that although he and Ewing had both

16. Campaign quotes from Busch, "Mistake of Your Life," 46. Busch researched the use of Bingham's painting in the 1879 Ohio gubernatorial campaign. He concluded that most biographers read the Missouri accounts without reviewing Ohio newspaper accounts. Busch email to author, June 2001. "Propaganda" and "mindless partisan clamor" from Taylor, "Business and Political Career," 331. Much of the Ohio gubernatorial campaign was covered by the *Lancaster Gazette;* see the issue of September 18, 1879, 3.

17. Taylor, "Business and Political Career," 333.

run the railroad into the ground, they should elect Foster instead of Ewing. The Republicans also alleged that Ewing's greenback "proclivities" were in danger of pushing the Democrats toward "communistic spirit." Historian Walter Busch indicates that Ewing's bluntness on the campaign might have alienated him from some former Union soldier votes. He would call for elections free of military presence, which might have made sense had he campaigned in Tennessee instead of Ohio. Finally, Republicans were able to mobilize their voters to get to the polls.[18]

One unexamined negative for Ewing was the impact of the National Independents (NIP). Ewing's campaigning for Tilden in 1876 angered Moses Field, who had offered Ewing a spot on the NIP ticket after the national Democratic convention in 1876. Ewing had good reasons to reject Field's overtures; he had switched parties on principle. Moving to a third party just for a vice-presidential nomination would make Ewing look like a flake. Field waited three years to get even and then fielded a strong third party candidate in Ohio, who siphoned off votes that would have gone to the Democratic nominee. Out of 667,000 votes cast, Foster beat Ewing by 17,000.

Some historians believe Ewing's loss in Ohio came about because of bad timing. This analysis has the most merit. The campaign came during an uptick in the economy. Ewing and the Democrats had failed to convince Ohioans to vote out the Republicans during good times. As proof that it was the economy that won it for the Republicans, the victories were regional in scope, not just in Ohio. The *Lancaster (Ohio) Gazette* headlined its story on the Republican landslide in other states, "Republican Victories Everywhere."[19]

Sometimes political events move to the candidate's detriment without the candidate's either seeing or anticipating the change. Ewing's bad timing and a stealth third-party candidate contributed much to his failed bid for governor. However, there is more to the problem than good economic times for the Republicans and bad timing by Democrats. Historian Richard Hofstadter points out that, by the 1880s, voters were tiring of capitalist entrepreneurs as candidates. Entrepreneurs such as Ewing—who believed they were giving of themselves in the time-honored mode of "public service"—were seen by a great many ordinary folks in a different light, as exploiters of labor. Ewing had been a lifelong supporter of the patronage system. He had once termed civil service reform as wrongheaded and the "rule by a class and a commission rather than people through the servants they

18. "Proclivities" and "communistic spirit" from "How the Figures Look in Ohio: The Republicans Can Win in a Fair and Square Fight," *Cincinnati Weekly Gazette,* June 18, 1879; Busch, "Mistake of Your Life," 47.

19. "Republican Victories Everywhere," *Lancaster (Ohio) Gazette,* November 6, 1879.

elect." It was another of Ewing's ideas that was right, in theory, but on the wrong side politically. His views supported the old system of influence that reporters claimed had corrupted the Gilded Age.[20]

Some of the Republicans simply outsmarted the Democrats, their word games lumping greenbackers and other "agrarian movements" as appealing only to misfits, unorthodox tradesmen, eggheads, and other neurotics. William Allen White summed it up best: over time the Republicans stole a good many of the issues from their ideological adversaries, catching the greenbackers and populists, as White put it, "in swimming" where they "stole all their clothing except the frayed under drawers of free silver."[21]

On October 22, 1869, Thomas Ewing Sr. collapsed while arguing a case before the U.S. Supreme Court. The stroke ended the old man's legal career and left him pretty much an invalid for the rest of his life. Two years after his stroke he passed quietly away, at home in Lancaster. Praise for his life came from all quarters, even from old political foes such as Rutherford Hayes, who served as a pallbearer. Orville Browning called him the "last of the great Senators" of the century. Ellen was crushed, locked into a permanent grief for her father, a grief that had begun before his death. She had begun writing a book on his life. Ellen wrote of her father, "To whom my heart went forth in Unselfish devotion / Thou wilt not return to me but I shall go to thee." She never wrote anything similar about her husband.[22]

The Old Salt Boiler as patriarch had set in motion a remarkable family. His place in history as the foster father of a general of international renown came about simply from his extending his hand to the son of a destitute neighbor. Not only was Thomas Ewing's career brilliant in its own right, as a preeminent real estate lawyer, U.S. senator, cabinet secretary for two presidents, and confidant to presidents of all parties for three decades, the legacies of his sons and daughters—in war and peace—were remarkable.

Hugh was the son whom everyone loved and for whom everyone was concerned. His independent streak and the wanderlust of his youth was noticed by everyone. From California in 1851 Cump Sherman had written, "it seems you are regarded as the wildest most prodigal son of the family, and ever since the Bible

20. Hofstadter views from Phillips, *Boiling Point,* 227; "rule by a class" from TEJr. to HBE, September 1, 1885, EFP/LC.

21. White quoted in Phillips, *Boiling Point,* 227.

22. Thomas Ewing Sr.'s illness came while he was arguing *Maguire v. Tyler* 75 U.S. (8 Wall.) 650 (1869); Browning, *Diary,* 2:301; EES tribute from Sherman, *Memorial,* 286.

was written parents and families have leaned toward such youth." He had long given up the desire for a Potomac farm. Instead, Hugh went back to Lancaster in his later life and achieved in those years a comfortable life in the idyllic lands of his youth, awaiting his own mortality. He had lost one daughter while traveling in Paris, and he lived to see another daughter, Eleanor, die as a missionary in 1894. His son became a priest, and the installation ceremony was joyous for both Hugh and Henrietta.[23]

Hugh's gout had grown progressively worse, leaving him feeble and invalid. Perhaps seeing his own mortality ahead, in his last years, he forgave his political enemies and joined the ranks of the Grand Army of the Republic, with General John Kountz of Toledo doing the honors, initiating into its fraternity an aging Democrat in his Lancaster home. The Republican tendencies of that organization had at long last been overlooked, or at least forgiven. In mid-June 1905, while the newspapers were filled with lurid descriptions of Russian battleship sailors revolting against the tsar, Hugh caught a cold. When his condition worsened, on June 30, 1905, Father Tom Sherman came to Lancaster to give him the last rites. Hugh Ewing slipped into a coma and died at age seventy-nine. He had been an adventurer and a nonconformist who marshaled a strong sense of self throughout his life. Pious to a strong degree but never overbearing in that realm he had, more than the other Ewing sons, a deep attachment to the land, to family, and to agrarian pursuits. He was willing to dream, and it hurt him hard when his dreams did not work out. He was not the strong and independent thinker Tom was. In battle he could be dogged and tough, and he soldiered with his regiment and brigades into several of the toughest fights of the war. In politics he was around long enough to see even his brother Tom come over to the Democratic side. Until late in life he was not particularly happy with the hand Fate dealt him. At the end, however, he finally made peace with his wanderlust. The subject of a Catholic service, Hugh Boyle Ewing was buried in his major general's uniform, not far from his father's grave at Lancaster's St. Mary's Cemetery, the obedient and reverent son, eternally at rest beside the father. His grave is marked by his GAR star.[24]

Tom Ewing's efforts to become governor of Ohio in 1879 marked his political high-water mark. The governor's office was to have been a step to higher office, the U.S. Senate or even president. Unlike many candidates who lose a close election,

23. WTS to HBE, May 6, December 8, 1851, HBE/OHS.

24. Obituary in *Lancaster Daily Eagle,* June 30, 1905; longer story on Hugh Ewing's life in *Lancaster (Ohio) Gazette,* July 6, 1905.

he found he had given into the bug once too often, and he refused to be bitten again. Never again did Tom Ewing seek public office. In 1880 while the Greenback-Labor Party he once led flirted with a platform including woman's suffrage and anti-monopolies laws, Ewing served out his last year in Congress. Then, unlike Hugh who had come back to Ohio for the remainder of his life, Tom left Ohio for good. He was burned out and recognized the brass ring of the Senate was something he no longer was destined to achieve. His fortunes having dipped with all his efforts in the political arena, he went back to doing what he did well, the practice of law and making money. In 1882 he moved his family to upscale Yonkers, New York, and partnered with Milton Southard in New York City, practicing patent law, an area of specialization he had begun early in his legal career in Cincinnati. In 1893, joined by his sons Thomas and Hampton, he established a larger firm—Ewing, Whitman & Ewing—with a Wall Street address. In addition to patent law he had an interest in investment banking. Ewing held a seat on the Yonkers Board of Trade. His clients included the New York City government.

A former supply sergeant in Hugh Ewing's old Kanawha brigade and the Twenty-Third Ohio, William McKinley, barnstormed the country in 1893 for the Republicans, ignoring the panic that had set into the national economy that year. He argued that the Panic of 1873 brought later prosperity, and this panic would give rise to another age of prosperity. Orators such as Democrat William Jennings Bryan had difficulty disproving McKinley's position. By 1893 Ewing watched with dismay as both parties embraced hard-money policies. Only Bryan railed against the swallowtails. Ewing no longer had the energy to lean into that political wind. Not wanting to give life to the labels his critics had given him, "anachronistic spokesman for a lost cause" among them, he delivered few speeches and offered little political advice to anyone during those years.[25]

Ewing's last affiliation had been with the Democratic Party. He did not campaign against his cousin James Blaine when in 1880 and 1884 Blaine ran losing campaigns for president on the Republican ticket. However, Ewing did make a half-hearted attempt to get Hugh Ewing an appointment as Grover Cleveland's minister to Guatemala or Columbia. Hugh's activities were severely reduced by his poor health, however, the gout by then having nearly crippled him.

Tom Ewing now had grandchildren. He was moderately wealthy and out of debt, thanks to his own efforts and also to his portion of his father's large estate in Lancaster. He had grown conservative in his older age, indulging in a little po-

25. "Lost cause" from Taylor, "Business and Political Career," 333–34; Tom Ewing's career in New York from his obituary in *New York Times,* January 22, 1896, 8.

litical nostalgia from time to time and suggesting reforms to those who would listen. In the spring of 1890, thirty-four years after he and Hamp Denman had put together a real estate firm and moved out to Leavenworth, Ewing came back to Topeka to address the seventh annual convention of the Kansas Bar Association (KBA). He was made an honorary member of that bar. He recommended to the Kansas bar, which he had once led as its chief justice, that it seek a state "civil code" and a less than unanimous jury verdict system to limit the number of hung juries. But Kansas was never a state to rush into anything, and it took the KBA another eight decades before a civil code and his jury idea were adopted.[26]

When William Tecumseh Sherman died in 1891 at age seventy-one, the general's passing in New York was a major news event, and it was a time when Tom Ewing stepped forward as the family spokesman. Hugh Ewing's health prevented him from attending the funeral, but he probably would not have gone even if he had been physically capable. Sherman's unwillingness in the last year of the war to assist Hugh's military career left a deep scar on their relationship, which continued after Reconstruction. Hugh always felt that, had Sherman exercised any initiative at all, he could have prevailed on Grant to overlook Hugh's Democratic affiliation and keep Hugh as an ambassador to some European country.

The majesty of Sherman's funeral rivaled that of Grant's and even Lincoln's. Tens of thousands lined up to view his casket and limber. His casket was hauled by special train to St. Louis where he wanted to be buried at Calvary Cemetery alongside his son, Willie, and Ellen, who had died three years earlier. A huge crowd maintained absolute silence. Several regiments of blue infantry fired volley after rolling rifle volley, the thunder of so many guns bringing back remembrance of the war to Tom and every other veteran there. Sherman was laid to rest in an integrated cemetery not far from the grave of Dred Scott.[27]

In a speech in 1894 Tom addressed the Loyal Legion of New York about his territorial days in Kansas when he had allied himself with Stephen Douglas and forced a president to abide by fair electoral processes and the rule of law. He had always admired men who stood up for what was right, and he took this time in his life to make sure that, if he could, he would remind newer generations of the importance of leadership. He had seen courage in many forms, on battlefields, in the White House, and in the U.S. Senate. In 1894 he spent some time mending ruptured alliances with friends such as Charles Robinson, to whom he wrote, "[I]

26. Suggestions to the KBA from Rev. Joab Spencer, "The Methodist-Episcopal Church South in Kansas," 150.

27. Ewing, *Sherman at War*, 180–83; burial from Johnson, *Sherman, Late Retired General*, 586–87, 476–80.

think oftener of you and Mrs. Robinson" than any other Kansas friends. "My respect and regard for you both have grown in the increasing years." He also wrote to Edmund Ross what was almost a parting letter of affection. As far as brevet Major General Thomas Ewing Jr. was concerned, the slightly built Edmund Ross, who never rose above the rank of captain, stood "preeminent for courage" among men—not only for his physical courage in battle but also for opposing the impeachment of a president of the other party. "In making [that] decision, you knew perfectly well that it could consign you to private life and the vehement denunciation of almost all your party friends." Ewing had seen few politicians in government stand up for the common man, the farmers, and the middle class that built the country. He found comfort in having known men such as Ross.[28]

Forty years had now passed since Ewing first came to the Kansas Territory filled with border ruffians and guerrilla war. His law office in New York was a great improvement on the drafty upstairs Leavenworth office. One cold January day in 1896, he took the trains to his New York City office as he always did. Although he could afford them, he did not use private carriages, preferring instead to ride the trains to upper Manhattan, then the trolleys to his office in the Equitable Building at 120 Broadway. New York was in the process of building its first subway, a project begun two years earlier and not yet completed. At Third Avenue he got off one cable car to make connections. Perhaps reading a newspaper, Ewing absentmindedly stepped in front of a second omnibus. The impact threw him several yards and his head struck the pavement.

Initially, everyone thought he would recover. Even the *Washington Post,* feeding off a *New York Times* article, claimed that Ewing was "badly bruised" and that stories of internal injuries were incorrect. This view of minor injuries was kept alive when Ewing was taken to his home in Yonkers instead of a hospital. The *Post* predicted he would be "out in two or three days." Ewing's head injury was far more serious, however. Dr. William Helmuth Jr. trepanned Ewing's skull to relieve the pressure of coagulating blood under the skull. Like Abraham Lincoln thirty-one years earlier, Ewing rallied briefly after the surgery but then sank back and breathed his last a day after being injured.[29]

Dr. Alexander Pitzer, a Presbyterian pastor whose first church was in Leavenworth, had been Ellen Cox Ewing's clergy. When the war came, the Presbyterian Church like the country split in half, and its pastors like soldiers went to their na-

28. "Think oftener" from TEJr. to Robinson, February 8, 1894, Robinson Papers, KSHS; TEJr. to Ross, July 16, 1894, TEJr./KSHS.

29. *Washington Post,* January 21, 1896, 6; "Death of Gen. Thomas Ewing, *New York Times,* January 22, 1896, 8; *Leavenworth Times,* January 22, 1896.

tive states. Pitzer had gone home to Virginia. After the war Tom Ewing happened to see the clergyman one day and persuaded Pitzer to charter a new church in Washington. Ewing's money seeded Pitzer's endeavor, which became the Central Presbyterian Church of Washington and from which Pitzer taught theology at Howard University for many years. It had taken a strong former Catholic to reconcile the Presbyterians, and it was Pitzer whom Ellen Ewing wired to come to New York and officiate at the general's funeral in the First Presbyterian Church in Yonkers.

At the funeral Pitzer spoke about Ewing as a man whose remarkable achievements characterized his life. He had fought against the Lecompton slave constitution. He had issued Order Number 11. A man without military training, he had led troops well in battle and defended Fort Davidson when under a death sentence by the Confederacy. He had fought for Mudd in court and against an improvident impeachment of Andrew Johnson. His fight for the common man characterized his greenback rhetoric. He was a man devoted to thinking about ordinary problems in unusual ways, and he had helped save a presidency at a time when a festering Reconstruction could have had more deadly consequences for the Union than war. These were Tom Ewing's "monuments to his efforts to build America." Pitzer described Ewing as "intelligent and enormously energetic, the type of man who could have adapted in any American Century." Having finally given up his Catholic roots, he was buried in the Protestant section of Oakland Cemetery in Yonkers.[30]

Retired Supreme Court justice Samuel Kingman had known Ewing well. He was an old friend, and his official words to Kansans were a fine eulogy:

> His moral character was of the best; no bad habits marred the beauty and symmetry of his life. He was honest, not merely honest in keeping his word and meeting his obligations, but honest with himself. He had strong convictions and stood by them manfully. He had great ambition but he never permitted it to dominate the integrity of his life. His life was his own . . . and he never pawned it for the gratification of his ambition. I was his senior in years, in nothing else. In the course of nature I ought to have preceded him. He has passed from earth while I still linger here feebly to bear witness to his worth. Citizen, jurist, soldier, statesman, friend. I grieve that I cannot lay a worthier tribute upon his grave.[31]

30. Rowland, "Thomas Ewing Jr.," 29; Pitzer's eulogy from Spencer, "Methodist-Episcopal Church," 149–50, A. W. Pitzer Manuscript Collection, KSHS; "monuments" from *Leavenworth Times,* January 22, 1896.

31. Samuel Kingman, "Memorial To Justice Thomas Ewing, Jr.," *56 Kansas Reports* (1896): xiv.

The best epitaph for Tom Ewing comes from his own words. The last paragraph of his 1894 discussion of the struggle for freedom in Kansas states:

> The importance of that [Kansas] struggle cannot be overestimated. It was the prelude to the War of the Rebellion, and prepared the people to realize its magnitude and to resolve that it should be a fight to the finish. But for this long preparation, it is not improbable that the Rebellion would have ended in a compromise, leaving slavery, though crippled, a lasting cause of bad blood and strife between the sections. Had John Brown's purpose to bring on a war between the sections succeeded [at Harper's Ferry], with the South in possession of all the power and prestige of the General government, and the North in rebellion, all the nations of the world would have stood by the South and the General government; while the North would have been divided, overwhelmed and conquered. But there was a higher power which foiled John Brown's mad scheme. The great sweep of events, from the Kansas Nebraska bill to the surrender at Appomattox, was no doubt divinely directed to unify and purify our people for their glorious mission. Whoever bore an honorable part, however humble, on the Northern side in the great struggle, has reason to thank God for having made him an instrument in preserving this beneficent Republic, which is the hope and light of the world.

BIBLIOGRAPHY

Manuscript Collections

Samuel and Florella Adair Family Papers. KSHS.
Edward Atkinson Papers. 79 volumes. Massachusetts Historical Society. Boston, Massachusetts.
James Buchanan Manuscript Collection. Historical Society of Pennsylvania, Philadelphia.
Charles Chadwick Manuscript Collection. KSHS.
Sidney Clarke Collection. Carl Albert Center, University of Oklahoma, Norman, Oklahoma.
William Connelley Collection. Public Library, Kansas City, Kansas.
Stephen A. Douglas Papers. Special Collections, Manuscripts. University of Chicago Library, Chicago, Illinois.
Hugh Boyle Ewing Papers. Ohio State Historical Society.
Joseph H. Ewing Private Collection. In possession of the family. Wheaton, Maryland.
Papers of the Thomas Ewing Family. Manuscript Division, Library of Congress.
Thomas Ewing Family Papers (SWI). University of Notre Dame Archives (UNDA), Notre Dame, IN 46556.
Thomas Ewing Jr. Papers. Manuscript division, Kansas State Historical Society, Topeka. Microfilm edition.
William C. Haynes Manuscript Collection. KSHS.
William Hutchinson Manuscript Collection. KSHS.
Kansas Collection. Kenneth Spencer Research Library and the Department of History of the University of Kansas. Available on the Internet.
Lecompton Constitution Manuscript Collection. KSHS.

Josephine Blakely Martin Manuscript Collection. KSHS.
James L. McDowell Manuscript Collection. KSHS.
James A. Pike Manuscript Collection. KSHS.
Alexander White Pitzer Manuscript Collection. KSHS.
Charles Robinson Papers. KSHS.
Edmund G. Ross Manuscript Collection. KSHS.
William T. Sherman Family Papers. Library of Congress
William T. Sherman Family Papers. Ohio Historical Society, Columbus, Ohio.
William T. Sherman Family Papers. University of Notre Dame Archives, Notre Dame, Indiana.
William T. Sherman Family Papers. Yonkers Collection of General Thomas Ewing (1831–1896). Microfilm.
Samuel Worthington Manuscript Collection. KSHS.

Journals, Letters, Speeches, and Diaries

Ewing, Hugh. "Autobiography of a Tramp." Manuscript 108, box 9, folders 1–3, Hugh Boyle Ewing Papers.
Ewing, Thomas Sr. "Address at the Centennial Celebration at Marietta." Speech presented in Marietta, Ohio, July 15, 1858. *Ohio Archaeological and Historical Quarterly* 28 (April 1919): 197, 206.
Ewing, Thomas Jr. *Speech of Maj. Gen. Thomas Ewing, Jr., of Kansas, at the Soldiers' and Sailors' National Convention, at Cooper Institute, July 4, 1868: reported and published by order of the convention.* New York: Printed by Wynkoop & Hallenbeck, [1868].
Ewing, Thomas III. "Some Happenings Fifty Years Ago, Address at the Banquet of the Kansas Society." New York, January 29, 1908. Lecompton Constitution Manuscript Collection, KSHS.
Guide to the Microfilm Edition of Thomas Ewing, Sr. Thomas Ewing Family Papers. University of Notre Dame Archives (UNDA), Notre Dame, Indiana.
Hodgson, Ira. "Reminiscences of an Old Civil War Veteran." KSHS Manuscripts, Topeka, Kansas.
Miller, Hon. Robert. "Thomas Ewing Jr.: First Chief Justice of the Kansas Supreme Court." Paper presented at the Jayhawker Club, April 29, 1981. Found at Kansas Supreme Court Law Library, Topeka (KFK 525.M5).

Books, Journals, Articles, Theses, and Treatises

Abel, Anna Heloise. "Indian Reservations in Kansas and the Extinguishment of Their Title." *Kansas Historical Collections* 8 (1904): 72–109.

Adams, Franklin G. "The Capitals of Kansas." *Kansas Historical Collections* 8 (1904): 331–51.

Anderson, T. J. *Report Of The Adjutant General Of The State Of Kansas, 1861–1865.* Topeka: State Printing Office, 1896.

Andreas, Alfred T. *History of the State of Kansas.* Chicago: Self-published, 1883; reproduction edition, Atchison County Historical Society, 1976.

Anthony, Daniel R. "Address To The Kansas Historical Society." *Kansas Historical Collections* 3 (1884): 410.

Athearn, Robert G. *Union Pacific Country.* Chicago: Rand McNally, 1971.

Austin, Edwin A. "The Supreme Court of the State of Kansas." *Kansas Historical Collections* 13 (1914): 95–125.

Bailey, Ronald H. *The Civil War, Battles for Atlanta; Sherman Moves East.* Alexandria, Va.: Time-Life Books, 1985.

Barnard, Harry. *Rutherford B. Hayes and His America.* New York: Russell and Russell, 1954.

Barnes, Lela. "Letters of Cyrus K. Holliday, 1854–1859." *Kansas Historical Quarterly* 6 (1937): 241–94.

Barrows, Chester. *William M. Evarts, Lawyer, Diplomat, Statesman.* Chapel Hill: University of North Carolina Press, 1941.

Basler, Roy. *The Collected Works of Abraham Lincoln.* New Brunswick, N.J.: Rutgers University Press, 1953.

Berwanger, Eugene. "Ross and the Impeachment: A New Look at a Critical Vote." *Kansas History: A Journal of the Central Plains* 1 (1978): 235–42.

Blaine, James G. *Twenty Years of Congress: From Lincoln To Garfield.* 2 volumes. Norwich, Conn.: Henry Bill Publishing Co., 1884–1886.

Blunt, James G. "General Blunt's Account of His Civil War Experiences." *Kansas Historical Collections* 18 (1932): 211–65.

Boatner, Mark. *The Civil War Dictionary.* New York: David McKay, 1959.

Bork, Robert. *The Tempting of America: The Political Seduction of the Law.* New York: Free Press; London: Collier Macmillan, 1990.

Boyd, Cyrus F. *The Civil War Diary of Cyrus F. Boyd, 15th Iowa Infantry.* Edited by Mildred Throne. Milwood, N.Y.: Kraus Reprint, 1977; Baton Rouge: Louisiana State University Press, 1998.

Bradford, Ned, ed. *Battles and Leaders of the Civil War.* New York: Appleton-Century-Crofts, 1956.

Brodhead, Michael J. *David J. Brewer: The Life of a Supreme Court Justice, 1837–1910.* Carbondale: Southern Illinois University Press, 1994.

Brodie, Fawn. *Thomas Jefferson: An Intimate History.* New York: W. W. Norton, 1974.

Brown, George W. *Reminiscences of Governor R. J. Walker: The True Story of the Rescue of Kansas from Slavery.* Rockford, Ill.: Self-published, 1902.

Browning, Orville H. *The Diary of Orville Hickman Browning.* Edited by Theodore C. Pease and James G. Randall. 2 volumes. Springfield: Illinois State Historical Library, 1927.

Brownson, Howard G. *History of Illinois Central Railroad.* Urbana: University of Illinois Press, 1915.

Busch, Walter E. "General, You Have Made the Mistake of Your Life." Masters diss., California State University, Dominguez Hills, 2001.

Carruth, William H. "The New England Emigrant Aid Company as an Investment Society." *Kansas Historical Collections* 6 (1900): 90–96.

Castel, Albert. *Civil War Kansas: Reaping the Whirlwind.* Lawrence: University of Kansas Press, 1997.

———. "Dead on Arrival: The Life and Death of General Albert Sidney Johnston." *Civil War Times Illustrated* (March 1997): 35–36.

———. *Decision in the West: The Atlanta Campaign of 1864.* Lawrence: University of Kansas Press, 1992.

———. *A Frontier State at War: Kansas, 1861–1865.* Ithaca, N.Y.: Cornell University Press, 1958.

———. *General Sterling Price and the Civil War in the West.* Baton Rouge: Louisiana State University Press, 1968.

Chappell, Phil E. "The History of the Missouri River." *Kansas Historical Collections* 9 (1905): 237–316.

Chesnut, Mary. *Mary Chesnut's Civil War.* Edited by C. Vann Woodward. New Haven: Yale University Press, 1982.

Chittenden, Lucius Eugene. *Report of the Debates and Proceedings in the Secret Sessions of the Conference Convention, for Proposing Amendments to the Constitution of the United States, Held At Washington, D.C. In February, A.D. 1861.* New York: D. Appleton & Company, 1864.

Connelley, William E. *James Henry Lane, The Grim Chieftain of Kansas.* Topeka, Kans.: Crane & Company, 1899.

———. "The Lane-Jenkins Claim Contest." *Kansas Historical Collections* 16 (1925): 21–176.

———. *Life of Preston B. Plumb.* Chicago: Browne and Howell, 1913.

———. *Quantrill and the Border Wars.* Cedar Rapids, Iowa: Cedar Rapids Torch, 1910.

Cox, Lawanda, and John H. Cox. *Politics, Principle and Prejudice 1865–1866: Dilemma of Reconstruction America.* New York: Free Press, 1963.

Cozzens, Peter. *The Shipwreck of Their Hopes.* Chicago: University of Illinois Press, 1994.

———. "The Tormenting Flame." *Civil War Times Illustrated* 35.1 (April 1996): 44–55.

Craik, Elmer L. "Southern Interest in Territorial Kansas, 1854–1858." *Kansas Historical Collections* 15 (1922): 334–450.

Crittenden, H. H. *The Crittenden Memoirs.* New York: G. P. Putnam and Sons, 1936.

Crook, George. *Autobiography.* Edited by Martin Schmitt. Norman: University of Oklahoma Press, 1946.

Cruise, John D. "Early Days on the Union Pacific." *Kansas Historical Collections* 11 (1910): 529–49.

Curry, Richard O. *Radicalism, Racism, and Party Realignment: The Border States during Reconstruction.* Baltimore: Johns Hopkins Press, 1969.

Davis, Kenneth S. *Kansas: A Bicentennial History.* New York: W. W. Norton, 1976.

———. "Portrait of a Changing Kansas." *Kansas Historical Quarterly* 42 (Spring 1976): 24–47.

Denison, W. W. "The Battle of Prairie Grove." *Kansas Historical Collections* 16 (1925): 586–90.

Douglass, Frederick. "Reconstruction." *Atlantic Monthly* 18 (1866): 761–65.

Downing, Alexander. *Downing's Civil War Diary.* Edited by Olynthus B. Clark. Des Moines: The Historical Department of Iowa, 1916.

Durham, James. "*U.S. v. Lewis L. Weld:* Judicial Creativity or Judicial Subversion?" *Journal of the Kansas Bar Association* (May–June 1987): 8–11.

Durkin, Joseph T. *General Sherman's Son: The Life of Thomas Ewing Sherman.* New York: Straus and Cudahy, 1959.

Eastin, Lucian J. "Notes on the Proslavery March against Lawrence." *Kansas Historical Quarterly* 11 (1942): 45–64.

Edwards, John N. *Shelby and His Men, The War in the West.* Cincinnati, Ohio: Miami Printing and Publishing Co., 1867.

Elbert, E. Duane. "The English Bill: An Attempt to Compromise the Lecompton Dilemma." *Kansas History: A Journal of the Central Plains* 1 (1978): 219–33.

Eldridge, Shalor. *Recollections of Early Days in Kansas.* Edited by Robert G. Elliott. Topeka: Kansas State Printing Division, 1920.

Elliott, Robert Gaston. "The Grasshopper Falls Convention and the Legislature of 1857." *Kansas Historical Collections* 10 (1908): 182–204.

Evans, Clement A., ed. *The Confederate Military History.* 12 volumes. Carmel, Ind.: Guild Press of Indiana, 1998. CD-ROM version.

Ewing, Joseph H. *Sherman at War.* Dayton, Ohio: Morningside Bookshop, 1992.

———. "Sherman Bashes the Press." *American Heritage* 38 (July–August 1987): 37.

Ewing, Thomas Jr. "Resumption of Specie Payments." *North American Review* 125.259 (1877): 412–16.

———. "The Struggle For Freedom In Kansas." *Cosmopolitan* 17 (1894): 1–11.

Fellman, Michael. *Citizen Sherman: A Life of William Tecumseh Sherman.* New York: Random House, 1995.

Foner, Eric. *Reconstruction: America's Unfinished Revolution.* New York: Harper and Row, 1988.

Foote, Shelby. *The Civil War: A Narrative.* 3 volumes. New York: Random House, 1974.

Frank, Joseph A., and George A. Reaves. *Seeing the Elephant: Raw Recruits at the Battle of Shiloh.* New York: Greenwood Press, 1989.

Gaeddert, G. Raymond. *The Birth of Kansas.* Topeka: Kansas State Printing Department, 1940.

Gates, Paul W. *Fifty Million Acres: Conflicts over Kansas Land Policy, 1854–1890.* Norman: University of Oklahoma Press, 1997.

———. "A Fragment of Kansas Land History: The Disposal of the Christian Indian Tract." *Kansas Historical Quarterly* 6 (1937): 227–40.

Glick, George. "The Railroad Convention of 1860." *Kansas Historical Collections* 9 (1905): 467–80.

Goodrich, Thomas. *Black Flag: Guerrilla Warfare on the Western Border, 1861–1865.* Bloomington: Indiana University Press, 1995.

Govan, Gilbert E., and James W. Livingwood. *A Different Valor: The Story of General Joseph E. Johnston, C.S.A.* New York: Konecky and Konecky, 1956.

Gower, Calvin. "The Pikes Peak Gold Rush and the Smoky Hill Route, 1859–1860." *Kansas Historical Quarterly* 25 (1959): 158–71.

Gowing, Clara. "Life among the Delaware Indians." *Kansas Historical Collections* 12 (1912): 153–89.

Grant, U. S. *The Papers of Ulysses S. Grant.* Edited by John Y. Simon. Carbondale: Southern Illinois University Press, 1967.

Greeley, Horace. *The American Conflict: A History of the Great Rebellion in the United States of America, 1860–1864.* 2 volumes. Chicago: O. D. Case & Co., 1866.

Grey, Thomas C. "The Constitution as Scripture." *Stanford Law Review* 37 (1984): 1–25.

Hamilton, Gail. *Biography of James G. Blaine.* Norwich, Conn.: Henry Bill Publishing Co., 1895.

Hannahs, Harrison. "General Thomas Ewing, Jr." *Kansas Historical Collections* 12 (1912): 276–82.

Hattaway, Herman, and Richard E. Beringer. *Jefferson Davis: Confederate President.* Lawrence: University of Kansas Press, 2002.

Hayes, Rutherford B. *Diary and Letters of Rutherford B. Hayes.* Volume 3. Rutherford B. Hayes Presidential Center, Fremont, Ohio.

Henderson, Frederic W. "Reconstruction: The Civil War Battle Yet to Be Won." *Executive Intelligence Review,* December 4, 1992. On the Internet at <http://american_almanac.tripod.com/fwhrecon.htm> last accessed April 8, 2008.

Hicken, Victor. *Illinois in the Civil War.* Urbana: University of Illinois Press, 1966.

Higdon, Hal. *The Union vs. Dr. Mudd.* Chicago: Follett, 1964.

Horton, Albert H. "The Judiciary of Kansas." *Kansas Historical Collections* 3 (1885): 389–96.

Horton, James C. "Business Then and Now." *Kansas Historical Collections* 8 (1904): 143–48.

Howe, Henry. *Historical Collections of Ohio.* Volume 28. Cincinnati: C. J. Krehbiel & Co., 1888.

Howe, Mark DeWolfe. *Home Letters of General Sherman.* New York: Scribner and Sons, 1909.

Hull, O. C. "Railroads in Kansas." *Kansas Historical Collections* 12 (1912): 37–43.

Johannsen, Robert W. *The Frontier, the Union, and Stephen A. Douglas.* Urbana: University of Illinois Press, 1989.

Johnson, W. Fletcher. *The Life of William Tecumseh Sherman, Late Retired General USA.* Chicago: Edgewood Publishing Co., 1891.

Kahn, Ali. "The Evolution of Money: A Story of Constitutional Nullification." *Cincinnati Law Review* 67 (1999): 393–427.

Kansas Statutes Annotated. Published by the State of Kansas.

Kelley, William D. "Resumption of Specie Payments." *North American Review* 125.259 (1877): 404–8.

Kempfer, Lester L. *The Salem Light Guard, Company G, 36th Regiment Ohio Volunteer Infantry, Marietta, Ohio, 1861–1865.* Chicago: Adams Press, 1973.

Kingman, Samuel. "Memorial To Justice Thomas Ewing, Jr." *56 Kansas Reports.* Preface (1896): xiv.

LaForte, Robert. "Cyrus Leland Jr. and the Lawrence Massacre: A Note and Document." *Kansas History: A Journal of the Central Plains* 9 (Winter 1986–1987): 175–81.

Langguth, A. J. *Patriots: The Men Who Started the American Revolution.* New York: Simon and Schuster, 1988.

Learnard, O. E. "Organization of the Republican Party." *Kansas Historical Collections* 6 (1900): 312–16.

Lee, J. V., ed. "Joint Discussions between Gen. Thomas Ewing, of Ohio, and Gov. Stewart L. Woodford, of New York, on the Finance Question." Columbus, Ohio (1876): 100.

Lee, Wayne. *Deadly Days in Kansas.* Caldwell, Idaho: Caxton Printers, 1997.

Lewis, Lloyd. *Sherman, Fighting Prophet.* New York: Harcourt, Brace, 1932.

Lincoln, Abraham. *New Letters and Papers of Lincoln.* Edited by Paul M. Angle. Boston: Houghton Mifflin, 1930.

Lomask, Milton. *Andrew Johnson: President on Trial.* New York: Farrar, Straus and Cudahy, 1960.

Lovejoy, Julia. "Letters from Kansas." *Kansas Historical Quarterly* 11 (1942): 29–44.

———. "Letters of Julia Louisa Lovejoy, 1856–1864." *Kansas Historical Quarterly* 15 (1947): 386–87.

Madison, James. *Notes of Debates in the Federal Convention of 1787, Reported by James Madison.* New York: W. W. Norton, 1966. On the Internet at <http://www.constitution.org/dfc/dfc_0822.htm> last accessed March 23, 2008.

Manning, Edwin C. "The Kansas State Senate of 1865 and 1866." *Kansas Historical Collections* 9 (1905): 359–75.

Marszalek, John F. *Sherman: A Soldier's Passion for Order.* New York: Macmillan, 1993.

Martin, George W. "The First Two Years of Kansas." *Kansas Historical Collections* 10 (1908): 123–32.

Martin, John A. *Proceedings and Debates of the Kansas Constitutional Convention.* Topeka: State Printer's Office, 1920.

McCook, Daniel, Jr. "The Second Division at Shiloh." *Harper's New Monthly Magazine* (May 1864): 1–6.

McCulloch, Hugh. "Resumption of Specie Payments." *North American Review* 125.259 (1877): 397–404.

McCullough, David. *Truman.* New York: Simon and Schuster, 1992.

McDonald, John. *Great Battles of the Civil War.* New York: Macmillan, 1988.

McDonough, James Lee. *Chattanooga: A Death Grip on the Confederacy.* Knoxville: University of Tennessee Press, 1984.

McFeely, William S. *Grant: A Biography.* New York: W. W. Norton, 1981.

McGonigle, James A. "First Kansas Infantry in the Battle of Wilson's Creek." *Kansas Historical Collections* 12 (1912): 292–95.

McPherson, James M. *Battle Cry of Freedom: The Civil War Era.* New York: Oxford University Press, 1988.

Meerse, David E. "No Propriety in the Late Course of the Governor: The Geary-Sherrard Affair Reexamined." *Kansas Historical Quarterly* 17 (Spring 1976): 238–55.

Meyer, Steve. *Iowa Valor.* Garrison, Iowa: Meyer, 1994.

Mitchell, Reid. *Civil War Soldiers.* New York: Viking Penguin, 1988.

Moline, Brian. "Early Kansas Judiciary." *Journal of the Kansas Bar Association* (June 1985): 25.

Monaghan, Jay. *Civil War on the Western Border, 1854–1865.* Lincoln: University of Nebraska Press, 1955.

Monnett, Howard. *Action before Westport, 1864.* Kansas City: Westport Historical Society/Lowell Press, 1964.

Moore, H. Miles. *Early History of Leavenworth City and County.* Leavenworth, Kans.: Samuel Dodsworth, 1906.

Morrow, Robert. "Emigration to Kansas in 1856." *Kansas Historical Collections* 8 (1904): 302–15.

Neely, Jeremy. *The Border between Them: Violence and Reconciliation on the Kansas–Missouri Line.* Columbia and London: University of Missouri Press, 2007.

Nice, Mary Jayne Newman. "Frontier Life in Northeast Kansas during the Territorial Days." PhD diss., Emporia State University, 1988.

Niepman, Ann Davis. "General Order Number 11 and Border Warfare during the Civil War." *Missouri Historical Review* 66 (1972): 185–210.

Oates, Stephen B. *With Malice toward None: The Life of Abraham Lincoln.* New York: Harper and Row, 1979.

Palmer, Henry E. "The Black Flag Character of the War on the Border." *Kansas Historical Collections* 9 (1905): 455–66.

———. "The Lawrence Raid." *Kansas Historical Collections* 6 (1900): 317–25.

Paludan, Phillip S. *The Presidency of Abraham Lincoln.* Lawrence: University of Kansas Press, 1994.

Peterson, Cyrus, and Joseph Hanson. *Pilot Knob: The Thermopylae of the West.* Cape Girardeau, Mo.: Ramfire Reprint Press, 1964.

Peterson, Norma L. *The Presidencies of Harrison and Tyler.* Lawrence: University of Kansas Press, 1989.

Phillips, Kevin. *Boiling Point: Republicans, Democrats and the Decline of Middle Class Prosperity.* New York: Random House, 1993.

Pitmann, Benn. *The Assassination of President Lincoln and the Trial of the Conspirators.* Edited by Philip Van Doren Stern. Reprint. New York: Funk and Wagnalls, 1954.

Plummer, Mark A. *Frontier Governor: Samuel J. Crawford of Kansas.* Lawrence: University of Kansas Press, 1971.

Randall, James G. "Captured and Abandoned Property during the Civil War." *American Historical Review* 19 (1913): 65–66.

Reid, Whitelaw. *Ohio In The War For The Suppression Of The Great Rebellion.* 2 volumes. Cincinnati, Ohio: Moore, Wilstach & Baldwin, 1868.

———. *Ohio In the War; Her Statesmen, Generals and Soldiers.* Volume 2. Columbus, Ohio: Eclectic Publishing Co., 1893.

"Resumption of Specie Payments." *North American Review* 125.259 (November 1877): 397–427. Available on the Internet at <http://cdl.library.cornell.edu/cgi-bin/moa/moa-cgi?notisid-ABQ7578-0125-54> last accessed April 12, 2008.

Rich, Everett. *The Heritage of Kansas: Selected Commentaries on Past Times.* Lawrence, Kans.: University of Kansas Press, 1960.

Richardson, Elmo, and Alan Farley. *John Palmer Usher: Lincoln's Secretary of the Interior.* Lawrence: University of Kansas Press, 1960.

Richmond, Robert, ed. *Requisite Learning and Good Moral Character: A History of the Kansas Bench and Bar.* Topeka: Kansas Bar Association, 1982.

Ridpath, John C. *Life and Work of James G. Blaine.* Philadelphia, Pa.: Historical Publishing Co., 1893.

Robinson, Charles. "Topeka and Her Constitution." *Kansas Historical Collections* 6 (1900): 291–305.

Robinson, Sara. "The Wakarusa War." *Kansas Historical Collections* 10 (1908): 457–71.

Roscoe, Theodore. *Web of Conspiracy.* Englewood Cliffs, N.J.: Prentice-Hall, 1959.

Rowland, Mary Scott. "Thomas Ewing: The Reluctant Chief Justice." *Journal of the Kansas Bar Association* (February 1988): 31–32.

———. "Thomas Ewing Jr." Unpublished manuscript. Mary S. Rowland Folder, December 14, 1972, 1–29. Miscellaneous Rowland Collection, KSHS.

Rutland, Robert. *The Papers of George Mason.* Chapel Hill: University of North Carolina Press, 1970.

Schofield, John M. *Forty Six Years in the Army.* New York: Century Co., 1897.

Scott, Kim. "The Preacher, the Lawyer, and the Spoils of War." *Kansas History: A Journal of the Central Plains* 13 (1991): 206–15.

Sears, Stephen W. "Civil War General." *American Heritage* 50 (May–June 1999): 1.

———. *Landscape Turned Red: The Battle of Antietam.* New York: Ticknor and Fields, 1983.

Shapiro, Larry, ed. *Abraham Lincoln: Mystic Chords of Memory; A Selection of Lincoln's Writings.* New York: Book of the Month Club, 1984.

Sherman, Ellen Ewing. *Memorial: Thomas Ewing of Ohio, 1789–1871.* New York: Catholic Public Society, 1873.

Sherman, John. *Recollections of Forty Years in the House, Senate and Cabinet.* 2 volumes. Chicago: Werner Publishing Co., 1895.

Sherman, William T. *Memoirs of General William T. Sherman; By Himself.* Foreword by B. H. Liddell Hart. 2 vols. Bloomington, Ind.: Indiana University Press, 1957.

Shively, S. J. "The Pottawatomie Massacre." *Kansas Historical Collections* 8 (1904): 177–87.

Smalley, Eugene V. "General Sherman." *Century Magazine* 27 (January 1884): 450–62.

Smith, Elbert B. *The Presidencies of Taylor and Fillmore.* Lawrence: University of Kansas Press, 1988.

Smith, Page. *The Rise of Industrial America: A People's History of the Post-Reconstruction Era.* New York: McGraw-Hill, 1984.

———. *Trial by Fire: A People's History of the Civil War and Reconstruction.* New York: McGraw-Hill, 1982.

Speer, John. "The Burning of Osceola Mo. by Lane and the Quantrill Massacre Contrasted." *Kansas Historical Collections* 6 (1900): 305–12.

Spencer, Rev. Joab. "The Methodist-Episcopal Church South in Kansas, 1854–1906." *Kansas Historical Collections* 12 (1912): 135–82.

Stampp, Kenneth M. *America in 1857: A Nation on the Brink.* New York: Oxford University Press, 1990.

Starr, Stephen Z. *Jennison's Jayhawkers: A Civil War Cavalry Regiment and Its Commander.* Baton Rouge: Louisiana State University Press, 1973.

Steers, Edward. "The Deceptive Doctor." *Columbiad* 2 (1988): 114.

Stewart, Nixon B. *Dan McCook's Regiment, 52nd OVI: A History of the Regiment, Its Campaigns and Battles.* Alliance, Ohio: Self-published, 1900.

Streeter, Floyd. *The Kaw: The Heart of the Nation.* New York: Farrar and Rinehart, 1941.

Suderow, Bryce A. *Thunder in Arcadia Valley: Price's Defeat, September 27, 1864.* Cape Girardeau, Mo.: The Center for Regional History and Cultural Heritage, Southeast Missouri State University, 1986.

Swierenga, Robert P. *Pioneers and Profits: Land Speculation on the Iowa Frontier.* Ames: Iowa State University Press, 1968.

Swinton, William. *Decisive Battles of the Civil War.* New York: Promontory Press, 1986.

Sword, Wiley. *Shiloh: Bloody April.* New York: William Morrow, 1974.

Taft, William H. "Kansas-Nebraska Bill and Decoration Day, an Address by the Secretary of War at Topeka, May 30, 1904." *Kansas Historical Collections* 9 (1905): 115–26.

Taylor, David G. "Business and Political Career of Thomas Ewing Jr.: A Study of Frustrated Ambition." PhD diss., University of Kansas, 1970.

———. "Hocking Valley Railroad Promotion in the 1870s: The Atlantic and Lake Erie Railway." *Ohio History* 81.4 (Autumn 1972): 263–78.

———. "Thomas Ewing Jr. and the Origins of the Kansas Pacific Railway Company." *Kansas Historical Collections* 42 (Summer 1976): 155–79.

Thorndike, Rachel Sherman, ed. *The Sherman Letters: Correspondence between General and Senator Sherman from 1837 to 1891.* New York: Scribner's & Sons, 1894.

Tocqueville, Alexis de. *Democracy in America.* 2 vols. 1840. On the Internet at <http://xroads.virginia.edu/~HYPER/DETOC/1_ch16.htm> last accessed on April 5, 2008.

Treadway, William E. "The Gilded Age in Kansas." *Kansas Historical Quarterly* 40 (Spring 1974): 14–15.

Turner, Thomas R. *Beware the People Weeping: Public Opinion and the Assassination of Abraham Lincoln.* Baton Rouge: Louisiana State University Press, 1982.

Verge, Laurie, ed. "From War Department Files. Statements Made By The Alleged Lincoln Conspirators Under Examination 1865." *Clinton: Surratt Society* (1980): 29–38.

Warner, Ezra. *Generals in Blue: Lives of the Union Commanders.* Baton Rouge: Louisiana State University Press, 1964.

The War of the Rebellion: A Compilation of the Official Records of the Union and Confederate Armies. 127 vols., index, and atlas. Washington, D.C.: Government Printing Office, 1880–1901. (Cited in notes as *O.R.* As abbreviated, *O.R.* 22:1:17 means *O.R.* series 1, volume 22, part 1, page 17.) The Civil War CD-ROM, developed at Guild Press on Indiana around 1995, is currently published by Oliver Computing LLC and available at <www.CivilWarAmerica.com>.

Weckesser, Elden C. *His Name Was Mudd: The Life of Dr. Samuel A. Mudd, Who Treated the Fleeing John Wilkes Booth.* Jefferson, N.C.: McFarland, 1991.

Wert, Jeffry D. *General James Longstreet, the Confederacy's Most Controversial Soldier: A Biography.* New York: Simon and Schuster, 1993.

Whalen, Charles, and Barbara Whalen. *The Fighting McCooks: America's Famous Fighting Family.* Bethesda, Md.: Westmoreland Press, 2006.

White, Leonard. *The Jacksonians.* New York: Macmillan, 1954.

Williams, Charles R. *Diary and Letters of Rutherford Birchard Hayes: Nineteenth President of the United States.* 5 vols. Columbus: Ohio State Archaeology and Historical Society, 1922.

Wilson, Paul E. "John Adams Halderman: Our Eldest Brother." *Journal of the Kansas Bar Association* 54 (1985): 84–95.

Wyman, Walker. "Atchison: A Great Frontier Depot." *Kansas Historical Quarterly* 11 (1942): 297–308.

Zywicki, Todd J. "Senators and Special Interests: A Public Choice Analysis of the Seventeenth Amendment." *Oregon Law Review* 73 (Winter 1994): 1007–55.

INDEX

Abbreviations used: HBE (Hugh Boyle Ewing); TEJr. (Thomas Ewing, Jr.); TESr. (Thomas Ewing, Sr.); WTS (William Tecumseh Sherman)

ABOUT THE AUTHOR

Ron Smith is a fifth-generation Kansan, an attorney, a grandfather, a Vietnam veteran, and a Civil War historian. Territorial Kansas, the Civil War, and the post–Civil War West are his writing subjects.